INSTANT POT COOKBOOK

Legal notice

This book is copyright (c) 2017 by Susan Moore. All rights are reserved. This book may not be duplicated or copied, either in whole or in part, via any means including any electronic form of duplication such as recording or transcription. The contents of this book may not be transmitted, stored in any retrieval system, or copied in any other manner regardless of whether use is public or private without express prior permission of the publisher.

This book provides information only. The author does not offer any specific advice, including medical advice, nor does the author suggest the reader or any other person engage in any particular course of conduct in any specific situation. This book is not intended to be used as a substitute for any professional advice, medical or of any other variety. The reader accepts sole responsibility for how he or she uses the information contained in this book. Under no circumstances will the publisher or the author be held liable for damages of any kind arising either directly or indirectly from any information contained in this book.

Instant Pot Cookbook

The Best 618 Instant Pot Recipes You'll Ever Eat

Fast, Easy and Delicious Recipes for Health and Rapid Fat Loss with Nutritional Facts for Every Recipe

Susan Moore

Contents

Chapter 1: Vegetarian 15

- Delicious Black Lentil Curry 16
- Frijoles Borrachos (Mexican "Drunken Beans") 16
- Navratan Korma 16
- Winter Veggie Soup 17
- Lentil Sweet Potato Beans Stew 17
- Cinnamon Carrots and Apples 17
- Broccoli Cauliflower Soup 18
- Perfect Carrot Soup 18
- Easy Taco Soup 18
- Spaghetti Squash Marinara 19
- Mushroom Stroganoff 19
- Creamy Mashed Potato 20
- Squash Curry Soup 20
- Creamy Split Pea Curry 20
- Easy Winter Veggie Soup 21
- Vegetable Coconut Curry 21
- Yummy Slow Cooked Potatoes 21
- Mushroom Potato Stew 22
- Delicious Three Bean Chili 22
- Lentil Curry 22
- Potato Red Lentil Curry 23
- Sweet Potato Peanut Stew 23
- Cranberry Apple Crisp 24
- Creamy Onion Soup 24
- Roasted Vegetables 24
- Tasty Tofu Curry 24
- Garam Masala Potatoes 25
- Cauliflower Potato Curry Soup 25
- Steamed Kale with Bacon 26
- Pumpkin Apple Curry Soup 26
- Scrumptious Spinach Paneer 26
- Cabbage Carrots Celery Soup 27
- Tomato Sauce 27
- Flavorful Red Lentils Curry 27
- Kale Potato Soup 27
- Tuscan Pinto Beans 28
- Mushroom Soup 28
- Creamy Carrot Squash Soup 29
- Yummy Cheese Soup 29
- Mashed Cauliflower 29
- Calico Beans 30
- Apple Cabbage and Beet Stew 30
- Almond Rice Pudding 30
- Spiced Cranberry Oatmeal 30
- Coconut Lime Cabbage 31
- Creamy Rice and Beans 31
- Potato Vegetable Soup 32
- Veggie Soup 32
- Simple Strawberry Sauce 32
- Creamy Kale Soup 33
- Chickpea Stew 33
- Veggie Quinoa Pilaf 33
- Creamy Tomato Soup 34
- Creamy Bow Tie Pasta 34
- Mixed Beans in Hot Sauce 35
- Honey Roasted Peanut Broccoli Salad 35
- Zucchini Curried Soup 35
- Barley Walnut Salad 36
- Delicious Sweet Potato Curry 36
- Savory Kale Garlic 36

Simple Black Eyed Peas 37	Coconut Crumble Nectarines 48
Red Wine Poached Pears 37	Curried Potatoes 48
Italian Vegetable Soup 37	Flavourful Vegetable Korma 48
Spiced Green Peas Rice 38	Curried Zucchini Eggplant 49
Mexican Rice and Beans 38	Cherry Almond Rice 49
Vegetable Scraps Stock 38	Butter Garlic Potatoes 49
Mix Vegetable Curry 38	Instant Pot Sambar 49
Frittata with Cheese and Broccoli 39	Corn on the Cob with Avocado Dressing .. 50
Butternut Squash Soup 39	Simple Yellow Lentil 50
Sweet Glazed Carrots 39	Vegetable Stew with Chickpeas 50
Perfect Curried Baked Beans 40	Lentil Cauliflower Curry 51
Turmeric Lentil Bean Chili 40	Simple Chickpea Curry 51
Tasty Spinach Potato 40	Mexican Rice 51
Potato Soup with Lentils 41	Vegetarian Chili Bowl 52
Chickpea Kale Sweet Potato Stew 41	Nutty Mocha Oatmeal 52
Asparagus Lemon Tender 41	Potato Chile Stew 52
Pumpkin Vegetable Stew 42	Spicy Winter Chickpeas 53
Quinoa Pilaf 42	Bean Soup 53
Sauteed Green Beans and Eggplant 42	Turkish Split Pea Stew 53
Barley with Mushrooms 43	Chickpea Pumpkin Lentil Curry 54
Cauliflower Lentil Curry 43	Tomato Lentil Soup 54
Cauliflower Curried Soup 43	Veggie Corn Soup 54
Buttered Peas Rice 44	Green Pea and Cauliflower Korma 55
Banana Bread 44	Red Beans with Bell Pepper 55
Chickpeas and Tofu 44	Vegetarian Curry 55
Soft Broccoli Quiche 45	Steamed Winter Veggies 56
Chickpea Spinach Soup 45	Delicious Carrot Potato Medley 56
Red Beans Bowl 46	Spicy Black Eyed Peas 56
Cauliflower "Mac" and Cheese 46	Pumpkin Pudding 57
Red Beans Cabbage Soup 46	Chickpea Lentil Chili 57
Potato Okra Curry 47	Parmesan Marinara Spaghetti Squash 57
Flavorful Vegetable Curry 47	Spicy Curried Chickpeas 58
Tempeh with Figs 47	Gluten Free Chickpea Curry 58

- Sloppy Joe Filling 58
- Spicy Vegetable Curry 59
- Zucchini Noodles 59
- Broccoli with Garlic Sauce 59
- North Indian red Beans 60
- Lentil Potato Coconut Curry 60
- Simple Slow Cooker Lentils 61
- Broccoli in Tomato Sauce 61
- Chickpea Coconut Quinoa Curry 61
- Garlic Smashed Potatoes 62
- Spicy Eggplant Potatoes 62
- Asparagus Cream Soup 62
- Delicious Tofu Coconut Curry 63
- Butternut Squash Risotto 63
- Baked Beans 63
- Spinach Coconut Lentil Soup 63
- Bulgur with Vegetables 64
- Butter Garlic Green Beans 64
- Chili with Cornmeal Dumplings 64
- Lentil Butternut Squash Curry 65
- Tomato Casserole with Onion 65
- Wild Rice with Mushrooms 65
- Simple Instant Pot Lentil 66
- Warm Broccoli Salad 66
- Lentil Sweet Potato Soup 66
- Creamy Cauliflower Soup 67
- Polenta Porridge 67
- Lentil Chicken Vegetable Curry 67
- Steamed Artichokes 68
- White Bean Wraps 68
- Red Beans and Lentils 68
- Wild Rice Soup 69
- Easy Whole Cauliflower Curry 69
- Easy Southwestern Soup 69
- Vegetable Curried Rice 70
- Original Brussel Sprouts Salads 70
- Coconut Tapioca Pudding 70
- Hearty Vegetarian Chili 71
- Red Bean Rice 71
- Brussels sprouts with Pine nuts 71
- Vegetable Fajitas 72
- Creamy Coconut Pumpkin Curry 72
- Easy Black Bean Soup 72
- Piña Colada Upside Down Cake 73
- Bitter Melon and Mushroom in Wrap 73
- Plum Slump 73
- Roasted Potato Wedges 74
- Sticky Mango Rice 74
- Brussels sprouts with Parmesan Cheese .. 74
- Broccoli Cheese Soup 75
- Harvest Couscous 75
- Lentil Vegetable Soup 75
- Delicious Lemon Lentils 75
- Spinach Curry with Lentils 75
- Cauliflower Casserole 76
- Tomato Rice with Zucchini 76
- Simple Quinoa Risotto 77
- Summer Vegetable Soup 77
- Perfect Mashed Potatoes 77
- Spicy Green Beans in Red Gravy 77
- Orange Sweet Potatoes 78
- Punjabi Red Bean Curry 78
- Green Lentil Curry 79
- Easy Cauliflower Rice 79
- Tangy Raspberry Lemon Curd 79
- Eggplant Chickpea Curry 80

- Root Vegetables 80
- Cazuela 80
- Nutritious Veggie Soup 80
- Rhubarb Strawberry Apple Crisp 81
- Tasty Carrot Lentils Soup 81
- Delicious Spiced Potatoes and Cauliflower 81
- Coconut Eggplant Curry 82
- Mushroom Veggie Soup with Tofu 82
- Green Beans Barley Soup 82
- Crisp and Tender Potatoes 83
- Hearty Potato Curry 83
- Broccoli Kale Soup 83
- Gluten Free Masala Lentils 84
- Riced Cauliflower 84
- Easy Lentils Rice 84
- Pea Chickpea Vegetable Curry 85
- Lentil Chili 85
- Spinach Lentils 85
- Vegetarian Chili 86
- Beet Borscht 86
- Lentil Soup with Spinach 86
- Chickpea Spinach Cauliflower Curry 87
- Butternut Squash Creamy Soup 87
- Eggplant Caponata 87
- Tasty Black Eyed Pea Curry 88
- Balsamic Tomato & Red Pepper Soup 88
- Smokey Lentil Soup 88
- Applesauce 89
- Quick Steamed Broccoli 89
- Spaghetti 89
- Spicy Lentil Stew 89
- Creamy Cauliflower Broccoli Soup 90
- Refried Black Beans 90
- Spring Veggie Soup 90
- Chilled Quinoa Salad 91
- Spiced Coconut Lentils 91
- Collard Green with Egg 92
- Creamy Curry Cauliflower Soup 92
- Blueberry Cobbler 92
- Chickpea Curry 93
- Potato Cheese Soup 93
- Creole Red Beans 93
- Sweet Potato Chili 94
- Split Pea Soup 94
- Fruity Butternut Squash 94
- Tasty Sweet Potato Soup 95
- Taco Beans & Rice Bowls 95
- Tempered Lentils 95
- Spicy Keema Lentils 96
- Tomato Basil Soup 96

Chapter 2: Beef 97
- Easy and Hearty Beef Stew 98
- Beef and Broccoli 98
- Stuffed Bell Peppers 98
- Slow Cooked Garlic Cinnamon Beef 99
- Beef in Gravy 99
- Beef Stroganoff 99
- Simple Beef Fajitas 100
- Classic Shepherd's Pie 100
- Mongolian Beef 101
- Boneless BBQ Beef Ribs 101
- Simple Beef Curry 101
- Mushroom Eggplant Potato Curry 102
- Refreshing Beef Mango 102
- Paprika Taco Meat 103

Simple Beef Bourguignon	103
Beef Short Ribs	103
Buttery Beef Ribs with Potatoes	104
Veggie Steak Soup	104
Beef Coconut Fritter	104
Spicy Beef Chuck Roast	105
Perfect Beef Stew	105
Beef Balls Light Soup	106
Instant Pot Roast	106
Hot Beef Ribs	107
Spicy Beef Roast	107
Apple Breadcrumb Meatloaf	107
Herb Garlic Pot Roast	108
Spicy and Tender Italian Beef	108
Simple Beef Bean Chili	108
Pot Roast	108
Ground Beef with Green Beans	109
Broccoli Beef Curry Stew	109
Hearty Spaghetti Sauce	110
Super Tender Italian Pot Roast	110
Tasty Beef Ragu	110
Slow cooked Fancy Beef	111
Beef Stew	111
Beef Couscous Stuffed Bell Peppers	112
Tender Greek Pot Roast	112
Tender Korean Beef	113
Sweet Crispy Beef	113
Low Carb Beef	113
Mexican Beef Stew	114
Steamed Beef in Coconut	114
Beef Heart	114
Gluten Free Pot Roast	115
Lasagna	115
Vegetable Beef Roast	115
Balsamic Beef Roast	116
Beef Pasta Black Pepper	116
Taco Bowls	116
Flavorful Jalapeno Beef	117
Juicy Roast Beef Sandwiches	117
Round Steak with Peppers	118
Beef Chili	118
Salty Beef Brisket	118
Tasty Mongolian Beef	119
Hot Pepper Shredded Beef	119
Spicy Habanero Chili	119
Beef Ragu	120
Curry Jalapeno Beef Stew	120
Beef Tender in Sweet Red Sauce	120
Cinnamon Honey Beef	121
Spicy Beef with Beans	121
Creamy Beef Stroganoff	121
Flavorful Slow Cooker Chili	122
Chunky Steak Chili	122
Chili Lime Shredded Beef	123
Bell Pepper Ground Beef Chili	123
Beef Mushroom Pie	124
Garlic Beef Short Ribs	124
Herb Pot Roast	124
Roasted Tomato Beef Curry	125
Spicy Orange Beef	125
Beef Stew	125
Juicy Beef Meatballs Marinara	126
Simple Beef Tacos	126
Beef Mix Vegetable Soup	126
Beef Bolognese Mushroom	127
Meatloaf	127

Beef Curry	128
Italian Beef	128
Bacon Cheeseburger Casserole	128
Beef and Potatoes	129
Beef Ribs	129
Beef Steak Black Pepper	129
Onion Chuck Roast	130
Tomato Beef Brisket	130
Braised Beef Ribs	130
Hot Beef with Herbs	131
Taco Meat	131
Oxtail Soup	132
Beef Tomato Soup	132
Chipotle Mexican Beef Stew	132
Sweet Beef Curry	133
Spicy Beef Stew	133
Chipotle Barbacoa	133
Smoky Beef Brisket	134
Meatballs with sauce	134
Mexican Meatloaf	134
Beanless Beef Chili	135
Simple Corned Beef	135
Corned Beef with Cabbage	135
Beef Potato Gratin	136

Chapter 3: Poultry ... 137

Tasty Cheeseburger Soup	138
Chicken Pot Pie	138
Spicy Chicken Curry	138
Chicken Vindaloo	139
Cinnamon Chicken Soup	139
Turkey with Sauerkraut	139
Savory Turkey Stew	140
Super easy Cashew Chicken	140
Sweet Chicken Wings with Black Pepper	141
Lemon Chicken	141
Classic Chicken Adobo	141
Lemon Garlic Chicken Breasts	142
Tasty Tso's Chicken	142
Simple BBQ Chicken	143
Chicken Garlic Rosemary	143
Spicy Cauliflower Chicken	143
Ranch Chicken Wings	144
Turkey Vaca Frita	144
Chicken Curry Tomato with Eggplant	144
Mushroom Leek Chicken	145
Turkey Soup	145
Chicken Wings Cola	146
Bacon and Mushroom with Honey Mustard Chicken	146
Original Salty Chicken	146
Turkey Sausage with Cabbage	146
Mediterranean Chicken Wings	147
Chicken Wings Barbecue	147
Chicken Taco Soup	147
Whole Turkey	148
Chicken Drumstick Soup	148
Slow Cooked Turkey Breast	148
Honey Chicken Apple	149
Curried Chicken Bowls	149
Easy White Chicken Chili	150
Spiced Chicken Cake	150
Chicken Quinoa Curry	151
Cafe Rio Chicken	151
Chicken Mushroom Stew	151
Yellow Chicken Curry	152

Turkey Sandwich Meat	152
Spicy Sour Chicken Soup	152
Creamy Chicken Vegetable Soup	153
Creamy Chicken Carrots	153
Chicken Soup	153
Honey Mustard Chicken	154
Rosemary Chicken	154
Sweet Brown Chicken	154
Teriyaki Chicken	155
Simple Turkey and Gravy	155
Tasty Chicken Enchilada Soup	156
Tasty Coconut Drumsticks	156
Tasty Leftover Turkey Stew	156
Salsa Verde Chicken	157
Chicken Potato with Lemon Sauce	157
Chicken Chili Verde	158
Shredded Chicken Wraps	158
Spicy Buffalo Chicken	158
Tasty Chicken Kheema	158
Japanese Chicken Teriyaki	159
Moroccan Chicken	159
Asian Chicken Legs	160
Shredded Chicken Pineapple	160
Creamy Coconut Chicken Curry	160
Chicken Vegetable Soup	161
Cranberry Turkey Wings	161
Sticky Honey Chicken	161
Tasty Fajita Soup	162
Shredded Chicken Garlic	162
Simple Shredded Chicken	163
Chicken Tomato Pasta	163
Tender and Juicy Turkey Breast	163
Chicken Salads in Cabbage Blanket	164
Black Pepper Chicken Thigh Stew	164
Easy 3 Ingredients Chicken	164
Moist and Tender Baked Chicken	164
Chicken Lettuce Wraps	165
Whole Turkey	165
Sweet Orange Honey Chicken	165
Caesar Chicken	166
Bacon-Wrapped Stuffed Chicken Breasts	166
Easy Chicken Wings	166
Chicken Stew	167
Easy Salsa Chicken	167
Perfect Chicken Curry	167
Chicken Rice Casserole	168
Simple Mustard Pulled Turkey	168
Simple Lime Chicken	168
Pulled Chicken Taco Salad	169
Quick Turkey Breast	169
Italian Chicken	169
Easy Pot Turkey	170
Chicken Potato Curry	170
Chicken Korma	171
Flavorful Chicken Curry	171
Bruschetta Chicken	171
Instant Pot Whole Chicken	172
Spicy White Chicken Chili	172
Easy Curried Chicken	172
Thai Red Curry with Chicken	173
Perfect Mexican Chicken	173
Adobo Chicken	173
Peanut Butter Chicken	174
Onion Balsamic Chicken	174
Chicken Cacciatore	174

Turkey Thighs 175	Easy Turkey Drumsticks 186
Rutabaga Chicken Soup 175	Garlicky Sweet Chicken 186
Chicken Leg Quarters with Lemon and Rosemary 175	Chicken Coconut Curry 186
Flavorful Chicken Cacciatore 176	Lemon Garlic Chicken Thighs with Green Beans 186
Red Pepper Chicken Tacos 176	Chicken Dumplings 187
Salsa Verde Shredded Chicken 176	Turkey and Bone Broth Gravy 187
Onion Garlic Chicken 177	Creamy Chicken Mushroom 188
Salsa Chicken 177	**Chapter 4: Pork** 189
Spicy Shredded Chicken 177	Pork Tender in Tropical Sauce 190
Chicken Tikka Masala 178	Tasty Sausage Soup 190
Olive Lemon Chicken 178	Pineapple Pork 190
Butter Chicken 178	Smoked Sausage & Cabbage 191
Easy Shredded Chicken 179	Pork Stew 191
Chicken Vegetable Curry 179	Pork Clear Soup with Collard Green 191
Tasty Chicken Fajitas 179	Citrusy Pork Carnitas 192
Chicken Tandoori 180	Appetizing Pork with Cabbage 192
Herbed Turkey Breast 180	Ginger-Honey Pork Tenderloin 192
Delicious Whole Chicken 180	Sweet Pork Belly 193
Lemon Garlic Quarter Chicken 181	Savory Pork Loin 193
Green Chicken Curry 181	Thai Pork Stew 193
Quick and Easy Turkey Breast 181	Hot Pork Ginger 194
Chicken Drumsticks 182	Tangy and Sticky Chicken 194
Tasty Chicken Tikka Masala 182	Simple Pork Ribs 194
Easy Dinner Turkey Roast 183	Apple Ginger Pork Stew 195
Garlic Lemon Dump Chicken 183	Apple Cider Shredded Pork 195
Orange Chicken Chunks 183	Smothered Pork Chops 195
Chicken Noodle Soup 184	Special Pork in Tomato Sticky Sauce ... 196
Shredded Turkey 184	Pork Ribs 196
Tasty Ranch Chicken 184	Savory Pork Belly in Fresh Basil 197
Basil Chicken Breasts 185	Pork Chops with Mushroom 197
Juicy and Tender Chicken Breasts 185	Simple Pork Garlic 197
Chicken Dinner 185	Peppercini Pot Roast 198

Easy Pork Sausage.................................198
Garlic Balsamic Pork Chops....................198
Salty and Spicy Pork..............................199
Delicious Pork Shoulder.........................200
Pork Meatballs in Sticky Sauce...............201
Tasty Pork Carnitas................................201
Simple Pulled Pork.................................201
Flavorful Shredded Pork........................202
Pork Belly Black Pepper.........................202
Pork Chops with Gravy..........................202
Pork Feet Stew with Vegetables.............203
Creamy Chicken....................................203
Cinnamon Honey Pork Chops................203
Baby Back Ribs......................................204
Chinese Steamed Pork Bags..................204
Green Chile Pork Stew..........................204
Crispy Pork in Sweet Sour Sauce............205
Easy Balsamic Pork Tenderloin..............205
Simple Cheesy Pork Meatloaf................206
Perfect Pork Ragu..................................206
Hot Chili Pork Ribs................................206
Honey Lime Shredded Pork with Chicken Stock..207
Pulled Pork Carnitas..............................207
Pork Roast Black Pepper.......................207
Pork Chops with Brussels sprouts..........208
Garlic Cumin Grapefruit Shredded Pork 208
Apple Pork Ribs.....................................209
Simple Kalua Pork.................................209
Crispy Pulled Pork.................................209
Kale Garlic Pork....................................210
Sirloin Tip Roast....................................210
Tender and Juicy shredded Pork............210

Ham & Asparagus Soup.........................211
Tasty Pork Stew.....................................211
Tomato Pulled Pork...............................211
Perfect Cuban Pork................................212
Jerk Pork Roast......................................212
Crustless Ham & Swiss Quiche..............212
Ranch Pork Chops..................................213
Herb Pork Tenderloin.............................213
Herb Pork Loin......................................213
Smoked Pulled Pork...............................214
Pork Carnitas...214
Garlic Thyme Pork Shoulder..................215
Pork Chops with Apples........................215
Loaded Cauliflower Bowls....................215
Shredded Pork.......................................216

Chapter 5: Seafood.................................217
Red Hot Fish...218
Creamy Coconut Fish Curry..................218
Sweet Soy Fish......................................218
Salmon with Broccoli............................219
Stuffed Squids in Tomato.......................219
Sea Bass Coconut Curry........................219
Vegetable Shrimps Tom Yum Soup.......220
Mahi Fillets...220
Steamed Lemon Crabs...........................220
Shrimp Scampi......................................221
Simple Steamed Salmon Fillet...............221
Quick Buttery Salmon...........................221
Tasty Seafood Chowder.........................222
Spicy Salmon Fillets..............................222
Easy Tuna Tender..................................222
Fish Chowder..223
Flavourful Salmon Fillets......................223

Creole Jambalaya	224
Clam Potato Chowder	224
Salty Spicy Salmon Balls	225
Pepper Lemon Salmon	225
Coconut Lime Catfish Curry	225
Chewy Fish in Tomato Light Soup	226
Spicy Fish in Savory Tomato Gravy	226
Crispy Salmon with Honey Glaze	227
Steamed Lobster Tails	227
Simple Salmon Fillets	227
Quick Salmon with Dill	228
Salsa Poached Cod	228
Warm Steamed Fish Ginger	228
Steamed Crabs Garlic	229
Salmon with Chili Lime Sauce	229
Brown Caramel Salmon	229
Teriyaki Salmon	230
Green Chili Tuna Pasta	230
Original Savory Shrimps	231
Mediterranean Cod	231
Squids Tomato Veggie	231
Ginger Scallion Tilapia	232
Chapter 6: Lamb	**233**
Ginger Goat (or Lamb) Curry	234
Easy Instant Pot Leg of Lamb	234
Easy Lamb Stew	234
Tomato Lamb Rogan Josh	235
Perfect Taco Mince	235
Cilantro Almond Lamb Curry	236
Coconut Milk Lamb Curry	236
Shredded Lamb	237
Spicy Lamb Curry	237
Shredded Lime Mint Lamb	237
Lamb Shanks with Ginger	238
Classic Lamb Curry	238
Coconut Milk Lamb Curry	239
Lamb Chops	239
Classic Lamb Rogan Josh	240
Spinach Lamb Curry	240
The "Dirty Dozen" and "Clean 15"	241
Measurement Conversion Tables	242
Recipe Index	243

Chapter 1: Vegetarian

Delicious Black Lentil Curry

Total Time: 12 hours 15 minutes; Serves: 8; Calories 186, Fat 4 g, Carbohydrates 27 g, Sugar 2 g, Protein 10 g, Cholesterol 9 mg

- 1 cup whole black gram lentils
- 3 cloves
- 1 tbsp ginger, chopped
- 8 garlic cloves, chopped
- 2 green chilies, cut lengthwise
- 1 tbsp coriander powder
- 1/2 tsp turmeric powder
- 1/2 cup kidney beans
- 1 bay leaf
- 1 cinnamon stick
- 3 cardamom pods
- 1/2 tsp chili powder
- 4 tomatoes, diced
- 1 tsp garam masala
- 1/4 cup cream
- 2 tbsp butter
- Salt

- Use the "Slow Cooker" setting on your Instant Pot.
- Soak black lentils and kidney beans in water for overnight.
- Add all ingredients except cream into the Instant Pot with 4 cups water and stir well.
- Cover and cook on low for 12 hours.
- Stir well and lightly mash using the back of a spoon.
- Add cream and stir well.
- Serve and enjoy.

Frijoles Borrachos (Mexican "Drunken Beans")

Serves: 8, Preparation time: 10 minutes, Cooking time: 40 minutes, Per Serving: Calories: 156; Total Fat: 3g; Saturated Fat: 1g; Protein: 8g; Carbs: 29g; Fiber: 18g; Sugar: 4g

- 1 white onion (diced)
- 1 green bell pepper (diced)
- 1 tablespoon vegetable oil
- 4 cloves garlic (minced)
- 1 pound dry Pinto beans (rinsed, drained)
- 8 cups vegetable stock or water
- 1 can (28 ounces) diced stewed tomatoes
- 1 can (12 ounces) Mexican beer
- 1 can (4 ounces) diced jalapenos (drained)
- 1 tablespoon salt, plus more to taste
- 2 teaspoons dried oregano
- 1 ½ teaspoons freshly ground black pepper, plus more to taste
- Salt, to taste
- 1 teaspoon ground chipotle chili pepper
- 3 whole dried bay leaves
- 1 teaspoon cumin
- 1 lime, cut into wedges

- In Instant Pot on sauté setting, cook onion and bell pepper in oil until softened, about 5 minutes. Add garlic and cook about 1 minute more.
- Add beans, vegetable stock, undrained tomatoes, beer, jalapenos, salt, oregano, black pepper, chipotle pepper, bay leaves and cumin to pot and mix thoroughly.
- Secure pot lid, close pressure valve and cook on bean/chili setting for 40 minutes. When cooking time ends, let pressure release naturally. Remove bay leaves, stir beans and season to taste with salt and pepper.
- If desired, mash beans with a fork to thicken the cooking juices. Garnish beans with lime wedges to serve. Enjoy!

Navratan Korma

Total Time: 8 hours 15 minutes; Serves: 2; Calories 237; Fat 10.6 g; Carbohydrates 33.6 g; Sugar 17.6 g; Protein 6.7 g; Cholesterol 5 mg

- 1/2 cup tomatoes, diced
- 1/2 cup peas
- 1 cup carrots, chopped
- 1 cup cauliflower florets
- 2 tbsp sour cream
- 1/4 cup almond milk
- 1 tbsp raisins
- 1/4 tsp chili powder

1/2 tsp ground coriander
1/2 tsp ground turmeric
1 tbsp ginger, grated
2 tbsp bell pepper, minced

1/4 cup onion
1/2 cup water
Salt

- Use the "Slow Cooker" setting on your Instant Pot.
- Add all ingredients except sour cream, milk, and salt into the slow cooker.
- Cover and cook on low for 8 hours.
- Just before serving add sour cream and milk and stir well.
- Season with salt and serve.

Winter Veggie Soup

Total Time: 8 hours 10 minutes; Serves: 2; Calories 134; Fat 1.4 g; Carbohydrates 28.7 g; Sugar 11.4 g; Protein 4.2 g; Cholesterol 0 mg

1 shallot, minced
1 garlic clove, minced
1/4 cup can tomatoes, diced
1/4 cup celery cubed
1 parsnip, diced
1 celery stalk, diced

1 small carrot, diced
1 tbsp fresh dill
1/4 tsp white pepper
1 tsp celery flakes
2 cup chicken stock
1/8 tsp salt

- Use the "Slow Cooker" setting on your Instant Pot.
- Add all ingredients to the slow cooker and stir well.
- Cover and cook on low for 8 hours.
- Serve and enjoy.

Lentil Sweet Potato Beans Stew

Total Time: 6 hours 30 minutes; Serves: 6; Calories 269, Fat 5.9 g, Carbohydrates 43.5 g, Sugar 4.8 g, Protein 10.8 g, Cholesterol 1 mg

3/4 cup dry lentils, rinsed and drained
3 cups sweet potatoes, cut into 1 inch cubed
1 1/2 cups green beans, cut into pieces
1 1/2 cups baby carrots
1/2 cup plain yogurt
1 3/4 cup vegetable broth
2 garlic cloves, minced

1 tsp fresh ginger, chopped
1 tsp ground cumin
1 tbsp curry powder
2 tbsp vegetable oil
1/4 cup onion, chopped
1/4 tsp black pepper
1/2 tsp salt

- Use the "Slow Cooker" setting on your Instant Pot.
- Add lentils, carrots, onion, and sweet potatoes into the Instant Pot.
- In a pan, heat oil over medium heat.
- Add garlic, ginger, pepper, cumin, curry powder, and salt and stir for 1 minute. Stir in broth.
- Pour mixture into the Instant Pot and mix well.
- Cover and cook on low for 6 hours.
- Turn heat to high and stir in green beans. Cover and cook for another 15 minutes.
- Top with plain yogurt and serve.

Cinnamon Carrots and Apples

Serves: 4, Preparation time: 15 minutes, Cooking time: 1 minute, Per Serving: Calories: 207; Total Fat: 4g; Saturated Fat: 3g; Protein: 2g; Carbs: 47g; Fiber: 7g; Sugar: 34g.

4 large carrots (peeled, sliced)
1 tablespoon coconut oil

4 Granny Smith apples (cored, sliced)
¼ cup brown sugar

1 teaspoon cinnamon
½ teaspoon nutmeg
½ cup almond milk
½ cup water
1 orange (zested, juiced)
Salt, to taste

- In Instant Pot on sauté setting, cook carrots in oil until softened, about 5 minutes. Add apples, brown sugar, cinnamon, nutmeg, almond milk, water and orange juice, season to taste with salt and mix well.
- Secure pot lid, close pressure valve and cook on high pressure for 1 minute. When cooking time ends, let pressure release naturally.
- Season carrots and apples to taste with salt, stir gently and spoon into bowls. Sprinkle orange zest over carrots and apples to serve. Enjoy!

Broccoli Cauliflower Soup

Serves: 6, Preparation time: 10 minutes, Cooking time: 30 minutes, Per Serving: Calories: 228; Total Fat: 16g; Saturated Fat: 9g; Protein: 9g; Carbs: 7g; Fiber: 5g; Sugar: 2g

1 tablespoon butter
3 stalks celery, trimmed and diced
1 small onion, diced
3 cloves garlic, peeled and minced
1 package (10 ounces) frozen broccoli
1 package (10 ounces) frozen cauliflower
4 cups chicken stock
1 package (3 ounces) cream cheese, softened
¼ teaspoon ground nutmeg
6 ounces sharp cheddar cheese, shredded
Salt and freshly ground black pepper, to taste

- In Instant Pot on sauté setting, melt butter and cook celery, onion and garlic until translucent, about 5 minutes.
- Add broccoli, cauliflower, chicken stock, cream cheese and nutmeg to pot and season to taste with salt and pepper.
- Secure pot lid, close pressure valve and cook on high setting for 30 minutes. When cooking time ends, let pressure release naturally.
- For chunky soup, serve immediately; otherwise puree soup with an immersion blender to desired texture. Garnish servings of soup with grated cheese and enjoy!

Perfect Carrot Soup

30 minutes, Serves: 4, Calories 363; Fat 30.8 g; Carbohydrates 20.3 g; Sugar 10.4 g; Protein 6 g; Cholesterol 8 mg

1 lb carrots, peeled and chopped
14 oz coconut milk, unsweetened
2 cups chicken broth, low sodium
1 Tsp fresh ginger, minced
1 garlic clove, minced
1 medium onion, chopped
1 tbsp extra virgin olive oil
1 tbsp clarified butter
Pepper
Salt

- Add oil in instant pot and select sauté.
- Add onion, ginger, and garlic and sauté for 1 minute.
- Add carrots and season with pepper and salt and sauté for 2 minutes.
- Stir in coconut milk and chicken broth.
- Seal pot with lid and cook on manual high pressure for 6 minutes.
- Allow releasing pressure naturally then open the lid.
- Using blender puree the soup until smooth.
- Season with pepper and salt.
- Serve warm and enjoy.

Easy Taco Soup

Serves: 12, Preparation time: 10 minutes, Cooking time: 25 minutes, Per Serving: Calories: 196; Total Fat: 2g; Saturated Fat: 0g; Protein: 12g; Carbs: 31g; Fiber: 7g; Sugar: 6g

1 onion (diced)
1 green bell pepper (diced)
1 red bell pepper (diced)
2 tablespoons olive oil
4 garlic cloves (minced)
2 cans (16 ounces each) pinto beans
2 cans (15 ounces each) great northern beans
2 cans (15 ounces each) hominy
2 cans (15 ounces each) whole kernel corn
2 cans (10 ounces each) diced tomatoes with chilies
1 tablespoon chili powder
2 teaspoons ground cumin
1 teaspoon dried oregano
1 teaspoon paprika
½ teaspoon cayenne pepper
½ teaspoon freshly ground black pepper
2 avocados (pitted, sliced)

- In Instant Pot on sauté setting, cook onion and bell peppers in oil until softened, stirring frequently, about 5 minutes. Add garlic and cook about 1 minute more.
- Add undrained cans of beans, hominy, corn and tomatoes to pot. Add chili powder, cumin, oregano, paprika, cayenne pepper and black pepper to pot and mix well.
- Secure pot lid, close pressure valve and cook on high setting for 20 minutes. When cooking time ends, let pressure release naturally.
- Stir soup thoroughly and ladle into deep bowls. Garnish with avocado slices and serve. Enjoy!

Spaghetti Squash Marinara

Serves: 4, Preparation time: 15 minutes, Cooking time: 30 minutes, Per Serving: Calories: 257; Total Fat: 12g; Saturated Fat: 0g; Protein: 7g; Carbs: 29g; Fiber: 9g; Sugar: 0g

1 large spaghetti squash
1 cup water
2 tablespoons olive oil (divided)
1 medium onion (finely diced)
1 small red bell pepper (finely diced)
4 garlic cloves (peeled, minced)
1 can (28 ounces) crushed tomatoes
1 can (6 ounces) tomato paste
1 tablespoon Italian herb blend
Salt and freshly ground black pepper, to taste

- Pierce spaghetti squash skin all over with a fork or the tip of a sharp knife. Pour water into Instant Pot, set trivet in pot and place squash on trivet. Secure pot lid, close pressure valve and cook on high setting for 10 minutes. When cooking time ends, let pressure release naturally. Remove trivet and set squash aside.
- Drain water from pot, set pot to sauté and cook onion and bell pepper in 1 tablespoon oil until softened, stirring frequently, about 4 minutes. Add garlic and cook about 1 minute more. Add tomatoes, tomato paste and herb blend to pot, season to taste with salt and pepper and mix thoroughly. Secure pot lid, close pressure valve and cook on high setting for 8 minutes. When cooking time ends, let pressure release naturally.
- While the sauce is cooking, cut the squash in half. Scoop out and discard squash seeds. Scrape the squash flesh from the shell into strings with a fork. Toss squash with remaining olive oil and season to taste with salt and pepper. Spoon squash into pasta bowls and top with the sauce to serve. Enjoy!

Mushroom Stroganoff

Total Time: 4 hours 20 minutes; Serves: 2; Calories 221; Fat 7.5 g; Carbohydrates 21.9 g; Sugar 10.1 g; Protein 10.2 g; Cholesterol 28 mg

1 lb mushrooms, sliced
1/4 cup sour cream
3 garlic cloves, sliced
3 tsp paprika
2 tbsp tomato ketchup
1 stock cube
1 tbsp butter
1 onion, diced

- Use the "Slow Cooker" setting on your Instant Pot.
- Melt butter in the pan.
- Add mushroom and onion to the pan and cook for 10 minutes.
- Transfer mushroom and onion mixture into the slow cooker.
- Add remaining ingredients to the slow cooker and mix well.
- Cover and cook on high for 4 hours.
- Serve over pasta and enjoy.

Creamy Mashed Potato

15 minutes, Serves: 6, Calories 282; Fat 13.6 g; Carbohydrates 37.4 g; Sugar 3.4 g; Protein 4.8 g; Cholesterol 15 mg

- 3 lbs potatoes, peeled and diced
- 1 tbsp mustard powder
- 1 tbsp fresh parsley, chopped
- 1/2 cup almond milk
- 1 tbsp coconut oil
- 3 tbsp clarified butter
- Pepper
- Salt

- Pour 1 cup water into the instant pot.
- Add potatoes in pot and season with pepper and salt.
- Seal pot with lid and cook on manual high pressure for 10 minutes.
- Release pressure using quick release method than open the lid carefully.
- Transfer potatoes in a large mixing bowl.
- Add remaining ingredients and using masher mash the potatoes.
- Serve and enjoy.

Squash Curry Soup

Serves: 4, Preparation time: 25 minutes, Cooking time: 35 minutes, Per Serving: Calories: 199; Total Fat: 4g; Saturated Fat: 1g; Protein: 4g; Carbs: 10g; Fiber: 2g; Sugar: 0g

- 1 onion (diced)
- 1 celery stalk (diced)
- 1 medium carrot (peeled, diced)
- 2 tablespoons olive oil
- 1 teaspoon curry powder
- Dash of ground cinnamon
- Dash of ground nutmeg
- 1 medium butternut squash (peeled, seeded, cubed)
- 4 cups vegetable stock
- 1 dried bay leaf
- ¼ cup coconut cream
- Salt and freshly ground black pepper, to taste
- 2 tablespoons pine nuts (toasted)

- In Instant Pot on sauté setting, cook onion, celery and carrot in oil until softened, stirring frequently, about 5 minutes. Add curry powder, cinnamon and nutmeg and stir until onion mixture is coated.
- Add squash, vegetable stock and bay leaf to pot, season to taste with salt and pepper and mix well.
- Secure pot lid, close pressure valve and cook at high pressure for 30 minutes. When cooking time ends, let pressure release naturally.
- Remove bay leaf from soup, add coconut cream and process soup with an immersion blender until smooth. Garnish soup with pine nuts to serve. Enjoy!

Creamy Split Pea Curry

Total Time: 6 hours 15 minutes; Serves: 6; Calories 425, Fat 23.8 g, Carbohydrates 42.4 g, Sugar 9 g, Protein 15.5 g, Cholesterol 27 mg

- 1 1/2 cups dried split peas
- 1 cup heavy cream
- 1/2 tsp ground ginger
- 2 tsp curry powder
- 1 tbsp turmeric
- 1 tbsp green curry paste
- 3 garlic cloves, minced
- 1/2 cup onion, diced
- 15 oz can coconut milk
- 28 oz can tomatoes, crushed
- 1 tsp salt

- Use the "Slow Cooker" setting on your Instant Pot.
- Add all ingredients except cream into the Instant Pot. Stir well.
- Cover and cook on low for 6 hours.
- Add cream and stir well.
- Serve with rice and enjoy.

Easy Winter Veggie Soup

30 minutes, Serves: 8, Calories 167; Fat 11.4 g; Carbohydrates 15 g; Sugar 4.7 g; Protein 3.8 g; Cholesterol 0 mg

- 1 medium onion, diced
- 3 cups butternut squash, diced
- 1 cup parsnips, diced
- 1 cup carrots, diced
- 1 cup celery, diced
- 2 tbsp extra virgin olive oil
- 1 cup coconut cream
- 3 cups chicken broth
- 3 garlic cloves, diced
- 2 fresh bay leaves
- 2 sprig rosemary
- 3 sprig fresh thyme
- 3 stalks fresh parsley
- 1/2 Tsp pepper
- 1 Tsp salt

- Add oil in instant pot and select sauté.
- Add onion, butternut squash, parsnips, carrots, and celery in pot and sauté for 8 minutes.
- Add garlic, herbs, pepper, and salt and sauté for 2 minutes.
- Add coconut cream and broth and stir well.
- Seal pot with lid and cook on soup setting for 15 minutes.
- Release pressure using quick release method than open the lid.
- Stir well and serve.

Vegetable Coconut Curry

Total Time: 4 hours 20 minutes; Serves: 8; Calories 370, Fat 18.3 g, Carbohydrates 48.8 g, Sugar 5.4 g, Protein 8.2 g, Cholesterol 0 mg

- 1/4 cup cilantro, chopped
- 1 cup green peas
- 1 1/2 cups carrots, peeled and cut into strips
- 14 oz can coconut milk
- 1 oz dry onion soup mix
- 2 bell pepper, cut into strips
- 1/2 tsp cayenne pepper
- 1/2 tsp red pepper flakes
- 1 tbsp chili powder
- 2 tbsp flour
- 1/4 cup curry powder
- 5 potatoes, peeled and cut into cubes
- Water as needed

- Use the "Slow Cooker" setting on your Instant Pot.
- Add all ingredients into the Instant Pot and mix well.
- Cover and cook on low for 4 hours.
- Stir well and serve.

Yummy Slow Cooked Potatoes

Total Time: 6 hours 15 minutes; Serves: 4; Calories 235, Fat 4.4 g, Carbohydrates 45.8 g, Sugar 6.2 g, Protein 5.7 g, Cholesterol 0 mg

- 2.2 lbs potatoes, peel and cut into cubes
- 1/2 tsp chili powder
- 1/2 tsp cumin
- 1 1/2 tsp turmeric
- 1 tsp garam masala
- 1 tsp ground ginger
- 1 tsp mustard seeds
- 4 tomatoes, chopped
- 1/4 tsp red chili flakes
- 1 tbsp vegetable oil
- 1 tsp salt

- Use the "Slow Cooker" setting on your Instant Pot.
- In a bowl, mix together chili flakes, chili powder, cumin, turmeric, garam masala, and ginger.
- Heat oil in the pan over medium heat.
- Add mustard seeds into the pan and stir until they start to pop then add onion and sauté until lightly brown.
- Add mixed spices and stir for a minute.
- Add tomatoes and salt and stir for a minute.

- Place potatoes in the Instant Pot then pour pan mixture over the potatoes.
- Cover and cook on low for 6 hours.
- Stir well and serve.

Mushroom Potato Stew

Serves: 8, Preparation time: 30 minutes, Cooking time: 25 minutes, Per Serving: Calories: 175; Total Fat: 4g; Saturated Fat: 1g; Protein: 5g; Carbs: 27g; Fiber: 5g; Sugar: 9g

1 yellow onion (diced)	3 cups vegetable stock
2 stalks celery (diced)	1 can (15 ounces) diced tomatoes
2 carrots (peeled, diced)	1 can (6 ounces) tomato paste
2 tablespoons olive oil	3 medium golden potatoes (peeled, cut into 1" chunks)
4 cups (about 24 ounces) assorted fresh mushrooms (cut into bite-size pieces as necessary)	2 teaspoons Italian herb mix
	2 tablespoons corn starch
2 garlic cloves (minced)	¼ cup cold water
1 cup dry sherry	

- In Instant Pot on sauté setting, cook onion, celery and carrots until slightly softened, stirring frequently, about 3 minutes. Add mushrooms and cook until wilted, about 4 minutes Add garlic and cook about 1 minute more, stirring constantly. Deglaze pot with sherry, scraping bottom of pot to release browned bits.
- Add vegetable stock, undrained tomatoes, tomato paste, potatoes and Italian herbs to pot, season to taste with salt and pepper and mix thoroughly. Secure pot lid, close pressure valve and cook on high pressure for 15 minutes. When cooking time ends, carefully turn venting knob from sealing to venting position for a quick pressure release.
- Season stew to taste with salt and pepper. Whisk cornstarch into water until smooth and gently stir into stew until thickened. Serve and enjoy!

Delicious Three Bean Chili

Total Time: 6 hours 10 minutes; Serves: 2; Calories 491; Fat 4.2 g; Carbohydrates 95 g; Sugar 16 g; Protein 26.7 g; Cholesterol 0 mg

7.5 oz can pinto beans, drained	1 garlic clove, minced
7.5 oz can black beans, drained	1/2 small onion, diced
15 oz can kidney beans, drained	3/4 cup corn kernels
1/2 tsp cayenne pepper	1 large bell pepper, diced
1/2 tsp cumin	7.5 oz can tomato, diced
1/2 cup salsa	Pepper
1 1/4 cups vegetable stock	Salt

- Use the "Slow Cooker" setting on your Instant Pot.
- Add all ingredients to the slow cooker and stir well.
- Cover and cook on low for 6 hours.
- Stir well and serve.

Lentil Curry

Total Time: 5 hours 10 minutes; Serves: 6; Calories 376, Fat 19 g, Carbohydrates 39 g, Sugar 4 g, Protein 15 g, Cholesterol 0 mg

1 1/2 cups green lentils, rinse and drained	1 onion, diced
3 tbsp tomato paste	3 garlic cloves, minced
14 oz can coconut milk	1 yellow pepper, diced
3 tsp curry powder	1/4 tsp pepper
	1/2 tsp ground ginger

2 tsp garam masala
2 tsp sugar
2 1/2 cups water
2 tbsp olive oil

1 tsp garlic powder
1 tsp cumin
1 1/2 tsp salt

- Use the "Slow Cooker" setting on your Instant Pot.
- Add olive oil, yellow pepper, garlic, and onion into the Instant Pot.
- Add lentils into the Instant Pot and stir well.
- Add all remaining ingredients and stir well.
- Cover and cook on low for 5 hours.
- Stir well and serve with rice.

Potato Red Lentil Curry

Total Time: 4 hours 15 minutes; Serves: 8;Calories 307, Fat 14 g, Carbohydrates 39 g, Sugar 3 g, Protein 13 g, Cholesterol 8 mg

1 cup red lentils, rinsed
2 potatoes, cut into cubed
1 cup brown lentil, rinsed
1 large onion, diced
1/2 tsp turmeric
1/2 tsp cumin seeds, toasted
1 tsp sugar

14 oz can tomato, diced
14 oz can coconut milk
1 tbsp garlic, minced
1 tsp ginger, minced
2 tbsp butter
2 tbsp curry powder
1/2 tsp red pepper flakes

- Use the "Slow Cooker" setting on your Instant Pot.
- Add all ingredients except coconut milk into the Instant Pot and stir well.
- Add water into the Instant Pot to cover lentil mixture.
- Cover and cook on high for 4 hours.
- Add coconut milk and stir well.
- Serve warm and enjoy.

Sweet Potato Peanut Stew

Serves: 4, Preparation time: 20 minutes, Cooking time: 15 minutes, Per Serving: Calories: 245; Total Fat: 7g; Saturated Fat: 1g; Protein: 10g; Carbs: 39g; Fiber: 10g; Sugar: 9g

1 onion (chopped)
2 celery stalks (chopped)
2 carrots (peeled, diced)
2 tablespoons coconut oil
2 garlic cloves (minced)
2 teaspoons paprika
Salt and freshly ground black pepper, to taste

3 cups vegetable stock
2 medium sweet potatoes (peeled, cut into 1" cubes)
1 can (15 ounces) diced tomatoes
½ cup smooth peanut butter
2 tablespoons tomato paste
2 bay leaves

- In Instant Pot on sauté setting, cook onion, celery and carrots in oil until softened, stirring frequently, about 5 minutes. Add garlic and paprika to pot, season to taste with salt and pepper and cook for about 1 minute, stirring constantly.
- Add vegetable stock, sweet potatoes, diced tomatoes, peanut butter, tomato paste and bay leaves to pot and mix thoroughly to combine. Secure pot lid, close pressure valve and cook on high pressure for 8 minutes. When cooking time ends, carefully turn venting knob from sealing to venting position for a quick pressure release.
- Remove bay leaves from stew, season stew to taste with salt and pepper and mix well. Serve and enjoy!

Cranberry Apple Crisp

Serves: 6, Preparation time: 15 minutes, Cooking time: 10 minutes, Per Serving: Calories: 320; Total Fat: 9g; Saturated Fat: 4g; Protein: 3g; Carbs: 65g; Fiber: 7g; Sugar: 43

- 6 medium apples (peeled, diced)
- ½ cup water
- ½ cup dried cranberries
- ¼ cup white sugar
- 2 teaspoons cinnamon, divided
- 1 teaspoon lemon juice
- 1 teaspoon nutmeg, divided
- 1 teaspoon corn starch
- ¼ teaspoon ground ginger
- ¾ cup rolled oats
- ¼ cup flour
- ¼ cup brown sugar
- 2 tablespoons coconut oil (melted)
- ¼ cup chopped pecans (lightly toasted)
- ¼ teaspoon salt

- Mix apples, water, dried cranberries, white sugar, 1 teaspoon cinnamon, lemon juice, ½ teaspoon nutmeg, corn starch and ginger, toss with apples and place in Instant Pot.
- For the topping, mix oats, flour, brown sugar, coconut oil, pecans, remaining cinnamon, remaining nutmeg and salt until crumbly and sprinkle in pot over apples.
- Secure pot lid, close pressure valve and cook on high pressure for 8 minutes. When cooking time ends, let pressure release naturally.
- Let crisp stand for about 10 minutes to allow sauce to thicken. Serve and enjoy!

Creamy Onion Soup

30 minutes, Serves: 6, Calories 111; Fat 6.7 g; Carbohydrates 16.3 g; Sugar 8.5 g; Protein 1.7 g; Cholesterol 0 mg

- 8 cups yellow onions, sliced
- 2 fresh thyme sprigs
- 2 bay leaves
- 6 cup vegetable stock
- 1 tbsp balsamic vinegar
- 2 tbsp coconut oil
- 1 Tsp salt

- Add oil in instant pot and select sauté.
- Add onion to the pot and sauté for 15 minutes.
- Add thyme, bay leaves, salt, stock, and vinegar and stir well.
- Seal pot with lid and cook on manual high pressure for 10 minutes.
- Allow releasing pressure naturally then open the lid.
- Discard thyme and bay leaves and using blender puree the soup until smooth.
- Stir well and serve.

Roasted Vegetables

Total Time: 3 hours 10 minutes; Serves: 2; Calories 348; Fat 15.2 g; Carbohydrates 48.3 g; Sugar 3 g; Protein 6.7 g; Cholesterol 2 mg

- 1 parsnip, peeled and chopped
- 1/2 cauliflower head, chopped
- 1/2 lb carrots, peeled and chopped
- 1/2 tsp cumin
- 1 tbsp honey
- 1 tbsp olive oil
- 1/2 onion, sliced
- 1/2 tsp salt

- Use the "Slow Cooker" setting on your Instant Pot.
- Add all ingredients to the slow cooker and mix well.
- Cover and cook on low for 3-4 hours or until vegetable are tender.
- Serve and enjoy.

Tasty Tofu Curry

Total Time: 2 hours 10 minutes; Serves: 2; Calories 338; Fat 24.2 g; Carbohydrates 25.9 g; Sugar 14.7 g; Protein 12.5 g; Cholesterol 0 mg

1/2 cup tofu, diced
1 tsp garlic, minced
1/2 cup onion, chopped
4 oz tomato paste
1 cup bell pepper, diced

1/2 tbsp garam masala
1 tbsp peanut butter
1/2 tbsp curry powder
5 oz coconut milk
3/4 tsp salt

- Use the "Slow Cooker" setting on your Instant Pot.
- Add all ingredients except tofu into the blender and blend until smooth.
- Add tofu to the slow cooker then pour blended mixture over the tofu.
- Cover and cook on low for 2 hours.
- Serve and enjoy.

Garam Masala Potatoes

Serves: 6, Preparation time: 20 minutes, Cooking time: 15 minutes, Per Serving: Calories: 238; Total Fat: 9g; Saturated Fat: 2g; Protein: 6g; Carbs: 29g; Fiber: 6g; Sugar: 6g

1 onion (chopped)
1 green bell pepper (chopped)
1 red bell pepper (chopped)
2 tablespoons vegetable oil
3 garlic cloves (minced)
1 tablespoon garam masala
1 teaspoon chili powder
2 large sweet potatoes (peeled, cut into 1/2" cubes)

2 large gold potatoes (peeled, cut into 1/2" cubes)
2 cans (15 ounces each) chopped tomatoes
1 can (15 ounces) coconut milk
1 can (4 ounces) tomato paste
Salt, freshly ground black pepper and cayenne pepper, to taste

- In Instant Pot on sauté setting, cook onion and bell peppers in oil until softened, stirring frequently, about 5 minutes. Add garlic, garam masala and chili powder and cook about 1 minute, stirring constantly.
- Add potatoes, undrained tomatoes, coconut milk and tomato paste to pot, season to taste with salt, pepper and cayenne pepper and mix well.
- Secure pot lid, close pressure valve and cook on high pressure for 8 minutes. When cooking time ends, carefully turn venting knob from sealing to venting position for a quick pressure release.
- Season garam masala potatoes to taste with salt, pepper and cayenne pepper, mix thoroughly and serve as desired. Enjoy!

Cauliflower Potato Curry Soup

Serves: 6, Preparation time: 15 minutes, Cooking time: ## minutes, Per Serving: Calories: 224; Total Fat: 13g; Saturated Fat: 10g; Protein: 4g; Carbs: 26g; Fiber: 2g; Sugar: 6g

1 small yellow onion (diced)
1 tablespoon olive oil
2 garlic cloves (minced)
1 piece fresh ginger (about 1", minced)
1 tablespoon curry powder
1 teaspoon cumin
2 cups vegetable stock

1 can (14 ounces) coconut milk
2 medium carrots (peeled, diced)
1 bag (10 ounces) frozen cauliflower florets
2 medium golden potatoes (peeled, diced)
Salt and freshly ground black pepper, to taste
1 small carrot (peeled, grated)
¼ cup coconut (lightly toasted)

- In Instant Pot on sauté setting, cook onion in oil until softened, stirring frequently, about 5 minutes. Add garlic and ginger and cook about 1 more minute, stirring constantly. Add curry powder and cumin and stir until onion mixture is coated.
- Add vegetable stock, coconut milk, carrots, cauliflower and potatoes to pot, season to taste with salt and pepper and mix well.
- Secure pot lid, close pressure valve and cook on high pressure for 10 minutes. When cooking time ends, let pressure release naturally.
- Process soup with an immersion blender until smooth and season to taste with salt and pepper. Ladle soup into bowls and garnish with grated carrot and coconut to serve. Enjoy!

Steamed Kale with Bacon

Serves: 4, Preparation time: 10 minutes, Cooking time: 10 minutes, Per Serving: Calories: 117; Total Fat: 5g; Saturated Fat: 3g; Protein: 6g; Carbs: 11g; Fiber: 4g; Sugar: 0g

1 bunch kale, about 8 cups chopped	4 slices bacon, diced
1 tablespoon butter	Salt and fresh coarsely ground black pepper, to taste
1 onion, diced	

- Pour 1 cup water into Instant Pot and set steamer basket in pot. Place kale in steamer basket.
- Secure pot lid, close pressure valve and cook on steam setting for 5 minutes. When cooking time ends, let pressure release naturally. Remove steamer basket from pot and drain pot.
- In Instant Pot on sauté setting, melt butter and cook onion and bacon until onion is translucent and bacon is crisped, about 5 minutes.
- Stir kale into onion mixture and season to taste with salt and pepper. Serve with a slotted spoon and enjoy!

Pumpkin Apple Curry Soup

Serves: 6, Preparation time: 15 minutes, Cooking time: 15 minutes, Per Serving: Calories: 149; Total Fat: 8g; Saturated Fat: 1g; Protein: 3g; Carbs: 21g; Fiber: 5g; Sugar: 11g

1 yellow onion (diced)	1 bay leaf
2 celery stalks (diced)	Salt, to taste
1 yellow apple (peeled, cored, diced)	1 cup plain unsweetened almond milk
2 tablespoons vegetable oil	2 tablespoons brown sugar
2 teaspoons curry powder	6 tablespoons plain unsweetened plant-based yogurt
3 cups vegetable stock	
1 can (15 ounces) pumpkin puree	

- In Instant Pot on sauté setting, cook onion, celery and apple in oil until softened, stirring frequently, about 5 minutes. Add curry powder and cook for 1 minute, stirring constantly.
- Add vegetable stock, pumpkin and bay leaf to pot, season to taste with salt and mix well. Secure pot lid, close pressure valve and cook on high pressure for 10 minutes. When cooking time ends, let pressure release naturally.
- Remove bay leaf from soup, stir in almond milk and brown sugar and season to taste with salt. Purée soup until smooth with an immersion blender.
- Ladle soup into bowls and top with spoonfuls of yogurt. Serve and enjoy!

Scrumptious Spinach Paneer

Total Time: 5 hours 15 minutes; Serves: 6; Calories 220, Fat 10 g, Carbohydrates 16 g, Sugar 6 g, Protein 20 g, Cholesterol 0 mg

12 oz paneer cheese	1 tbsp ground coriander
8 oz fresh spinach, chopped	1 tbsp garam masala
30 oz frozen spinach, thawed	1 1/2 cups can tomato sauce
14 oz can coconut milk	3 tbsp fresh ginger, minced
1/8 tsp cayenne pepper	4 garlic cloves, chopped
1 tbsp ground cumin	1 tsp salt

- Use the "Slow Cooker" setting on your Instant Pot.
- Add all ingredients except fresh spinach and paneer into the Instant Pot.
- Cover and cook on low for 3 hours.
- Add fresh spinach and cook for 1 hour.
- Using immersion blender blend mixture until smooth.
- Add paneer cheese and cook for 1 hour.
- Serve and enjoy.

Cabbage Carrots Celery Soup

25 minutes, Serves: 4, Calories 148; Fat 1.7 g; Carbohydrates 27.1 g; Sugar 15.2 g; Protein 8.6 g; Cholesterol 0 mg

- 1 small cabbage head, chopped
- 3 cups chicken broth
- 1 tbsp lemon juice
- 3 tbsp apple cider vinegar
- 3 garlic cloves, minced
- 28 oz jar tomatoes, chopped
- 3 celery stalks, chopped
- 3 carrots, chopped
- 1 onion, chopped

- Add all ingredients into the instant pot and stir well.
- Seal pot with lid and cook on manual high pressure for 15 minutes.
- Release pressure using quick release method than open the lid.
- Stir well and serve.

Tomato Sauce

Serves: 8, Preparation time: 15 minutes, Cooking time: 10 minutes, Per Serving: Calories: 90; Total Fat: 1g; Saturated Fat: 0g; Protein: 3g; Carbs: 13g; Fiber: 4g; Sugar: 8g

- 1 small onion (finely chopped)
- 1 tablespoon olive oil
- 1 garlic clove (minced)
- ½ teaspoon dried red pepper flakes
- 2 pounds fresh plum-style tomatoes (diced)
- Salt and freshly ground black pepper, to taste

- In Instant Pot on sauté setting, cook onion in oil until translucent, stirring frequently, about 5 minutes. Add garlic and red pepper flakes and cook for about 1 minute, stirring constantly.
- Add tomatoes and basil leaves to pot, season to taste with salt and pepper and mix well. Secure pot lid, close pressure valve and cook on high pressure for 10 minutes. When cooking time ends, carefully turn venting knob from sealing to venting position for a quick pressure release. Remove basil leaves.
- If desired, strain the cooked mixture through a food mill or strainer to remove the tomato skins.
- Puree sauce to desired consistency with an immersion blender. Serve and enjoy!

Flavorful Red Lentils Curry

Total Time: 8 hours 15 minutes; Serves: 16; Calories 261, Fat 6 g, Carbohydrates 37 g, Sugar 4 g, Protein 13 g, Cholesterol 8 mg

- 4 cups brown lentils, rinsed and drained
- 5 tbsp red curry paste
- 1 tbsp garam masala
- 1 1/2 tsp turmeric
- 2 tsp sugar
- 1/2 cup coconut milk
- 29 oz can tomato puree
- 2 onions, diced
- 4 garlic cloves, minced
- 1 tbsp ginger, minced
- 4 tbsp butter
- 7 cups water
- 1 tsp salt

- Use the "Slow Cooker" setting on your Instant Pot.
- Add all ingredients except coconut milk into the Instant Pot and stir well.
- Cover and cook on low for 8 hours.
- Add coconut milk and stir well.
- Serve with rice and enjoy.

Kale Potato Soup

25 minutes, Serves: 8, Calories 166; Fat 4.7 g; Carbohydrates 24.9 g; Sugar 2.7 g; Protein 6.8 g; Cholesterol 0 mg

- 2 lbs potatoes, peeled and diced
- 8 oz kale, chopped
- 2 garlic cloves, minced
- 6 cups vegetable broth
- 2 leeks, sliced
- 2 tbsp extra virgin olive oil
- 1/2 Tsp apple cider vinegar
- Pepper
- Salt

- Add oil in instant pot and select sauté.
- Add leeks and sauté until softened.
- Add garlic, broth, and potatoes and stir well.
- Seal pot with lid and cook on manual high pressure for 6 minutes.
- Release pressure using quick release method than open the lid carefully.
- Using masher mash the potatoes lightly.
- Stir in chopped kale and stir well.
- Seal pot and cook on manual high pressure for 2 minutes.
- Release pressure using quick release method than open the lid.
- Stir in apple cider vinegar, pepper and salt.
- Serve and enjoy.

Tuscan Pinto Beans

Serves: 8, Preparation time: 10 minutes, Cooking time: 45 minutes, Per Serving: Calories: 128; Total Fat: 2g; Saturated Fat: 0g; Protein: 8g; Carbs: 29g; Fiber: 16g; Sugar: 4g

1 yellow onion (chopped)
1 celery stalk (chopped)
1 small carrot (peeled, stocked)
1 tablespoon olive oil
2 garlic cloves (minced)
1 teaspoon cumin
1 pound dry pinto beans (picked, rinsed)
6 cups vegetable stock or water
½ teaspoon dried red pepper flakes
Salt and freshly ground black pepper, to taste
2 Roma tomatoes (chopped)

- In Instant Pot on sauté setting, cook onion, celery and carrot in oil until softened, stirring frequently, about 5 minutes. Add garlic and cumin and cook about 1 minute more, stirring constantly.
- Add pinto beans, vegetable stock and red pepper flakes to pot, season to taste with salt and pepper and mix well.
- Secure pot lid, close pressure valve and cook on high pressure for 40 minutes. When cooking time ends, carefully turn venting knob from sealing to venting position for a quick pressure release.
- Add tomatoes to beans, season to taste with salt and pepper and mix well. Serve and enjoy!

Mushroom Soup

Serves: 6, Preparation time: 15 minutes, Cooking time: 20 minutes, Per Serving: Calories: 136; Total Fat: 5g; Saturated Fat: 1g; Protein: 6g; Carbs: 20g; Fiber: 4g; Sugar: 4g

2 tablespoons olive oil (divided)
12 ounces cremini mushrooms (sliced, divided)
1 yellow onion (diced)
1 celery stalk (diced)
12 ounces white button mushrooms (sliced)
2 medium white potatoes (peeled, diced)
2 garlic cloves (minced)
2 tablespoons flour
8 cups vegetable stock or water
1 cup unsweetened almond milk
2 teaspoons soy sauce
½ teaspoon dried thyme
1 dried bay leaf
Salt and freshly ground black pepper, to taste

- For garnish, in Instant Pot on sauté setting, cook a handful of cremini mushroom slices in 1 tablespoon olive oil until browned, stirring frequently, about 5 minutes. Remove mushrooms from pot and set aside until serving.
- Cook onion and celery in remaining oil until softened, stirring frequently, about 5 minutes. Add remaining cremini mushrooms and button mushrooms and cook until wilted, stirring frequently, about 5 minutes. Add garlic and cook for about 1 minute, stirring constantly. Sprinkle flour over onion mixture and stir to coat.
- Add potatoes, vegetable stock, almond milk, soy sauce, thyme and bay leaf to pot and season to taste with salt and pepper. Secure pot lid, close pressure valve and cook on high pressure for 10 minutes. When cooking time ends, let pressure release naturally.
- Remove bay leaf from soup. Season soup to taste with salt and pepper and process to desired consistency with an immersion blender. Ladle soup into bowls and garnish with reserved mushrooms to serve. Enjoy!

Creamy Carrot Squash Soup

Total Time: 6 hours 15 minutes; Serves: 8; Calories 163, Fat 11.3 g, Carbohydrates 15.8 g, Sugar 5.1 g, Protein 3.8 g, Cholesterol 0 mg

1 lb butternut squash, peeled and diced
1/2 lb carrots, peeled and cut into chunks
13.5 oz can coconut milk
1/4 tsp ground sage
1 tsp pepper
1 bay leaf
3 cups vegetable broth
1 apple, peeled and sliced
1 medium onion, diced
1 tsp salt

- Use the "Slow Cooker" setting on your Instant Pot.
- Add squash, bay leaf, apple, carrots, onion, and broth into the Instant Pot.
- Cover and cook on low for 6 hours.
- Discard bay leaf and using immersion blender blend until smooth.
- Add coconut milk, sage, pepper, and salt. Stir well.
- Serve and enjoy.

Yummy Cheese Soup

Total Time: 1 hour 50 minutes; Serves: 2; Calories 640; Fat 51.3 g; Carbohydrates 14.9 g; Sugar 2.1 g; Protein 31.2 g; Cholesterol 147 mg

2 cups cheddar cheese, shredded
1/2 cup half and half
1/2 tsp Worcestershire sauce
1/2 tsp paprika
10 oz condensed cream of celery soup
Black pepper
Salt

- Use the "Slow Cooker" setting on your Instant Pot.
- Add Worcestershire sauce, paprika, shredded cheese, and cream of celery soup into the slow cooker. Stir well.
- Cover and cook on low for 1 1/2 hours.
- Add half and half and stir well.
- Cover and cook on low for 10 minutes.
- Season with pepper and salt.
- Serve hot and enjoy.

Mashed Cauliflower

Serves: 4, Preparation time: 5 minutes, Cooking time: 15 minutes, Per Serving: Calories: 128; Total Fat: 8g; Saturated Fat: 5g; Protein: 4g; Carbs: 11g; Fiber: 5g; Sugar: 5g

1 cup chicken, beef or vegetable stock
Salt and freshly ground black pepper, to taste
1 large head cauliflower (about 3 pounds), cut into large chunks
2 tablespoons butter
2 tablespoons heavy cream

- Pour stock into Instant Pot. Place cauliflower in steamer basket and set in pot. Season cauliflower to taste with salt and pepper.
- Secure pot lid, close pressure valve and cook on steam setting for 6 minutes. When cooking time ends, let pressure release naturally.
- Remove cauliflower from steamer basket to a large bowl and add butter and heavy cream. Mash cauliflower to desired consistency with a fork, potato ricer, or immersion blender.
- Season cauliflower to taste with salt and pepper to serve. Enjoy!

Calico Beans

Serves: 8, Preparation time: 5 minutes, Cooking time: 65 minutes, Per Serving: Calories: 176; Total Fat: 5g; Saturated Fat: 1g; Protein: 12g; Carbs: 36g; Fiber: 25g; Sugar: 5g

1 cup dried kidney beans	1 tablespoon olive oil
1 cup dried great northern beans	1 cup tomato sauce
1 cup dried butter beans	½ cup brown sugar
6 cups vegetable stock or water	¼ cup ketchup
1 onion (diced)	3 tablespoons white wine vinegar
2 stalks celery (chopped)	1 teaspoon ground mustard

- Rinse and drain beans and place in Instant Pot. Pour vegetable stock over beans and mix well.
- Secure pot lid, close pressure valve and cook on high pressure for 45 minutes. When cooking time ends, let pressure release naturally. Drain beans and set aside.
- In Instant Pot on sauté setting, cook onion and celery in oil until softened, stirring constantly, about 5 minutes. Stir tomato sauce, brown sugar, ketchup, vinegar and mustard into onion mixture until thoroughly combined. Stir beans into sauce.
- Secure pot lid, close pressure valve and cook on high pressure for 15 minutes. When cooking time ends, carefully turn venting knob from sealing to venting position for a quick pressure release. Stir beans and serve. Enjoy!

Apple Cabbage and Beet Stew

40 minutes, Serves: 4, Calories 134; Fat 1.8 g; Carbohydrates 23.9 g; Sugar 15.4 g; Protein 7.6 g; Cholesterol 0 mg

1/2 cabbage head, chopped	2 small carrots, chopped
2 beets, chopped	1 small onion, chopped
1 apple, diced	4 cups chicken broth
2 tbsp parsley	Salt
1 tbsp fresh ginger, grated	

- Add all ingredients into the instant pot and stir well.
- Seal pot with lid and cook on manual high pressure for 20 minutes.
- Release pressure using quick release method than open the lid.
- Stir well and serve.

Almond Rice Pudding

Serves: 6, Preparation time: 20 minute, Cooking time: 20 minutes, Per Serving: Calories: 274; Total Fat: 7g; Saturated Fat: 0g; Protein: 7g; Carbs: 47g; Fiber: 2g; Sugar: 20g

1 cup dry white rice	1 vanilla bean (seeded, scraped)
4 cups almond milk (sweetened, unsweetened or vanilla)	½ cup coconut cream
1/4 cup white sugar	½ cup sliced almonds (toasted)

- Place rice in a fine mesh colander, rinse thoroughly and drain. Mix rice, almond milk and salt in Instant Pot. Add vanilla bean and stir gently.
- Secure pot lid, close pressure valve and cook on high pressure for 20 minutes. When cooking time ends, let pressure release naturally for 10 minutes, then carefully turn venting knob from sealing to venting position to quickly release remaining pressure.
- Remove vanilla bean from pudding and stir in coconut cream. Spoon pudding into cups or bowls and sprinkle with sliced almonds to serve. Enjoy!

Spiced Cranberry Oatmeal

Serves: 4 / Preparation time: 30 minutes / Cooking time: 3 minutes

Steel cut oats are also known as "Irish oats" or "Scottish oats." They're made by chopping whole oat groats into pieces. When cooked, steel cut oats have a chewy texture and retain most of their shape.

1 teaspoon coconut oil	½ teaspoon salt
1 cup steel cut oats	½ teaspoon ground cinnamon
3 cups almond milk	¼ teaspoon ground nutmeg
¾ cup dried cranberries	Pinch of dried cloves
2 tablespoons brown sugar	¼ cup chopped walnuts (toasted, if desired)

- Grease the inside bottom of the Instant Pot with coconut oil. Add oats, almond milk, cranberries, brown sugar, salt, cinnamon, nutmeg and cloves to pot and mix gently.
- Secure pot lid, close pressure valve and cook on manual setting for 3 minutes. When cooking time ends, let pressure release naturally.
- Mix oatmeal thoroughly, spoon into bowls and sprinkle with chopped walnuts. Serve and enjoy!

Per Serving:
Calories: 170; Total Fat: 3g; Saturated Fat: 1g; Protein: 4g; Carbs: 34g; Fiber: 3g; Sugar: 12g

Coconut Lime Cabbage

20 minutes, Serves: 4, Calories 192; Fat 11.2 g; Carbohydrates 23.9 g; Sugar 10.6 g; Protein 4.5 g; Cholesterol 0 mg

1 medium cabbage, shredded	1 tbsp curry powder
1/3 cup water	1 Tsp mustard powder
1 tbsp extra virgin olive oil	1/2 red chili, sliced
1/2 cup coconut, unsweetened and desiccated	2 garlic cloves, diced
2 tbsp fresh lime juice	1 medium onion, sliced
1 medium carrot, peeled and sliced	1 tbsp coconut oil
1 tbsp turmeric powder	1 1/2 Tsp salt

- Add coconut oil in instant pot and select sauté.
- Add onion and 1/2 Tsp salt and sauté for 4 minutes.
- Add spices, chili, and garlic and stir for 30 seconds.
- Add carrots, extra virgin olive oil, coconut, lime juice, and cabbage and stir well.
- Add water and stir until well combined.
- Seal pot with lid and cook on manual high pressure for 5 minutes.
- Allow releasing pressure naturally then open the lid.
- Stir well and serve.

Creamy Rice and Beans

Serves: 10, Preparation time: 20 minutes, Cooking time: 36 minutes, Per Serving: Calories: 429; Total Fat: 7g; Saturated Fat: 1g; Protein: 9g; Carbs: 37g; Fiber: 17g; Sugar: 2g

1 onion (minced)	4 cups vegetable stock or water
1 red bell pepper (minced)	2 cans (15 ounces each) coconut milk
1 celery stalk (minced)	2 cups dry kidney beans (rinsed)
2 tablespoons vegetable oil	2 cups long-grain white rice
5 garlic cloves (minced)	Salt and freshly ground black pepper, to taste
2 teaspoons cumin	Fresh cilantro for garnish

- In Instant Pot on sauté setting, cook onion, bell pepper and celery in oil until softened, stirring frequently, about 5 minutes. Add garlic and cumin and cook 1 minute more, stirring constantly.
- Add vegetable stock, coconut milk, kidney beans and rice, season to taste with salt and pepper and mix thoroughly.
- Secure pot lid, close pressure valve and cook on high pressure for 30 minutes. When cooking time ends, let pressure release naturally.

- Season rice and beans to taste with salt and pepper, mix thoroughly and garnish with sprigs of cilantro. Serve and enjoy!

Potato Vegetable Soup

Serves: 4, Preparation time: 20 minutes, Cooking time: 20 minutes, Per Serving: Calories: 149; Total Fat: 6g; Saturated Fat: 1g; Protein: 5g; Carbs: 21g; Fiber: 3g; Sugar: 5g

2 sweet onions	1 tablespoon white wine vinegar
3 tablespoons olive oil, divided	2 cups vegetable stock
1 celery stalk (diced)	1 pound gold potatoes (peeled, cut into 1/2" pieces)
1 carrot (peeled, diced)	
2 garlic cloves (minced)	1 cup plain unsweetened almond milk

- Cut one onion into julienne strips. In Instant Pot on sauté setting, cook julienned onion in 1 tablespoon oil until caramelized, stirring frequently, 6-7 minutes. Remove caramelized onion from pot and set aside for garnish.
- Dice remaining onion and cook with carrots and celery in remaining oil until softened, stirring frequently, about 5 minutes. Add vinegar and garlic and cook until vinegar evaporates, about 2 minutes.
- Add vegetable stock and potatoes to pot, season to taste with salt and pepper and mix well. Secure pot lid, close pressure valve and cook on manual setting for 7 minutes. When cooking time ends, carefully turn venting knob from sealing to venting position for a quick pressure release.
- Mash soup to desired texture with a potato masher. Stir almond milk into soup, season to taste with salt and pepper and re-heat, if necessary.
- Ladle soup into bowls and garnish with caramelized onions to serve. Enjoy!

Veggie Soup

Serves: 2 / Preparation time: 5 minutes / Cooking time: 10 minutes, Per Serving: Calories: 248; Total Fat: 9.9g; Saturated Fat: 2.2g; Protein: 14.9g; Carbs: 22.6g; Fiber: 6.5g; Sugar: 6.8g

¼ cup of diced carrots	3 cups chopped spinach
¼ cup of diced potatoes	1 cup diced tomatoes
¼ cup of diced celery	1 teaspoon garlic powder
½ cup diced onion	1 teaspoon basil
2 teaspoons minced garlic	1 teaspoon oregano
1 tablespoon vegetable oil	½ teaspoon salt
4 cups of low sodium vegetable broth	1 tablespoon chopped parsley

- Turn on the sauté function of your Instant pot and preheat it. When it is ready, put olive oil, minced garlic, diced potatoes, carrots, and celery then sauté them.
- Once the veggies look softer, put the other ingredients.
- After a while, close the pot and push the cancel button. Choose the "Soup" setting and set the time to 10 minutes.
- Once it is done, quickly release the pressure through the pressure valve. You can also let the pot release the pressure naturally, but it will take another 15 minutes. If you do so, the veggies will be too soft.
- Transfer to a serving bowl then serve.
- Enjoy.

Simple Strawberry Sauce

Serves: 16, Preparation time: 25 minutes, Cooking time: 1 minute, Per Serving: Calories: 42; Total Fat: 0g; Saturated Fat: 0g; Protein: 0g; Carbs: 11g; Fiber: 1g; Sugar: 9g

2 pounds fresh ripe strawberries (hulled, halved)	½ cup sugar
1 tablespoon lemon juice	2 teaspoons cornstarch

- Place strawberries in Instant Pot, drizzle with lemon juice and mix well. Combine sugar and cornstarch, sprinkle over strawberries and mix well.

- Secure pot lid, close pressure valve and cook on high pressure for 1 minute. When cooking time ends, let pressure release naturally.
- Serve sauce as desired. Sauce can be served immediately or slightly cooled. Or, let sauce cool, ladle into four 8-ounce jars and refrigerate or freeze. Unopened jars will keep in the freezer for up to 6 months. Once opened, store jars in the refrigerator and use sauce within 5-7 days. Enjoy!

Creamy Kale Soup

Serves: 4, Preparation time: 5 minutes, Cooking time: 5 minutes, Per Serving: Calories: 267; Total Fat: 15g; Saturated Fat: 10g; Protein: 10; Carbs: 24g; Fiber: 7g; Sugar: 4g

1 onion, diced
4 stalks celery, trimmed and chopped
8 cloves garlic, peeled and minced
1 tablespoon butter
1 package (16 ounces) frozen chopped kale
1 package (16 ounces) frozen cauliflower florets
4 cups beef or chicken stock
1 tablespoon balsamic vinegar
Salt and freshly ground pepper, to taste
½ cup heavy cream
4 tablespoons finely grated Parmesan cheese

- In Instant Pot on sauté setting, cook onion, celery and garlic in butter until slightly softened, about 2 minutes.
- Add kale, cauliflower, stock and balsamic vinegar to pot and season to taste with salt and pepper.
- Secure pot lid, close pressure valve and cook on high for 3 minutes. Let pressure release naturally.
- Slowly pour cream into soup, stirring constantly. Mash some of the cauliflower if desired for a thicker consistency.
- Ladle soup into bowls and garnish with Parmesan cheese to serve. Enjoy!

Chickpea Stew

Serves: 6, Preparation time: 15 minutes, Cooking time: 15 minutes, Per Serving: Calories: 225; Total Fat: 8g; Saturated Fat: 4g; Protein: 8g; Carbs: 30g; Fiber: 8g; Sugar: 5g

1 onion (diced)
2 carrots (peeled, diced)
1 small cauliflower (cored, diced)
1 red bell pepper (diced)
1 tablespoon coconut oil
2 cans (15 ounces each) chickpeas (rinsed and drained)
1 can (28 ounces) crushed tomatoes
1 can (14 ounces) coconut milk
2 tablespoons tomato paste
1 teaspoon cumin
1 teaspoon coriander
Salt and freshly ground black pepper, to taste
2 Roma tomatoes (diced)

- In Instant Pot on sauté setting, cook onion, carrots, cauliflower and bell pepper in coconut oil until softened, stirring frequently, about 5 minutes.
- Add chickpeas, *undrained* tomatoes, coconut milk, tomato paste, cumin and coriander to pot, season to taste with salt and pepper and mix thoroughly.
- Secure pot lid, close pressure valve and cook stew on soup setting for 10 minutes. When cooking time ends, let pressure release naturally.
- Mix stew thoroughly. If desired, mash some of the chickpeas with a fork to thicken the stew. Sprinkle Roma tomatoes over the stew and serve. Enjoy!

Veggie Quinoa Pilaf

Total Time: 1 hour 15 minutes; Serves: 2; Calories 330; Fat 17.8 g; Carbohydrates 36 g; Sugar 2 g; Protein 9.2 g; Cholesterol 0 mg

1/2 cup quinoa, soak for 5 minutes, rinse and drained
2 tbsp parsley, minced
7/8 cup boiling water

1/8 tsp dried ginger	1/8 tsp asafetida
1/4 tsp cumin	1 tbsp olive oil
1/4 tsp ground coriander	1/4 cup cashews
1/8 tsp turmeric	1/4 cup red pepper, chopped
1/4 tsp thyme	1/2 cup celery, chopped
1 bay leaf	1/4 tsp salt

- Use the "Slow Cooker" setting on your Instant Pot.
- Heat olive oil in the saucepan over medium heat.
- Add cashews, red pepper, celery, asafetida, red pepper, and celery and sauté until cashews are golden brown.
- Add remaining spices except for parsley.
- Add quinoa and stir well.
- Transfer saucepan mixture to the slow cooker.
- Add boiling water and cover and cook on low for 1 hour.
- Add parsley and stir well.
- Serve and enjoy.

Creamy Tomato Soup

30 minutes, Serves: 6, Calories 86; Fat 5.3 g; Carbohydrates 7.8 g; Sugar 4.2 g; Protein 2.8 g; Cholesterol 0 mg

14 oz tomatoes, diced	2 large carrots, diced
2 cups vegetable broth	2 large celery stalks, diced
2 bay leaves	1 medium onion, diced
2 Tsp basil, dried	1/2 Tsp black pepper
1/4 Tsp red pepper flakes	1 Tsp salt
2 tbsp extra virgin olive oil	

- Add oil in instant pot and select sauté.
- Add carrots, celery, and onion to the pot and sauté for 5 minutes.
- Add basil, red pepper flakes, black pepper, and salt and sauté for 1 minute.
- Add remaining ingredients and stir well.
- Seal pot with lid and cook on manual high pressure for 15 minutes.
- Allow releasing pressure naturally then open the lid.
- Discard bay leaves and using blender puree the soup until smooth.
- Serve and enjoy.

Creamy Bow Tie Pasta

Serves: 4, Preparation time: 15 minutes, Cooking time: 10 minutes, Per Serving: Calories: 223; Total Fat: 17g; Saturated Fat: 12g; Protein: 9g; Carbs: 39g; Fiber: 3g; Sugar: 6g

1 onion (diced)	3 cups vegetable stock
1 tablespoon olive oil	1 package (8 ounces) uncooked bow tie pasta
4 garlic cloves (minced)	Salt and freshly ground black pepper, to taste
1 cup coconut milk	

- In Instant Pot on sauté setting, cook onion in oil until translucent, stirring frequently, about 5 minutes. Add garlic and cook about 1 minute, stirring constantly.
- Add vegetable stock, coconut milk and pasta to pot, season to taste with salt and pepper and mix well.
- Secure pot lid, close pressure valve and cook on high pressure for 4 minutes. When cooking time ends, carefully turn venting knob from sealing to venting position for a quick pressure release.
- Season pasta to taste with salt and pepper and mix thoroughly. Pasta sauce will thicken as it stands. Serve and enjoy!

Mixed Beans in Hot Sauce

Serves: 2 / Preparation time: 5 minutes / Cooking time: 15 minutes, Per Serving: Calories: 387; Total Fat: 7.6g; Saturated Fat: 1.3g; Protein: 23.1g; Carbs: 61.4g; Fiber: 17.5g; Sugar: 10.9g

¼ cup chopped onion	1 cup chipotle pepper
2 teaspoons minced garlic	1 teaspoon chipotle pepper sauce
¼ cup red chili flakes	½ cup cooked kidney beans
1 ½ teaspoons oregano	1 cup cooked black beans
1 ½ teaspoons cumin	1 cup cannellini beans
1 cup diced tomatoes	½ teaspoon salt
2 teaspoons olive oil	1 tablespoon chopped parsley
1 ½ cups vegetable broth	

- Turn on the sauté function of your Instant Pot and preheat it.
- When it is ready, put the olive oil then followed by the onion until it is softened.
- Add the garlic, oregano, chili flakes, cumin, and oregano then stir for another minute.
- Put the vegetable broth, chipotle pepper and its sauce, and also all kinds of the beans.
- Add salt and stir.
- Set the time to 10 minutes.
- Release the steam through the valve 5 minutes after the timer is done.
- Add the parsley and serve.

Honey Roasted Peanut Broccoli Salad

Serves: 4, Preparation time: 5 minutes, Cooking time: 8 minutes, Per Serving: Calories: 330; Total Fat: 27g; Saturated Fat: 4g; Protein: 4g; Carbs: 20g; Fiber: 3g; Sugar: 13g

1 small red onion (julienned)	Salt and freshly ground black pepper, to taste
1 tablespoon peanut oil	2 tablespoons extra-virgin olive oil
1 bag (12 ounces) broccoli slaw mix	1 tablespoon red wine vinegar
½ teaspoon dried ginger	2 teaspoons sugar
1 lime (zested, juiced)	2 tablespoons honey-roasted peanuts (chopped)

- In Instant Pot on sauté setting, cook onion in peanut oil until translucent, stirring frequently, about 5 minutes. Add broccoli, ginger and lime zest to pot, season to taste with salt and pepper and mix well.
- Secure pot lid, close pressure valve and cook on manual setting for 1 minute. Carefully turn venting knob from sealing to venting position for a quick pressure release.
- Mix olive oil, vinegar and sugar, season to taste with salt and pepper and sprinkle over broccoli mixture. Divide salad onto plates and garnish with peanuts to serve. Enjoy!

Zucchini Curried Soup

35 minutes, Serves: 10, Calories 108; Fat 9.2 g; Carbohydrates 6.4 g; Sugar 3.5 g; Protein 2.5 g; Cholesterol 0 mg

10 cups zucchini, chopped
32 oz chicken stock
13 oz coconut milk
1 tbsp Thai curry paste

- Add all ingredients into the instant pot and stir well.
- Seal pot with lid and cook on manual high pressure for 10 minutes.
- Release pressure using quick release method than open the lid carefully.
- Using blender puree the soup until smooth.
- Stir well and serve.

Barley Walnut Salad

Serves: 4, Preparation time: 10 minutes, Cooking time: 30 minutes, Per Serving: Calories: 286; Total Fat: 9g; Saturated Fat: 7g; Protein: 6g; Carbs: 39g; Fiber: 8g; Sugar: 8g

½ cup chopped walnuts	1 lemon (zested, juiced)
1 tablespoon coconut oil	Salt and freshly ground black pepper, to taste
4 cups water	2 fresh ripe pears (diced)
1 cup pearl barley	

- In Instant Pot on sauté setting, cook walnuts in oil until toasted, about 5 minutes, stirring frequently. Remove walnuts from pot and set aside.
- Pour water into Instant Pot and stir in barley and lemon zest. Add salt to barley mixture if desired, up to ½ teaspoon. Secure pot lid, close pressure valve and cook on high pressure for 25 minutes. When cooking time ends, let pressure release naturally.
- Add walnuts to barley and season to taste with salt and pepper. Stir salad until combined and spoon into salad bowls.
- Toss diced pears with lemon juice and sprinkle over barley salads. Serve and enjoy!

Delicious Sweet Potato Curry

Total Time: 6 hours 15 minutes; Serves: 6;Calories 275, Fat 19.5 g, Carbohydrates 24 g, Sugar 8.3 g, Protein 5.5 g, Cholesterol 0 mg

1 sweet potato, diced	4 tbsp flour
1 courgette, diced	14 oz can coconut milk
1/4 cup cashew nuts	1 tsp garlic, minced
14 oz can tomatoes, chopped	2 onions, diced
1 tsp curry powder	4 tomatoes, diced
1/2 tsp chili powder	1 tsp ginger, minced
1/2 tsp black pepper	2 tsp garam masala
2 tbsp tomato puree	1 tbsp vegetable oil

- Use the "Slow Cooker" setting on your Instant Pot.
- Heat oil in the pan over medium heat.
- Add ginger, onion, and garlic to the pan and sauté for 5 minutes.
- Add tomato paste, flour, and spices and cook for a minute.
- Add coconut milk and stir well and cook until thickened.
- Transfer pan mixture into the Instant Pot along with remaining ingredients and mix well.
- Cover and cook on low for 6 hours.
- Serve and enjoy.

Savory Kale Garlic

Serves: 2 / Preparation time: 3 minutes / Cooking time: 3 minutes, Per Serving: Calories: 61; Total Fat: 2.4g; Saturated Fat: 0.3g; Protein: 2.4g; Carbs: 8.6g; Fiber: 1.1g; Sugar: 0.2g

2 cups chopped kale	1 teaspoon fish sauce
1 teaspoon olive oil	1 teaspoon oyster sauce
3 teaspoons garlic	¼ teaspoon salt
1 cup water	

- Preheat the Instant Pot for about 30 seconds then select the "Sauté" menu.
- Pour olive oil into the pot then stir in minced garlic. Sauté until lightly golden and aromatic.
- Next, add chopped kale to the pot then season with fish sauce, oyster sauce, and salt.
- Pour water into the Instant Pot then cover the Instant Pot with the lid and make sure that it is completely locked.
- Press "Cancel" button then choose "Manual" menu and cook on high for 3 minutes.
- Once it is done, naturally release the Instant Pot then open the lid.
- Transfer the kale garlic to a serving dish then serve.

- Enjoy.

Simple Black Eyed Peas

Total Time: 6 hours 15 minutes; Serves: 6; Calories 203,nFat 0.5 g, Carbohydrates 48.8 g, Sugar 2.8 g, Protein 20.2 g, Cholesterol 0 mg

1 lb dried black-eyed peas, soak for overnight	1 small onion, diced
1 tsp ground sage	2 cups water
1/8 tsp thyme	2 cups vegetable broth
1 bay leaf	1/2 tsp pepper
1 garlic clove, diced	1 tsp sea salt

- Use the "Slow Cooker" setting on your Instant Pot.
- Add all ingredients into the Instant Pot and mix well.
- Cover and cook on low for 6 hours.
- Serve and enjoy.

Red Wine Poached Pears

Serves: 6, Preparation time: 30 minutes, Cooking time: 25 minutes, Per Serving: Calories: 210; Total Fat: 0g; Saturated Fat: 0g; Protein: 0g; Carbs: 40g; Fiber: 4g; Sugar: 33g

3 cups water	3 cinnamon sticks
2 cups dry red wine	3 cloves
1 orange (zested, juiced)	6 firm ripe Bartlett pears
½ cup sugar	

- Set Instant Pot to sauté setting. Mix water, red wine, orange juice, sugar, cinnamon sticks and cloves in pot and bring to a simmer, stirring occasionally, until sugar is dissolved.
- While sauce is simmering, peel pears, leaving intact. Cut thin slices from bottoms of pears if necessary so pears will stand vertically.
- Set pears in syrup mixture in Instant Pot. Secure pot lid, close pressure valve and cook on high pressure for 3 minutes. When cooking time ends, carefully turn venting knob from sealing to venting position for a quick pressure release.
- Remove pears from the pot with a slotted spoon and stand them up in serving bowls. Set Instant Pot to sauté setting and simmer syrup until reduced to desired consistency. Skim cinnamon sticks and cloves from syrup and discard. Ladle syrup over pears and sprinkle with orange zest to serve. Enjoy!

Italian Vegetable Soup

25 minutes, Serves: 4, Calories 105; Fat 5.8 g; Carbohydrates 16 g; Sugar 7.3 g; Protein 3.6 g; Cholesterol 0 mg

6 large mushrooms, sliced	1 small zucchini, diced
2 medium carrots, peeled and sliced	4 oz kale, chopped
2 celery sticks, sliced	1 cup tomatoes, chopped
1 onion, diced	4 garlic cloves, diced
1 tbsp extra virgin olive oil	1/2 red chili, sliced
1 bay leaf	1/4 Tsp salt
4 cups vegetable stock	

- Add oil in instant pot and select sauté.
- Add carrots, celery, onion, and salt and sauté for 2 minutes.
- Add garlic, chili, and mushrooms and stir for 2 minutes.
- Add bay leaves, stock, tomatoes, zucchini, and kale and stir well.
- Seal pot with lid and cook on manual high pressure for 10 minutes.
- Allow releasing pressure naturally then open the lid.

- Stir well and serve.

Spiced Green Peas Rice

Total Time: 2 hours 20 minutes; Serves: 6; Calories 214, Fat 3 g, Carbohydrates 41.8 g, Sugar 3.4 g, Protein 5.3 g, Cholesterol 0 mg

- 1 cup green peas
- 2 tsp chili powder
- 2 tomatoes, pureed
- 1 tsp turmeric powder
- 2 green chilies, chopped
- 1 tsp cumin seeds
- 1 tbsp vegetable oil
- 2 potatoes, peeled and chopped
- 1 cup basmati rice, rinsed and drained
- 2 cups water

- Use the "Slow Cooker" setting on your Instant Pot.
- Add water, rice, and potatoes into the Instant Pot.
- Heat oil in the pan over medium heat.
- Add cumin seeds, turmeric, chili powder, tomato puree, green chilies, and salt to the pan and sauté for 2 minutes.
- Transfer pan mixture into the Instant Pot and stir well.
- Cover and cook on high for 1 1/2 hours.
- Add green peas and cook for another 30 minutes.
- Serve and enjoy.

Mexican Rice and Beans

Total Time: 1 hour 40 minutes; Serves: 2; Calories 347; Fat 0.2 g; Carbohydrates 70.7 g; Sugar 5.7 g; Protein 10.8 g; Cholesterol 0 mg

- 1/2 jalapeno, remove seed and minced
- 1 garlic clove, minced
- 1/2 cup vegetable broth
- 1 packet, taco seasoning
- 7 oz can black beans
- 1/2 jar salsa
- 1/2 cup rice, uncooked

- Use the "Slow Cooker" setting on your Instant Pot.
- Add all ingredients to the slow cooker and stir well.
- Cover and cook on high for 1 1/2 hours.
- Serve and enjoy.

Vegetable Scraps Stock

Serves: 8, Preparation time: 10 minutes, Cooking time: 30 minutes, Per Serving: Calories: 15; Total Fat: 0g; Saturated Fat: 0g; Protein: 0g; Carbs: 2g; Fiber: 0g; Sugar: 0g

1 gallon-size bag of vegetable scraps   8 cups water

- Place vegetable scraps and water in Instant Pot and stir, making sure scraps are covered with water. Secure lid, close pressure valve and cook on high pressure for 30 minutes. When cooking time ends, let pressure release naturally.
- Strain stock through a colander into a large container, pressing gently on the scraps in the colander to release as much flavor as possible into your stock. Stock can be used immediately or stored, tightly covered, in the freezer for up to 6 months.

Mix Vegetable Curry

Total Time: 6 hours 10 minutes; Serves: 4; Calories 313, Fat 22 g, Carbohydrates 28.3 g, Sugar 5.1 g, Protein 6.3 g, Cholesterol 0 mg

- 3 1/2 cups broccoli florets
- 2.5 oz green beans
- 2 medium carrots, peeled and sliced
- 2 large sweet potatoes, diced

3 tbsp tomato puree	2 tsp ground cumin
14 oz can coconut milk	1 tsp chili powder
1 red chili, seeded and chopped	1 tsp ginger, grated
1 tsp garam masala	1 tsp garlic, grated
1 tsp ground turmeric	1 onion, diced
2 tsp ground coriander	

- Use the "Slow Cooker" setting on your Instant Pot.
- Add all ingredients except green beans into the Instant Pot and mix well.
- Cover and cook on low for 5 hours.
- Add green beans and stir well and cook for another 1 hour.
- Serve with rice.

Frittata with Cheese and Broccoli

Serves: 4, Preparation time: 10 minutes, Cooking time: 30 minutes, Per Serving: Calories: 462; Total Fat: 34g; Saturated Fat: 16g; Protein: 28g; Carbs: 7g; Fiber: 2g; Sugar: 2g

2 tablespoons butter	½ cup plain whole-milk yogurt
1 onion, diced	½ teaspoon dried dill
4 cloves garlic, peeled and minced	8 ounces mild cheddar cheese, shredded
2 cups bite-size broccoli florets	Salt and freshly ground black pepper, to taste
8 eggs	

- Set Instant Pot to sauté, melt butter and cook onion and garlic until transparent, stirring occasionally, about 5 minutes. Add broccoli florets and cook until slightly softened, about 4 minutes. Remove broccoli mixture from pot and set aside.
- Whisk eggs and yogurt until thoroughly combined. Stir in cheese and broccoli mixture and season to taste with salt and pepper.
- Select a casserole dish that fits inside the Instant Pot. Grease casserole dish with butter or spray with nonstick cooking spray. Pour egg mixture into casserole dish and cover with aluminum foil.
- Set trivet inside pot and pour about 1 cup water into pot. Carefully set casserole dish on trivet. Secure pot lid, close pressure valve and cook on manual setting until done, about 20 minutes. When cooking time ends, let pressure release naturally.
- Using oven mitts, carefully remove casserole from instant pot. Cut frittata into wedges and serve immediately, or let cool. Enjoy!

Butternut Squash Soup

Total Time: 6 hours 10 minutes; Serves: 2; Calories 168; Fat 1.7 g; Carbohydrates 33.8 g; Sugar 9.2 g; Protein 8 g; Cholesterol 0 mg

3 cups butternut squash, peeled, seeded, and diced	1/2 medium onion, diced
	1 medium carrots, peeled and diced
1/4 tsp cayenne	2 cups chicken broth
1/2 tsp cinnamon	1/2 tsp salt
1 chipotle peppers	

- Use the "Slow Cooker" setting on your Instant Pot.
- Add all ingredients to the slow cooker and stir well.
- Cover and cook on low for 6 hours.
- Using blender puree the soup until smooth.
- Serve and enjoy.

Sweet Glazed Carrots

Total Time: 6 hours 5 minutes; Serves: 2; Calories 250; Fat 11.8 g; Carbohydrates 36.5 g; Sugar 28.4 g; Protein 1.6 g; Cholesterol 31 mg

1 lb baby carrots 2 tbsp butter
1/4 cup brown sugar

- Use the "Slow Cooker" setting on your Instant Pot.
- Spray slow cooker from inside with cooking spray.
- Add baby carrots to the slow cooker.
- Top with sugar and butter.
- Cover and cook on low for 6 hours.
- Serve and enjoy.

Perfect Curried Baked Beans

Total Time: 8 hours 10 minutes; Serves: 8; Calories 485, Fat 13 g, Carbohydrates 70.4 g, Sugar 7.4 g, Protein 22.9 g, Cholesterol 0 mg

4 cups pinto beans, cooked 1 garlic cloves, minced
1 tbsp vegetable oil 1 tbsp fresh ginger, minced
1 medium onion, diced 3 tsp curry powder
14 oz can coconut milk 1/8 tsp red pepper flakes
6 oz can tomato paste 1/2 tsp cumin
2 tbsp brown sugar 1/2 tsp salt

- Use the "Slow Cooker" setting on your Instant Pot.
- Add cooked beans into the Instant Pot.
- Heat oil in the pan over medium heat.
- Add onion and sauté for 5 minutes.
- Add garlic and sauté for another 1 minute.
- Stir in crushed red peppers, cumin, curry powder, ginger, and salt.
- Reduce heat and stir in coconut milk, brown sugar, and tomato paste.
- Pour pan mixture over the beans and stir well.
- Cover Instant Pot and cook on low for 8 hours.
- Serve and enjoy.

Turmeric Lentil Bean Chili

Total Time: 4 hours 15 minutes; Serves: 6; Calories 598, Fat 11.5 g, Carbohydrates 92.6 g, Sugar 9.2 g, Protein 35.5 g, Cholesterol 0 mg

15 oz can red beans, rinsed and drained 6 oz can tomato paste
1 cup coconut milk 2 cups water
1 tsp turmeric 32 oz vegetable stock
1 tsp chili powder 1 small onion, chopped
1 tsp ground cumin 2 cups green lentils, rinsed and drained

- Use the "Slow Cooker" setting on your Instant Pot.
- Add all ingredients except coconut milk into the Instant Pot and stir well.
- Cover and cook on high for 4 hours.
- Add coconut milk and stir well.
- Stir well and serve.

Tasty Spinach Potato

Total Time: 3 hours 15 minutes; Serves: 4; Calories 168, Fat 3.9 g, Carbohydrates 30.4 g, Sugar 2.8 g, Protein 4.7 g, Cholesterol 0 mg

1 1/2 lbs potatoes, peel and cut into chunks 1/2 tsp garam masala
1/2 lb fresh spinach, chopped 1/2 tsp ground coriander
1/2 tsp chili powder 1/2 tsp cumin
  1 tbsp vegetable oil

1/4 cup water
1/2 onion, sliced
Pepper
Salt

- Use the "Slow Cooker" setting on your Instant Pot.
- Add all ingredients into the Instant Pot and stir well.
- Cover and cook on low for 3 hours.
- Serve and enjoy.

Potato Soup with Lentils

Serves: 6, Preparation time: 15 minutes, Cooking time: 10 minutes, Per Serving: Calories: 186; Total Fat: 5g; Saturated Fat: 1g; Protein: 10g; Carbs: 26g; Fiber: 12g; Sugar: 2g

- 1 medium onion (chopped)
- 2 carrots (peeled, diced)
- 2 celery stalks (diced)
- 1 tablespoon olive oil
- 3 garlic cloves (minced)
- 2 teaspoons cumin
- 1 ½ teaspoons paprika
- Salt and freshly ground black pepper, to taste
- 1 pound mixed colors new potatoes (or other waxy potatoes, cut into 1" pieces)
- 1 cup red lentils (rinsed)
- 8 cups vegetable stock
- 1 small bunch Swiss chard (about 8 ounces, chopped)

- In Instant Pot on sauté setting, cook onion, carrots and celery in oil until softened, stirring frequently, about 5 minutes. Add garlic, cumin and paprika, season to taste with salt and pepper and cook about 1 minute more.
- Add potatoes and lentils to pot, mix well and stir in vegetable stock. Secure pot lid, close pressure valve and cook on high pressure for 3 minutes. When cooking time ends, carefully turn venting knob from sealing to venting position for a quick pressure release.
- Stir chard into soup, season to taste with salt and pepper and serve. Enjoy!

Chickpea Kale Sweet Potato Stew

Total Time: 4 hours 20 minutes; Serves: 8; Calories 323, Fat 12.6 g, Carbohydrates 47.7 g, Sugar 4.7 g, Protein 8 g, Cholesterol 0 mg

- 15.5 oz can chickpeas, drained and rinsed
- 5 oz kale, chopped
- 2 red bell peppers, diced
- 1 1/2 lbs sweet potatoes, peeled and cut into pieces
- 2 tbsp curry powder
- 1 tsp fresh ginger, peeled and minced
- 3 garlic cloves, minced
- 2 cups vegetable broth
- 14.5 oz can tomatoes, drained and diced
- 1/4 tsp black pepper
- 14 oz can coconut milk
- 1 tsp vegetable oil
- 1 large onion, diced
- 1 tbsp kosher salt

- Use the "Slow Cooker" setting on your Instant Pot.
- Heat oil in the pan over medium heat.
- Add onion and 1 tsp salt and sauté for 5 minutes.
- Add potatoes and 1 tsp salt and sauté for another 5 minutes.
- Add curry powder, garlic, and ginger and stir for 2 minutes.
- Add pan mixture into the Instant Pot along with remaining ingredients except for kale and coconut milk.
- Cover and cook on high for 4 hours.
- Add coconut milk and kale and stir well. Cook for another 10 minutes.
- Serve and enjoy.

Asparagus Lemon Tender

Serves: 2 / Preparation time: 3 minutes / Cooking time: 2 minutes, Per Serving: Calories: 35; Total Fat: 2.5g; Saturated Fat: 0.5g; Protein: 1.4g; Carbs: 2.5g; Fiber: 1.3g; Sugar: 1.4g

¼ lb. Asparagus
1 cup water
2 tablespoons lemon juice
1 teaspoon olive oil

- Trim the asparagus and cut the woody parts.
- Drizzle lemon juice and olive oil over the asparagus then toss to combine.
- Turn on the sauté function of your Instant Pot and preheat it.
- Pour water into the Instant Pot then place a trivet in it.
- Place the asparagus on the trivet then cover the Instant Pot with the lid. Lock it properly.
- Select "Manual" menu then cook the asparagus on high for 2 minutes.
- Once it is done, naturally release the Instant Pot then open the lid.
- Transfer the steamed asparagus to a serving dish then enjoy.

Pumpkin Vegetable Stew

Serves: 4, Preparation time: 15 minutes, Cooking time: 10 minutes, Per Serving: Calories: 180; Total Fat: 7g; Saturated Fat: 1g; Protein: 4g; Carbs: 30g; Fiber: 6g; Sugar: 11g

2 onions (coarsely chopped)
2 tablespoons olive oil
2 teaspoons ground cumin
1 teaspoon curry powder
1 teaspoon ground coriander
2 cups raw pumpkin flesh (peeled, cut into 1" cubes)
2 golden potatoes (peeled, cut into 1" chunks)
2 carrots (peeled, diced)
1 can (14.5 ounces) diced tomatoes
1 ½ cups water
Salt and freshly ground black pepper, to taste

- In Instant Pot on sauté setting, cook onions in oil until translucent, stirring frequently, about 5 minutes. Add cumin, curry powder and coriander to onions and stir to coat.
- Add pumpkin, potatoes, carrots, tomatoes and water to pot and season to taste with salt and pepper. Secure pot lid, close pressure valve and cook on high pressure for 5 minutes. When cooking time ends, carefully turn venting knob from sealing to venting position for a quick pressure release.
- To thicken stew, mash some of the vegetables with a fork. Season stew to taste with salt and pepper and stir gently. Serve and enjoy!

Quinoa Pilaf

Serves: 4, Preparation time: 20 minutes, Cooking time: 20 minutes, Per Serving: Calories: 260; Total Fat: 4g; Saturated Fat: 1g; Protein: 7g; Carbs: 36g; Fiber: 4g; Sugar: 4g

1 white onion (diced)
2 carrots (peeled, diced)
1 green bell pepper (diced)
2 cups sliced mushrooms
1 tablespoon vegetable oil
2 garlic cloves (minced)
1 cup white quinoa (rinsed and drained)
1 ½ cups vegetable stock
Salt and freshly ground black pepper, to taste
½ cup chopped fresh parsley leaves

- In Instant Pot on sauté setting, cook onion, carrots, bell pepper and mushrooms in oil until softened, stirring frequently, about 5 minutes. Add garlic and cook for about 1 minute, stirring frequently. Add quinoa and mix until coated with onion mixture.
- Stir stock into pot, scraping bottom and sides of pot to loosen any quinoa and browned bits. Season to taste with salt and pepper.
- Secure pot lid, close pressure valve and cook on high pressure for 10 minutes. When coking time ends, let pressure release naturally for 5 minutes, then carefully turn venting knob from sealing to venting position to release remaining pressure quickly.
- Season pilaf to taste with salt and pepper and fluff with a fork. Garnish with parsley leaves to serve. Enjoy!

Sauteed Green Beans and Eggplant

Serves: 2 / Preparation time: 5 minutes / Cooking time: 3 minutes, Per Serving: Calories: 44; Total Fat: 0.2g; Saturated Fat: 0g; Protein: 3.1g; Carbs: 9g; Fiber: 3.5g; Sugar: 2.6g

1 cup chopped green beans
1 cup chopped eggplant
2 teaspoons minced garlic
2 tablespoons soy sauce
1 tablespoons oyster sauce
1 tablespoons fish sauce
½ teaspoon olive oil
½ cup water

- Preheat an Instant Pot for 30 seconds then select "Sauté" menu.
- Pour olive oil into the pot then stir in minced garlic. Sauté until lightly golden and aromatic.
- Add green beans and eggplant to the pot then season with soy sauce, oyster sauce, and fish sauce.
- Pour water over the vegetables then stir well.
- Cover the Instant Pot with the lid and make sure that it is completely locked.
- Choose "Manual" menu and cook on high for 3 minutes.
- Once it is done, quickly release the Instant Pot then open the lid.
- Transfer to a serving dish then enjoy immediately.

Barley with Mushrooms

Serves: 4, Preparation time: 15 minutes, Cooking time: 35 minutes, Per Serving: Calories: 149; Total Fat: 7g; Saturated Fat: 1g; Protein: 4g; Carbs: 32g; Fiber: 03g; Sugar: 0g

2 onions (sliced)
2 tablespoons olive oil
12 ounces cremini mushrooms (sliced)
1 ½ cups pearl barley (rinsed, drained)
3 cups vegetable stock
Salt and freshly ground black pepper, to taste
½ teaspoon dried dill

- In Instant Pot on sauté setting, cook onions until nearly caramelized, stirring frequently, 8-10 minutes. Add mushrooms and cook until softened, 2-3 minutes more. Remove onion mixture from pot and set aside.
- Add barley and vegetable stock to pot and season to taste with salt and pepper. Scrape bottom of pot to loosen any browned bits.
- Secure pot lid, close valve and cook on high pressure for 25 minutes. At the end of cooking time, let pressure release naturally.
- Fluff barley with a fork and stir in reserved onion mixture. Sprinkle dill over barley and serve. Enjoy!

Cauliflower Lentil Curry

Total Time: 5 hours 15 minutes; Serves: 6; Calories 247, Fat 9 g, Carbohydrates 29 g, Sugar 6 g, Protein 12 g, Cholesterol 0 mg

1 cup red lentils
3 cups cauliflower, cut into florets
3 dates, pitted and chopped
2/3 cup coconut milk
1 1/2 tsp turmeric
1 tsp ginger, grated
2 tbsp Thai red curry paste
3 garlic cloves, minced
1/2 onion, chopped
3 cups vegetable broth
1/4 tsp sea salt

- Use the "Slow Cooker" setting on your Instant Pot.
- Add all ingredients except coconut milk into the Instant Pot and stir well.
- Cover and cook on low for 5 hours.
- Add coconut milk and stir well.
- Serve with rice and enjoy.

Cauliflower Curried Soup

40 minutes, Serves: 6, Calories 240; Fat 17.8 g; Carbohydrates 16.6 g; Sugar 5.3 g; Protein 6.8 g; Cholesterol 0 mg

1 small cauliflower head, chopped
4 cups chicken broth
14 oz can coconut milk
1 Tsp turmeric
2 tbsp curry powder
1 Tsp ginger, grated

2 Tsp garlic, minced
1 large sweet potato, peeled and diced
1 cup onion, diced
1 cup carrots, diced
1 tbsp extra virgin olive oil

- Add oil in instant pot and select sauté.
- Add onion and carrots and sauté for 3 minutes.
- Add turmeric, curry powder, ginger, garlic, cauliflower, and sweet potato and stir well.
- Add broth and coconut milk and stir well.
- Seal pot with lid and select soup function.
- Release pressure using quick release method than open the lid carefully.
- Using blender puree the soup until smooth.
- Season with pepper and salt and serve.

Buttered Peas Rice

Total Time: 2 hours 15 minutes; Serves: 4; Calories 265, Fat 7.2 g, Carbohydrates 44.4 g, Sugar 3.4 g, Protein 6 g, Cholesterol 15 mg

1 cup brown rice, uncooked
2 tbsp green onion, sliced
1 cup frozen peas
1 bell pepper, chopped
2 tbsp butter
1 1/4 cup water
Pepper
Salt

- Use the "Slow Cooker" setting on your Instant Pot.
- Add all ingredients into the Instant Pot and mix well.
- Cover and cook on high for 2 hours.
- Serve and enjoy.

Banana Bread

Serves: 12, Preparation time: 15 minutes, Cooking time: 55 minutes, Per Serving: Calories: 294; Total Fat: 16g; Saturated Fat: 11g; Protein: 3g; Carbs: 39g; Fiber: 2g; Sugar: 21g

2/3 cup coconut oil, divided
1 cup water
2 cups flour
1 cup sugar
1 ½ teaspoons baking soda
½ teaspoon salt
¼ teaspoon nutmeg
1 ½ cups mashed ripe bananas (about 3 medium bananas)
¼ cup vanilla almond milk
1 teaspoon vanilla
½ cup chopped walnuts

- Grease a 6-cup bundt cake pan with 2 tablespoons coconut oil and set aside. Pour water into Instant Pot and set trivet in pot.
- In a large bowl, mix flour, sugar, baking soda, salt and nutmeg. Melt remaining coconut oil and add to flour mixture with mashed bananas, almond milk and vanilla. Mix batter well and stir in walnuts. Pour batter into prepared pan, cover pan with aluminum foil and set pan on trivet in Instant Pot.
- Secure pot lid, close pressure valve and cook on high pressure for 55 minutes. When cooking time ends, let pressure release naturally. Remove pan from Instant Pot, loosen foil and set pan on a baking rack to let banana bread cool completely.
- Carefully loosen bread from pan with a butter knife. Set a serving plate over the pan and invert to remove bread onto plate. Cut into slices and serve. Enjoy!

Chickpeas and Tofu

Total Time: 4 hours 15 minutes; Serves: 6; Calories 294, Fat 18.5 g, Carbohydrates 26.2 g, Sugar 3.3 g, Protein 10.8 g, Cholesterol 0 mg

12 oz firm tofu
15 oz can chickpeas, rinsed and drained
1/8 cup cilantro, chopped
1/2 tsp ground ginger
2 tsp chili powder
1 tbsp curry powder

1 tbsp garam masala	1 medium onion, diced
1 cup tomato puree	1 tsp vegetable oil
14 oz can coconut milk	Pepper
4 garlic cloves, minced	Salt

- Use the "Slow Cooker" setting on your Instant Pot.
- Rinse tofu well and pat dry with paper towel. Squeeze out all liquid from tofu and cut tofu into the pieces.
- Heat oil in the saucepan over medium heat.
- Add onion to the pan and sauté for 5 minutes.
- Add garlic and cook for 1 minute.
- Whisk in coconut milk, ginger, chili powder, curry powder, garam masala, tomato puree, pepper, and salt. Cook for 5 minutes.
- Add chickpeas and tofu into the Instant Pot.
- Pour pan mixture into the Instant Pot.
- Cover and cook on low for 4 hours.
- Garnish with cilantro and serve.

Soft Broccoli Quiche

Serves: 2 / Preparation time: 5 minutes / Cooking time: 8 minutes, Per Serving: Calories: 241; Total Fat: 13.9g; Saturated Fat: 6.5g; Protein: 17.5g; Carbs: 12.7g; Fiber: 1.9g; Sugar: 8.1g

1-cup broccoli florets	3 organic eggs
½ cup chopped onion	½ teaspoon black pepper
1-½ cups fresh milk	¼ cup grated cheese

- Pour water into the Instant Pot then place a trivet in it.
- Coat a small heatproof casserole dish then set aside.
- Crack the eggs then place in a bowl.
- Add fresh milk to the eggs then season with black pepper. Stir well.
- Sprinkle broccoli florets and chopped onion in the prepared casserole.
- Pour the eggs mixture over the broccoli then sprinkle grated cheese on top.
- Place the casserole dish on the trivet then cover the Instant Pot with the lid. Lock it properly.
- Select "Manual" setting then cook the beef on high for 8 minutes.
- Once it is done, naturally release the Instant Pot then open the lid.
- Remove the casserole dish from the Instant Pot then enjoy warm.

Chickpea Spinach Soup

Serves: 4, Preparation time: 5 minutes, Cooking time: 30 minutes, Per Serving: Calories: 194; Total Fat: 3g; Saturated Fat: 1g; Protein: 7g; Carbs: 23g; Fiber: 7g; Sugar: 3g

1 small onion (diced)	1 teaspoon dried thyme
2 carrots (peeled, diced)	4 cups vegetable stock
1 celery stalk (sliced)	1 can (12 ounces) garbanzo beans, drained
1 tablespoon olive oil	Salt and freshly ground black pepper, to taste
4 garlic cloves (minced)	1 package (10 ounces) frozen chopped spinach
1 teaspoon cumin	(thawed, drained)
1 teaspoon turmeric	

- In Instant Pot on sauté setting, cook onion, carrots and celery in oil until softened, stirring frequently, about 5 minutes. Add garlic, cumin, turmeric and thyme and cook, stirring constantly, about 1 minute more.
- Add vegetable stock and garbanzo beans to pot, season to taste with salt and pepper and mix thoroughly.
- Secure pot lid, close pressure valve and cook on high pressure for 12 minutes. When cooking time ends, carefully turn venting knob from sealing to venting position for a quick pressure release.
- Stir spinach into soup, season soup to taste with salt and pepper and mix well. Serve and enjoy!

Red Beans Bowl

Total Time: 8 hours 15 minutes; Serves: 4; Calories 399, Fat 2.1 g, Carbohydrates 72.2 g, Sugar 7.4 g, Protein 25.6 g, Cholesterol 2 mg

- 14 oz can kidney beans, drained and rinsed
- 1/2 tsp garam Masala
- 1/2 tsp turmeric powder
- 2 cups onion, chopped
- 1 tomato, chopped
- 1/2 inch cinnamon stick
- 1 bay leaf
- 2 cloves
- 1 tsp ginger, minced
- 5 garlic cloves, minced
- 1 green chili, chopped
- 1/2 tbsp cumin seeds
- 1 tsp cayenne pepper
- 1 tbsp paprika
- Salt

- Use the "Slow Cooker" setting on your Instant Pot.
- Add all ingredients except yogurt into the Instant Pot and stir well.
- Add 4 cups water and stir to combine.
- Cover and cook on high for 8 hours.
- Using back of spoon mash few beans.
- Stir well and serve with rice.

Cauliflower "Mac" and Cheese

Serves: 4, Preparation time: 15 minutes, Cooking time: 5 minutes, Per Serving: Calories: 280; Total Fat: 19; Saturated Fat: 15g; Protein: 13g; Carbs: 14g; Fiber: 5g; Sugar: 6g

- 1 large head cauliflower (about 3 pounds), cut into bite-size pieces
- 1 tablespoon butter
- ½ teaspoon salt
- 1 3-ounce package cream cheese, cut into pieces
- 1 cup plain whole-milk yogurt
- 2 ounces sharp cheddar cheese, shredded
- 2 ounces white cheddar cheese, shredded
- ¼ teaspoon garlic powder
- Salt and freshly ground black pepper, to taste

- Pour 1 cup water into Instant Pot. Place cauliflower pieces in steamer basket and set in pot. Secure pot lid, close pressure valve and cook on steam setting until softened, about 5 minutes. When cooking time ends, let pressure release naturally.
- Remove steamer basket, drain water from pot and set pot to warm. Mix cauliflower, butter, salt, cream cheese, yogurt, cheddar cheeses and garlic powder in pot, season to taste with salt and pepper and stir until cheese is melted.
- Serve immediately and enjoy!

Red Beans Cabbage Soup

Total Time: 8 hours 10 minutes; Serves: 6; Calories 275, Fat 0.9 g, Carbohydrates 51.9 g, Sugar 8.6 g, Protein 18.4 g, Cholesterol 0 mg

- 15 oz can red beans, drained and rinsed
- 4 cups water
- 4 garlic cloves, minced
- 1 bay leaf
- 1 tsp dried thyme
- 5 oz can tomato paste
- 1/2 head green cabbage, chopped
- 1 green bell pepper, seeded and diced
- 1 medium onion, diced
- 1 medium carrots, peeled and diced
- 1/4 tsp black pepper
- Salt

- Use the "Slow Cooker" setting on your Instant Pot.
- Add all ingredients into the Instant Pot and stir well.
- Cover and cook on high for 8 hours.
- Stir well and serve.

Potato Okra Curry

Total Time: 3 hours 15 minutes; Serves: 6; Calories 290, Fat 17.8 g, Carbohydrates 31.8 g, Sugar 5.3 g, Protein 5.5 g, Cholesterol 0 mg

- 1 1/2 lbs potatoes, peeled and cut into pieces
- 1 lb okra, cut the ends and sliced
- 2 cups vegetable stock
- 13 oz can coconut milk
- 1 1/2 tbsp curry powder
- 3/4 tsp red pepper flakes
- 2 tsp fresh ginger, grated
- 4 garlic cloves, minced
- 1 large onion, chopped
- 1 1/2 tbsp vegetable oil
- 1 bell pepper, seeded and chopped
- 1 1/2 tsp salt

- Use the "Slow Cooker" setting on your Instant Pot.
- Add potatoes, bell pepper, and okra into the Instant Pot.
- Heat oil in a pan over medium heat.
- Add garlic, onion, and ginger to the pan and sauté for 5 minutes.
- Remove pan from heat and stir in spices.
- Transfer pan mixture into the Instant Pot and stir well.
- Cover and cook on low for 3 hours.
- Stir well and serve with rice.

Flavorful Vegetable Curry

Total Time: 7 hours 15 minutes; Serves: 4; Calories 367, Fat 3.1 g, Carbohydrates 75.3 g Sugar 11.8 g, Protein 12.6 g, Cholesterol 1 mg

- 15 oz can chickpeas, rinsed and drained
- 8 oz fresh green beans, cut into 1-inch pieces
- 4 medium carrots, sliced
- 2 medium potatoes, cut into 1/2 inch cubes
- 1 cup onion, chopped
- 14 oz can vegetable broth
- 14 oz can tomatoes, diced
- 2 tbsp tapioca
- 2 tsp curry powder
- 1 tsp ground coriander
- 3 garlic cloves, minced
- 1/8 tsp ground cinnamon
- 1/4 tsp red pepper, crushed
- 1/4 tsp salt

- Use the "Slow Cooker" setting on your Instant Pot.
- Add all ingredients into the Instant Pot and stir well.
- Cover and cook on low for 7 hours.
- Stir well and serve with rice.

Tempeh with Figs

Total Time: 4 hours 15 minutes; Serves: 2; Calories 308; Fat 13.6 g; Carbohydrates 29.3 g; Sugar 17.5 g; Protein 11.7 g; Cholesterol 0 mg

- 1/2 fresh thyme sprig
- 1/2 fresh rosemary sprig
- 1/2 tbsp chicken bouillon
- 1/2 tbsp balsamic vinegar
- 1/2 cup port wine
- 1/4 cup water
- 4 fresh figs, cut into wedges
- 4 oz package tempeh, cubed
- 1 garlic clove, minced
- 1/2 small onion, minced
- 1 tbsp olive oil
- Pepper
- Salt

- Use the "Slow Cooker" setting on your Instant Pot.
- The night before, heat olive oil in a pan over medium heat.

- Add onion to the pan and sauté for 3 minutes.
- Add garlic and sauté for 1 minute.
- Transfer onion and garlic mixture into the airtight container with figs and tempeh and store in the refrigerator.
- Next day, add all ingredients to the slow cooker and cook on low for 4 hours.
- Serve and enjoy.

Coconut Crumble Nectarines

Serves: 6, Preparation time: 25 minutes, Cooking time: 15 minutes, Per Serving: Calories: 264; Total Fat: 14g; Saturated Fat: 12g; Protein: 3g; Carbs: 39g; Fiber: 2g; Sugar: 20g

6 firm but ripe nectarines	½ teaspoon cinnamon
¼ cup white flour	¼ teaspoon nutmeg
¼ cup brown sugar	¼ cup toasted coconut
2 tablespoons coconut oil (melted)	

- Cut about ½" off the tops of the nectarines and set aside. Carefully remove pits with a sharp paring knife, leaving a hollowed shell with about ½" of nectarine flesh inside peel.
- From the set-aside nectarine TOPS, scrape any flesh that remains and chop finely. Mix the chopped nectarine flesh with flour, sugar, coconut oil, cinnamon and nutmeg until crumbly. Stuff mixture into hollowed nectarine shells.
- Pour 1 cup water into Instant Pot and set steamer insert in place. Carefully arrange stuffed nectarines in steamer insert.
- Secure pot lid, close pressure valve and cook on high pressure for 3 minutes. When cooking time ends, carefully turn venting knob from sealing to venting position for a quick pressure release.
- Carefully remove steamer insert from pot, set in a dish and let nectarines stand for about 10 minutes. Sprinkle nectarines with toasted coconut to serve. Enjoy!

Curried Potatoes

Total Time: 6 hours 15 minutes; Serves: 6; Calories 218, Fat 2.9 g, Carbohydrates 45.1 g, Sugar 6.7 g, Protein 5.1 g, Cholesterol 0 mg

7 potatoes, washed and cut into chunks	2 tsp paprika
2 tsp sugar	14.5 oz can tomatoes, diced
2 tsp chili powder	1 tbsp vegetable oil
2 tsp curry powder	1/2 tsp kosher salt

- Use the "Slow Cooker" setting on your Instant Pot.
- Add all ingredients into the Instant Pot and stir well.
- Cover and cook on low for 6 hours.
- Serve and enjoy.

Flavourful Vegetable Korma

Total Time: 5 hours 15 minutes; Serves: 4; Calories 295, Fat 19.4 g, Carbohydrates 28.7 g, Sugar 11.8 g, Protein 9.1 g, Cholesterol 0 mg

2 tbsp almond meal	1 cup green beans, chopped
1 tbsp red pepper flakes	1/2 cup frozen green peas
1 tsp garam masala	2 large carrots, chopped
2 tbsp curry powder	1 large cauliflower head, cut into florets
10 oz coconut milk	
2 garlic cloves, minced	1 tsp sea salt
1/2 large onion, chopped	

- Use the "Slow Cooker" setting on your Instant Pot.
- Add all ingredients into the Instant Pot and stir well.

- Cover and cook on high for 5 hours.
- Serve and enjoy.

Curried Zucchini Eggplant

Total Time: 4 hours 15 minutes; Serves: 4; Calories 307, Fat 23.6 g, Carbohydrates 24.3 g, Sugar 10.9 g, Protein 7.2 g, Cholesterol 0 mg

4 cups zucchini, chopped	1/4 tsp cayenne pepper
4 cups eggplant, peeled and chopped	1 tbsp garam masala
1/4 cup vegetable broth	1 tbsp curry powder
15 oz can coconut milk	4 garlic cloves, minced
6 oz can tomato paste	1 onion, chopped
1/4 tsp cumin	1 tsp salt

- Use the "Slow Cooker" setting on your Instant Pot.
- Add all ingredients into the Instant Pot and mix well.
- Cover and cook on low for 4 hours.
- Stir well and serve with rice.

Cherry Almond Rice

Serves: 6 / Preparation time: 10 minutes / Cooking time: 22 minutes, Per Serving: Calories: 250; Total Fat: 7g; Saturated Fat: 0g; Protein: 5g; Carbs: 44g; Fiber: 3g; Sugar: 180g

2 cups brown rice	2 tablespoons brown sugar
3 cups vanilla almond milk	Salt, to taste
½ cup dried cherries	½ cup sliced almonds (toasted)

- Pour almond milk into Instant Pot. Stir rice, dried cherries and brown sugar into pot and season to taste with salt.
- Secure pot lid, close pressure valve and cook at high pressure for 22 minutes. When cooking time ends, let pressure release naturally.
- Mix rice thoroughly and spoon into bowls. Sprinkle almonds over rice to serve. Enjoy!

Butter Garlic Potatoes

10 minutes, Serves: 2, Calories 319; Fat 15.4 g; Carbohydrates 43.5 g; Sugar 4.1 g; Protein 5.9 g; Cholesterol 0 mg

1 lb new potatoes	1/4 cup fresh herbs, chopped
3 Tsp garlic puree	Pepper
3 tbsp coconut butter	Salt

- Pour 1 cup water into the instant pot and place steamer rack in pot.
- Add all ingredients into the steamer rack.
- Seal pot with lid and cook on manual high pressure for 4 minutes.
- Release pressure using quick release method than open the lid carefully.
- Serve warm and enjoy.

Instant Pot Sambar

Total Time: 6 hours 10 minutes; Serves: 2; Calories 130, Fat 0.6 g, Carbohydrates 24.7 g, Sugar 5.3 g, Protein 7.5 g, Cholesterol 0 mg

1/4 cup pink lentils	1/4 cup tomatoes, chopped
1 cup water	1/4 cup eggplants, cut into pieces
1/2 tsp tamarind paste	1/4 cup pumpkin, cut into pieces
1 tsp sambar powder	1 medium onion, sliced
4 curry leaves	1 drumstick, peeled and cut into pieces

Salt
- Use the "Slow Cooker" setting on your Instant Pot.
- Add all ingredients into the Instant Pot and stir well.
- Cover and cook on low for 6 hours.
- Stir well and serve hot with rice.

Corn on the Cob with Avocado Dressing

Serves: 6, Preparation time: 20 minutes, Cooking time: 2 minutes, Per Serving: Calories: 127; Total Fat: 6g; Saturated Fat: 2g; Protein: 1g; Carbs: 20g; Fiber: 5g; Sugar: 3g

1 cup water	1 lime (zested, juiced)
6 ears corn on the cob (husks and silk removed)	1 tablespoon water
1 avocado (halved, pitted)	½ teaspoon ground chipotle chili pepper
2 garlic cloves (minced)	¼ teaspoon cayenne pepper
3 tablespoons fresh cilantro (chopped)	Salt and freshly ground black pepper, to taste

- Pour water into Instant Pot and place trivet in pot. Arrange ears of corn in criss-crossed layers in pot.
- Secure pot lid, close pressure valve and cook on high pressure for 2 minutes. When cooking time ends, carefully turn venting knob from sealing to venting position for a quick pressure release.
- While Instant Pot is coming to pressure, make the dressing. In a small mixing bowl, mash avocado flesh, garlic, cilantro, lime juice, water, chipotle chili pepper and cayenne pepper and season to taste with salt and pepper.
- Place cooked corn on the cob in a shallow casserole dish. Spread avocado dressing over corn, turning corn to coat evenly. Sprinkle lime zest over corn and serve. Enjoy!

Simple Yellow Lentil

Total Time: 3 hours 15 minutes; Serves: 2; Calories 265; Fat 1.1 g; Carbohydrates 37.6 g; Sugar 7.6 g; Protein 13.6 g; Cholesterol 0 mg

1/2 cup yellow split peas, soaked in water for 1 hour	1/2 medium onion, chopped
2 tbsp cilantro, minced	1/4 tsp mustard seeds
1/8 tsp cayenne	1/4 tsp cumin seeds
1/8 tsp ground turmeric	1 tbsp olive oil
1/2 tsp ground coriander seeds	1 1/2 tomatoes, diced
2 garlic cloves, sliced	1 1/2 cups water

- Use the "Slow Cooker" setting on your Instant Pot.
- Add lentils, salt, and water into the slow cooker.
- Cover and cook on high for 3 hours or until lentils are cooked.
- Heat oil in the pan over medium heat.
- Once the oil is hot then add cumin seeds and mustard seeds and cook for 30 seconds.
- Add remaining ingredients and sauté for 4 minutes.
- Transfer pan mixture to the slow cooker and stir well.
- Serve over rice and enjoy.

Vegetable Stew with Chickpeas

Serves: 2 / Preparation time: 5 minutes / Cooking time: 5 minutes, Per Serving: Calories: 260; Total Fat: 6.3g; Saturated Fat: 0.9g; Protein: 14.3g; Carbs: 39.1g; Fiber: 11.6g; Sugar: 8.5g

¼ cup diced carrot	½ cup chickpeas
½ cup cauliflower florets	1 teaspoon minced garlic
2 cups chopped spinach	2 teaspoons sliced shallot
2 tablespoons chopped leek	¼ teaspoon turmeric
1 cup chopped cabbage	½ teaspoon thyme

½ teaspoon pepper 1-teaspoon olive oil
1-cup vegetable broth

- Soak the chickpeas overnight then wash and rinse them.
- Preheat an Instant Pot for 30 seconds then select "Sauté" menu.
- Stir in minced garlic and sliced shallot with olive oil then sauté until wilted and aromatic.
- Next, add chickpeas together with carrots, cauliflower, cabbage, and chopped leek then season with turmeric, thyme, and pepper.
- Pour vegetable broth over the vegetables then stir well.
- Cover the Instant Pot with the lid and make sure that it is locked properly.
- Select "Manual" setting then cook the beef on high for 55 minutes.
- Once it is done, quickly release the Instant Pot then open the lid.
- Stir in chopped spinach then mix well.
- Transfer to a serving dish then serve.
- Enjoy.

Lentil Cauliflower Curry

Total Time: 6 hours 10 minutes; Serves: 2; Calories 180; Fat 1.2 g; Carbohydrates 36.4 g; Sugar 13 g; Protein 10.5 g; Cholesterol 0 mg

- 12.5 oz water
- 12.5 oz tomato sauce
- 1 1/2 tbsp curry powder
- 1/2 cauliflower head, cut into florets
- 1 carrot, chopped
- 1 cup brown lentils, rinsed
- 1/2 tbsp ginger, grated
- 1 garlic clove, minced
- 1/2 onion, diced
- Black pepper
- Salt

- Use the "Slow Cooker" setting on your Instant Pot.
- Add all ingredients to the slow cooker and stir well.
- Cover and cook on low for 6 hours.
- Serve over rice and enjoy.

Simple Chickpea Curry

Total Time: 6 hours 10 minutes; Serves: 6; Calories 265, Fat 16.3 g, Carbohydrates 27.1 g, Sugar 4.1 g, Protein 6.4 g, Cholesterol 0 mg

- 15 oz can chickpeas
- 15 oz can coconut milk
- 15 oz can tomatoes, diced
- 1/4 tbsp cilantro, chopped
- 2 tbsp curry powder
- 1 tsp ginger, minced
- 4 garlic cloves, minced
- 2 onions, diced
- Salt

- Use the "Slow Cooker" setting on your Instant Pot.
- Add all ingredients except cilantro into the Instant Pot and stir well.
- Cover and cook on low for 6 hours.
- Garnish with cilantro and serve.

Mexican Rice

Serves: 8, Preparation time: 5 minutes, Cooking time: 8 minutes, Per Serving: Calories: 199; Total Fat: 4g; Saturated Fat: 0g; Protein: 3g; Carbs: 28g; Fiber: 2g; Sugar: 5g

- 2 cups long-grain white rice
- 1 tablespoon vegetable oil
- 3 cups water
- 2 teaspoons chili powder
- 2 teaspoons salt
- 2 teaspoons bottled hot sauce

- In Instant Pot on sauté setting, cook rice in oil until toasted, stirring frequently, about 5 minutes.
- Add water, chili powder, salt and hot sauce and mix thoroughly.

- Secure pot lid, close pressure valve and cook on high pressure for 3 minutes. When cooking time ends, let pressure release naturally for 5 minutes, then carefully turn venting knob from sealing to venting position to quickly release remaining pressure.
- Fluff rice with a fork and serve immediately. Enjoy!

Vegetarian Chili Bowl

Total Time: 4 hours 20 minutes; Serves: 8; Calories 135, Fat 5.7 g, Carbohydrates 19.5 g, Sugar 6.7 g, Protein 4.4 g, Cholesterol 0 mg

1 tsp garam masala	2 tbsp fresh cilantro, chopped
4 large tomatoes, peeled, seeded and chopped	2 tbsp vegetable oil
	2 green chili, minced
1/3 cup can black beans, drained and rinsed	1/2 medium zucchini, cut into pieces
	1 cup celery, chopped
1/3 cup can chickpea, rinsed and drained	1/2 tbsp chili powder
	1/2 tbsp ground coriander
1 1/2 cups onions, chopped	1/2 tsp cumin powder
1 cup green bell peppers, chopped	1 tsp dried oregano
3 garlic cloves, minced	1 tsp dried thyme
1/3 cup can red beans, rinsed and drained	1 tsp fresh ginger
	1/4 tsp turmeric
1 1/2 cup vegetable stock	1 1/4 tsp salt

- Use the "Slow Cooker" setting on your Instant Pot.
- Heat oil in the pan over medium heat.
- Add onion, celery, green chilies, and ginger into the pan and sauté for 5 minutes.
- Add spices and stir for another 2 minutes.
- Add remaining all ingredients into the Instant Pot along with pan mixture. stir well.
- Cover and cook on low for 8 hours.
- Serve and enjoy.

Nutty Mocha Oatmeal

Serves: 4, Preparation time: 10 minutes, Cooking time: 10 minutes, Per Serving: Calories: 213; Total Fat: 3g; Saturated Fat: 0g; Protein: 6g; Carbs: 42g; Fiber: 4g; Sugar: 15g

1 teaspoon coconut oil	2 tablespoons sugar
4 cups water	¼ cup sliced almonds (toasted)
2 cups old-fashioned oats	¼ cup vegan chocolate chips
1 ½ tablespoons unsweetened cocoa powder	1 cup sweetened or vanilla almond milk (warmed)
2 teaspoons instant espresso powder	
¼ teaspoon salt	

- Grease the inside bottom of the Instant Pot with coconut oil. Add water, oats, cocoa powder, espresso powder and salt to pot and mix gently.
- Secure pot lid, close pressure valve and cook on manual setting for 4 minutes. When cooking time ends, carefully turn venting knob from sealing to venting position for a quick pressure release. Let oatmeal stand in pot for about 5 minutes.
- Stir sugar into oatmeal and spoon into bowls. Sprinkle almonds and chocolate chips over oatmeal to serve. Add warmed almond milk to servings as desired. Enjoy!

Potato Chile Stew

20 minutes, Serves: 4, Calories 254; Fat 4.5 g; Carbohydrates 49.6 g Sugar 6.4 g; Protein 6.3 g; Cholesterol 0 mg

3 large potatoes, peeled and chopped	2 garlic cloves, minced
4 cups chicken stock	1/4 Tsp cumin

1/2 Tsp coriander
1 small onion, diced
1 tbsp extra virgin olive oil

3 green chilies, peeled and chopped
Pepper
Salt

- Add oil in instant pot and select sauté.
- Add garlic and onion and sauté for 2 minutes.
- Add chicken stock, chilies, potatoes, cumin, and coriander and stir well.
- Seal pot with lid and cook on manual high pressure for 7 minutes.
- Allow releasing pressure naturally then open the lid.
- Season with pepper and salt.
- Serve and enjoy.

Spicy Winter Chickpeas

Total Time: 6 hours 15 minutes; Serves: 4; Calories 425, Fat 14.3 g, Carbohydrates 60.5 g, Sugar 12.6 g, Protein 16.3 g, Cholesterol 0 mg

1 1/2 cups dried chickpeas, rinsed and drained
2 tbsp parsley, chopped
1 tbsp lemon juice
1 bay leaf
1/2 butternut squash, cut into 1-inch cubes
10 green olive, pitted
1 tsp tamarind paste
2 garlic cloves, minced

2 tomatoes, diced
1 large onion, chopped
2 tbsp vegetable oil
1/2 tsp ground black pepper
1 tsp curry powder
1 tsp ground ginger
1 tsp garam masala
1 tsp smoked paprika
1 tsp turmeric
1/2 tsp salt

- Use the "Slow Cooker" setting on your Instant Pot.
- Heat oil in the pan over medium heat.
- Add garlic, ginger, and onion to the pan and sauté for 5 minutes.
- Add spices and sauté for 1 minute. Transfer mixture into the Instant Pot.
- Add remaining ingredients into the Instant Pot and stir well.
- Cover and cook on low for 6 hours.
- Serve and enjoy.

Bean Soup

Total Time: 8 hours 10 minutes; Serves: 2; Calories 250; Fat 2.3 g; Carbohydrates 42.3 g; Sugar 2.7 g; Protein 16.6 g; Cholesterol 10 mg

2/3 cups dry great northern beans, Soaked overnight and drained
2 cups water
1/4 cup ham, chopped
1 bay leaf

1/2 cup onion, chopped
2 tbsp celery, chopped
Pepper
Salt

- Use the "Slow Cooker" setting on your Instant Pot.
- Add all ingredients to the slow cooker and stir well.
- Cover and cook on low for 8 hours.
- Serve and enjoy.

Turkish Split Pea Stew

Serves: 4, Preparation time: 20 minutes, Cooking time: 15 minutes, Per Serving: Calories: 280; Total Fat: 8g; Saturated Fat: 1g; Protein: 10g; Carbs: 46g; Fiber: 13g; Sugar: 16g

1 onion (diced)
1 carrot (peeled, chopped)

1 small golden potato (peeled, chopped)
2 tablespoons olive oil

4 garlic cloves (minced)
1 ½ teaspoons cumin
1 teaspoon sweet paprika
½ teaspoon chili powder
¼ teaspoon cayenne pepper
¼ teaspoon ground cinnamon
5 cups vegetable stock

1 ½ cups yellow split peas (rinsed, drained)
1 can (14.5 ounces) diced tomatoes
Salt and freshly ground black pepper, to taste
1 lemon (cut into wedges)
1 carton (6 ounces) unsweetened plain plant-based yogurt

- In Instant Pot on sauté setting, cook onion, carrot and potato in oil until softened, stirring frequently, about 5 minutes. Add garlic and cook, stirring constantly, about 1 minute more. Add cumin, paprika, chili powder, cayenne pepper and cinnamon to onion mixture and stir to coat.
- Add vegetable stock, split peas, undrained tomatoes and bay leaf to pot, season to taste with salt and pepper and mix thoroughly. Secure pot lid, close pressure valve and cook on high pressure for 10 minutes. When cooking time ends, let pressure release naturally.
- Season stew to taste with salt and pepper and mix gently. Ladle stew into deep bowls and garnish with lemon wedges and dollops of yogurt to serve. Enjoy!

Chickpea Pumpkin Lentil Curry

Total Time: 8 hours 40 minutes; Serves: 6; Calories 376, Fat 17 g, Carbohydrates 43.5 g, Sugar 3.1 g, Protein 15.7 g, Cholesterol 0 mg

15 oz can chickpeas, rinsed and drained
1 cup pumpkin puree
1 cup lentils, rinsed and drained
15 oz can coconut milk
1/4 tsp ground cayenne pepper

1 tbsp curry powder
2 cups vegetable broth
2 garlic cloves, minced
1 medium onion, diced
1 tsp kosher salt

- Use the "Slow Cooker" setting on your Instant Pot.
- Add all ingredients except coconut milk into the Instant Pot and stir well.
- Cover and cook on low for 8 hours.
- Add coconut milk and stir well. Cook for another 30 minutes.
- Serve with rice and enjoy.

Tomato Lentil Soup

Total Time: 6 hours 10 minutes; Serves: 2; Calories 354; Fat 2.4 g; Carbohydrates 58.6 g; Sugar 10.3 g; Protein 25.9 g; Cholesterol 0 mg

5 oz can tomatoes
1/4 tsp ground cumin
1/4 tsp dried thyme
1/4 tsp dried basil
1 garlic clove, minced
1/2 small onion, diced

2 oz tomato paste
1 carrot, cut into chunks
2 cups vegetable broth
3/4 cup red lentils, dried
1/8 tsp black pepper
Salt

- Use the "Slow Cooker" setting on your Instant Pot.
- Add all ingredients to the slow cooker and stir well.
- Cover and cook on low for 6 hours.
- Stir well and serve.

Veggie Corn Soup

Serves: 2 / Preparation time: 5 minutes / Cooking time: 25 minutes, Per Serving: Calories: 115; Total Fat: 3g; Saturated Fat: 0.5g; Protein: 4g; Carbs: 18.8g; Fiber: 4.5g; Sugar: 7.1g

½ cup corn kernels
¼ cup diced carrots

2 tablespoons chopped leek
¼ cup chopped green beans

¼ cup green peas
¼ cup chopped onion
½ teaspoon pepper
½ teaspoon salt

¼ teaspoon nutmeg
2 cups unsweetened tomato juice
1 teaspoon olive oil

- Heat up an Instant Pot for 30 seconds then press the "Sauté" menu.
- Stir in chopped onion then sauté in olive oil.
- Add corn kernels, green peas, carrots, and green beans to the pot then pour tomato juice into the pot.
- Season with salt, pepper, and nutmeg then stir well.
- Cover the Instant pot with the lid and lock it properly.
- Select "Soup" setting then cook on high and set the time to 25 minutes.
- Once it is done, open the lid then add chopped leek to the pot. Stir immediately.
- Transfer the soup to a serving bowl then serve warm.

Green Pea and Cauliflower Korma

Total Time: 4 hours 15 minutes; Serves: 4; Calories 295, Fat 21.9 g, Carbohydrates 21.8 g, Sugar 9.8 g, Protein 7.6 g, Cholesterol 0 mg

10 oz green peas
1 cauliflower head, cut into florets
1 cup water
1 1/2 cups coconut milk
1/4 tsp cayenne

1 tsp turmeric
1/4 tsp cumin
2 tsp garam masala
1 medium onion, diced

- Use the "Slow Cooker" setting on your Instant Pot.
- Add all ingredients into the Instant Pot and stir well.
- Cover and cook on low for 4 hours.
- Stir well and serve.

Red Beans with Bell Pepper

Total Time: 5 hours 10 minutes; Serves: 4; Calories 525, Fat 29 g, Carbohydrates 35.8 g, Sugar 4.1 g, Protein 30.8 g, Cholesterol 83 mg

3/4 cup celery, chopped
1 tsp dried thyme
1 tsp paprika
3/4 tsp ground red pepper
1/2 tsp ground black pepper
3 cups water
1 cup dried red beans

1 cup onion, chopped
1 cup green bell pepper, chopped
14 oz turkey sausage, sliced
1 bay leaf
5 garlic cloves, minced
1/2 tsp salt

- Use the "Slow Cooker" setting on your Instant Pot.
- Add all ingredients into the Instant Pot and stir well.
- Cover and cook on high for 5 hours.
- Stir well and serve with rice.

Vegetarian Curry

Total Time: 4 hours 10 minutes; Serves: 2; Calories 475; Fat 25.4 g; Carbohydrates 57.7 g; Sugar 15.4 g; Protein 11.3 g; Cholesterol 0 mg

1/2 cup spinach
1 tbsp curry powder
1 sweet potato, diced
1/2 cup butternut squash, diced

1/2 small onion, chopped
7 oz can chickpeas, drained
7 oz can coconut milk
14 oz can tomatoes, chopped

- Use the "Slow Cooker" setting on your Instant Pot.
- Add all ingredients except spinach into the slow cooker and stir well.
- Cover and cook on low for 4 hours.
- Add spinach and stir well.
- Serve and enjoy.

Steamed Winter Veggies

Serves: 4, Preparation time: 20 minutes, Cooking time: 5 minutes, Per Serving: Calories: 147; Total Fat: 6g; Saturated Fat: 1g; Protein: 5g; Carbs: 23g; Fiber: 8g; Sugar: 6g

1 cup water
2 medium carrots (peeled, cut into 1" chunks)
1 pound Brussels sprouts (rinsed, trimmed, cut in half)
2 tablespoons olive oil
4 cloves garlic (minced)
2 tablespoons chopped sun dried tomatoes

- Pour water into Instant Pot and set steamer basket in pot. Season carrots and Brussels sprouts with salt and pepper to taste and place in steamer basket.
- Secure pot lid, close pressure valve and cook vegetables on high pressure for 2 minutes. When cooking time ends, let pressure release naturally for 5 minutes, then carefully turn venting knob from sealing to venting position to quickly release remaining pressure.
- Carefully remove steamer basket from pot and drain pot. On sauté setting, cook garlic in oil for 1 minute, stirring constantly. Add sun dried tomatoes and vegetables to pot and stir until coated with oil.
- Season vegetables to taste with salt and pepper and serve immediately. Enjoy!

Delicious Carrot Potato Medley

25 minutes, Serves: 6, Calories 326; Fat 5.3 g; Carbohydrates 64.8 g; Sugar 11.9 g; Protein 7 g; Cholesterol 1 mg

2 lbs carrots, chopped
4 lbs potatoes, cut into chunks
1 Tsp Italian seasoning
1/2 cup vegetable broth
3 garlic cloves, chopped
1 onion, diced
2 tbsp extra virgin olive oil

- Add oil in instant pot and select sauté.
- Add onion to the pot and sauté for 5 minutes.
- Add carrots and sauté for another 5 minutes.
- Add remaining ingredients and stir well.
- Seal pot with lid and cook on manual high pressure for 10 minutes.
- Allow releasing pressure naturally then open the lid.
- Stir well and serve.

Spicy Black Eyed Peas

Total Time: 6 hours 30 minutes; Serves: 10; Calories 122, Fat 0.2 g, Carbohydrates 30.7 g, Sugar 2.4 g, Protein 11.4 g, Cholesterol 0 mg

1 lb dried black-eyed peas, rinsed and drained
1 tsp ground black pepper
1 1/2 tsp cumin
1/2 tsp cayenne pepper
1 jalapeno pepper, seeded and minced
1 red bell pepper, seeded and diced
2 garlic cloves, diced
1 onion, diced
6 cups water
Salt

- Use the "Slow Cooker" setting on your Instant Pot.
- Add all ingredients into the Instant Pot and stir well.
- Cover and cook on low for 6 hours.
- Serve and enjoy.

Pumpkin Pudding

Serves: 6, Preparation time: 30 minutes, plus cooling and refrigerating, Cooking time: 30 minutes, Per Serving: Calories: 195; Total Fat: 10g; Saturated Fat: 3g; Protein: 2g; Carbs: 30g; Fiber: 4g; Sugar: 14g

1 tablespoon coconut oil	¼ cup brown sugar
1 can (15 ounces) pumpkin pureé	2 teaspoons pumpkin pie spice
1 2/3 cup almond milk	¼ teaspoon salt
3 tablespoons cornstarch	1 cup water
2 tablespoons molasses	½ cup chopped pecans (toasted)

- For a pudding mold, choose a 3-cup heat-proof baking pan, gelatin mold or glass dish that will fit inside the Instant Pot. Thoroughly grease the inside of the pudding mold with the coconut oil.
- In a mixing bowl, process pumpkin, almond milk, cornstarch and molasses with an immersion blender until smooth. Add brown sugar, pie spice and salt, process until combined and pour into prepared mold. Tightly cover mold with aluminum foil.
- Pour water into Instant Pot, place trivet in pot and carefully set mold on trivet. Secure pot lid, close pressure valve and cook on high pressure for 30 minutes. When cooking time ends, carefully turn venting knob from sealing to venting position for a quick pressure release.
- Carefully remove pudding mold from Instant Pot and let pudding stand, undisturbed, until cooled. Refrigerate cooled pudding for 4-6 hours until completely set.
- Remove foil and loosen pudding from mold with a butter knife. Set a serving plate over the mold and invert to turn pudding out onto the serving plate. Sprinkle pecans over pudding to serve. Enjoy!

Chickpea Lentil Chili

Total Time: 8 hours 15 minutes; Serves: 6; Calories 388, Fat 3.3 g, Carbohydrates 73.3 g, Sugar 17.3 g, Protein 19.6 g, Cholesterol 0 mg

1 cup dried chickpeas, soaked overnight	1 cup lentils
1/2 cup raisins	1/2 tsp chili powder
2 1/2 cups vegetable broth	1/2 tsp ground cinnamon
1/2 cup water	1/4 tsp ground turmeric
28 oz can whole tomatoes, undrained and crushed	1 cup onion, chopped
2 cups sweet potatoes, cut into cubes	5 garlic cloves, minced
	1 1/2 tsp ground cumin
	1 tsp kosher salt

- Use the "Slow Cooker" setting on your Instant Pot.
- Add all ingredients into the Instant Pot and stir well.
- Cover and cook on low for 8 hours.
- Stir well and serve.

Parmesan Marinara Spaghetti Squash

Serves: 4, Preparation time: 15 minutes, Cooking time: 30 minutes, Per Serving: Calories: 300; Total Fat: 12g; Saturated Fat: 5g; Protein: 2g; Carbs: 9g; Fiber: 2g; Sugar: 4g

1 large spaghetti squash	1 can (6 ounces) tomato paste
1 tablespoon olive oil	1 teaspoon Italian herb blend
¼ cup finely chopped onion	½ cup finely grated Parmesan cheese
¼ cup finely chopped red bell pepper	1 tablespoon butter
1 can (28 ounces) crushed tomatoes	Salt and freshly ground pepper, to taste

- Pierce spaghetti squash skin all over with a fork or the tip of a sharp knife. Place squash in steamer basket and set in Instant Pot. Secure pot lid, close pressure valve and cook on high setting for 20 minutes. When cooking time ends, let pressure release naturally.
- Remove steamer basket and set squash aside. Drain water from pot, set pot to sauté and cook onion and bell pepper in olive oil until translucent, stirring frequently. Add tomatoes, tomato paste, and herb blend

- to pot, season to taste with salt and pepper and mix thoroughly. Secure pot lid, close pressure valve and cook on high setting for 8 minutes.
- While sauce is cooking, cut squash in half. Scoop out and discard squash seeds. Scrape squash flesh from shell into strings with a fork. Toss squash with butter and season to taste with salt and pepper. At the end of sauce cooking time, let pressure release naturally.
- Divide squash among serving plates, drizzle with sauce and garnish with grated Parmesan cheese. Serve remaining sauce and cheese on the side and enjoy!

Spicy Curried Chickpeas

Total Time: 6 hours 20 minutes; Serves: 4; Calories 540, Fat 12.6 g, Carbohydrates 85.7 g, Sugar 18.5 g, Protein 25.8 g, Cholesterol 0 mg

1.1 lbs chickpeas, rinsed and drained
1/2 tsp dried herbs
1/2 tsp nutmeg
1/2 tsp garam masala
1/2 tsp coriander powder
1 tsp tomato puree
14 oz tomatoes, chopped

2 garlic cloves, minced
2 onion, chopped
1 tsp cumin seeds
4 tsp vegetable oil
2 bay leaves
Salt

- Use the "Slow Cooker" setting on your Instant Pot.
- Soaked chickpeas in a water for overnight.
- Heat oil in the pan over medium heat.
- Add cumin seeds, garlic, and onion into the pan and sauté for 5 minutes.
- Add tomato paste, tomatoes and spices and sauté for 2 minutes. Transfer pan mixture into the blender and blend until smooth.
- Add chickpeas, bay leaves, and blended puree into the Instant Pot and stir well.
- Cover and cook on low for 6 hours.
- Serve with rice and enjoy.

Gluten Free Chickpea Curry

Total Time: 4 hours 10 minutes; Serves: 4; Calories 636, Fat 17.9 g, Carbohydrates 113.6 g, Sugar 54.1 g, Protein 8.7 g, Cholesterol 0 mg

14 oz can chickpeas, drained
3 cup sweet potatoes, peeled and chopped
1/2 tsp chili flakes
1 tbsp honey
1 tsp ground cumin
2 tsp ground turmeric

2 tsp garam masala
13 oz can cream
1 tsp vegetable oil
1 tbsp fresh ginger, grated
4 garlic cloves, minced
1 large onion, chopped

- Use the "Slow Cooker" setting on your Instant Pot.
- Heat oil in the pan over medium heat.
- Add onion, garlic, and ginger to the pan and sauté for 5 minutes.
- Add onion mixture into the blender along with honey, spices, cream, and salt and blend until smooth.
- Add remaining ingredients and curry blend into the Instant Pot and stir well.
- Cover and cook on high for 4 hours.
- Serve and enjoy.

Sloppy Joe Filling

Serves: 4, Preparation time: 15 minutes, Cooking time: 20 minutes, Per Serving: Calories: 241; Total Fat: 3g; Saturated Fat: 1g; Protein: 12g; Carbs: 37g; Fiber: 6g; Sugar: 8g

1 onion (diced)
4 stalks celery (diced)

1 tablespoon olive oil
4 garlic cloves (minced)
3 cups vegetable stock or water
1 cup dry green or brown lentils
1 can (8 ounces) tomato sauce
1 tablespoon balsamic vinegar
1 tablespoon brown sugar
1 teaspoon Worcestershire sauce
1 teaspoon Dijon mustard
1 teaspoon chili powder
Salt and freshly ground black pepper, to taste

- In Instant Pot on sauté setting, cook onion and celery in oil until softened, stirring frequently, about 5 minutes. Add garlic and cook for 1 minute, stirring constantly.
- Add vegetable stock, lentils, tomato sauce, vinegar, brown sugar, Worcestershire sauce, mustard and chili powder to pot, season to taste with salt and pepper and mix well.
- Secure pot lid, close pressure valve and cook on high pressure for 12 minutes. When cooking time ends, let pressure release naturally.
- Season filling to taste with salt and pepper and mix thoroughly. Serve and enjoy!

Spicy Vegetable Curry

Serves: 2 / Preparation time: 5 minutes / Cooking time: 10 minutes, Per Serving: Calories: 234; Total Fat: 17.3g; Saturated Fat: 13.2g; Protein: 4.2g; Carbs: 20.8g; Fiber: 4.4g; Sugar: 8g

½ cup broccoli florets
½ cup chopped cabbage
½ cup chopped carrots
3 teaspoons red chili flakes
1-teaspoon olive oil
2 teaspoons sliced garlic
3 teaspoons sliced shallot
½ teaspoon turmeric
¼ teaspoon ginger
¼ teaspoon cumin
1-inch galangal
1 bay leaf
2 kaffir lime leaves
½ cup coconut milk
1-½ cups water

- Preheat the Instant Pot for 30 seconds then select "Sauté" menu.
- Stir in sliced garlic, shallot, and red chili flakes then sauté together with olive oil.
- Add carrot, cabbage, and broccoli florets then season with turmeric, ginger, cumin, galangal, bay leaf, and kaffir lime leaves. Stir well.
- Cover the Instant Pot with the lid and lock it properly.
- Select "Soup" setting then cook the vegetable on high for 8 minutes.
- Once it is done, quickly release the Instant Pot then open the lid.
- Select "Sauté" menu then pour coconut milk into the pot. Mix well.
- Transfer the soup to a serving bowl then serve immediately.

Zucchini Noodles

10 minutes, Serves: 2, Calories 179; Fat 14.7 g; Carbohydrates 12.2 g; Sugar 5.8 g; Protein 4.3 g; Cholesterol 0 mg

2 large zucchini, spiralized
1 tbsp fresh mint, sliced
1 tbsp lemon juice
2 garlic cloves, diced
2 tbsp extra virgin olive oil
1/2 lemon zest
1/2 Tsp sea salt

- Add oil in instant pot and select sauté.
- Add garlic, salt and lemon zest and stir for 30 seconds.
- Add zucchini noodles and lemon juice and stir for 30 seconds.
- Stir well and serve warm.

Broccoli with Garlic Sauce

Serves: 6, Preparation time: 5 minutes, Cooking time: 15 minutes, Per Serving: Calories: 216; Total Fat: 8g; Saturated Fat: 2g; Protein: 9g; Carbs: 30g; Fiber: 5g; Sugar: 12g

1 ¼ cup water, divided
2 stalks broccoli (cut into bite-size pieces)

Salt and freshly ground black pepper, to taste	¼ cup soy sauce
2 garlic cloves (minced)	¼ cup packed brown sugar
1 tablespoon ginger (minced)	½ teaspoon red pepper flakes
1 tablespoon olive oil	2 tablespoons cornstarch
2 cups vegetable stock	¼ cup chopped salted cashews

- Pour 1 cup water into Instant Pot and set steamer basket in pot. Place broccoli in basket and season to taste with salt.
- Secure pot lid, close pressure valve and cook on steam setting for 4 minutes. When cooking time ends, carefully turn venting knob from sealing to venting for a quick pressure release. Transfer broccoli to a serving dish, cover to keep warm and set aside. Drain water from pot.
- For the sauce, set Instant Pot to sauté setting and cook garlic and ginger in olive oil for 1 minute. Add vegetable stock, soy sauce, brown sugar and red pepper flakes to pot, season to taste with salt and pepper and heat sauce to a simmer, stirring frequently, about 8 minutes.
- Dissolve cornstarch in ¼ cup water, whisk into sauce and cook until thickened, stirring constantly, about 2 minutes.
- Pour sauce over broccoli and stir gently to coat. Sprinkle cashews over broccoli and serve. Enjoy!

North Indian red Beans

Total Time: 4 hours 15 minutes; Serves: 4; Calories 376, Fat 4.8 g, Carbohydrates 64.1 g, Sugar 5.9 g, Protein 22.2 g, Cholesterol 0 mg

2 cups dry red beans, soak for overnight	1 tbsp lemon juice
2 tbsp cilantro, chopped	4 garlic cloves, minced
1 cup tomato sauce	1 tsp ginger, minced
1 cinnamon stick	1 medium onion, chopped
1/4 tsp turmeric	1 tsp cumin seeds
1/4 tsp cayenne pepper	1 bay leaf
1/4 tsp ground coriander	1 tbsp vegetable oil
	1 1/2 tsp salt

- Use the "Slow Cooker" setting on your Instant Pot.
- Heat oil in the pan over medium heat.
- Add onion, bay leaf, and cumin seeds into the pan and cook for 5 minutes.
- Add dry spices and lemon juice and stir for 2 minutes.
- Add beans, cinnamon stick, tomato sauce, and salt into the Instant Pot.
- Transfer pan mixture into the Instant Pot and stir well.
- Cover and cook on high for 4 hours.
- Using spoon lightly mash the red beans it helps to thicken the gravy.
- Garnish with cilantro and serve.

Lentil Potato Coconut Curry

Total Time: 8 hours 15 minutes; Serves: 10; Calories 152, Fat 3 g, Carbohydrates 22 g, Sugar 6 g, Protein 9 g, Cholesterol 0 mg

2 cups brown lentils	3 tbsp curry powder
14 oz can coconut milk	2 medium carrots, peel and diced
3 cups vegetable broth	1 sweet potato, peel and diced
15 oz can tomato sauce	2 garlic cloves, minced
15 oz can tomatoes, diced	1 medium onion, diced
1/4 tsp ground cloves	

- Use the "Slow Cooker" setting on your Instant Pot.
- Add all ingredients except coconut milk into the Instant Pot and stir well.
- Cover and cook on low for 8 hours.
- Stir in coconut milk and serve with rice.

Simple Slow Cooker Lentils

Total Time: 2 hours 10 minutes; Serves: 10; Calories 382; Fat 5.3 g; Carbohydrates 58.8 g; Sugar 3.5 g; Protein 24.5 g; Cholesterol 0 mg

- 3/4 cup green lentils, rinsed
- 1 cup fresh spinach
- 2 tbsp green curry paste
- 1 small sweet potatoes, cut into chunks
- 1/2 onion, diced
- 2 cups vegetable broth
- Salt

- Use the "Slow Cooker" setting on your Instant Pot.
- Add all ingredients to the slow cooker except spinach and mix well.
- Cover and cook on high for 2 hours or until all liquid is absorbed.
- Add spinach and stir well.
- Serve and enjoy.

Broccoli in Tomato Sauce

Serves: 2 / Preparation time: 5 minutes / Cooking time: 5 minutes, Per Serving: Calories: 116; Total Fat: 3.1g; Saturated Fat: 0.5g; Protein: 4.6g; Carbs: 21.6g; Fiber: 5.2g; Sugar: 10.6g

- 1 cup broccoli florets
- 1 ½ cup tomato puree
- ½ teaspoon nutmeg
- ¼ cup chopped onion
- 1 teaspoon olive oil
- ¼ teaspoon pepper
- ¼ teaspoon salt

- Preheat an Instant Pot for 30 seconds then press the "Sauté" menu.
- Pour olive into the Instant Pot the stir in chopped onion. Sauté until translucent and aromatic. Press the "Cancel" button.
- Add broccoli florets and tomato puree to the Instant Pot then season with nutmeg, pepper, and salt.
- Cover the Instant Pot with the lid and make sure that it is completely locked.
- Choose "Manual" menu and cook on high for 5 minutes.
- Once it is done, naturally release the Instant Pot then open the lid.
- Transfer to a serving dish then serve.
- Enjoy.

Chickpea Coconut Quinoa Curry

Total Time: 4 hours 20 minutes; Serves: 8; Calories 291, Fat 12.2 g, Carbohydrates 41.3 g, Sugar 9.3 g, Protein 7.9 g, Cholesterol 0 mg

- 3 cups sweet potato, peeled and cut into cubes
- 2 cups broccoli florets
- 14.5 oz can coconut milk
- 1/4 cup quinoa
- 2 garlic cloves, minced
- 1 tbsp ginger, grated
- 1 cup onion, diced
- 15 oz can chickpeas, drained and rinsed
- 28 oz can tomatoes, diced
- 1 tsp ground turmeric
- 2 tsp tamari
- 1 tsp chili flakes

- Use the "Slow Cooker" setting on your Instant Pot.
- Add all ingredients into the Instant Pot and stir well.
- Cover and cook on high for 4 hours.
- Serve and enjoy.

Garlic Smashed Potatoes

Serves: 6, Preparation time: 10 minutes, Cooking time: 17 minutes, Per Serving: Calories: 240; Total Fat: 4g; Saturated Fat: 0g; Protein: 4g; Carbs: 25g; Fiber: 2g; Sugar: 2g

- 1 ½ pounds new potatoes
- 4 garlic cloves
- 1 tablespoon dried chives
- 1 teaspoon onion powder
- 2 tablespoons olive oil
- 1 cup vegetable stock

- In Instant Pot on sauté setting, cook potatoes, garlic, chives and onion powder in oil, stirring frequently until potatoes are lightly browned on all sides, about 10 minutes.
- Pour vegetable stock into pot, secure pot lid, close pressure valve and cook at high pressure for 7 minutes. When cooking time ends, let pressure release naturally.
- Remove potatoes from Instant Pot and coarsely mash with a fork or potato masher, being sure to crush the garlic cloves. Add cooking liquid from the pot if necessary to achieve desired consistency. Serve and enjoy!

Spicy Eggplant Potatoes

Total Time: 2 hours 40 minutes; Serves: 8; Calories 147, Fat 7.5 g, Carbohydrates 19.4 g, Sugar 5.2 g, Protein 2.9 g, Cholesterol 0 mg

- 2 medium eggplants, cut into 1-inch cubes
- 1 large potato, peeled and cut into 1/2 inch cubes
- 2 jalapeño chilies, seeded and minced
- 1 tbsp ground cumin
- 1 tbsp chili powder
- 1 medium onion, chopped
- 1 tsp ginger, grated
- 6 garlic cloves, minced
- 1 tbsp garam masala
- 1 tsp turmeric
- 2 tbsp fresh cilantro, chopped
- 1/4 cup vegetable oil
- 1 tbsp kosher salt

- Use the "Slow Cooker" setting on your Instant Pot.
- Add all ingredients into the Instant Pot and stir well.
- Cover and cook on high for 2 hours.
- Remove lid and cook on low for another 30 minutes.
- Serve and enjoy.

Asparagus Cream Soup

Serves: 2 / Preparation time: 5 minutes / Cooking time: 5 minutes, Per Serving: Calories: 216; Total Fat: 18.2g; Saturated Fat: 11.4g; Protein: 5.8g; Carbs: 10.5g; Fiber: 3.9g; Sugar: 4g

- ¾ lb. chopped asparagus
- 1 tablespoon butter
- 2 tablespoons chopped onion
- 1 ½ cups water
- ½ cup sour cream
- 1 tablespoon lemon juice
- ¼ teaspoon pepper
- ¼ teaspoon salt
- ¼ teaspoon nutmeg

- Heat up an Instant Pot for 30 seconds then press the "Sauté" menu.
- Add butter to the Instant Pot then let it melt.
- Put the chopped onion in the Instant Pot then sauté until translucent and aromatic. Press the "Cancel" button.
- Stir in chopped asparagus then season with lemon juice, salt, pepper, and nutmeg.
- Pour water into the Instant Pot then cover it with the lid. Lock the Instant Pot properly.
- Choose "Manual" menu and cook on high for 5 minutes.
- Once it is done, quickly release the Instant Pot then open the lid.
- Stir in sour cream then using an immersion blender, blend the soup until smooth.
- Transfer to a serving bowl then serve.
- Enjoy immediately.

Delicious Tofu Coconut Curry

Total Time: 4 hours 15 minutes; Serves: 4 ;Calories 179, Fat 9.1 g, Carbohydrates 20.4 g, Sugar 11.6 g, Protein 8.9 g, Cholesterol 15 mg

- 1 cup firm tofu, diced
- 2 tsp garlic cloves, minced
- 1 cup onion, chopped
- 8 oz tomato paste
- 2 cups bell pepper, chopped
- 1 tbsp garam masala
- 2 tbsp butter
- 1 tbsp curry powder
- 10 oz can coconut milk
- 1 1/2 tsp sea salt

- Use the "Slow Cooker" setting on your Instant Pot.
- Add all ingredients into the Instant Pot and stir well.
- Cover and cook on low for 4 hours.
- Stir well and serve with rice.

Butternut Squash Risotto

Total Time: 2 hours 10 minutes; Serves: 2; Calories 458; Fat 17.7 g; Carbohydrates 71.1 g; Sugar 4.7 g; Protein 8.2 g; Cholesterol 23 mg

- 3/4 cup Arborio rice
- 1 tbsp butter
- 1 1/2 tbsp parmesan cheese
- 1 1/2 tbsp cheddar cheese
- 1/8 tsp black pepper
- 1/2 tsp dried sage
- 1 garlic cloves, chopped
- 1/2 small onion, chopped
- 6 oz butternut squash
- 2 cups vegetable stock
- 1 tbsp olive oil
- 1/2 tsp salt

- Use the "Slow Cooker" setting on your Instant Pot.
- Add all ingredients to the slow cooker and stir well.
- Cover and cook on high for 2 hours.
- Serve hot and enjoy.

Baked Beans

Serves: 10, Preparation time: 30 minutes, Cooking time: 20 minutes, Per Serving: Calories: 161; Total Fat: 3g; Saturated Fat: 1g; Protein: 9g; Carbs: 38g; Fiber: 17g; Sugar: 13g

- 1 pound dry navy beans (picked, rinsed)
- 6 cups water
- 1 white onion (chopped)
- 1 green bell pepper (chopped)
- 1 teaspoon chopped jalapeño pepper
- 2 tablespoons vegetable oil
- 2 garlic cloves (minced)
- 1 can (6 ounces) tomato paste
- ¼ cup blackstrap molasses
- ¼ cup packed brown sugar
- 1 tablespoon apple cider vinegar
- 2 teaspoons Dijon mustard
- 1 teaspoon chipotle chili pepper
- Salt and freshly ground black pepper, to taste

- Place beans and water in Instant Pot and cook on high pressure for 1 minute. At the end of cooking time, let pressure release naturally. Drain the beans and rinse the pot.
- In Instant Pot on sauté setting, cook onion, bell pepper and jalapeño pepper in oil until softened, stirring frequently, about 5 minutes. Add garlic and cumin and cook about 1 minute more, stirring constantly.
- Add beans, tomato paste, molasses, brown sugar, vinegar, mustard and chipotle pepper to pot, season to taste with salt and pepper and mix well until thoroughly combined.
- Secure pot lid, close pressure valve and cook at high pressure for 15 minutes. When cooking time ends, let pressure release naturally. Season beans to taste with salt and pepper and mix thoroughly.
- If necessary, set pot to sauté and simmer beans to reduce sauce to desired consistency. Serve and enjoy!

Spinach Coconut Lentil Soup

Total Time: 4 hours 45 minutes; Serves: 6; Calories 368, Fat 20 g, Carbohydrates 37 g, Sugar 5 g, Protein 14.9 g, Cholesterol 0 mg

4 cups fresh spinach, chopped	1 tsp ground coriander seed
14 oz coconut milk	1 tsp ground cumin
4 cups vegetable stock	2 tsp garlic, minced
1 1/2 cup red lentils, rinsed and drained	1 large onion, chopped
1 tsp ground cinnamon	1 tbsp vegetable oil
1/2 tsp garam masala	Pepper
1 tsp ground turmeric	Salt

- Use the "Slow Cooker" setting on your Instant Pot.
- Heat oil in the pan over medium heat.
- Add onion to the pan and sauté for 5 minutes or until golden brown.
- Add cinnamon, garam masala, turmeric, coriander, cumin, and garlic and cook for 2 minutes.
- Transfer onion-spice mixture into the Instant Pot.
- Add lentils and stock into the Instant Pot and stir well.
- Cover and cook on low for 4 hours.
- Add coconut milk and spinach. Stir well and cook for another 30 minutes.
- Season with pepper and salt.
- Serve and enjoy.

Bulgur with Vegetables

Serves: 4, Preparation time: 10 minutes, Cooking time: 17 minutes, Per Serving: Calories: 207; Total Fat: 3g; Saturated Fat: 1g; Protein: 6g; Carbs: 49g; Fiber: 10g; Sugar: 3g

1 white onion (diced)	1 cup fresh or frozen peas
1 red bell pepper (diced)	1 tablespoon curry powder
2 medium carrots (peeled, diced)	Salt and freshly ground black pepper, to taste
1 tablespoon vegetable oil	2 cups vegetable stock or water
4 asparagus stalks (trimmed, cut into 1" pieces)	1 cup bulgur

- In Instant Pot on sauté setting, cook onion, bell pepper and carrots in oil until softened, stirring frequently, about 4 mintues. Add asparagus, peas and curry powder and stir until coated.
- Add vegetable stock and bulgur to pot and mix well. Secure pot lid, close pressure valve and cook on low pressure for 10 minutes. When cooking time ends, let pressure release naturally.
- Fluff bulgur with a fork and serve immediately. Enjoy!

Butter Garlic Green Beans

15 minutes, Serves: 4, Calories 87; Fat 5.9 g; Carbohydrates 8.4 g; Sugar 1.6 g; Protein 2.2 g; Cholesterol 15 mg

1 lb fresh green beans	2 tbsp clarified butter
1 1/4 cup water	Pepper
1 garlic clove, minced	Salt

- Add all ingredients into the instant pot and stir well.
- Seal pot with lid and cook on manual low pressure for 5 minutes.
- Release pressure using quick release method than open the lid.
- Serve and enjoy.

Chili with Cornmeal Dumplings

Serves: 8, Preparation time: 30 minutes, Cooking time: 25 minutes, Per Serving: Calories: 354; Total Fat: 9g; Saturated Fat: 3g; Protein: 14g; Carbs: 42g; Fiber: 9g; Sugar: 21g

1 yellow onion (diced)	4 cloves garlic (minced)
1 green bell pepper (diced)	1 tablespoon chili powder
2 celery stalks (diced)	2 teaspoons cumin
3 tablespoons olive oil, divided	2 teaspoons paprika

½ teaspoon cayenne pepper
Salt and freshly ground black pepper, to taste
6 cups water
1 can (28 ounces) crushed tomatoes
2 cups dry beans

1 can (6 ounces) tomato paste
2/3 cup flour
1/3 cup cornmeal
2 teaspoons baking powder
½ cup soy milk

- In Instant Pot on sauté setting, cook onion, bell pepper and celery in 1 tablespoon oil until softened, stirring frequently, about 5 minutes. Add garlic, chili powder, cumin, paprika and cayenne pepper, season to taste with salt and pepper and stir until onion mixture is coated with the spices.
- Add water, crushed tomatoes, dry beans and tomato paste to pot, season with salt and pepper and mix well. Mix flour, cornmeal, baking powder, soy milk and remaining olive oil until moistened and drop by tablespoonful over the chili.
- Secure pot lid, close pressure valve and cook on the beans/chili setting for 20 minutes. When cooking time ends, let pressure release naturally. Spoon chili and dumplings into bowls to serve. Enjoy!

Lentil Butternut Squash Curry

Total Time: 12 hours 15 minutes; Serves: 8; Calories 329, Fat 11 g, Carbohydrates 45 g, Sugar 5 g, Protein 15 g, Cholesterol 0 mg

2 cups red lentils
4 cups butternut squash, cut into cubes
2 tbsp ginger, minced
1 1/2 tsp curry powder
1 tsp ground coriander
1 onion, minced
2 garlic cloves, minced

1 tsp garam masala
1 tsp turmeric
14 oz can coconut milk
19 oz can tomatoes, diced
3 cups vegetable stock
1 tsp ground cumin
1/2 tsp salt

- Use the "Slow Cooker" setting on your Instant Pot.
- Add all ingredients into the Instant Pot and stir well.
- Cover and cook on low for 8 hours.
- Serve and enjoy.

Tomato Casserole with Onion

Serves: 2 / Preparation time: 5 minutes / Cooking time: 10 minutes, Per Serving: Calories: 203; Total Fat: 15.6g; Saturated Fat: 2.8g; Protein: 4.1g; Carbs: 14.7g; Fiber: 3.7 g; Sugar: 7.2g

1 lb. red tomatoes
½ lb. onion
½ cup grated Mozzarella cheese

2 tablespoons olive oil
½ teaspoon salt
½ teaspoon pepper

- Cut the tomatoes and onion into slices then alternately arrange them in a heatproof casserole dish.
- Drizzle olive oil then sprinkle salt and pepper over the tomatoes and onion.
- Top with Mozzarella cheese then set aside.
- Preheat the Instant Pot for 30 seconds then pour water into the Instant Pot.
- Place a trivet in the Instant Pot then lay the casserole dish on it.
- Cover the Instant Pot with the lid and lock it properly.
- Select "Soup" setting then cook the vegetable on high for 10 minutes.
- Once it is done, naturally release the Instant Pot then open the lid.
- Take the casserole out from the Instant Pot then serve.
- Enjoy.

Wild Rice with Mushrooms

Serves: 8, Preparation time: 20 minutes, Cooking time: 30 minutes, Per Serving: Calories: 130; Total Fat: 3g; Saturated Fat: 1g; Protein: 3g; Carbs: 25g; Fiber: 3g; Sugar: 20g

1 white onion (diced)

2 carrots (peeled, diced)

2 stalks celery (diced)
8 ounces fresh baby portabella mushrooms (sliced)
2 tablespoons vegetable oil
2 garlic cloves (minced)
½ cup uncooked wild rice
½ cup uncooked brown rice
2 ½ cups vegetable stock or water
½ teaspoon dried rosemary, crushed
½ teaspoon dried thyme
Salt and freshly ground black pepper, to taste

- In Instant Pot on sauté setting, cook onion, carrots, celery and mushrooms in oil until softened, stirring frequently, about 5 minutes. Add garlic and cook about 1 minute more. Add wild rice and brown rice and cook until lightly toasted, stirring frequently, 2-3 minutes.
- Stir vegetable stock into pot, scraping bottom and sides to loosen any browned bits or rice. Add rosemary and thyme to rice mixture and season to taste with salt and pepper.
- Secure pot lid, close pressure valve and cook on high pressure for 20 minutes. When cooking time ends, let pressure release naturally.
- Fluff rice with a fork before serving. Enjoy!

Simple Instant Pot Lentil

Total Time: 6 hours 15 minutes; Serves: 6; Calories 265, Fat 1 g, Carbohydrates 46 g, Sugar 4 g, Protein 18 g, Cholesterol 0 mg

2 cups red lentils, rinsed and drained
1 bay leaf
1 tbsp ground turmeric
1 tbsp fresh ginger, grated
1 medium onion, diced
15 oz can tomatoes, diced
5 cups water
1 tsp fennel seeds
2 tsp mustard seeds
2 tsp cumin seeds
1/4 tsp ground black pepper
1 tsp kosher salt

- Use the "Slow Cooker" setting on your Instant Pot.
- Heat pan over medium heat and toast fennel seeds, mustard seeds, and cumin seeds in a pan until fragrant for 2-3 minutes.
- Add toasted spices and remaining all ingredients into the Instant Pot and stir well.
- Cover and cook on low for 6 hours.
- Stir well and serve.

Warm Broccoli Salad

Serves: 4, Preparation time: 15 minutes, Cooking time: 8 minutes, Per Serving: Calories: 193; Total Fat: 11g; Saturated Fat: 8g; Protein: 7g; Carbs: 17g; Fiber: 5g; Sugar: 8g

1 head broccoli (about 1 pound)
1 small red onion, sliced
2 tablespoons coconut oil
½ teaspoon dried ginger
1 lime, zested and juiced
Salt and freshly ground black pepper, to taste
1 cup unflavored whole-milk yogurt
2 tablespoons finely chopped roasted peanuts

- Peel broccoli stalks if necessary and cut into julienne strips. Cut broccoli florets into bite-size pieces. Set broccoli aside.
- In Instant Pot on sauté setting, melt coconut oil and cook onion until translucent, about 5 minutes.
- Add broccoli, ginger and lime zest to pot, season to taste with salt and pepper and mix well.
- Secure pot lid, close pressure valve and cook on manual setting until broccoli is crisp-tender, about 3 minutes. Carefully turn venting knob from sealing to venting position for a quick pressure release.
- Stir yogurt and lime juice into broccoli mixture and sprinkle with chopped peanuts to serve. Enjoy!

Lentil Sweet Potato Soup

Total Time: 6 hours 20 minutes; Serves: 4; Calories 395, Fat 17 g, Carbohydrates 54 g, Sugar 11 g, Protein 23 g, Cholesterol 1 mg

1 1/2 cups brown lentils
1 large sweet potato, cut into 1/2 inch cubes
6 cups vegetable broth
1 cup coconut milk
1/2 tbsp chili paste
1 medium onion, diced
3 garlic cloves, minced

1/2 tbsp ginger, grated
2 tsp ground cumin
1 tsp garam masala
2 tsp lime juice
1/4 cup fresh cilantro, chopped
14 oz can tomatoes, diced
Pepper
Salt

- Use the "Slow Cooker" setting on your Instant Pot.
- Add all ingredients except tomatoes and lime juice into the Instant Pot and stir well.
- Cover and cook on low for 6 hours.
- Stir in tomatoes and lime juice.
- Cook soup for another 10 minutes to blend the flavors.
- Season with pepper and salt.
- Serve warm and enjoy.

Creamy Cauliflower Soup

Total Time: 4 hours 20 minutes; Serves: 6; Calories 276, Fat 18.5 g, Carbohydrates 25.1 g, Sugar 20.1 g, Protein 6.2 g, Cholesterol 2 mg

1 cauliflower head
2 cups vegetable broth
3 garlic cloves
1/4 cup dried cranberries
1/4 cup pine nuts
13.5 oz can coconut milk

5.3 oz plain yogurt
1 tbsp curry powder
1 tbsp water
3/4 tsp garam masala
1/2 cup sugar
1/2 tsp salt

- Use the "Slow Cooker" setting on your Instant Pot.
- Add cauliflower, broth, and garlic into the Instant Pot. Cover and cook on low for 4 hours.
- Add cauliflower mixture into the blender along with yogurt and coconut milk and blend until smooth.
- Pour into the six serving bowls.
- In a pan, cook over medium heat pine nuts with water, garam masala, and sugar. Cook until sugar is crystallized.
- Sprinkle pan mixture over the soup.
- Serve and enjoy.

Polenta Porridge

Serves: 4, Preparation time: 10 minutes, Cooking time: 25 minutes, Per Serving: Calories: 130; Total Fat: 0g; Saturated Fat: 0g; Protein: 3g; Carbs: 27g; Fiber: 2g; Sugar: 0g

4 cups vegetable stock
2 tablespoons olive or vegetable oil

½ teaspoon salt, plus more to taste if necessary
1 cup polenta

- Set Instant Pot to sauté. Mix vegetable stock, olive oil and salt in pot and heat to a simmer. In a thin, steady stream, pour polenta into pot, whisking constantly to keep mixture smooth.
- Secure pot lid, close valve and cook for 8 minutes on porridge setting, then let stand on the "Keep Warm" setting for 15 minutes longer. At the end of the 15 minutes, carefully turn venting knob from sealing to venting position for a quick pressure release.
- Stir polenta, scraping the bottom and sides of pot if necessary. Season polenta to taste with additional salt, if desired. Serve and enjoy!

Lentil Chicken Vegetable Curry

Total Time: 4 hours 20 minutes; Serves: 8; Calories 473, Fat 10 g, Carbohydrates 42 g, Sugar 4.6 g, Protein 51 g, Cholesterol 101 mg

1 lb dried lentils, rinsed and drained	2 lbs chicken thighs, boneless and cut into pieces
4 cups fresh spinach, chopped	6 garlic cloves, minced
4 cups vegetable broth	1 small cauliflower head, cut into florets
1/4 tsp cinnamon	2 cups carrots, chopped
1 1/2 tsp turmeric	1 large onion, chopped
1/2 tsp cayenne	1 tsp salt
1 tbsp curry powder	

- Use the "Slow Cooker" setting on your Instant Pot.
- Add all ingredients except spinach into the Instant Pot and stir well.
- Cover and cook on high for 3 1/2 hours.
- Add spinach and stir well. Cover and cook for another 30 minutes.
- Stir well and serve with rice.

Steamed Artichokes

35 minutes, Serves: 2, Calories 61; Fat 0.2 g; Carbohydrates 13.8 g; Sugar 1.4 g; Protein 4.2 g; Cholesterol 0 mg

2 medium artichokes, wash, trimmed and cut top	1 cup water
	1 lemon, cut into wedges

- Rub lemon wedges on top of artichokes.
- Pour 1 cup water into the instant pot.
- Place steam rack into the instant pot and place artichokes on the rack.
- Seal pot with lid and select manual and set timer for 20 minutes.
- Allow releasing pressure naturally for 10 minutes then release using quick release method.
- Open lid carefully and serve warm.

White Bean Wraps

Serves: 4, Preparation time: 15 minutes, Cooking time: 16 minutes, Per Serving: Calories: 268; Total Fat: 7g; Saturated Fat: 1g; Protein: 12g; Carbs: 34g; Fiber: 18g; Sugar: 2g

1 red onion (diced)	Salt and freshly ground black pepper, to taste
1 tablespoon olive oil	1 tablespoon pimentos (chopped)
2 garlic cloves (minced)	1 tablespoon dried chives
1 cup dry navy beans (rinsed, drained)	½ cup plain unsweetened plant-based yogurt
3 cups vegetable stock or water	4 large lettuce leaves
1 lemon (zested, juiced)	4 vegan whole wheat tortillas

- In Instant Pot on sauté setting, cook onion in oil until translucent, stirring frequently, about 5 minutes. Add garlic and cook for about 1 minute, stirring constantly.
- Add beans, vegetable stock and lemon juice to pot, season to taste with salt and pepper and mix well.
- Secure pot lid, close pressure valve and cook on high pressure for 12 minutes. When cooking time ends, let pressure release naturally.
- Add lemon zest, pimentos and chives to beans and season to taste with salt and pepper. Mash beans with a fork or process with an immersion blender to desired consistency. Stir yogurt into bean mixture.
- Layer lettuce leaves on tortillas, top with bean mixture and wrap up to serve. Enjoy!

Red Beans and Lentils

Total Time: 4 hours 15 minutes; Serves: 10; Calories 288, Fat 2.8 g, Carbohydrates 49.1 g, Sugar 2 g, Protein 18.4 g, Cholesterol 0 mg

3 cups red beans, cooked	1/4 tsp ground mustard
1 cup black lentils, rinsed and drained	1/4 tsp ground nutmeg

1 tsp ground turmeric
1 tsp ground cardamom
1 1/2 tsp chili powder
3 tsp ground cumin
2 tbsp ginger, grated
6 garlic cloves, minced
5 cups water

For serving:
1 tsp garam masala
2 tsp ginger, grated
2 tsp tomato paste
1/2 cup cashew creamer
Salt

- Use the "Slow Cooker" setting on your Instant Pot.
- Add all ingredients except serving ingredients into the Instant Pot and stir well.
- Cover and cook on high for 4 hours.
- Add all serving ingredients and stir well.
- Serve with rice and enjoy.

Wild Rice Soup

Serves: 4, Preparation time: 15 minutes, Cooking time: 50 minutes, Per Serving: Calories: 223; Total Fat: 5g; Saturated Fat: 0g; Protein: 6g; Carbs: 38g; Fiber: 3g; Sugar: 4g

1 onion (chopped)
4 carrots (peeled, chopped)
4 celery stalks (diced)
2 tablespoons vegetable oil
4 garlic cloves (minced)
1 cup dry wild rice
4 cups vegetable stock
2 dried bay leaves
½ teaspoon dried thyme
½ teaspoon dried sage
½ teaspoon rosemary (crushed)
Salt and freshly ground black pepper, to taste
2 cups leftover mashed potatoes

- In Instant Pot on sauté setting, cook onion, carrots and celery in vegetable oil until softened, stirring frequently, about 5 minutes. Add garlic and cook about 1 minute.
- Add wild rice, vegetable stock, bay leaves, thyme, sage and rosemary to pot, season to taste with salt and pepper and mix well.
- Secure pot lid, close pressure valve and cook on high pressure for 45 minutes. When cooking time ends, let pressure release naturally. Remove bay leaves and thoroughly mix mashed potatoes into soup. Serve and enjoy!

Easy Whole Cauliflower Curry

Total Time: 4 hours 15 minutes; Serves: 4; Calories 383, Fat 25.8 g, Carbohydrates 34.3 g, Sugar 8.6 g, Protein 11.4 g, Cholesterol 0 mg

1 large cauliflower head, trimmed
2 garlic cloves, sliced
1/2 onion, chopped
2 small potatoes, quartered
1 red pepper, sliced
For sauce:

1/2 tsp cayenne pepper
1 tsp cumin
2 tbsp curry powder
2 cups can coconut milk
2 cups vegetable broth

- Use the "Slow Cooker" setting on your Instant Pot.
- Add red pepper, potatoes, onion, garlic, and cauliflower into the Instant Pot.
- In a bowl, whisk together all sauce ingredients and pour over cauliflower.
- Cover and cook on low for 4 hours.
- About 15 minutes before serving add coconut milk and stir well.
- Serve and enjoy.

Easy Southwestern Soup

Total Time: 6 hours 10 minutes; Serves: 2; Calories 104; Fat 0.8 g; Carbohydrates 15.5 g; Sugar 4.4 g; Protein 8.5 g; Cholesterol 0 mg

4 oz can tomatoes, crushed
1 garlic clove, minced
1/2 cup potatoes, diced
1/4 cup onion, diced
1/4 cup carrots, sliced
14 oz can chicken broth
1/2 tbsp Worcestershire sauce

- Use the "Slow Cooker" setting on your Instant Pot.
- Add all ingredients to the slow cooker and stir well.
- Cover and cook on low for 6 hours.
- Stir well and serve.

Vegetable Curried Rice

Total Time: 4 hours 10 minutes; Serves: 4; Calories 237, Fat 2.9 g, Carbohydrates 42.1 g, Sugar 2.7 g, Protein 10.7 g, Cholesterol 0 mg

1 1/2 ups green cabbage, chopped
2 cups mushrooms, chopped
1 cup broccoli, chopped
1 cup brown rice
1 tsp curry powder
2 tbsp apple cider vinegar
1/4 tsp dried thyme
1/2 tsp garlic powder
1/2 tsp black pepper
4 cups vegetable broth
1 tsp salt

- Use the "Slow Cooker" setting on your Instant Pot.
- Add all ingredients into the Instant Pot and mix well.
- Cover and cook on low for 4 hours.
- Using fork fluff the rice.
- Serve and enjoy.

Original Brussel Sprouts Salads

Serves: 2 / Preparation time: 5 minutes / Cooking time: 3 minutes, Per Serving: Calories: 139; Total Fat: 5.5g; Saturated Fat: 0.9g; Protein: 7.8g; Carbs: 20.8g; Fiber: 8.6g; Sugar: 4.9g

1 lb. Brussels Sprouts
½ teaspoon salt
¼ teaspoon pepper
2 teaspoons olive oil

- Preheat an Instant Pot for 30 seconds then pour water into the Instant Pot.
- Place a trivet in the Instant Pot then put the Brussels sprouts on the trivet.
- Cover the Instant Pot with the lid and make sure that it is completely locked.
- Choose "Manual" menu and cook on high for 3 minutes.
- Once it is done, quickly release the Instant Pot then open the lid.
- Transfer to a salad bowl then quickly drizzle olive oil over the Brussels sprouts.
- Sprinkle salt and pepper on top then toss to combine.
- Serve and enjoy.

Coconut Tapioca Pudding

Serves: 6, Preparation time: 5 minutes, Cooking time: 20 minutes, Per Serving: Calories: 324; Total Fat: 20g; Saturated Fat: 17g; Protein: 2g; Carbs: 36g; Fiber: 0g Sugar: 18g

2 ½ cups water (divided)
½ cup small pearl tapioca (rinsed and drained)
1 can (14 ounces) full-fat coconut milk
½ cup sugar
1 medium orange (zested, juiced)
¼ teaspoon salt
1/3 cup coconut (toasted)

- Pour 1 cup water into Instant Pot, place steamer basket in pot and set aside.
- In a heat-proof bowl that fits into the Instant Pot, mix tapioca, remaining 1 ½ cups water, coconut milk, sugar, orange juice and orange zest. Carefully place bowl in steamer basket in pot.

- Secure pot lid, close pressure valve and cook at high pressure for 8 minutes. When cooking time ends, let pressure release naturally. Let pudding stand in pot for 5 more minutes before removing lid.
- Thoroughly mix pudding with a fork, then spoon into individual serving cups or bowls. Pudding can be served immediately, or let stand and serve warm. To serve chilled, cover cooled pudding with plastic wrap and refrigerate for at least 3 hours. Sprinkle toasted coconut over pudding before serving. Enjoy!

Hearty Vegetarian Chili

Total Time: 6 hours 10 minutes; Serves: 2; Calories 513; Fat 3.9 g; Carbohydrates 97.6 g; Sugar 12.5 g; Protein 30.1 g; Cholesterol 0 mg

2 cups butternut squash, peeled and diced
1/2 tsp dried oregano
1/2 tbsp smoked paprika
1/2 tbsp chili powder
1 tbsp cumin
1 garlic clove, minced

1/2 cup fresh corn
1 cup vegetable broth
7 oz kidney beans, rinsed and drained
7 oz tomatoes, roasted and diced
1/2 red pepper, seeded and diced
1/2 onion, diced

- Use the "Slow Cooker" setting on your Instant Pot.
- Add all ingredients to the slow cooker and stir well.
- Cover and cook on low for 6 hours.
- Serve and enjoy.

Red Bean Rice

Total Time: 3 hours 40 minutes; Serves: 2; Calories 405; Fat 2.3 g; Carbohydrates 78.1 g; Sugar 7.6 g; Protein 18.6 g; Cholesterol 0 mg

1/2 cup rice
1/8 tsp cayenne pepper
1/2 tsp smoked paprika
1 bay leaf
1 1/4 cup vegetable broth
1 garlic clove, minced

1 tsp dried thyme
1/2 cup celery, chopped
1/2 cup green bell pepper, chopped
1/2 cup onion, chopped
15 oz can red beans, rinsed and drained

- Use the "Slow Cooker" setting on your Instant Pot.
- Add red beans, cayenne pepper, smoked paprika, bay leaf, broth, garlic, thyme, celery, green pepper, and onion into the slow cooker and mix well.
- Cover and cook on low for 3 hours.
- Add rice and stir well. Season with pepper and salt.
- Cover and cook on high for 30 minutes or until rice is cooked.
- Serve and enjoy.

Brussels sprouts with Pine nuts

15 minutes, Serves: 4, Calories 124; Fat 6.5 g; Carbohydrates 11.7 g; Sugar 2.8 g; Protein 5.3 g; Cholesterol 0 mg

1 lb Brussels sprouts, washed and cut in half
1 cup pomegranate seeds

1/4 cup pine nuts, toasted
Pepper
Salt

- Pour 1 cup water in instant pot and place steamer basket in pot.
- Add Brussels sprouts to the steamer basket.
- Seal pot with lid and cook on high pressure for 3 minutes.
- Release pressure using quick release method than open the lid carefully.
- Transfer sprouts to a serving dish and season with pepper and salt.

- Sprinkle with pomegranate seeds and pine nuts.
- Serve and enjoy.

Vegetable Fajitas

Total Time: 3 hours 40 minutes; Serves: 2; Calories 162; Fat 1.1 g; Carbohydrates 23.4 g; Sugar 13.9 g; Protein 3.5 g; Cholesterol 0 mg

1 cup cherry tomatoes, halved	1 tbsp olive oil
1/2 tsp ground coriander	3 bell peppers, cut into strips
1 tsp smoked paprika	1 onion, sliced
1 tsp chili powder	

- Use the "Slow Cooker" setting on your Instant Pot.
- Add onion, bell peppers, oil, chili powder, smoked paprika, and coriander into the slow cooker and stir well.
- Cover and cook on high for 1 1/2 hours.
- Now add tomatoes and cook for another 2 hours.
- Serve over tortillas and enjoy.

Creamy Coconut Pumpkin Curry

Total Time: 6 hours 15 minutes; Serves: 6; Calories 357, Fat 17.7 g, Carbohydrates 35 g, Sugar 7.4 g, Protein 17.6 g, Cholesterol 43 mg

15 oz can coconut milk, unsweetened	1/4 tsp ground black pepper
2 cups pumpkin puree	1/2 large onion, diced
1 cup vegetable stock	1 garlic clove, minced
3 carrots, cut into 1-inch pieces	2 chicken breasts, cut into 1-inch cubes
3 cups sweet potatoes, cut into 1-inch cubes	1 lime juice
1/2 tbsp curry powder	2 tsp garam masala
1/4 tsp turmeric powder	1/2 tsp kosher salt

- Use the "Slow Cooker" setting on your Instant Pot.
- Add all ingredients into the Instant Pot and mix well.
- Cover and cook on low for 6 hours.
- Serve with rice and enjoy.

Easy Black Bean Soup

Total Time: 8 hours 10 minutes; Serves: 2; Calories 208; Fat 1 g; Carbohydrates 38.6 g; Sugar 3.7 g; Protein 11.9 g; Cholesterol 0 mg

14 oz can black beans, rinsed and drained	1 tbsp red wine
3 tbsp salsa	14 oz vegetable stock

- Use the "Slow Cooker" setting on your Instant Pot.
- Add all ingredients to the slow cooker and stir well.
- Cover and cook on low for 8 hours.
- Using blender puree the soup until smooth.
- Serve and enjoy.

Piña Colada Upside Down Cake

Serves: 8, Preparation time: 10 minutes, Cooking time: 18 minutes, Per Serving: Calories: 323; Total Fat: 15g; Saturated Fat: 13g; Protein: 3g; Carbs: 54g; Fiber: 1g; Sugar: 24g

- 1/3 cup coconut oil (divided)
- ¾ cup light brown sugar (divided)
- 1 can (8 ounces) pineapple slices
- 1 2/3 cups all-purpose flour
- ½ teaspoon baking powder
- ¼ teaspoon baking soda
- ¼ teaspoon salt
- ½ cup coconut milk
- 1 teaspoon vanilla extract
- ¼ cup coconut (toasted)

- Choose a cake pan that will fit inside Instant Pot. Grease bottom of cake pan with 2 tablespoons of the coconut oil and sprinkle with ¼ cup of the brown sugar. Drain pineapple slices, reserving juice. Arrange pineapple slices in a single layer on the bottom of the cake pan, cutting the rings into pieces if necessary for fit.
- Mix flour, brown sugar, baking powder, baking soda and salt; set aside. Melt remaining coconut oil and mix with reserved pineapple juice, coconut milk and vanilla. Add wet mixture to dry mixture, stir until combined and pour over pineapples in cake pan. Tightly cover cake pan with foil.
- Pour 1 cup water into Instant Pot and place trivet in pot. Carefully set cake pan on trivet. Secure pot lid, close pressure valve and cook on high pressure for 18 minutes. When cooking time ends, let pressure release naturally.
- Remove cake from Instant Pot, remove foil and let cake stand on a cooling rack for 10 minutes. Loosen cake from pan by running a butter knife around the edge of the pan. Set a serving plate over the cake and invert to remove cake from pan onto plate. Sprinkle toasted coconut over cake to serve. Enjoy!

Bitter Melon and Mushroom in Wrap

Serves: 2 / Preparation time: 5 minutes / Cooking time: 10 minutes, Per Serving: Calories: 116; Total Fat: 1g; Saturated Fat: 0.1g; Protein: 7.6g; Carbs: 24.5g; Fiber: 4.9 g; Sugar: 3.8g

- 1 lb. bitter melon
- 1 lb. oyster mushroom
- 2 cloves garlic
- 4 shallots
- ¼ cup red chili
- 2 tablespoons chopped tomatoes
- ½ cup basil

- Pour water into the pan then place a trivet in it.
- Cut the bitter melon into slices then place in a bowl.
- Place garlic, shallots, and red chili in a food processor then process until smooth.
- Combine bitter melon with oyster mushroom and basil then season with the spice mixture. Mix well.
- Place the mixture on a sheet of aluminum foil then wrap it tightly.
- After that, place it in the trivet then cover the Instant Pot properly.
- Select "manual" setting then cook on high for 10 minutes.
- Once it is done, naturally release the Instant Pot then open the lid.
- Transfer to a serving dish then serve immediately.
- Enjoy warm.

Plum Slump

Serves: 8, Preparation time: 20 minutes, Cooking time: 10 minutes, Per Serving: Calories: 245; Total Fat: 5g; Saturated Fat: 4g; Protein: 4g; Carbs: 52g; Fiber: 2g; Sugar: 24g

- ¾ cup water
- 1 lemon (zested, juiced)
- ½ cup brown sugar
- ¼ cup flour
- ¼ teaspoon cardamom
- ¼ teaspoon nutmeg
- 12 fresh medium-size ripe plums (peeled, pitted, sliced)
- 2 cups flour
- 2 teaspoons baking powder
- ¼ teaspoon cinnamon
- ¼ teaspoon salt
- ½ cup almond milk
- 3 tablespoons coconut oil (melted)
- 1 teaspoon vanilla

- Pour water and lemon juice into Instant Pot. Mix brown sugar, flour, lemon zest, cardamom and nutmeg, toss with plum slices and set aside.
- For the dumpling batter, mix flour, baking powder, cinnamon and salt. Add almond milk, coconut oil and vanilla to flour mixture and stir just until combined.
- Add plums to water in Instant Pot. Dollop tablespoonfuls of dumpling batter into plum mixture.
- Secure pot lid, close pressure valve and cook on high pressure for 10 minutes. When cooking time ends, let pressure release naturally. Spoon slump into bowls to serve. Enjoy!

Roasted Potato Wedges

20 minutes, Serves: 6, Calories 100; Fat 1.6 g; Carbohydrates 19.2 g; Sugar 1.7 g; Protein 3 g; Cholesterol 0 mg

1 1/2 lbs russet potatoes, peel and cut into wedges
1 cup vegetable broth
1/2 Tsp paprika
1 Tsp garlic powder
1/2 Tsp onion powder
1/4 cup avocado oil
1/4 Tsp black pepper
1 Tsp sea salt

- Add oil in instant pot and select sauté.
- Add potatoes and sauté for 5 minutes.
- Add remaining all ingredients and stir well.
- Seal pot with lid and cook on manual high pressure for 7 minutes.
- Release pressure using quick release method than open the lid.
- Stir well and serve.

Sticky Mango Rice

Serves: 6, Preparation time: 10 minutes, Cooking time: 30 minutes, Per Serving: Calories: 301; Total Fat: 17g; Saturated Fat: 14g; Protein: 3g; Carbs: 38g; Fiber: 1g; Sugar: 19g

1 tablespoon coconut oil
2 cups glutinous rice
2 cups vanilla or sweetened almond milk
1 teaspoon salt
1 can (15 ounces) coconut milk
¼ cup brown sugar
1 ripe mango (peeled, diced)

- Grease inside of Instant Pot with coconut oil. Add rice, almond milk and salt to Instant pot and mix well.
- Secure pot lid, close pressure valve and cook on high pressure for 10 minutes. Let pressure release naturally for 10 minutes, then carefully turn venting knob from sealing to venting position to quickly release remaining pressure.
- Stir coconut milk and brown sugar into rice mixture and replace pot lid. Set pot to warming setting and let rice stand until heated through, about 10 minutes.
- Mix rice, spoon into shallow bowls and sprinkle with mango to serve. Enjoy!

Brussels sprouts with Parmesan Cheese

Total Time: 1 hour 40 minutes; Serves: 2; Calories 632; Fat 14.4 g; Carbohydrates 81.5 g; Sugar 17.9 g; Protein 51.8 g; Cholesterol 20 mg

1 1/2 lbs Brussels sprouts, trimmed and halved
2 tbsp parmesan cheese, grated
1/4 cup pecans, chopped
1 tbsp olive oil
1 1/2 tbsp maple syrup
2 tbsp balsamic vinegar
1/8 tsp black pepper
1/4 tsp sea salt

- Use the "Slow Cooker" setting on your Instant Pot.
- Add all ingredients to the slow cooker and stir well.
- Cover and cook on low for 1 1/2 hours.
- Serve and enjoy.

Broccoli Cheese Soup

Serves: 8, Preparation time: 15 minutes, Cooking time: 10 minutes, Per Serving: Calories: 268; Total Fat: 22g; Saturated Fat: 15g; Protein: 8g; Carbs: 5g; Fiber: 4g; Sugar: 2g

2 tablespoons butter	4 cups broccoli florets
1 medium onion, diced	1 cup heavy cream
4 cloves garlic, peeled and minced	8 ounces Colby cheese, shredded
4 cups chicken stock	

- In Instant Pot on sauté setting, melt butter and cook onion and garlic until translucent, about 5 minutes. Add broccoli and chicken stock to pot and season to taste with salt and pepper.
- Secure pot lid, close pressure valve and cook on high setting for 5 minutes. When cooking time ends, carefully turn venting knob from sealing to venting position for a quick pressure release.
- Add heavy cream and Colby cheese to soup and stir until cheese is melted. Season soup to taste with salt and pepper, serve and enjoy!

Harvest Couscous

Serves: 8, Preparation time: 10 minutes, Cooking time: 5 minutes, Per Serving: Calories: 170; Total Fat:1g; Saturated Fat: 0g; Protein: 6g; Carbs: 34g; Fiber: 2g; Sugar: 2g

2 ½ cups vegetable stock	1 tablespoon olive oil
1 cup couscous	½ teaspoon onion powder
½ cup orzo	½ teaspoon garlic powder
½ cup red quinoa	Salt and freshly ground black pepper, to taste

- Mix vegetable stock, couscous, orzo, quinoa, olive oil, onion powder and garlic powder in Instant Pot and season to taste with salt and pepper.
- Secure pot lid, close pressure valve and cook on high pressure for 5 minutes. When cooking time ends, carefully turn venting knob from sealing to venting position for a quick pressure release.
- Season couscous to taste with salt and pepper, fluff with a fork and serve. Enjoy!

Lentil Vegetable Soup

Total Time: 8 hours 15 minutes; Serves: 8; Calories 288, Fat 2.6 g, Carbohydrates 49 g, Sugar 6.7 g, Protein 18.5 g, Cholesterol 0 mg

1 1/2 cups green lentils, rinsed and drained	2 tsp oregano
9 cups vegetable broth	1 tbsp garlic powder
5 peppercorns	2 cups corn
3 bay leaves	4 cups potatoes, diced
3 tbsp soy sauce	3 large carrots, diced
1 tsp thyme	3 large celery stalks, diced
	2 medium onion, diced

- Use the "Slow Cooker" setting on your Instant Pot.
- Add all ingredients into the Instant Pot and mix well.
- Cover and cook on low for 8 hours.
- Discard peppercorns and bay leaves from soup and using blender puree the soup until you get desired texture.
- Serve hot and enjoy.

Delicious Lemon Lentils

Spinach Curry with Lentils

Serves: 2 / Preparation time: 5 minutes / Cooking time: 10 minutes, Per Serving: Calories: 244; Total Fat: 7.8g; Saturated Fat: 1.1g; Protein: 13.5g; Carbs: 31.3g; Fiber: 15.7 g; Sugar: 1.2g

2 cups chopped spinach
½ cup lentils
3 teaspoons olive oil
1 teaspoon minced garlic
¼ teaspoon cumin

½ teaspoon coriander
½ teaspoon turmeric
½ teaspoon curry powder
¼ teaspoon pepper
1-½ cups water

- Heat up the Instant Pot then select "Sauté" menu.
- Pour olive oil into the pot then stir in minced garlic, cumin, coriander, turmeric, curry powder, and pepper. Sauté until aromatic.
- Add lentils to the pot then pour water over the lentils.
- Cover the Instant Pot with the lid and lock it properly.
- Select "manual" setting then cook on high for 30 minutes.
- Once it is done, quickly release the Instant Pot then open the lid.
- Quickly add spinach to the pot then stir until wilted.
- Transfer to a serving bowl then serve immediately.
- Enjoy warm.

Cauliflower Casserole

Total Time: 2 hours 10 minutes; Serves: 2; Calories 357; Fat 20.7 g; Carbohydrates 30.7 g; Sugar 8.5 g; Protein 15.4 g; Cholesterol 56 mg

1 cauliflower head, cut into pieces
2 tbsp parmesan cheese, shredded
1/4 cup cheddar cheese, shredded
20 oz cream of celery soup

1/4 cup celery, chopped
1/2 onion, diced
1/4 cup vegetable broth

- Use the "Slow Cooker" setting on your Instant Pot.
- Spray slow cooker from inside with cooking spray.
- Add water, onion, celery, and cauliflower into the slow cooker.
- Add remaining ingredients.
- Cover and cook on low for 2 hours.
- Serve and enjoy.

Tomato Rice with Zucchini

Serves: 4, Preparation time: 15 minutes, Cooking time: 25 minutes, Per Serving: Calories: 192; Total Fat: 3g; Saturated Fat: 0g; Protein: 3g; Carbs: 35g; Fiber: 4g; Sugar: 6g

1 can (28 ounces) crushed tomatoes
1 green bell pepper (diced)
1 onion (diced)
1 cup white rice
½ cup water

1 teaspoon chili powder
Salt and freshly ground black pepper, to taste
2 small zucchini (julienned)
1 tablespoon olive oil

- Mix crushed tomatoes, bell pepper, onion, rice, water and chili powder in Instant Pot and season to taste with salt and pepper. Secure pot lid, close pressure valve and cook on rice setting for 22 minutes. When cooking time ends, let pressure release naturally for 10 minutes, then carefully turn venting knob from sealing to venting position to quickly release remaining pressure.
- While the rice is cooking, sauté zucchini in olive oil in a small saucepan on the stove top until lightly browned, about 5 minutes, stirring frequently.
- Season rice to taste with salt and pepper and mix thoroughly. Spoon rice into bowls and top with zucchini to serve. Enjoy!

Simple Quinoa Risotto

Total Time: 1 hour 40 minutes;Serves: 2; Calories 279; Fat 11.3 g; Carbohydrates 32 g; Sugar 1.9 g; Protein 12.4 g; Cholesterol 21 mg

- 1/2 cup quinoa, rinsed
- 3 tbsp parmesan cheese
- 1/2 cup water
- 1 1/4 cup vegetable broth
- 1 garlic cloves, minced
- 1 tbsp butter
- 1 small onion, diced
- 1/8 tsp pepper
- 1/4 tsp salt

- Use the "Slow Cooker" setting on your Instant Pot.
- Add butter, garlic, and onion in the microwave safe bowl and microwave for 5 minutes. Stir every 1 minute.
- Add butter mixture to the slow cooker.
- Add remaining ingredients to the slow cooker and stir well.
- Cover and cook on low for 1 1/2 hour.
- Serve and enjoy.

Summer Vegetable Soup

20 minutes, Serves: 8, Calories 153; Fat 0.6 g; Carbohydrates 15.4 g; Sugar 6.6 g; Protein 23 g; Cholesterol 0 mg

- 1 cup green beans
- 1 cup corn
- 1 medium summer squash, sliced
- 1 medium zucchini, sliced
- 2 large tomatoes, seeded and sliced
- 1 small eggplant, sliced
- 5 garlic cloves, smashed
- 1 medium onion, diced
- 8 cups bone broth
- 1/2 cup fresh basil
- 1 green bell pepper, seeded and sliced
- 1 red bell pepper, seeded and sliced
- Pepper
- Salt

- Add all ingredients into the instant pot and stir well.
- Seal pot with lid and cook on manual high pressure for 10 minutes.
- Allow releasing pressure naturally then open the lid.
- Using blender puree the soup until smooth.
- Season with pepper and salt.
- Serve and enjoy.

Perfect Mashed Potatoes

Serves: 6, Preparation time: 10 minutes, Cooking time: 20 minutes, Per Serving: Calories: 210; Total Fat: 7g; Saturated Fat: 2g; Protein: 4g; Carbs: 33g; Fiber: 3g; Sugar: 3g

- 2 pounds gold potatoes (peeled, cut into 1" chunks)
- Water, to cover potatoes
- 1 teaspoon salt
- ½ cup plain unsweetened almond milk
- 1 tablespoon olive oil
- Salt and freshly ground black pepper, to taste

- Place potatoes in Instant Pot, add salt and pour in enough water to cover, about 4 cups.
- Secure pot lid, close pressure valve and cook on steam setting for 12 minutes. When cooking time ends, turn venting knob from sealing to venting position for a quick pressure release.
- Drain potatoes and return to pot. Add almond milk and olive oil to potatoes, season to taste with salt and pepper and mash to desired consistency with a potato masher. Serve and enjoy!

Spicy Green Beans in Red Gravy

Serves: 2 / Preparation time: 5 minutes / Cooking time: 8 minutes, Per Serving: Calories: 75; Total Fat: 3.1g; Saturated Fat: 0.5g; Protein: 4g; Carbs: 8.7g; Fiber: 1.5g; Sugar: 3.2g

¾ cup chopped green beans
1-teaspoon olive oil
1 teaspoon minced garlic
1 tablespoon sliced shallots
¼ cup red chili flakes
½ cup unsweetened tomato juice
1-cup vegetable broth

- Pour water into the Instant Pot then place a trivet in it.
- Coat a small heatproof casserole dish then set aside.
- Combine crackers crush with butter then place the mixture in the casserole dish. Using your hand, press it.
- Combine eggplant, zucchini, onion, pepper, ginger, nutmeg, and salt then mix well.
- Place on the cracker mixture.
- Crack the egg then whisk until incorporated.
- Pour the egg over the eggplant then place the casserole dish on the trivet.
- Cover the Instant Pot with the lid and make sure that it is locked properly.
- Select "Manual" setting then cook on high for 15 minutes.
- Once it is done, naturally release the Instant Pot then open the lid.
- Remove the casserole dish from the Instant Pot then enjoy warm.

Orange Sweet Potatoes

Serves: 6, Preparation time: 15 minutes, Cooking time: 5 minutes, Per Serving: Calories: 215; Total Fat: 6g; Saturated Fat: 1g; Protein: 4g; Carbs: 37g; Fiber: 5g; Sugar: 13g

2 medium sweet potatoes (peeled, quartered)
1 cup water
1 orange (zested, juiced)
1 tablespoon canola oil
¼ cup brown sugar
¼ teaspoon salt

- Place sweet potatoes in Instant Pot. Mix orange zest into water and pour over sweet potatoes.
- Secure pot lid, close valve and cook on high pressure for 5 minutes. When cooking time ends, carefully turn venting knob from sealing to venting position for a quick pressure release.
- Drain sweet potatoes, drizzle with orange juice and canola oil and sprinkle with brown sugar and salt. Mash sweet potatoes to desired consistency with a fork. Serve and enjoy!

Punjabi Red Bean Curry

Serves: 4, Preparation time: 30 minutes, Cooking time: 40 minutes, Per Serving: Calories: 151; Total Fat: 3g; Saturated Fat: 1g; Protein: 8g; Carbs: 30g; Fiber: 17g; Sugar:2g

1 cup dry kidney beans (rinsed)
2 cups water, plus more as needed
1 onion (diced)
1 tablespoon vegetable oil
1 knob fresh ginger (minced)
2 garlic cloves (minced)
1 teaspoon cumin
1 teaspoon coriander
½ teaspoon chili powder
½ teaspoon cayenne pepper
¼ teaspoon turmeric
2 medium tomatoes (diced)
Salt and freshly ground black pepper, to taste
Additional water, to cover beans

- Place beans and water in Instant Pot and cook on high pressure for 1 minute. At the end of cooking time, let pressure release naturally. Drain the beans and rinse the pot.
- In Instant Pot on sauté setting, cook onion in oil until translucent, stirring frequently, about 5 minutes. Add ginger, garlic, cumin, coriander, chili powder, cayenne pepper and turmeric and cook about 1 minute more, stirring constantly.
- Add beans and tomatoes to pot, season to taste with salt and pepper and mix thoroughly. Add enough water to pot to cover bean mixture. Secure pot lid, close pressure valve and cook at high pressure for 30 minutes. When cooking time ends, let pressure release naturally.
- Season beans to taste with salt and pepper, mix thoroughly and serve. Enjoy!

Green Lentil Curry

Total Time: 6 hours 15 minutes; Serves: 6; Calories 404, Fat 15.9 g, Carbohydrates 49 g, Sugar 5.9 g, Protein 19.7 g, Cholesterol 0 mg

- 2 cups green lentils, rinsed and drained
- 3 cups water
- 6 oz can tomato paste
- 14 oz can coconut milk
- 1 tsp cumin
- 1 tsp curry powder
- 1/2 tsp ground coriander
- 1 tsp turmeric
- 1 tsp vegetable oil
- 6 garlic cloves, minced
- 1 large onion, chopped
- 1 1/4 tsp salt

- Use the "Slow Cooker" setting on your Instant Pot.
- Heat oil in the pan over medium heat.
- Add garlic and onion to the pan and sauté for 5 minutes.
- Add cumin, curry powder, coriander, turmeric, and salt and sauté for 1 minute.
- Transfer pan mixture to the Instant Pot with remaining all ingredients. Stir well.
- Cover and cook on low for 6 hours.
- Serve warm with rice and enjoy.

Easy Cauliflower Rice

Serves: 2 / Preparation time: 5 minutes / Cooking time: 15 minutes, Per Serving: Calories: 110; Total Fat: 7.2g; Saturated Fat: 1g; Protein: 3.3g; Carbs: 10.8g; Fiber: 4.4 g; Sugar: 4.8g

- 3 cups cauliflower florets
- 3 teaspoons olive oil
- ½ teaspoon salt
- ½ teaspoon chopped parsley
- ¼ teaspoon turmeric
- ½ cup chopped onion

- Pour water into an Instant Pot then place a trivet in it.
- Place the cauliflower florets in the trivet then cover the Instant Pot with the lid properly.
- Select "Manual" setting then cook on high for 3 minutes.
- Quickly release the Instant Pot then open the lid.
- Take the cauliflower from the Instant Pot then set aside.
- Discard water from the Instant Pot then select "Sauté" menu.
- Pour olive oil into the Instant Pot then stir in chopped onion. Sauté until wilted.
- Add cooked cauliflower to the Instant Pot then season with salt, turmeric, and chopped parsley. Stir well.
- Turn off the Instant Pot then open the lid.
- Using a potato masher, mash the cauliflower florets until crumbled.
- Transfer to a serving dish then enjoy.

Tangy Raspberry Lemon Curd

Serves: 24, Preparation time: 10 minutes, plus cooling and refrigerating, Cooking time: 1 minute, Per Serving: Calories: 70; Total Fat: 1g; Saturated Fat: 0g; Protein: 0g; Carbs: 16g; Fiber: 1g; Sugar: 13g

- 12 ounces fresh raspberries
- 4 tablespoons cornstarch
- 1 ½ cups white sugar
- 1 cup water
- ½ cup lemon juice
- 1/8 teaspoon salt
- 6 tablespoons soy milk
- 2 tablespoons margarine

- Toss raspberries with cornstarch to coat, then mix with sugar, water, lemon juice and salt in Instant Pot.
- Secure pot lid, close pressure valve and cook on high pressure for 1 minute. When cooking time ends, let pressure release naturally.
- Puree raspberry mixture through a strainer to remove seeds. Thoroughly whisk soy milk and margarine into raspberry mixture. Let curd cool before spooning into three 8-ounce jars. Refrigerate jars until ready to serve. Enjoy!

Eggplant Chickpea Curry

Total Time: 8 hours 40 minutes; Serves: 6; Calories 203, Fat 2.3 g, Carbohydrates 39.2 g, Sugar 11.3 g, Protein 9.7 g, Cholesterol 0 mg

- 15 oz can chickpeas, rinsed and drained
- 1 tbsp fresh ginger, minced
- 2 tsp cumin
- 1 tbsp garam masala
- 1 tbsp curry powder
- 3 cups vegetable broth
- 15 oz can tomatoes
- 4 garlic cloves, minced
- 3 lbs eggplant, diced
- 2 cups onion, diced
- 2 tsp salt

- Use the "Slow Cooker" setting on your Instant Pot.
- Add all ingredients except chickpeas into the Instant Pot.
- Cover and cook on low for 8 hours.
- Add chickpeas and cook for another 30 minutes.
- Stir well and serve.

Root Vegetables

Total Time: 2 hours 40 minutes; Serves: 2; Calories 93; Fat 0.6 g; Carbohydrates 17.6 g; Sugar 8.8 g; Protein 0.6 g; Cholesterol 0 mg

- 3/4 lb of your favorite mixed root vegetables
- 2 garlic cloves, peeled
- 1/2 large onion, sliced
- 1/8 tsp salt

- Use the "Slow Cooker" setting on your Instant Pot.
- Add all ingredients to the slow cooker and mix well.
- Cover and cook on high for 2 1/2 hours.
- Serve and enjoy.

Cazuela

Serves: 6, Preparation time: 15 minutes, Cooking time: 15 minutes, Per Serving: Calories: 140; Total Fat: 5g; Saturated Fat: 3g; Protein: 3g; Carbs: 25g; Fiber: 5g; Sugar: 5g

- 1 yellow onion (diced)
- 2 celery stalks (diced)
- 2 tablespoons vegetable oil
- 4 garlic cloves (minced)
- 1 small butternut squash (peeled, cut into ½" cubes)
- 3 medium gold potatoes (peeled, cut into ½" cubes)
- 2 ears corn on the cob (cut into 2" chunks)
- 6 cups vegetable stock
- 1 teaspoon dried oregano
- 1 teaspoon cumin
- Salt and freshly ground black pepper, to taste
- Chopped fresh cilantro

- In Instant Pot on sauté setting, cook onion and celery in oil until softened, stirring frequently, about 5 minutes. Add garlic and cook about 1 minute, stirring constantly.
- Add squash, potatoes, corn, vegetable stock, oregano and cumin to pot, season to taste with salt and pepper and mix well. Secure pot lid, close pressure valve and cook at high pressure for 8 minutes. When cooking time ends, carefully turn venting knob from sealing to venting position for a quick pressure release.
- Ladle cazuela into shallow bowls and sprinkle with cilantro to serve. Enjoy!

Nutritious Veggie Soup

30 minutes, Serves: 4, Calories 409; Fat 25.3 g; Carbohydrates 41.8 g; Sugar 13.9 g; Protein 9.9 g; Cholesterol 0 mg

- 1 medium onion, chopped
- 1 large sweet potato, peeled and chopped
- 2 cups carrots, cut into chunks
- 4 cups butternut squash, cubed
- 14 oz coconut milk

3 1/2 cups vegetable broth, low sodium
1/4 Tsp cayenne pepper
1 Tsp curry powder
1 Tsp garam masala
2 Tsp turmeric powder
1 Tsp fresh ginger, grated
2 Tsp garlic, minced

- Add all ingredients into the instant pot and stir well.
- Seal pot with lid and cook on manual high pressure for 20 minutes.
- Release pressure using quick release method than open the lid.
- Using blender puree the soup until smooth.
- Serve and enjoy.

Rhubarb Strawberry Apple Crisp

Serves: 8, Preparation time: 30 minutes, Cooking time: 8 minutes, Per Serving: Calories: 337; Total Fat: 16g; Saturated Fat: 14g; Protein: 3g; Carbs: 53g; Fiber: 4g; Sugar: 25g

1/3 cup coconut oil, divided
6 rhubarb stalks (chopped)
2 apples (peeled, chopped)
1 pound strawberries (hulled, chopped)
1/3 cup white sugar
1 tablespoon corn starch
1 teaspoon ground cinnamon, divided
1/2 teaspoon ground nutmeg, divided
3/4 cup flour, divided
½ cup brown sugar
½ cup quick-cooking oats
1 teaspoon baking powder
½ cup coconut (toasted)

- Grease inside of Instant Pot with 1 tablespoon coconut oil. Toss rhrubarb, apples and strawberries with white sugar, corn starch, ½ teaspoon cinnamon and ¼ teaspoon nutmeg until coated and place in Instant Pot.
- Combine flour, brown sugar, oats, baking powder with remaining coconut oil, cinnamon and nutmeg, mix with a fork until crumbly and spread over rhubarb mixture.
- Secure pot lid, close pressure valve and cook at high pressure for 8 minutes. When cooking time ends, let pressure release naturally, then let crisp stand for about 10 more minutes to allow sauce to thicken.
- Spoon crisp into bowls and sprinkle with coconut to serve. Enjoy!

Tasty Carrot Lentils Soup

Total Time: 8 hours 15 minutes; Serves: 8; Calories 158, Fat 1.1 g, Carbohydrates 30.6 g Sugar 15.3 g Protein 7 g, Cholesterol 0 mg

1/2 cup lentils
2 lbs carrots, peeled and cut into 1-inch pieces
1/2 tsp harissa
1/4 cup maple syrup
1 cup orange juice
4 cups vegetable broth
1 tsp fresh ginger, grated
1/2 tbsp ground cumin
1/2 tbsp curry powder
1 medium onion, peeled and chopped
Pepper
Salt

- Use the "Slow Cooker" setting on your Instant Pot.
- Add orange juice, broth, ginger, curry powder, onion, and carrots into the Instant Pot and mix well.
- Cover and cook on low for 6 hours.
- Add lentils, harissa, and maple syrup. Stir well and cook on high for another 2 hours.
- Season with pepper and salt.
- Serve and enjoy.

Delicious Spiced Potatoes and Cauliflower

Total Time: 4 hours 15 minutes; Serves: 8; Calories 123, Fat 5.6 g, Carbohydrates 16.7 g, Sugar 4 g, Protein 3.6 g, Cholesterol 0 mg

1 large cauliflower head, cut into florets	1 tbsp cumin seeds
1 large potato, peeled and diced	1 tsp turmeric
1 tsp fresh ginger, grated	3 tbsp vegetable oil
2 cloves garlic, minced	1 tbsp fresh cilantro, chopped
2 jalapeno peppers, sliced	1/4 tsp cayenne pepper
1 medium onion, peeled and diced	1 tbsp garam masala
1 medium tomato, diced	1 tbsp kosher salt

- Use the "Slow Cooker" setting on your Instant Pot.
- Add all ingredients except cilantro into the Instant Pot and mix well.
- Cover and cook on low for 4 hours.
- Garnish with cilantro and serve.

Coconut Eggplant Curry

Total Time: 4 hours 10 minutes; Serves: 6;Calories 216, Fat 15.2 g, Carbohydrates 20.7 g, Sugar 9.8 g, Protein 4.8 g, Cholesterol 0 mg

2 lbs eggplant, cut into 1 inch cubed	1 green bell pepper, seeded and chopped
4 garlic cloves, minced	2 Serrano peppers, seeded and minced
14.5 oz can coconut milk	1 tbsp garam masala
6 oz tomato paste	1 tsp salt
1 tbsp curry powder	
1 medium onion, chopped	

- Use the "Slow Cooker" setting on your Instant Pot.
- Add all ingredients into the Instant Pot and stir well.
- Cover and cook on low for 4 hours.
- Serve and enjoy.

Mushroom Veggie Soup with Tofu

Serves: 2 / Preparation time: 5 minutes / Cooking time: 8 minutes, Per Serving: Calories: 184; Total Fat: 7.1g; Saturated Fat: 1.7g; Protein: 19g; Carbs: 11.6g; Fiber: 4.1g; Sugar: 4.6g

¼ cup chopped mushroom	¼ cup chopped onion
¼ cup chopped carrots	2 tablespoons chopped leek
¼ cup chopped cabbage	1-teaspoon rosemary
¼ cup broccoli florets	½ teaspoon pepper
½ cup chopped green collard	1 tablespoon lemon juice
½ lb. firm tofu	1-teaspoon salt
¼ cup zucchini	3 cups vegetable broth
2 tablespoons chopped tomatoes	

- Place all ingredients except zucchini and tomatoes in an Instant Pot.
- Cover the Instant Pot with the lid and make sure that it is locked properly.
- Select "Manual" setting then cook vegetables on high and set the time to 5 minutes.
- Once it is done, quickly release the Instant Pot then open the lid.
- Add zucchini and tomatoes to the pot then stir until wilted.
- Transfer the soup to a serving bowl then serve immediately.

Green Beans Barley Soup

Total Time: 4 hours 10 minutes; Serves: 2; Calories 173; Fat 3.3 g; Carbohydrates 26.6 g; Sugar 2.3 g; Protein 11.1 g; Cholesterol 10 mg

7.5 oz can green beans, cut into pieces	1/4 cup barley, uncooked
1/4 cup ham, chopped	12 oz chicken broth

- Use the "Slow Cooker" setting on your Instant Pot.
- Add all ingredients to the slow cooker and stir well.
- Cover and cook on low for 4 hours.
- Serve and enjoy.

Crisp and Tender Potatoes

Total Time: 1 hour 40 minutes; Serves: 2; Calories 348; Fat 15.2 g; Carbohydrates 48.3 g; Sugar 3 g; Protein 6.7 g; Cholesterol 2 mg

4 cups small red potatoes, cut into wedges
2 tbsp parmesan cheese
1/2 tsp dried oregano
1/2 tsp dried thyme
1 garlic clove, minced
2 tbsp olive oil
1/8 tsp black pepper
1/8 tsp salt

- Use the "Slow Cooker" setting on your Instant Pot.
- Add all ingredients to the slow cooker and stir well.
- Cover and cook on high for 1 1/2 hours.
- Serve and enjoy.

Hearty Potato Curry

Total Time: 8 hours 10 minutes; Serves: 4; Calories 476, Fat 36.5 g, Carbohydrates 37.2 g, Sugar 8.8 g, Protein 7 g, Cholesterol 0 mg

1 lb potatoes, cut into 1-inch cubes
1/2 tsp cumin
1/2 tsp coriander
1/2 tsp peppercorns
1 cinnamon stick
1 cups vegetable stock
1 tsp tamarind paste
1 bay leaf
1/4 tsp red pepper, crushed
1/2 tsp garam masala
4 garlic cloves, minced
2 tsp ginger, minced
1 onion, diced
2 tbsp vegetable oil
1 1/2 tsp paprika
1 1/2 tsp turmeric
1/2 cup frozen peas
2 cups coconut milk
2 tbsp all purpose flour
Pepper
Salt

- Use the "Slow Cooker" setting on your Instant Pot.
- Heat 1 tbsp oil in the pan over medium heat.
- Add onion and cook until golden brown, about 3 minutes.
- Add powder spices and stir for 1 minute.
- Transfer onion mixture to the blender with tamarind, ginger, garlic, and coconut milk and blend until smooth.
- Pour blended mixture into the Instant Pot with remaining ingredients except for peas and flour.
- Cover and cook on low for 8 hours.
- Add peas and stir well. Whisk flour in little water and pour into the Instant Pot.
- Stir well and serve.

Broccoli Kale Soup

Serves: 4, Preparation time: 5 minutes, Cooking time: 8 minutes, Per Serving: Calories: 206; Total Fat: 12g; Saturated Fat: 4g; Protein: 8g; Carbs: 17g; Fiber: 2g; Sugar: 10g

1 onion (coarsely chopped)
4 celery stalks (coarsely chopped)
4 garlic cloves (minced)
1 tablespoon olive oil

1 package (16 ounces) frozen chopped kale
1 package (16 ounces) frozen broccoli florets
4 cups vegetable stock
1 tablespoon balsamic vinegar
Salt and freshly ground black pepper, to taste
¼ cup tahini
1 lemon, cut into wedges

- In Instant Pot on sauté setting, cook onion and celery in oil until softened, stirring frequently, about 4 minutes. Add garlic and cook about 1 minute longer.
- Add kale, broccoli, vegetable stock and balsamic vinegar to pot and season to taste with salt and pepper.
- Secure pot lid, close pressure valve and cook on high pressure for 3 minutes. At the end of cooking time, let pressure release naturally.
- Stir tahini into soup, season to taste with salt and pepper and purée to desired consistency with an immersion blender. Ladle soup into bowls and garnish with lemon wedges to serve. Enjoy!

Gluten Free Masala Lentils

Total Time: 6 hours 10 minutes; Serves: 8; Calories 306, Fat 9 g, Carbohydrates 41 g, Sugar 5 g, Protein 17 g, Cholesterol 0 mg

2 1/4 cups brown lentils
4 cups vegetable broth
15 oz can tomatoes, diced
1 medium onion, chopped
3 garlic cloves, minced
1 tbsp fresh ginger, minced
1/4 cup tomato paste
2 tsp tamarind paste
1 tsp maple syrup
1 1/2 tsp garam masala
1 cup coconut milk
3/4 tsp salt

- Use the "Slow Cooker" setting on your Instant Pot.
- Add all ingredients except coconut milk into the Instant Pot and stir well.
- Cover and cook on low for 6 hours.
- Stir in coconut milk and serve.

Riced Cauliflower

Serves: 4, Preparation time: 5 minutes, Cooking time: 15 minutes, Per Serving: Calories: 103; Total Fat: 6g; Saturated Fat: 4g; Protein: 4g; Carbs: 11g; Fiber: 5g; Sugar: 5g

1 large head cauliflower (about 3 pounds), cut into large chunks
1 teaspoon lemon juice
2 tablespoons butter
½ teaspoon salt

- Pour 1 cup of water into Instant Pot. Place cauliflower in steamer basket and set in pot. Drizzle lemon juice over cauliflower.
- Secure pot lid, close pressure valve and cook on manual setting for 1 minute. Carefully turn venting knob from sealing to venting position for a quick pressure release.
- Remove steamer basket, drain water from pot, and set pot to sauté.
- Melt butter in pot, add cauliflower and salt, and mash cauliflower to desired consistency with a fork or a potato masher. Fluff cauliflower with a fork if necessary. Serve and enjoy!

Easy Lentils Rice

Total Time: 4 hours 10 minutes; Serves: 6; Calories 204, Fat 1.3 g, Carbohydrates 37 g, Sugar 1.7 g, Protein 9.6 g, Cholesterol 0 mg

1/2 cup lentils, rinsed and drained
1 tsp garlic powder
3 1/2 cups vegetable broth
1 tbsp curry powder
1 cup white rice, rinsed and drained
1 onion, diced
1/4 tsp pepper
Salt

- Use the "Slow Cooker" setting on your Instant Pot.
- Add all ingredients into the Instant Pot and stir well.
- Cover and cook on high for 4 hours.
- Stir well and serve.

Pea Chickpea Vegetable Curry

Total Time: 2 hours 15 minutes; Serves: 8;Calories 201, Fat 12.4 g, Carbohydrates 19 g, Sugar 2.7 g, Protein 5.7 g, Cholesterol 0 mg

- 1 cup can chickpeas, drained
- 1 cup green peas
- 1 tsp red pepper flakes
- 1 tsp ground coriander
- 1 tsp ginger powder
- 2 tbsp curry powder
- 15 oz can coconut milk
- 2 cups vegetable broth
- 1 medium onion, diced
- 3/4 cup carrot, diced
- 1 1/2 cups potatoes, chopped
- 2 tsp sea salt

- Use the "Slow Cooker" setting on your Instant Pot.
- Add all ingredients into the Instant Pot and stir well.
- Cover and cook on high for 2 hours.
- Stir well and serve.

Lentil Chili

Serves: 8, Preparation time: 20 minutes, Cooking time: 25 minutes, Per Serving: Calories: 317; Total Fat: 5g; Saturated Fat: 1g; Protein: 35g; Carbs: 66g; Fiber: 25g; Sugar: 13g

- 2 colored bell peppers (diced)
- 1 large onion (diced)
- 1 tablespoon olive oil
- 4 garlic cloves (peeled, minced)
- 1 can (15 ounces) kidney beans (drained, rinsed)
- 1 can (15 ounces) great northern beans, (drained, rinsed)
- 2 cups dried brown or green lentils (rinsed, drained)
- 3 cups vegetable broth or water
- 1 can (6 ounces) tomato paste
- 1 tablespoon chili powder
- 1 tablespoon cumin
- 1 tablespoon paprika
- 1 teaspoon dried oregano
- Salt, freshly ground black pepper, and cayenne pepper, to taste
- 1 can (28 ounces) crushed tomatoes
- 1 avocado (pitted, sliced)

- In Instant Pot on sauté setting, cook bell peppers and onion in oil until softened, stirring frequently, about 4 minutes. Add garlic and cook about 2 minutes more.
- Add kidney beans, great northern beans, lentils, broth, tomato paste, chili powder, cumin, paprika and oregano to pot, season to taste with salt, pepper, and cayenne pepper and mix well.
- Secure pot lid, close pressure valve and cook chili at high pressure for 15 minutes. When cooking time ends, let pressure release naturally.
- Add crushed tomatoes to chili, season to taste with salt and pepper and stir until heated through. Ladle chili into bowls and garnish with avocado slices to serve. Enjoy!

Spinach Lentils

Total Time: 4 hours 30 minutes; Serves: 4; Calories 236, Fat 1.4 g, Carbohydrates 43 g, Sugar 9 g, Protein 16.1 g, Cholesterol 0 mg

- 1 cup yellow split peas
- 3 1/2 cups water
- 10 oz spinach, chopped
- 1 tsp cumin seeds
- 1 tbsp fresh ginger, peeled and minced
- 3 garlic cloves, minced
- 1 tsp mustard seeds
- 1 medium onion, diced
- 15 oz can tomatoes, drained and diced
- 2 jalapeno pepper, cored and diced
- 1 tsp turmeric
- 1/2 tsp coriander
- 1/4 tsp cayenne
- 1 tsp salt

- Use the "Slow Cooker" setting on your Instant Pot.
- Add all ingredients except spinach into the Instant Pot and stir well.
- Cover and cook on high for 4 hours.
- Add spinach and cook for another 20.

- Stir well and serve.

Vegetarian Chili

Total Time: 6 hours 10 minutes; Serves: 2; Calories 460; Fat 3 g; Carbohydrates 84.7 g; Sugar 8.7 g; Protein 31.1 g; Cholesterol 0 mg

1 bay leaf	7.5 oz can black beans
1/4 tbsp basil, dried	7.5 oz can white beans
1 packet chili seasoning	7.5 oz can chili with beans
3 tsp chili powder	1/2 cup lentils
1 cup vegetable broth	1/2 tsp garlic salt
4 oz tomato sauce	1/8 tsp black pepper
7 oz can tomatoes, diced	1/8 tsp salt

- Use the "Slow Cooker" setting on your Instant Pot.
- Add all ingredients to the slow cooker and stir well.
- Cover and cook on low for 6 hours.
- Discard bay leaf and serve.

Beet Borscht

55 minutes, Serves: 8, Calories 108; Fat 1.9 g; Carbohydrates 24.4 g; Sugar 17.4 g; Protein 3.9 g; Cholesterol 0 mg

8 cups beets, peeled and diced	1 medium onion, diced
1/4 cup fresh dill, chopped	2 garlic cloves, diced
1/2 tbsp thyme	2 large carrots, diced
6 cups vegetable stock	3 celery stalks, diced
3 cups cabbage, shredded	1 tbsp salt

- Pour 1 cup water into the instant pot.
- Place steamer rack in instant pot and add beets in steamer rack.
- Seal pot with lid and cook on manual high pressure for 7 minutes.
- Release pressure using quick release method than open the lid.
- Now add beets, stock, bay leaf, cabbage, onions, garlic, celery, carrots, thyme, and salt in instant pot.
- Seal pot with lid and select soup setting and adjust the timer to 45 minutes.
- Allow releasing pressure naturally then open the lid.
- Stir well and serve.

Lentil Soup with Spinach

Serves: 4, Preparation time: 5 minutes, Cooking time: 30 minutes, Per Serving: Calories: 186; Total Fat: 5g; Saturated Fat: 0g; Protein: 10g; Carbs: 27g; Fiber: 12g; Sugar: 2g

1 medium onion (diced)	Salt and freshly ground black pepper, to taste
2 celery stalks (diced)	4 cups vegetable stock
2 carrots (peeled, diced)	1 cup dry brown or green lentils (rinsed)
1 tablespoon olive oil	8 ounces fresh baby spinach (stems removed, torn)
4 garlic cloves (minced)	
1 tablespoon curry powder	1 lemon (cut into wedges)

- In Instant Pot on sauté setting, cook onions, celery and carrots in olive oil until softened, stirring frequently, about 5 minutes. Add garlic and cook for about 1 minute. Add curry powder, season to taste with salt and pepper and cook for about 1 minute.
- Add vegetable stock and lentils to pot and mix well. Secure pot lid, close pressure valve and cook on high pressure for 12 minutes. When cooking time ends, let pressure release naturally.
- Add spinach to soup, season to taste with salt and pepper and mix well. Ladle soup into bowls and garnish with lemon wedges to serve. Enjoy!

Chickpea Spinach Cauliflower Curry

Total Time: 6 hours 15 minutes; Serves: 6; Calories 323, Fat 12.6 g, Carbohydrates 47.7 g, Sugar 4.7 g, Protein 8 g, Cholesterol 0 mg

- 2 cups baby spinach, chopped
- 15 oz can chickpeas
- 1/2 tbsp curry powder
- 1 tbsp garam masala
- 1 cup vegetable broth
- 14 oz can coconut milk
- 1 sweet potato, peeled and diced
- 2 cups cauliflower florets
- 2 cups can tomatoes, chopped
- 1 tbsp ginger, minced
- 1 garlic clove, minced
- 1/2 onion, chopped
- 1 tsp vegetable oil
- 1 tsp salt

- Use the "Slow Cooker" setting on your Instant Pot.
- Heat oil in the pan over medium heat.
- Add ginger, garlic, and onion to the pan and sauté for 5 minutes.
- Add pan mixture into the Instant Pot with remaining ingredients except for spinach.
- Cover and cook on low for 6 hours.
- Add spinach and stir well.
- Serve with rice and enjoy.

Butternut Squash Creamy Soup

Serves: 2 / Preparation time: 5 minutes / Cooking time: 8 minutes, Per Serving: Calories: 106; Total Fat: 1.4g; Saturated Fat: 0.4g; Protein: 6.6g; Carbs: 17.6g; Fiber: 3.5g; Sugar: 4.3g

- 3 cups butternut squash cubes
- ½ teaspoon pepper
- 2 cups vegetable broth
- ¼ cup chopped onion
- ½ teaspoon salt

- Preheat the Instant Pot for 30 seconds then place all ingredients in the pot.
- Cover the Instant Pot with the lid and lock it properly.
- Select "Manual" setting then cook the butternut squash on high for 8 minutes.
- Once it is done, quickly release the Instant Pot then open the lid.
- Using an immersion blender, blend the soup until smooth.
- Transfer the creamy soup to a soup bowl.
- Serve and enjoy warm.

Eggplant Caponata

Total Time: 6 hours 10 minutes; Serves: 2; Calories 287; Fat 21.9 g; Carbohydrates 24.1 g; Sugar 12.6 g; Protein 3.8 g; Cholesterol 0 mg

- 1 baby eggplant, peeled and cut into slices
- 1 tomato, diced
- 1 tbsp red wine vinegar
- 1 tsp Italian parsley, chopped
- 1 tsp capers
- 1 small onion, chopped
- 1 olive, chopped
- 3 tbsp olive oil
- 1/2 tsp garlic, minced
- 1/4 tsp balsamic vinegar
- 1/2 red bell pepper
- 1 celery stalk
- Black pepper
- Salt

- Use the "Slow Cooker" setting on your Instant Pot.
- Add all ingredients to the slow cooker and stir well.
- Cover and cook on low for 6 hours.
- Stir well and serve with crackers.

Tasty Black Eyed Pea Curry

Total Time: 4 hours 15 minutes; Serves: 4; Calories 128, Fat 0.4 g, Carbohydrates 31.4 g, Sugar 4.3 g, Protein 10.4 g, Cholesterol 0 mg

- 1 cup dried black-eyed peas, soaked for overnight
- 1 bay leaf
- 6 garlic cloves, minced
- 1/2 tsp black pepper
- 1/4 tsp cayenne
- 2 tomatoes, chopped
- 3 cups water
- 1 tsp ginger, minced
- 1 tsp turmeric
- 1/2 tsp cumin seeds
- 1 large onion, diced
- 1 tsp garam masala
- 1 tsp salt

- Use the "Slow Cooker" setting on your Instant Pot.
- Add all ingredients into the Instant Pot and stir well.
- Cover and cook on high for 4 hours.
- Stir well and serve.

Balsamic Tomato & Red Pepper Soup

Serves: 6, Preparation time: 20 minutes, Cooking time: 10 minutes, Per Serving: Calories: 100; Total Fat: 3g; Saturated Fat: 1g; Protein: 5g; Carbs: 16g; Fiber: 1g; Sugar: 10g

- 1 onion (diced)
- 1 red bell pepper (diced)
- 1 tablespoon vegetable oil
- 2 tablespoons tomato paste
- 2 cans (28 ounces each) whole tomatoes
- 3 cups vegetable stock
- 1 teaspoon dried oregano
- 1 teaspoon dried basil
- 2 dried bay leaves
- Salt and freshly ground black pepper, to taste
- 1 tablespoon balsamic vinegar
- ¼ cup sugar
- Red pepper flakes for garnish

- In Instant Pot on sauté setting, cook onion and bell pepper until lightly browned, stirring frequently, about 6 minutes. Stir tomato paste into pot and mix well.
- Add *undrained* tomatoes, vegetable stock, oregano, basil and bay leaves to pot and mix well, scraping the bottom of the pot to loosen any browned bits.
- Secure pot lid, close pressure valve and cook on soup setting for 10 minutes. When cooking time ends, let pressure release naturally.
- Remove bay leaves from soup and stir in balsamic vinegar and sugar. Pureé soup to desired consistency with an immersion blender. Ladle soup into bowls and sprinkle with red pepper flakes to serve. Enjoy!

Smokey Lentil Soup

Total Time: 6 hours 15 minutes; Serves: 6; Calories 474, Fat 9.9 g, Carbohydrates 67.6 g, Sugar 7 g, Protein 25.8 g, Cholesterol 0 mg

- 2 cups red lentils
- 2 tbsp smoked paprika
- 2 carrots, chopped
- 4 garlic cloves, minced
- 8 cups vegetable broth
- 1 onion, chopped
- 3 tbsp fresh parsley, chopped
- 1/4 cup hulled pumpkin seeds
- 2 potatoes, peeled and chopped
- 1/3 cup tomato paste
- 3 tbsp lemon juice
- 3 tbsp vegetable oil

- Use the "Slow Cooker" setting on your Instant Pot.
- Add lentils, lemon juice, tomato paste, garlic, paprika, carrots, potato, onion, and broth into the Instant Pot and stir well.
- Cover and cook on low for 6 hours.
- Meanwhile, in a small bowl, combine together parsley and oil.
- Ladle soup into the bowls and drizzle with parsley and oil mixture.
- Sprinkle pumpkin seeds over the soup.
- Serve and enjoy.

Applesauce

Serves: 6, Preparation time: 20 minutes, Cooking time: 3 minutes, Per Serving: Calories: 96; Total Fat: 0g; Saturated Fat: 0g; Protein: 0g; Carbs: 48g; Fiber: 10g; Sugar: 38g

12 Golden Delicious apples (peeled, quartered, cored)
1 cup water
½ cup sugar
1 teaspoon cinnamon
½ teaspoon nutmeg
Dash salt

- Add all ingredients to Instant Pot and mix gently. Secure pot lid, close pressure valve and cook on high pressure for 3 minutes. When cooking time ends, let pressure release naturally.
- Mash or pureé applesauce to desired consistency with a fork, potato masher or immersion blender. Serve immediately or let cool and refrigerate. Enjoy!

Quick Steamed Broccoli

5 minutes, Serves: 4, Calories 39; Fat 0.4 g; Carbohydrates 7.6 g; Sugar 1.9 g; Protein 3.2 g; Cholesterol 0 mg

5 cups broccoli florets
Pepper
Salt

- Add 1 cup water into the instant pot and place steamer rack to the pot.
- Add broccoli florets into the pot.
- Seal pot with lid and cook on manual high pressure for 2 minutes,
- Allow releasing pressure naturally then open the lid.
- Season broccoli with pepper and salt.
- Serve and enjoy.

Spaghetti

Serves: 8, Preparation time: 20 minutes, Cooking time: 10 minutes, Per Serving: Calories: 246; Total Fat: 7g; Saturated Fat: 1g; Protein: 6g; Carbs: 41g; Fiber: 5g; Sugar: 14g

1 onion (diced)
1 red bell pepper (diced)
8 ounces fresh mushrooms (sliced)
1 tablespoon olive oil
4 cloves garlic (minced)
1 can (29 ounces) crushed tomatoes
3 cans (8 ounces each) tomato sauce
1 can (6 ounces) tomato paste
2 tablespoons Italian herb mix
1 tablespoon sugar
Salt and freshly ground black pepper, to taste
1 package (16 ounces) uncooked spaghetti noodles
2 whole dried bay leaves
Water, as needed

- In Instant Pot on sauté setting, cook onion, bell pepper and mushrooms in olive oil until softened, stirring frequently, about 5 minutes. Add garlic and cook 1 minute more, stirring constantly.
- Add crushed tomatoes, tomato sauce, tomato paste, Italian herb mix and sugar to pot, season to taste with salt and pepper and stir to combine.
- Break spaghetti noodles in half, place in pot and stir gently to coat with tomato mixture. Gently press noodles into pot and add enough water to cover noodles.
- Secure pot lid, close pressure valve and cook on high pressure for 8 minutes. When cooking time ends, carefully turn venting knob from sealing to venting position for a quick pressure release. Season spaghetti to taste with salt and pepper and mix thoroughly. Serve and enjoy!

Spicy Lentil Stew

Total Time: 6 hours 15 minutes; Serves: 8; Calories 318, Fat 2 g, Carbohydrates 51 g, Sugar 5 g, Protein 23 g, Cholesterol 0 mg

3 cups red lentils, rinsed and drained
3 1/2 cup tomatoes, crushed
1/2 tbsp black pepper
1/2 tbsp curry powder

1/2 tbsp paprika
1/2 tbsp chili powder
1/2 tbsp garam masala
1/2 tbsp turmeric powder
6 cups vegetable broth
1 onion, diced
2 garlic cloves, minced

3 Serrano chili, diced
2 tbsp cilantro, minced
1 tbsp Creole seasoning
1 tbsp garlic powder
1 tbsp onion powder
1/2 tbsp ginger powder

- Use the "Slow Cooker" setting on your Instant Pot.
- Add all ingredients into the Instant Pot and stir well.
- Cover and cook on high for 5 hours.
- Uncover the Instant Pot and cook for another 50 minutes.
- Serve and enjoy.

Creamy Cauliflower Broccoli Soup

Total Time: 6 hours 10 minutes; Serves: 2; Calories 452; Fat 30.7 g; Carbohydrates 23 g; Sugar 11 g; Protein 23.5 g; Cholesterol 48 mg

1/2 cup plain yogurt
3 oz cheddar cheese, shredded
1/2 cup almond milk
1 3/4 cups chicken broth
1 medium carrot, diced
1/4 cup shallots, diced

1 garlic clove, minced
1 cup cauliflower florets, chopped
1 1/2 cups broccoli florets, chopped
Pepper
Salt

- Use the "Slow Cooker" setting on your Instant Pot.
- Add all ingredients except milk, cheese, and yogurt into the slow cooker and stir well.
- Cover and cook on low for 6 hours.
- Using blender puree the soup until smooth.
- Add cheese and milk and blend until cheese is melted.
- Add yogurt and stir well to combine.
- Serve and enjoy.

Refried Black Beans

Serves: 6, Preparation time: 15 minutes, Cooking time: 20 minutes, Per Serving: Calories: 173; Total Fat: 2g; Saturated Fat:0g; Protein: 8g; Carbs: 24g; Fiber: 16g; Sugar: 2g

1 medium onion (finely diced)
1 red bell pepper (finely diced)
1 tablespoon olive oil
4 garlic cloves (peeled, minced)
2 cans black beans (undrained)

½ cup vegetable broth or water
1 teaspoon chili powder
1 teaspoon cumin
½ teaspoon chipotle chili powder
Salt and freshly ground black pepper, to taste

- In Instant Pot on sauté setting, cook onion and bell pepper in oil until softened, stirring frequently, about 4 minutes. Add garlic and cook about 1 minute more.
- Add undrained beans, vegetable broth, chili powder, cumin, chipotle chili powder. Season mixture to taste with salt and pepper and mix well.
- Secure pot lid, close pressure valve and cook beans at high pressure for about 15 minutes. When cooking time ends, let pressure release naturally.
- Mash beans to desired texture with a fork or potato masher. Serve and enjoy!

Spring Veggie Soup

25 minutes, Serves: 8, Calories 124; Fat 0.2 g; Carbohydrates 8.6 g; Sugar 3.2 g; Protein 22 g; Cholesterol 0 mg

1 medium leek, chopped
1 bunch asparagus, trimmed
10 radishes, remove tops

5 small carrots, remove tops
1/2 lb spinach
5 garlic cloves

1 medium onion, diced
8 cups bone broth

Pepper
Salt

- Add all ingredients into the instant pot and stir well.
- Seal pot with lid and cook on soup setting for 10 minutes.
- Allow releasing pressure naturally then open the lid.
- Using blender puree the soup until smooth.
- Serve and enjoy.

Chilled Quinoa Salad

Serves: 4, Preparation time: 20 minutes, plus cooling and refrigerating, Cooking time: 20 minutes, Per Serving: Calories: 220; Total Fat: 12g; Saturated Fat: 2g; Protein: 6g; Carbs: 24g; Fiber: 4g; Sugar: 2g

1 red onion (diced)
2 tablespoons olive oil, divided
2 garlic cloves (minced)
1 cup white quinoa (rinsed and drained)
1 lemon (zested, juiced)
2 cups vegetable stock or water
Salt and freshly ground black pepper, to taste
4 Roma tomatoes (diced)
½ cup canned black olives (sliced)
1 avocado (pitted, sliced)

- In Instant Pot on sauté setting, cook onion in 1 tablespoon olive oil until translucent, stirring frequently, about 5 minutes. Add garlic and cook for about 1 minute, stirring frequently. Add quinoa, lemon zest and lemon juice and mix briefly.
- Stir stock into pot, scraping bottom and edges of pot to loosen any quinoa and browned bits. Season to taste with salt and pepper.
- Secure pot lid, close pressure valve and cook on high pressure for 10 minutes. When coking time ends, let pressure release naturally for 5 minutes, then carefully turn venting knob from sealing to venting position to release remaining pressure quickly.
- Let quinoa cool to room temperature, then cover and refrigerate until chilled through, about 2 hours.
- Drizzle remaining olive oil over quinoa, season to taste with salt and pepper and fluff with a fork. Stir tomatoes and black olives into quinoa and garnish with avocado slices to serve. Enjoy!

Spiced Coconut Lentils

Total Time: 8 hours 20 minutes; Serves: 12; Calories 258, Fat 8 g, Carbohydrates 33 g, Sugar 4 g, Protein 13 g, Cholesterol 0 mg

3 cups yellow lentils, Soak for 10 minutes
14 oz coconut milk
1/4 cup cilantro
1 tbsp fresh ginger, peeled and chopped
2 tbsp curry powder
2 tsp ground cumin
2 tsp ground turmeric
1 tsp chili powder
4 chilies, stemmed and seeded
1 large onion, chopped
5 garlic cloves
1/2 tsp sugar
28 oz can tomatoes, diced
Kosher salt

- Use the "Slow Cooker" setting on your Instant Pot.
- Rinse lentil and drain well. Add lentil into the Instant Pot.
- Add sugar, chili powder, turmeric, cumin, curry powder, ginger, garlic, onion, and Serrano chilies into the food processor and process until mixture becomes a paste. Add into the Instant Pot.
- Stir in tomatoes and 6 cups of water.
- Cover Instant Pot and cook on low for 8 hours.
- Season with salt and stir well.
- Add coconut milk and stir well.
- Garnish with cilantro and serve.

Collard Green with Egg

Serves: 2 / Preparation time: 5 minutes / Cooking time: 5 minutes, Per Serving: Calories: 117; Total Fat: 7.6g; Saturated Fat: 1.9g; Protein: 9g; Carbs: 3.7g; Fiber: 1.5g; Sugar: 0.9g

2 cups chopped collard	1-cup vegetable broth
2 organic eggs	½ teaspoon pepper
1-teaspoon olive oil	1-teaspoon oyster sauce
1-¾ teaspoons minced garlic	2 tablespoons water

- Crack the eggs then place in a bowl. Stir well.
- Heat up the Instant Pot for 30 seconds then select "Sauté" menu.
- Pour olive oil then stir in eggs into the Instant Pot. Stir and fold until becoming scrambled.
- Add minced garlic to the Instant pot then sauté until aromatic and lightly golden.
- Add chopped collard then season with pepper and oyster sauce.
- Pour water into the pot then stir well.
- Cover the Instant Pot with the lid and make sure that it is locked properly.
- Select "Manual" setting then cook the beef on high for 5 minutes.
- Once it is done, quickly release the Instant Pot then open the lid.
- Transfer to a serving dish then serve.
- Enjoy.

Creamy Curry Cauliflower Soup

Total Time: 6 hours 10 minutes; Serves: 2; Calories 47; Fat 0.4 g; Carbohydrates 10 g; Sugar 4 g; Protein 2.9 g; Cholesterol 0 mg

1/2 lb cauliflower florets	1 garlic clove, minced
1/8 tsp cumin	1/2 onion, minced
1 1/2 tsp curry powder	1 1/4 cup water

- Use the "Slow Cooker" setting on your Instant Pot.
- Add all ingredients to the slow cooker and stir well.
- Cover and cook on low for 6 hours.
- Using blender puree the soup until smooth.
- Serve and enjoy.

Blueberry Cobbler

Serves: 6, Preparation time: 15 minutes, Cooking time: 10 minutes, Per Serving: Calories: 339; Total Fat: 18g; Saturated Fat: 16g; Protein: 2g; Carbs: 44g; Fiber: 2g; Sugar: 27g

½ cup coconut oil, divided	1 ½ teaspoons baking powder
2 cups blueberries	¼ teaspoon salt
2/3 cup sugar	½ cup almond milk
1 lemon (zested, juiced)	1 teaspoon vanilla
1 teaspoon vanilla extract	½ teaspoon cinnamon
1 cup flour	

- Grease the inside bottom and 2" up the sides of the Instant Pot with 1 tablespoon coconut oil. Toss blueberries with 1/3 cup sugar, lemon juice and lemon zest until coated and place in Instant Pot.
- For the topping, mix flour, ¼ cup sugar, baking powder and salt. Melt remaining coconut oil, add to flour mixture with almond milk and vanilla and stir until smooth.
- Spread topping mixture over blueberries in Instant Pot. Secure pot lid, close pressure valve and cook on high pressure for 10 minutes. When cooking time ends, let pressure release naturally.
- Mix remaining sugar with cinnamon and sprinkle over cobbler. Spoon cobbler into bowls and serve. Enjoy!

Chickpea Curry

Serves: 6, Preparation time: 10 minutes, Cooking time: 10 minutes, Per Serving: Calories: 328; Total Fat: 20g; Saturated Fat: 14g; Protein: 7g; Carbs: 33g; Fiber: 11g; Sugar: 5g

2 sweet onions (diced)
2 celery stalks (diced)
2 tablespoons vegetable oil
2 garlic cloves (minced)
1 tablespoon curry powder
2 cans (15 ounces each) chickpeas (rinsed and drained)
1 can (14 ounces) coconut milk
2 gold potatoes (peeled, diced)
2 cups peas (fresh or frozen)
1 cup vegetable broth or water (plus more if needed)
Salt and freshly ground black pepper, to taste
1 lime (zested and juiced)

- In Instant Pot on sauté setting, cook onions and celery in oil until onion is translucent, stirring frequently, about 5 minutes. Add garlic and curry powder and cook for about 1 minute, stirring constantly.
- Add chickpeas, potatoes, peas, coconut milk, vegetable stock and lime zest, season to taste with salt and pepper and mix thoroughly. Stir in additional vegetable stock to cover ingredients if necessary.
- Secure pot lid, close pressure valve and cook curry on high pressure for 5 minutes. When cooking time ends, let pressure release naturally.
- Stir lime juice into curry and season to taste with salt and pepper. Serve and enjoy!

Potato Cheese Soup

Total Time: 6 hours 15 minutes; Serves: 2; Calories 438; Fat 20.4 g; Carbohydrates 41.1 g; Sugar 5.1 g; Protein 22.7 g; Cholesterol 60 mg

2 tbsp green onions, sliced
4 oz shredded cheese
1 1/2 tbsp cornstarch
2 1/2 cups potatoes, peeled and diced
3/4 cup onion, chopped
2 cups chicken broth

- Use the "Slow Cooker" setting on your Instant Pot.
- Spray slow cooker from inside with cooking spray.
- Add green onion, potatoes, onion, and chicken broth into the slow cooker.
- Cover and cook on low for 6 hours.
- Add cornstarch to the little water and stir well and pour into the slow cooker.
- Add cheese and stir until cheese is melted.
- Serve and enjoy.

Creole Red Beans

Serves: 8, Preparation time: 15 minutes, Cooking time: 41 minutes, Per Serving: Calories: 128; Total Fat: 4g; Saturated Fat: 1g; Protein: 9g; Carbs: 27g; Fiber: 3g; Sugar: 2g

1 yellow onion (diced)
1 green bell pepper (diced)
4 celery stalks (diced)
2 tablespoons vegetable oil
4 garlic cloves (minced)
1 teaspoon Creole seasoning
1 pound dry red beans
4 cups vegetable stock or water
2 dried bay leaves
1 ½ teaspoons smoked paprika
1 teaspoon dried thyme
1 teaspoon dried oregano
Salt, cayenne pepper and freshly ground black pepper, to taste
Cooked white rice, if desired, for serving

- In Instant Pot on sauté setting, cook onion, bell pepper and celery in oil until softened, stirring frequently, about 5 minutes. Add garlic and Creole seasoning and cook about 1 minute, stirring constantly.
- Add beans, vegetable stock, bay leaves, paprika, thyme and oregano to pot, season to taste with salt, pepper and cayenne pepper and mix well.

- Secure pot lid, close pressure valve and cook on high pressure for 35 minutes. When cooking time ends, let pressure release naturally. Remove bay leaves and mix beans well, mashing some of them to thicken the cooking juices to a creamy texture.
- Spoon beans into bowls to serve, topping with scoops of white rice if desired. Enjoy!

Sweet Potato Chili

Total Time: 4 hours 10 minutes; Serves: 2; Calories 179; Fat 1.1 g; Carbohydrates 37.3 g; Sugar 13.9 g; Protein 8.3 g; Cholesterol 0 mg

1 sweet potatoes, peeled and cut into chunks	7 oz can tomatoes
1/4 cup orange juice	1/2 bell pepper, seeded and chopped
1/2 cup water	7.5 oz can red kidney beans, rinsed and drained
1/2 tsp chipotle chili powder	1 garlic clove, minced
1/2 tsp smoked paprika	1/2 onion, diced
1/2 tbsp chili powder	1/4 tsp kosher salt

- Use the "Slow Cooker" setting on your Instant Pot.
- Add all ingredients to the slow cooker and stir well.
- Cover and cook on low for 4 hours.
- Stir well and serve.

Split Pea Soup

Total Time: 8 hours 10 minutes; Serves: 2; Calories 392; Fat 1.7 g; Carbohydrates 71.7 g; Sugar 9.9 g; Protein 25.8 g; Cholesterol 0 mg

1 cup dry split peas	1 cup potato, diced
1/4 tsp ground rosemary	1 bouillon cube
1 tsp thyme	3 cups water
1 tsp turmeric	Black pepper
2 bay leaves	Salt
1/2 cup carrot, diced	

- Use the "Slow Cooker" setting on your Instant Pot.
- Add all ingredients to the slow cooker and stir well.
- Cover and cook on low for 8 hours.
- Serve and enjoy.

Fruity Butternut Squash

Serves: 6, Preparation time: 15 minutes, Cooking time: 10 minutes, Per Serving: Calories: 178; Total Fat: 4g; Saturated Fat: 2g; Protein: 2g; Carbs: 38g; Fiber: 6g; Sugar: 2g

1 tablespoon coconut oil	1 cup vanilla almond milk
4 cups shredded butternut squash	½ teaspoon ground cinnamon
1 lemon (zested, juiced)	¼ teaspoon ground nutmeg
1 cup golden raisins	½ cup chopped pecans (toasted)
1 apple (peeled, chopped)	

- Grease inside of Instant Pot with coconut oil. Place shredded squash, lemon juice, lemon zest, raisins, apple, almond milk, cinnamon and nutmeg in Instant Pot and mix well.
- Secure pot lid, close pressure valve and cook at high pressure for 10 minutes. When cooking time ends, let pressure release naturally. Thoroughly stir squash mixture and spoon into bowls. Garnish squash with pecans to serve. Enjoy!

Tasty Sweet Potato Soup

Total Time: 8 hours 10 minutes; Serves: 2; Calories 314; Fat 0.8 g; Carbohydrates 73.8 g; Sugar 5.1 g; Protein 4.7 g; Cholesterol 0 mg

- 1 lb sweet potatoes, peel and diced
- 1/2 cinnamon stick
- 1/2 tbsp curry powder
- 1/2 tbsp fresh ginger, grated
- 1 medium carrot, diced
- 1 onion, diced
- 3 cups water
- Pepper
- Salt

- Use the "Slow Cooker" setting on your Instant Pot.
- Add all ingredients to the slow cooker and stir well.
- Cover and cook on low for 8 hours.
- Discard cinnamon stick form slow cooker.
- Using blender puree the soup until smooth.
- Serve and enjoy.

Taco Beans & Rice Bowls

Serves: 8, Preparation time: 10 minutes, Cooking time: 35 minutes, Per Serving: Calories: 184; Total Fat: 3g; Saturated Fat: 1g; Protein: 9g; Carbs: 37g; Fiber: 17g; Sugar: 2g

- 1 white onion (diced)
- 1 red bell pepper (diced)
- 1 tablespoon vegetable oil
- 2 garlic cloves (minced)
- 1 tablespoon chili powder
- 1 tablespoon dried cumin
- 9 cups water
- 2 cups dry black beans
- 2 cups brown rice
- 1 teaspoon salt
- ½ teaspoon cayenne pepper
- Additional salt and freshly ground black pepper, to taste
- Optional toppings: shredded lettuce, diced tomatoes, sliced avocados

- In Instant Pot on sauté setting, cook onion and bell pepper in oil until softened, stirring frequently, about 5 minutes. Add garlic and cook for about 1 more minute, stirring constantly. Add chili powder and cumin and mix briefly.
- Pour water into pot and add beans, rice, and salt. Season mixture to taste with pepper and mix thoroughly.
- Secure pot lid, close pressure valve and cook on high pressure for 28 minutes. When cooking time ends, let pressure release naturally. Season beans and rice to taste with salt and pepper, mix well and scoop into large bowls to serve. Add toppings as desired and enjoy!

Tempered Lentils

Total Time: 6 hours 20 minutes; Serves: 6; Calories 208, Fat 5.2 g, Carbohydrates 28 g, Sugar 1.5 g, Protein 12.7 g, Cholesterol 0 mg

- 1 1/2 cups yellow split lentils, rinsed and drained
- 1/4 cup fresh cilantro, chopped
- 1 tsp turmeric powder
- 2 tsp garlic, minced
- 2 medium tomatoes, chopped
- 1/2 medium onion, chopped
- 1 tsp salt

For tempering:
- 2 tbsp vegetable oil
- 1/4 tsp chili powder
- 1/2 tsp coriander powder
- 1/2 tsp cumin powder
- 1 garlic cloves, minced
- 1/2 tsp whole cumin seeds

- Use the "Slow Cooker" setting on your Instant Pot.
- Add lentils into the Instant Pot with 4 cups water.

- Add turmeric powder, garlic, tomatoes, onion, and salt into the Instant Pot and stir well.
- Cover and cook on low for 5 hours.
- Heat vegetable oil in the pan over medium-high heat.
- Once the oil is hot then turn off the heat and add cumin, garlic, and spices. Mix well.
- Stir prepared tempering into the hot lentil.
- Add cilantro and stir well.
- Cook lentils for another 1 hour to blend all flavors.
- Serve hot with rice and enjoy.

Spicy Keema Lentils

Total Time: 4 hours 15 minutes; Serves: 4; Calories 206, Fat 0.9 g, Carbohydrates 37 g, Sugar 2 g Protein 15 g, Cholesterol 0 mg

- 3 cups green lentils, cooked
- 1 tsp dried chili flakes
- 1/2 tsp ground turmeric
- 2 tsp garam masala
- 2 tsp ground coriander
- 2 tsp ground cumin
- 1 large onion, chopped
- 3 tbsp fresh ginger, grated
- 6 garlic cloves, chopped
- 1 1/2 cup vegetable broth
- 2 tbsp tamari
- 1 tsp pepper
- 1 tsp salt

- Use the "Slow Cooker" setting on your Instant Pot.
- Add all ingredients into the Instant Pot and stir well.
- Cover and cook on low for 4 hours.
- Stir well and serve.

Tomato Basil Soup

Total Time: 4 hours 10 minutes; Serves: 2; Calories 219; Fat 12 g; Carbohydrates 20.9 g; Sugar 10.8 g; Protein 7.9 g; Cholesterol 0 mg

- 13.5 oz can whole tomatoes, peeled
- 5 basil leaves
- 2 cups chicken broth
- 1/2 tsp red pepper flakes, crushed
- 2 garlic cloves, peeled
- 1 medium onion, diced
- 1 1/2 large carrots, peeled and diced
- 1 1/2 tbsp olive oil
- 1/2 tbsp salt

- Use the "Slow Cooker" setting on your Instant Pot.
- Add all ingredients to the slow cooker and stir well.
- Cover and cook on low for 4-6 hours.
- Using blender puree the soup until smooth.
- Stir well and serve.

Chapter 2: Beef

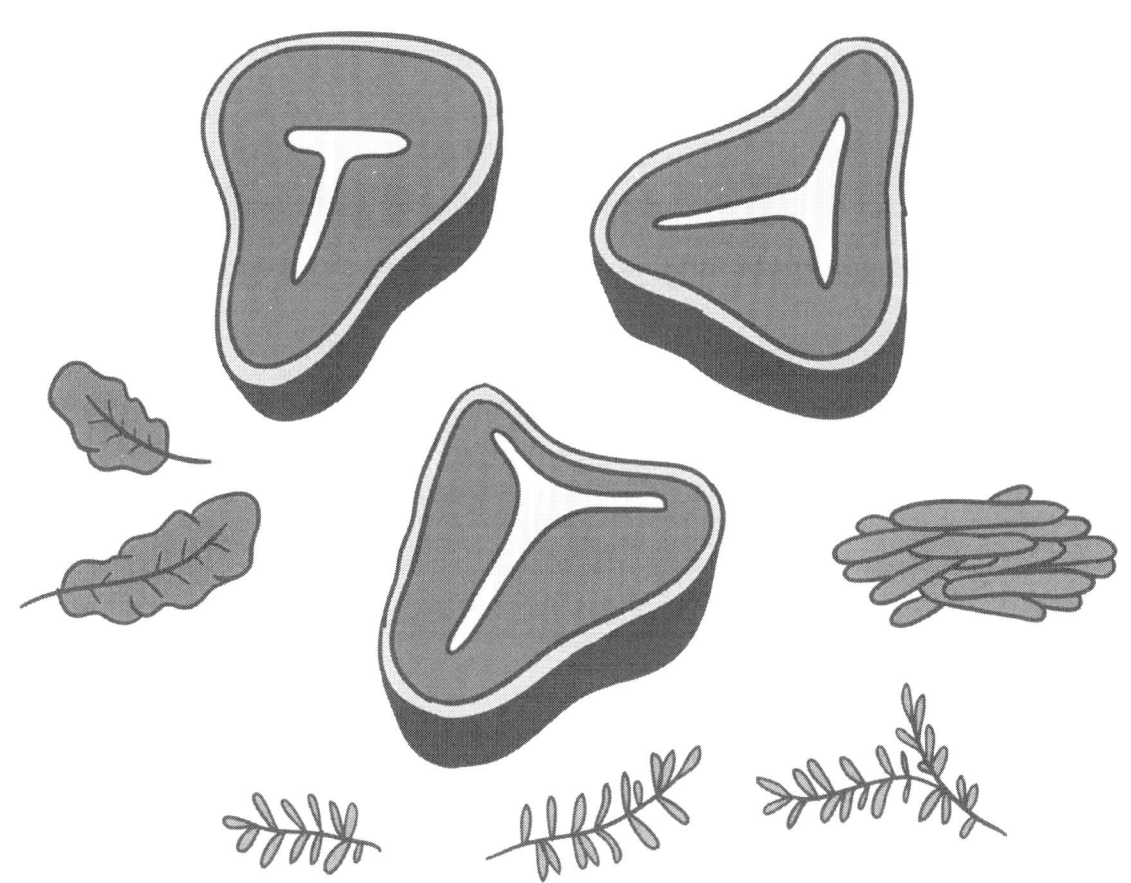

Easy and Hearty Beef Stew

Total Time: 6 hours 10 minutes; Serves: 2; Calories 622; Fat 15.5 g; Carbohydrates 39 g; Sugar 5.7 g; Protein 76.8 g; Cholesterol 203 mg

1 lb beef stew meat, cut into 1-inch pieces
1 bay leaf
1/2 tsp Worcestershire sauce
1 1/2 cups beef broth
2 carrots, diced
1 1/2 cup potatoes, peeled and diced
1/2 tsp garlic powder
1 tsp onion powder
4 tbsp all purpose flour
1/2 tsp ground black pepper
1/2 tsp kosher salt

- Use the "Slow Cooker" setting on your Instant Pot.
- Add all-purpose flour, garlic powder, onion powder, black pepper, and salt into the large zip-lock bag and mix well.
- Add meat pieces to the flour mixture and coat well.
- Place coated meat pieces in the slow cooker.
- Add carrots and potatoes over the meat.
- Mix together Worcestershire sauce and beef broth and pour into the slow cooker. Top with bay leaf.
- Cover and cook on low for 6 hours.
- Discard bay leaf and serve.

Beef and Broccoli

Total Time: 2 hours 20 minutes; Serves: 2; Calories 775; Fat 51.4 g; Carbohydrates 26.4 g; Sugar 14 g; Protein 50.1 g; Cholesterol 175 mg

0.75 lb beef chuck roast, sliced into strips
1 1/2 cup broccoli florets
1 1/4 tbsp cornstarch
2 garlic cloves, minced
2 1/2 tbsp brown sugar
1/2 tbsp sesame oil
1/4 cup soy sauce
1/2 cup beef broth
1/2 onion, sliced
Pepper
Salt

- Use the "Slow Cooker" setting on your Instant Pot.
- Add beef and onion into the slow cooker.
- In a bowl, mix together broth, garlic, brown sugar, sesame oil, and soy sauce. Season with pepper and salt.
- Pour mixture over beef.
- Cover and cook on low for 2 hours or until meat has cooked.
- Ladle out little broth from slow cooker and pour into the bowl.
- Add cornstarch and whisk until smooth. Return broth and cornstarch mixture into the slow cooker and stir gently.
- Add broccoli florets to the slow cooker.
- Cover and cook for 10 minutes or until broccoli is tender.
- Serve and enjoy.

Stuffed Bell Peppers

Total Time: 8 hours 10 minutes; Serves: 2; Calories 623; Fat 21.9 g; Carbohydrates 54.5 g; Sugar 11.7 g; Protein 51.1 g; Cholesterol 146 mg

2 large bell peppers, cut the top and discard seeds
3/4 cup shredded cheese
1/2 lb ground beef
7 oz tomato sauce
1/8 tsp garlic, minced
1/2 cup cooked rice
1/2 onion, diced
1/2 tsp salt

- Use the "Slow Cooker" setting on your Instant Pot.
- In a bowl, combine together ground beef, 1/2 tomato sauce, garlic, rice, 1/2 cup cheese, onion, and salt.

- Stuff beef mixture into the bell peppers.
- Pour 1/4 cup water into the slow cooker.
- Place stuff bell peppers into the slow cooker.
- Pour remaining tomato sauce over the stuff peppers.
- Cover and cook on low for 8 hours.
- Uncover the slow cooker and top bell pepper with remaining cheese.
- Again cover and cook for 5 minutes or until cheese is melted.
- Serve and enjoy.

Slow Cooked Garlic Cinnamon Beef

Total Time: 6 hours 15 minutes; Serves: 4; Calories 651, Fat 29.9 g, Carbohydrates 19.7 g, Sugar 5 g, Protein 71.8 g, Cholesterol 203 mg

- 2 lbs beef chuck steak, diced
- 1/2 cup coriander, chopped
- 2 cardamom pods
- 1 cinnamon stick
- 14 oz can tomatoes, diced
- 1/4 cup curry paste
- 1 red chili, chopped
- 1 tsp ginger, grated
- 2 garlic cloves, crushed
- 1 large onion, sliced
- 2 tbsp vegetable oil
- 1/4 cup plain flour

- Use the "Slow Cooker" setting on your Instant Pot.
- Add beef and flour into the ziplock bag and shake well.
- Heat oil in the saucepan over medium heat.
- Add beef into the saucepan and cook for 3-4 minutes or until lightly brown. Transfer beef into the Instant Pot.
- In the same pan, add onion, ginger, and garlic and sauté for 4 minutes.
- Add curry paste and chili and stir for 1 minute.
- Add 3/4 cup water, tomatoes, cardamom, and cinnamon and stir well. Transfer mixture into the Instant Pot.
- Cover and cook on low for 5 1/2 hours or until beef is tender.
- Add coriander and stir well.
- Serve and enjoy.

Beef in Gravy

Total Time: 8 hours 10 minutes; Serves: 2; Calories 508; Fat 18.3 g; Carbohydrates 10.9 g; Sugar 2.2 g; Protein 70.2 g; Cholesterol 203 mg

- 1 lb beef stew meat, cut into 1-inch pieces
- 1 tbsp tapioca
- 2 tbsp beef broth
- 2 tbsp onion soup mix
- 10 oz cream of mushroom soup

- Use the "Slow Cooker" setting on your Instant Pot.
- Add tapioca, broth, soup mix, and mushroom soup into the slow cooker and stir well.
- Add meat pieces to the slow cooker. Mix well.
- Cover and cook on low for 8 hours.
- Serve and enjoy.

Beef Stroganoff

Total Time: 8 hours 10 minutes; Serves: 2; Calories 477; Fat 28.2 g; Carbohydrates 15.3 g; Sugar 3.5 g; Protein 40 g; Cholesterol 127 mg

- 1/2 lb beef stew meat
- 1/2 cup sour cream
- 1/8 tsp pepper
- 2 1/2 oz mushrooms, sliced and drained
- 10 3/4 oz mushroom soup
- 1/4 cup onion, chopped

- Use the "Slow Cooker" setting on your Instant Pot.
- Add all ingredients except sour cream into the slow cooker and mix well.
- Cover and cook on low for 8 hours.
- Add sour cream and stir well.
- Serve and enjoy.

Simple Beef Fajitas

Total Time: 8 hours 10 minutes; Serves: 2; Calories 191; Fat 5.6 g; Carbohydrates 11 g; Sugar 5.1 g; Protein 26.3 g; Cholesterol 70 mg

1/2 lb beef chuck stew meat	1 bell pepper, sliced
2 tbsp soy sauce	1 tbsp lime juice
1/2 tsp ground cumin	1/4 tsp pepper
1 tsp chili powder	1/4 tsp salt
1/2 large onion, sliced	

- Use the "Slow Cooker" setting on your Instant Pot.
- Add meat, onion and bell pepper into the slow cooker and mix well.
- In a small bowl, whisk together lime juice, soy sauce, cumin, chili powder, pepper, and salt.
- Pour bowl mixture over the meat mixture.
- Cover and cook on low for 8 hours.
- Using fork shred the meat and stirs well in slow cooker juices.
- Serve over tortillas with your choice of toppings.

Classic Shepherd's Pie

Total Time: 4 hours 45 minutes; Serves: 2; Calories 617; Fat 29.4 g; Carbohydrates 38.4 g; Sugar 10 g; Protein 49.6 g; Cholesterol 165 mg

1/2 lb ground beef	1 garlic cloves, minced
1/2 cup frozen peas	Pepper
1/2 cup carrots, chopped	Salt
1 tbsp all purpose flour	For mashed potatoes:
1 tsp onion powder	1/2 lb potatoes, peeled and diced
1 tsp garlic powder	1/2 cup cheddar cheese, shredded
1/2 tsp dried oregano	2 tbsp butter, melted
1 tsp Worcestershire sauce	1/3 cup milk
2 tbsp tomato paste	1/4 tsp ground black pepper
1/4 cup beef broth	1/2 tsp salt
1/4 cup mushrooms, diced	

- Use the "Slow Cooker" setting on your Instant Pot.
- Add beef, mushrooms, and garlic into the slow cooker and stir well.
- In a bowl, whisk together broth, onion powder, garlic powder, oregano, and Worcestershire sauce.
- Pour bowl mixture into the slow cooker and stir well.
- Cover and cook on low for 4 hours or until beef is cooked.
- For mashed potatoes, add potatoes in a saucepan and cover them with water. Bring to boil. Stir in salt and boil for 15 minutes.
- Drain potatoes well and return to the saucepan.
- Add butter, milk, pepper, and salt. Using masher gently mash the potatoes.
- In a small bowl, mix together 2 tbsp water and flour then slowly stir into the slow cooker.
- Add carrots and peas to the slow cooker and stir well.
- Season with pepper and salt.

- Add cheese to the mashed potatoes and mix well. Spread mashed potatoes in an even layer over the top of beef mixture.
- Cover slow cooker and cook on high for 30 minutes.
- Serve and enjoy.

Mongolian Beef

Total Time: 4 hours 10 minutes; Serves: 2; Calories 544; Fat 14.2 g; Carbohydrates 28.8 g; Sugar 18.3 g; Protein 71.1 g; Cholesterol 203 mg

- 1 lb sirloin steak, sliced
- 1 green onion, sliced
- For sauce:
- 2 tbsp cornstarch
- 1/4 tsp red pepper flakes
- 1/4 cup brown sugar
- 1 tsp garlic, minced
- 1/4 tsp ground ginger
- 1/4 cup water
- 1/4 cup soy sauce

- Use the "Slow Cooker" setting on your Instant Pot.
- In a small bowl, combine together all sauce ingredients and pour into the slow cooker.
- Add sliced steak and green onion into the slow cooker.
- Cover and cook on low for 4 hours.
- Serve over rice and enjoy.

Boneless BBQ Beef Ribs

Serves: 4, Preparation time: 10 minutes, Cooking time: 30 minutes, Per Serving: Calories: 374; Total Fat: 31g; Saturated Fat: 11g; Protein: 16g; Carbs: 5g; Fiber: 1g; Sugar: 1g

- 2 teaspoons onion powder
- 1 teaspoon garlic powder
- 1 teaspoon cumin
- 1 teaspoon chili powder
- ¼ teaspoon chipotle chili powder
- 1 pound boneless beef ribs
- 2 tablespoons peanut oil
- 4 slices bacon, diced
- 1 large onion, diced
- 1 ½ cups beef stock
- 2 tablespoons red wine vinegar
- 2 tablespoons tomato paste
- 1 tablespoon arrowroot flour
- 1 tablespoon water

- Mix onion powder, garlic powder, cumin, chili powder and chipotle chili powder and rub over ribs. Season ribs with salt and pepper.
- Heat oil in Instant Pot on sauté setting and cook ribs until lightly browned on all sides, about 8 minutes. Remove ribs from pot and set aside.
- Cook bacon in pot until lightly browned. Add onion and cook for 3 more minutes.
- Add stock to pot and mix thoroughly, scraping bottom of pot to loosen browned bits. Stir vinegar and tomato paste into pot and return ribs to pot, stirring lightly to coat ribs.
- Secure pot lid, close pressure valve and cook at high pressure for 20 minutes. When cooking time ends, let pressure release naturally.
- Remove ribs from pot and cover to keep warm. Strain fat from juices in pot and set pot to sauté. Whisk arrowroot flour into water, add to pot and stir until sauce is thickened.
- Turn Instant Pot off, return ribs to pot and stir lightly to coat with sauce. Let ribs stand in sauce for about 10 minutes before serving. Enjoy!

Simple Beef Curry

Total Time: 8 hours 40 minutes; Serves: 4; Calories 375, Fat 20.2 g, Carbohydrates 16.7 g, Sugar 9.3 g, Protein 30.8 g, Cholesterol 79 mg

- 12 oz beef steak, cut into 1-inch pieces
- 2 onions, chopped
- 14 oz can tomatoes, chopped
- 2 tsp garam masala
- 4 garlic cloves, chopped
- 4 tsp ground cumin

4 tsp ground coriander	1 tsp ginger, grated
2 tsp ground turmeric	7 oz yogurt
2 chilies, chopped	4 tbsp vegetable oil

- Use the "Slow Cooker" setting on your Instant Pot.
- Heat oil in the pan over medium heat.
- Add beef to the pan and cook for 4-5 minutes or until lightly brown. Transfer beef into the Instant Pot.
- In the same pan, sauté onion, ginger, chili, and garlic for 2 minutes.
- Add spices and stir-fry for 1 minute. Transfer pan mixture to the Instant Pot.
- Add remaining ingredients except for yogurt into the Instant Pot and stir well.
- Cover and cook on low for 8 hours.
- Add yogurt and stir well and cook for another 30 minutes.
- Serve and enjoy.

Mushroom Eggplant Potato Curry

Total Time: 4 hours 15 minutes; Serves: 6;Calories 173, Fat 5.3 g, Carbohydrates 29.4 g, Sugar 6.7 g, Protein 4.6 g, Cholesterol 0 mg

8 mushrooms, quartered	1/2 cup red pepper, chopped
1 large eggplant, peeled and cut into 1-inch pieces	1 tsp black pepper
	1 tbsp ground cumin
3 potatoes, peeled and cut into 1/2 inch cubes	2 garlic cloves, minced
	1 large onion, chopped
1 bay leaf	2 tbsp vegetable oil
2 tsp fresh ginger, grated	1 tsp lime juice
14 oz can tomatoes, chopped	Salt

- Use the "Slow Cooker" setting on your Instant Pot.
- Heat oil in the pan over medium heat.
- Add eggplant to the pan and sauté until lightly brown.
- Transfer eggplant to the Instant Pot.
- In the same pan, add onion and sauté for 3 minutes. Add garlic, pepper, and cumin and sauté for a minute.
- Transfer onion mixture to the Instant Pot along with remaining all ingredients and stir well.
- Cover and cook on high for 4 hours.
- Stir well and serve.

Refreshing Beef Mango

Serves: 2 / Preparation time: 5 minutes / Cooking time: 10 minutes, Per Serving: Calories: 173; Total Fat: 6.9g; Saturated Fat: 6.9g; Protein: 14.3g; Carbs: 13.6g; Fiber: 1g; Sugar: 12.2g

¾ lbs. beef tenderloin	1 tablespoon lemon juice
1-teaspoon olive oil	½ teaspoon ginger
½ cup chopped ripe mango	2 teaspoons raw honey
2 tablespoons chopped onion	½ cup low sodium beef broth

- Heat up the Instant Pot then select "Sauté" menu.
- Stir in olive oil and chopped onion then sauté until aromatic. Press the "Cancel" button.
- Cut the beef into thin slices then add to the Instant Pot.
- Season with ginger and lemon juice then pour raw honey and beef broth over the beef.
- Cover the Instant Pot with the lid then make sure that it is locked properly.
- Select "Manual" setting then cook the beef on high for 10 minutes.
- Quickly release the Instant Pot then open the lid.
- Press the "Sauté" menu on the Instant Pot then add sliced mango to the pot. Stir well.
- Once it is done, turn the Instant Pot off then transfer the beef mango to a serving dish.
- Serve and enjoy.

Paprika Taco Meat

45 minutes, Serves: 6, Calories 392; Fat 19.2 g; Carbohydrates 6.9 g; Sugar 3.2 g; Protein 46.9 g; Cholesterol 135 mg

2 lbs ground beef	1/2 tbsp chili powder
1/2 Tsp cumin	1/4 Tsp chipotle powder
1/2 Tsp smoked paprika	1 Tsp cayenne
1/2 Tsp turmeric	4 tbsp extra virgin olive oil
2 Tsp oregano	2 garlic cloves, minced
2 large bell peppers, diced	1/4 Tsp black pepper
1 large onion, diced	1 Tsp salt

- Add all ingredients except meat into the instant pot.
- Select sauté and sauté for 5 minutes.
- Add ground beef and stir until lightly brown.
- Seal pot with lid and cook on manual high pressure for 30 minutes.
- Allow releasing pressure naturally then open the lid.
- Select sauté function and stir for 10 minutes.
- Garnish cilantro and serve.

Simple Beef Bourguignon

Total Time: 6 hours 15 minutes; Serves: 2; Calories 604; Fat 24.5 g; Carbohydrates 8 g; Sugar 3 g; Protein 74.5 g; Cholesterol 210 mg

1 lb beef, cut into cubed	1/2 oz pancetta, sliced
1/2 cup beef stock	1 tsp thyme
4 oz mushrooms, sliced	1 tbsp olive oil
1 garlic cloves, crushed	1/2 cup red wine
1 small onions, diced	1/2 tsp black pepper

- Use the "Slow Cooker" setting on your Instant Pot.
- Add beef, black pepper, thyme, and red wine into the large ziplock bag and shake well.
- Place in refrigerator and marinate for 2 hours.
- Heat large pan over medium-high heat.
- Add pancetta to the hot pan and cook for few minutes.
- Remove cooked pancetta from pan and set aside.
- Add onion to the same pan and sauté for 2-3 minutes then add garlic and sauté for a minute.
- Transfer onion and garlic mixture into the slow cooker.
- Drain beef well and browned the marinated meat from all the sides.
- Add remaining ingredients and marinade reserved into the slow cooker.
- Cover and cook on low for 6 hours.
- Serve over noodles and enjoy.

Beef Short Ribs

35 minutes, Serves: 6, Calories 705; Fat 32.3 g; Carbohydrates 8.6 g; Sugar 3.8 g; Protein 89.4 g Cholesterol 275 mg

4 lbs beef short ribs	2 cups onion, diced
2 tbsp extra virgin olive oil	1 tbsp thyme, dried
1 1/2 cups chicken broth	Pepper
4 carrots, cut into pieces	Salt
3 garlic cloves, minced	

- Season ribs with pepper and salt.
- Add oil in instant pot and select sauté.

- Add season ribs in the pot and cook until brown about 5 minutes per side.
- Remove ribs from pot and place on a plate.
- Add garlic in a pot and sauté for 1 minute.
- Add thyme, carrots, onion, pepper, and salt and sauté for 4 minutes.
- Add broth and ribs into the pot.
- Seal pot with lid and cook on manual high pressure for 35 minutes.
- Allow releasing pressure naturally then open the lid.
- Serve hot and enjoy.

Buttery Beef Ribs with Potatoes

Serves: 2 / Preparation time: 10 minutes / Cooking time: 35 minutes, Per Serving: Calories: 373; Total Fat: 31.6 g; Saturated Fat: 18g; Protein: 10.4g; Carbs: 12.8g; Fiber: 2g; Sugar: 2.1g

1 lb. beef ribs	¼ cup butter
2 teaspoons minced garlic	½ cup beef broth
½ cup chopped onion	¼ lb. potatoes

- Heat up the Instant Pot for 30 seconds then select "Sauté" menu.
- Add butter to the Instant pot then stir in chopped onion, minced garlic, and beef ribs. Sauté until the beef ribs are brown. Press the "Cancel" button.
- Pour beef broth into the pot then place a trivet over the beef ribs.
- Peel and cut the potatoes into medium cubes then place on the trivet.
- Cover the Instant Pot with the lid and make sure that it is locked properly.
- Select "Manual" setting then select "High" menu and set time for 35 minutes.
- Once it is done, naturally release the Instant Pot then open the lid.
- Place the beef ribs on a platter next to the potatoes.
- Serve and enjoy warm.

Veggie Steak Soup

25 minutes, Serves: 4, Calories 316; Fat 6.6 g; Carbohydrates 17.8 g; Sugar 8.4 g; Protein 46.5 g; Cholesterol 102 mg

1 lb steak, trimmed and diced	8 oz mushrooms, sliced
1 bay leaf	2 cups water
3 medium carrots, diced	2 cups beef stock
1 onion, diced	1 cup tomatoes, crushed
1/2 tbsp thyme	1 large bell pepper, diced
1 1/2 tbsp oregano	1 large celery stalk, diced
2 tbsp garlic powder	1 tbsp salt

- Start instant pot and select sauté mode.
- Add steak meat into the pot and sauté until brown.
- Add onion, celery, carrots, and pepper and cook until softened.
- Add mushrooms and cook until softened.
- Add spices, stock, water, and salt and stir well.
- Seal pot with lid and cook on soup setting for 15 minutes.
- Release pressure using quick release method than open lid carefully.
- Stir well and serve.

Beef Coconut Fritter

Serves: 2 / Preparation time: 5 minutes / Cooking time: 15 minutes, Per Serving: Calories: 229; Total Fat: 17.6g; Saturated Fat: 9.3g; Protein: 13.6g; Carbs: 4.9g; Fiber: 2.7g; Sugar: 1.8g

¾ lbs. ground beef	1 egg
½ cup grated coconut	2 teaspoons chopped red chili
1-tablespoon coconut flour	¼ teaspoon salt

½ teaspoon pepper   1-teaspoon olive oil

- Place ground beef, coconut flour, red chili, salt, and pepper in food processor. Pulse until smooth.
- Shape the mixture into fritter forms then set aside.
- Crack the egg then place in a bowl. Whisk until incorporated.
- Dip the fritter in the egg then roll in the grated coconut.
- Place the fritter in the trivet then spray with olive oil.
- Pour water into the Instant Pot then place the trivet in it.
- Cover the Instant Pot with the lid then make sure that it is locked properly.
- Turn on the Instant Pot then choose "Manual" setting.
- Cook the beef balls on high and set the time for 15 minutes.
- Once it is done, naturally release the Instant Pot then open the lid.
- Remove the fritters from the Instant Pot then arrange on a serving dish.
- Serve and enjoy.

Spicy Beef Chuck Roast

1 hour 30 minutes, Serves: 4, Calories 557; Fat 23.1 g; Carbohydrates 6.8 g; Sugar 4.3 g; Protein 76.8 g; Cholesterol 229 mg

2 lbs chuck roast, cut in half   1 tbsp olive oil
1 tbsp lime juice   1 Tsp garlic powder
1/4 cup fresh cilantro   2 Tsp cumin
1/2 cup beef broth   2 Tsp chili powder
2 tbsp chipotle sauce   1/2 Tsp pepper
8 oz tomato sauce   1 Tsp salt

- Season meat with garlic powder, pepper, cumin, chili powder, and salt.
- Add oil in instant pot and select sauté.
- Add seasoned roast in pot and sauté for 5 minutes on each side.
- Add remaining ingredients and stir well.
- Seal pot with lid and cook on manual high pressure for 70 minutes.
- Allow releasing pressure naturally then open the lid.
- Using fork shred the beef and serves.

Perfect Beef Stew

Total Time: 8 hours 10 minutes; Serves: 2; Calories 550; Fat 24.7 g; Carbohydrates 38.9 g; Sugar 7.2 g; Protein 41.9 g; Cholesterol 101 mg

1/2 lb beef stew meat   2 garlic cloves, minced
1 bay leaf   1 small onion, chopped
1/4 tsp cumin   1 tsp canola oil
1 tsp old bay seasoning   2 tbsp olive oil
1 1/4 cups beef broth   1/4 tsp garlic powder
2 tbsp Worcestershire sauce   1/4 cup flour
1 celery stalk, chopped   1/2 tsp pepper
1 potato, diced   1/2 tsp salt
1/2 cup carrots

- Use the "Slow Cooker" setting on your Instant Pot.
- In a large zip lock bag combine the garlic powder, flour, pepper, and salt. Add meat to the bag and shake bag to coat meat well.
- In a large pan, heat 1 tbsp olive oil and canola oil over medium heat.
- Add coated meat to the pan and brown them from all the sides then transfer meat into the slow cooker.
- Heat remaining oil in the same pan over medium heat.

- Add onion to the pan and sauté for 5 minutes.
- Add garlic and sauté for 1 minute.
- Add onion and garlic mixture over the beef.
- Top with celery, potatoes, and carrots.
- Add remaining ingredients to the slow cooker.
- Cover and cook on low for 8 hours.
- Stir well and serve.

Beef Balls Light Soup

Serves: 2 / Preparation time: 5 minutes / Cooking time: 20 minutes, Per Serving: Calories: 376; Total Fat: 13g; Saturated Fat: 4.8g; Protein: 57.3g; Carbs: 4.7g; Fiber: 0.6g; Sugar: 0.9g

¾ lbs. ground beef
¼ cup chopped onion
1 organic egg
1-tablespoon sesame flour
¼ lb. beef bones

2 teaspoons minced garlic
½ teaspoon pepper
½ teaspoon salt
3 cups water

- Combine ground beef with egg, chopped onion, and sesame flour then mix well.
- Shape the mixture into balls forms then arrange in a casserole dish. Set aside.
- Pour water into the Instant Pot then season with minced garlic, pepper, and salt.
- Add beef bone in the Instant Pot then place a trivet over the bones.
- Place the casserole dish with beef balls in the trivet.
- Cover the Instant Pot with the lid then make sure that it is locked properly.
- Turn on the Instant Pot then choose "Manual" setting.
- Cook the beef balls on high and set the time to 20 minutes.
- Once it is done, naturally release the Instant Pot then open the lid.
- Take the casserole dish out from the Instant Pot then transfer the beef balls to a serving bowl.
- Pour the gravy over the beef balls then serve hot.
- Enjoy.

Instant Pot Roast

Serves: 6 / Preparation time: 10 minutes / Cooking time: 60 minutes, Per Serving: Calories: 734; Total Fat: 30.1g; Saturated Fat: 9.9g; Protein: 102.3g; Carbs: 7.8g; Fiber: 1.9g; Sugar: 3.9g;

4 lbs chuck roast
1 tbsp vinegar
2 cups homemade beef stock
1 onion, chopped
2 bay leaves
2 thyme sprigs
2 celery stalks, chopped
2 carrots, peeled and chopped

3 garlic cloves, mashed
1/3 cup tomato paste
2 tbsp olive oil
1/2 cup hot water
1/4 cup dried porcini
Black pepper
Salt

- Add hot water and dried porcini into the bowl and set aside.
- Heat olive oil in the pan over high heat.
- Season chuck roasts with pepper and salt and sear until golden brown, about 10 minutes.
- Transfer seared roast into the instant pot.
- Add tomato paste, bay leaves, thyme, celery, carrots, garlic, and onion and sauté for 5 minutes.
- Deglaze pan with vinegar and stock and pour into the instant pot with porcini.
- Seal pot with lid and cook on high pressure for 45 minutes.
- Remove roast from pot and cut into slices and season with pepper and salt.
- Top with vegetables and serve.

Hot Beef Ribs

Serves: 2 / Preparation time: 5 minutes / Cooking time: 30 minutes, Per Serving: Calories: 356; Total Fat: 15.8g; Saturated Fat: 5.4g; Protein: 43.2g; Carbs: 8.7g; Fiber: 1.5g; Sugar: 2g

- 1-½ lbs. beef ribs
- 1-teaspoon olive oil
- 3 cloves garlic
- 4 shallots
- ¼ cup red chili
- 1-teaspoon ginger
- 1 kaffir lime leaf

- Brush the beef ribs with olive oil then set aside.
- Place garlic, shallots, red chili, and ginger in a food processor then pulse until smooth.
- Rub the beef ribs with the spice then place in a casserole dish.
- Pour water into the Instant Pot then place a trivet in it.
- Place the casserole dish in the trivet then add kaffir lime leaf.
- Cover the Instant Pot with the lid and lock it properly.
- Select "Manual" setting then cook the beef on high and set the time for 30 minutes.
- Once it is done, naturally release the Instant Pot then open the lid.
- Take the casserole dish out from the Instant Pot then sprinkle chopped tomato on top,
- Serve right away.

Spicy Beef Roast

Total Time: 5 hours 15 minutes; Serves: 6; Calories 421, Fat 16.8 g, Carbohydrates 6.2 g, Sugar 1.9 g, Protein 58.4 g, Cholesterol 169 mg

- 2 1/2 lbs beef roast
- 25 curry leaves
- 1 tbsp ginger, grated
- 1 Serrano pepper, minced
- 2 tbsp lemon juice
- 2 tbsp garlic, minced
- 1 tbsp garam masala
- 1 tsp coriander powder
- 2 tsp chili powder
- 1 tsp turmeric
- 1/2 tsp black pepper
- 2 onions, chopped
- 2 tbsp coconut oil
- 1 tsp mustard seeds
- 1 tsp salt

- Use the "Slow Cooker" setting on your Instant Pot.
- Add all ingredients into the Instant Pot and mix well.
- Cover and cook on high for 5 hours.
- Using fork shred the meat and serves.

Apple Breadcrumb Meatloaf

45 minutes, Serves: 4, Calories 412; Fat 10.2 g; Carbohydrates 38.6 g; Sugar 16 g; Protein 41.2 g; Cholesterol 148 mg

- 1 lb ground beef
- 1 tbsp Dijon mustard
- 1 large egg
- 1/2 cup ketchup
- 1 medium onion, chopped
- 1 apple, chopped
- 1 cup Italian bread crumbs
- 1/2 Tsp garlic powder
- 1/2 Tsp thyme, dried
- 2 Tsp parsley, dried
- 1/4 Tsp pepper
- 1/4 Tsp salt

- Take one loaf pan which fits into your instant pot and sprays with cooking spray.
- In a bowl, combine together all ingredients and pour into the prepared loaf pan.
- Pour 1 cup water into the instant pot then place a trivet in the pot.
- Place loaf pan on a trivet.
- Seal pot with lid and select manual and set timer for 35 minutes.
- Release pressure using quick release method than open the lid carefully.

- Cut meatloaf into slices and serve.

Herb Garlic Pot Roast

Serves: 8 / Preparation time: 10 minutes / Cooking time: 45 minutes, Per Serving: Calories: 910; Total Fat: 67.1g; Saturated Fat: 25.7g; Protein: 65g; Carbs: 7.2g; Fiber: 1.7g; Sugar: 3.5g;

4 lbs beef chuck roast, cut into cubes
1/2 tsp dried thyme
6 large carrots, peeled and diced
2 cups homemade bone broth
1 onion, diced

2 tbsp olive oil
1 tbsp Italian seasoning
1 tsp garlic powder
1 tsp pepper
1 tsp salt

- Season meat with spices and set aside.
- Add oil into the instant pot and select sauté.
- Add onion to the pot and sauté for 5 minutes or until lightly browned.
- Add onion and broth and stir well.
- Seal pot with lid and select manual setting and set the timer for 40 minutes.
- Release pressure using quick release method than open the lid.
- Stir well and serve.

Spicy and Tender Italian Beef

1 hour 20 minutes, Serves: 8, Calories 665; Fat 25.8 g; Carbohydrates 11.6 g; Sugar 0.3 g; Protein 93.7 g; Cholesterol 286 mg

5 lbs chuck roast
1 cup water
1/2 onion, sliced

16 oz pepperoncini peppers, sliced
1 packet Italian seasoning mix
1 tbsp extra virgin olive oil

- Add oil in instant pot and select sauté.
- Brown roast in a pot from both the sides, about 5 minutes from each side.
- Add Italian seasoning, 1/2 pepperoncini, onion, and water.
- Seal pot with lid and select manual and set timer for 55 minutes.
- Release pressure using quick release method than open the lid.
- Using fork shred the roast and add remaining pepperoncini and stir well.
- Serve and enjoy.

Simple Beef Bean Chili

Total Time: 6 hours 10 minutes; Serves: 2; Calories 658; Fat 9.4 g; Carbohydrates 87.2 g; Sugar 9.5 g; Protein 58.4 g; Cholesterol 101 mg

1 cup ground beef, cooked
15 oz can pinto beans, drained
1 packet taco seasoning mix

2 tbsp dry onion, minced
15 oz can tomato sauce

- Use the "Slow Cooker" setting on your Instant Pot.
- Add all ingredients to the slow cooker and mix well.
- Cover and cook on low for 6 hours.
- Stir well and serve.

Pot Roast

Serves: 6 / Preparation time: 10 minutes / Cooking time: 55 minutes, Per Serving: Calories: 695; Total Fat: 25.3g; Saturated Fat: 9.2g; Protein: 101.1g; Carbs: 9g; Fiber: 1.6g; Sugar: 2.7g;

4 lbs chuck roast, boneless
2 tbsp arrowroot powder
2 garlic cloves, crushed
3 bay leaves
1 thyme sprig
2 celery sticks, cut into pieces
2 carrots, peeled and chopped
2 onions, chopped
1 cup homemade beef stock
Black pepper
Salt

- Spray instant pot from inside with cooking spray and set on sauté mode.
- Add chuck roast into the instant pot and sauté until lightly brown.
- Add remaining ingredients except for arrowroot powder and stir well.
- Seal pot with lid and select manual and set timer for 50 minutes.
- Allow releasing pressure naturally then open the lid.
- Remove meat from instant pot and place onto the dish.
- Mix little water and arrowroot powder together in a small bowl and pour into the instant pot.
- Set the instant pot on sauté mode and cook until gravy thickened.
- Strain out veggies and pour over meat.
- Serve and enjoy.

Ground Beef with Green Beans

Serves: 2 / Preparation time: 5 minutes / Cooking time: 10 minutes, Per Serving: Calories: 213; Total Fat: 16.3g; Saturated Fat: 8.9g; Protein: 9.6g; Carbs: 8.4g; Fiber: 3.2g; Sugar: 2.4g

½ lb. ground beef
1 cup chopped green beans
3 teaspoons sliced garlic
3 tablespoons chopped red chili
¼ teaspoon salt
¼ teaspoon oregano
½ teaspoon black pepper
2 tablespoons butter
½ cup beef broth

- Heat up the Instant Pot for 30 seconds.
- Select "Sauté" menu then add butter to the Instant Pot.
- Put sliced garlic and chopped red chili into the Instant Pot then sauté until lightly golden and aromatic.
- Stir in ground beef then season with salt, oregano, and pepper.
- Add green beans to the Instant Pot then pour beef broth over the ground beef.
- Cover the Instant Pot then lock it properly.
- Select "Manual" setting then cook the beef on high for 10 minutes.
- Once it is done, naturally release the Instant Pot then open the lid.
- Transfer to a serving dish then serve.
- Enjoy.

Broccoli Beef Curry Stew

55 minutes, Serves: 6, Calories 556; Fat 28.3 g; Carbohydrates 14.2 g; Sugar 5.6 g; Protein 62.7 g; Cholesterol 169 mg

2 1/2 lbs beef stew meat, cut into cubes
14 oz coconut milk
1 tbsp garlic powder
2 tbsp curry powder
1/2 cup water
3 zucchini, chopped
1 lb broccoli florets
Salt

- Add all ingredients into the instant pot and stir well.
- Seal pot with lid and cook on manual high pressure for 45 minutes.
- Release pressure using quick release method than open the lid.
- Stir well and serve.

Hearty Spaghetti Sauce

Serves: 4, Preparation time: 10 minutes, Cooking time: 15 minutes, Per Serving: Calories: 358; Total Fat: 15g; Saturated Fat: 6g; Protein: 37g; Carbs: 17g; Fiber: 4g; Sugar: 8g

1 pound lean ground beef	1 can (28 ounces) crushed tomatoes
1 link Italian sausage, casing removed	8 ounces fresh mushrooms, sliced
1 onion, diced	1 tablespoon Italian herb mix
1 red bell pepper, diced	½ teaspoon dried red pepper flakes
4 cloves garlic, peeled and minced	½ cup freshly grated Parmesan cheese
Salt and freshly ground black pepper, to taste	

- Set Instant Pot to sauté. Crumble ground beef and sausage into pot and add onion, bell pepper and garlic. Season beef mixture to taste with salt and pepper and cook until browned, 5-6 minutes. If necessary, drain fat from pot.
- Add crushed tomatoes, mushrooms, herb mix and red pepper flakes to pot and mix well.
- Secure pot lid, close pressure valve and cook at high pressure for 8 minutes. When cooking time ends, carefully turn venting knob from sealing to venting position for a quick pressure release.
- Transfer sauce to a large bowl and sprinkle with Parmesan cheese to serve. Enjoy!

Super Tender Italian Pot Roast

Serves: 8 / Preparation time: 10 minutes / Cooking time: 30 minutes, Per Serving: Calories: 719; Total Fat: 49.5g; Saturated Fat: 19.2g; Protein: 47g; Carbs: 19.3g; Fiber: 4.9g; Sugar: 6.8g;

3 lbs beef chuck roast, boneless and trimmed	1 celery stalks, chopped
3 parsnips, peeled and cut into pieces	2 tbsp tomato paste
4 carrots, peeled and cut into pieces	1 tbsp coconut aminos
1 lb onions, chopped	2 cups homemade beef broth
1 tbsp fresh basil leaves, chopped	1/4 tsp black pepper
2 tsp fresh oregano, chopped	1 tbsp olive oil
2 tsp fresh thyme	3 garlic cloves, sliced
1 bay leaf	1/4 tsp salt

- Using sharp knife make small slits all over the roast then stuff sliced garlic all over the roast.
- Season roast with pepper and salt.
- Add oil into the instant pot and select sauté mode.
- Place roast into the pot and brown roast on all the sides.
- Add broth, basil, oregano, thyme, bay leaf, celery, tomato paste, and coconut aminos into the pot.
- Seal pot with lid and cook for 45 minutes.
- Release pressure using quick release method than open the lid.
- Add parsnips, carrots, and onion and again seal pot with lid and cook for another 10 minutes.
- Release pressure using quick release method.
- Transfer roast and vegetables to serving the dish and serve.

Tasty Beef Ragu

Total Time: 6 hours 10 minutes; Serves: 2; Calories 851; Fat 28 g; Carbohydrates 47.7 g; Sugar 30.8 g; Protein 95.1 g; Cholesterol 239 mg

1 lb chuck roast	3 oz tomato paste
1/4 cup red wine	14 oz can tomatoes, crushed
1/4 cup water	1/2 tsp basil

1/2 tsp oregano
1 beef bouillon
1/2 tbsp garlic, minced
1/2 celery stalk, diced
1 small carrot, diced
1/4 cup onion, diced
1/4 tsp black pepper
1/2 tsp salt

- Use the "Slow Cooker" setting on your Instant Pot.
- Add all ingredients to the slow cooker and mix well.
- Cover and cook on low for 6 hours.
- Using fork shred the meat.
- Serve over pasta and enjoy.

Slow cooked Fancy Beef

Total Time: 8 hours 10 minutes; Serves: 2; Calories 885; Fat 55.2 g; Carbohydrates 33.6 g; Sugar 19.2 g; Protein 49.3 g; Cholesterol 175 mg

0.75 lbs beef chuck roast, cut into pieces
1 tbsp flour
2 bay leaves
1 tbsp soy sauce
1 tbsp brown sugar
4 oz tomato sauce
1 cup broth
1/2 cup red wine
3 thyme sprigs
1 tbsp garlic, minced
2 celery stalk, minced
2 cup baby carrots
1/2 onion, chopped
1 tbsp olive oil
Pepper
Salt

- Use the "Slow Cooker" setting on your Instant Pot.
- Heat olive oil in the pan over medium heat.
- Add onions, carrots, and celery and sauté until onion soften.
- Add garlic and sauté for minutes.
- Transfer pan mixture to the slow cooker.
- Season beef with pepper and salt.
- Season flour with pepper and salt.
- Coat beef with seasoned flour then browned beef in the pan from all the sides.
- Transfer beef to the slow cooker over veggies.
- Add remaining ingredients to the slow cooker.
- Cover and cook on low for 8 hours.
- Serve and enjoy.

Beef Stew

Serves: 4, Preparation time: 15 minutes, Cooking time: 40 minutes, Per Serving: Calories: 273; Total Fat: 16g; Saturated Fat: 9g; Protein: 25g; Carbs: 180g; Fiber: 1g; Sugar: 5g

1 pound lean beef stew meat
Salt and freshly ground black pepper, to taste
2 tablespoons butter
2 cloves garlic, peeled and minced
2 cups beef stock
2 teaspoons Worcestershire sauce
2 teaspoons soy sauce
1 teaspoon paprika
4 stalks celery, trimmed and cut into 1-inch pieces
1 package (14 ounces) frozen pearl onions
8 ounces sliced mushrooms
2 bay leaves
1 tablespoon arrowroot flour
1 tablespoon water

- Season beef with salt and pepper. In Instant Pot on sauté setting, melt butter and cook stew meat until lightly browned on all sides, about 5 minutes. Add garlic to pot and cook until softened, about 2 minutes.
- Add beef stock, Worcestershire sauce, soy sauce and paprika to pot and stir to deglaze pot.

- Add celery, pearl onions, mushrooms and bay leaves to pot, season stew to taste with salt and pepper and mix thoroughly.
- Secure pot lid, close pressure valve and cook at high pressure for about 30 minutes until done. When cooking time ends, let pressure release naturally. Remove bay leaves from stew.
- Whisk arrowroot flour into water and stir into stew to thicken gravy. Serve and enjoy!

Beef Couscous Stuffed Bell Peppers

Total Time: 4 hours 15 minutes; Serves: 2; Calories 288; Fat 4.3 g; Carbohydrates 39.5 g; Sugar 11.5 g; Protein 51.1 g; Cholesterol 51 mg

1/4 lb ground beef	1 garlic clove, chopped
1/2 cup water	1/4 cup onion, chopped
1/3 cup couscous, uncooked	2 large bell pepper, cut the top and discard seeds
1/8 tsp ground cinnamon	
1/4 tsp ground cumin	1/4 tsp salt
8 oz tomato sauce	

- Use the "Slow Cooker" setting on your Instant Pot.
- Place trivet into the slow cooker then pours water into the slow cooker.
- In a bowl, combine together all ingredients except bell peppers.
- Cook bowl mixture in a pan over medium heat for about 5 minutes.
- Stuff beef mixture into the bell peppers.
- Place stuffed bell peppers on a trivet.
- Cover slow cooker and cook on low for 4 hours or until beef mixture is cooked.
- Serve and enjoy.

Tender Greek Pot Roast

Serves: 6 / Preparation time: 10 minutes / Cooking time: 35 minutes, Per Serving: Calories: 560; Total Fat: 24g; Saturated Fat: 7.6g; Protein: 76.8g; Carbs: 5.3g; Fiber: 1.3g; Sugar: 2.4g;

3 lbs chuck roast, boneless and cut into slices	1 tsp dill
	1 tbsp oregano
1 tsp vinegar	1 tbsp dried basil
1 cup homemade beef broth	1/2 tsp marjoram
1/2 cup sundried tomatoes	2 tbsp olive oil
5 garlic cloves	1/2 tsp pepper
1 small onion, sliced	2 tsp kosher salt

- In a small bowl, mix together all spices.
- Drizzle meat with 1 tbsp olive oil. Rub spice mixture all over the meat.
- Add remaining oil into the instant pot and select sauté mode.
- Add onion and tomatoes into the instant pot and sauté for 5 minutes.
- Add garlic and sauté for 30 seconds.
- Place meat into the instant pot then pours broth over the meat.
- Seal pot with lid and cook on high pressure for 30 minutes.
- Allow releasing pressure naturally then open the lid.
- Remove meat from instant pot and place onto the plate and using fork shred the meat.
- Return shredded meat to the instant pot and toss well.
- Season with pepper and salt.
- Serve and enjoy.

Tender Korean Beef

Total Time: 4 hours 10 minutes; Serves: 2;
Calories 553; Fat 6.9 g; Carbohydrates 38.1 g; Sugar 27.6 g; Protein 50.2 g; Cholesterol 94 mg

0.75 lb flank steak, cut into strips	1/4 cup soy sauce
1/8 tsp red pepper flakes	1/4 tsp garlic, minced
1/2 small onion, chopped	1 tbsp sesame oil
6 tbsp brown sugar	2 tbsp cornstarch
1/4 cup beef broth	

- Use the "Slow Cooker" setting on your Instant Pot.
- Add cornstarch and flank steak pieces into the ziplock bag and shake well to coat.
- Add remaining ingredients to the slow cooker and stir well.
- Add coated steak pieces to the slow cooker. Stir well.
- Cover and cook on low for 4 hours.
- Serve and enjoy.

Sweet Crispy Beef

Serves: 2 / Preparation time: 5 minutes / Cooking time: 30 minutes, Per Serving: Calories: 351; Total Fat: 4.8g; Saturated Fat: 1.6g; Protein: 21.3g; Carbs: 54.3g; Fiber: 3.2g; Sugar: 3g

¾ lb. beef tenderloin	1-cup flour
1-teaspoon olive oil	½ cup chopped onion
½ teaspoon salt	3 tablespoons soy sauce
½ teaspoon pepper	1/2 cup chopped tomato

- Cut the beef into slices then place in a plastic bag.
- Combine flour with salt and pepper then add to the plastic bag. Shake until the beef is completely coated with flour.
- Heat up the Instant Pot then select the "Sauté" setting.
- Place the coated beef in the Instant Pot then sauté until the beef is crispy and lightly brown.
- Take the beef out from the Instant Pot then place in a casserole dish.
- Pour water into an Instant Pot then place a trivet in it.
- Place the casserole dish with beef in the trivet then drizzle soy sauce over the beef.
- Sprinkle chopped onion on top then cover the Instant Pot with the lid. Lock it properly.
- Select "Manual" setting then cook the beef on high and set the time to 30 minutes.
- Once it is done, naturally release the Instant Pot then open the lid.
- Take the casserole dish out from the Instant Pot then sprinkle chopped tomato on top,
- Serve right away.

Low Carb Beef

Serves: 6 / Preparation time: 10 minutes / Cooking time: 50 minutes, Per Serving: Calories: 542; Total Fat: 23.8g; Saturated Fat: 7.6g; Protein: 75.8g; Carbs: 1g; Fiber: 0.2g; Sugar: 0.2g;

3 lbs chuck roast	1/2 tsp rosemary
1 cup homemade beef broth	3 garlic cloves, sliced
1/4 cup balsamic vinegar	1/2 tsp pepper
1/2 tsp thyme	1 tsp salt
2 tbsp olive oil	

- Using knife cut little slits in the roast the stuff garlic slices in all over the chuck roast.
- In a small bowl, mix together thyme, rosemary, pepper, and salt and rub all over the roast.
- Add oil into the instant pot and select sauté.
- When the oil is hot then add roast into the instant pot and brown on both the sides, about 5 minutes on each side.

- Remove roast from instant pot and set aside.
- Add broth and vinegar into the instant pot and stir well.
- Return roast to the instant pot.
- Seal pot with lid and cook for 40 minutes.
- Allow releasing pressure naturally then open the lid.
- Serve and enjoy.

Mexican Beef Stew

40 minutes, Serves: 6, Calories 462; Fat 24.8 g; Carbohydrates 8.2 g; Sugar 3.4 g; Protein 48.8 g; Cholesterol 160 mg

2 lbs stew meat, thawed	1 Tsp oregano, dried
6 oz can green chilies, diced	1 Tsp smoked paprika
15 oz can tomatoes	2 Tsp cumin
1 cup chicken broth	1 medium onion, diced
1/2 Tsp chipotle powder	2 tbsp coconut oil
1/2 Tsp white pepper	2 Tsp salt

- Add oil in instant pot and select sauté.
- Add onion and sauté for 2 minutes.
- In a bowl, mix together spice and meat.
- Add season meat into the pot and cook for 2 minutes.
- Pour in green chilies, tomatoes, and broth.
- Seal pot with lid and select manual and set timer for 30 minutes.
- Release pressure using quick release method than open the lid carefully.
- Stir well and serve.

Steamed Beef in Coconut

Serves: 2 / Preparation time: 5 minutes / Cooking time: 30 minutes, Per Serving: Calories: 377; Total Fat: 32.7 g; Saturated Fat: 26.9g; Protein: 15.6g; Carbs: 9g; Fiber: 2.9g; Sugar: 4.1g

¾ lb. beef tenderloin	1-inch galangal
2 teaspoons sliced garlic	1 bay leaf
2 teaspoons sliced shallot	1-cup coconut milk

- Pour water into an Instant Pot then place a trivet in it.
- Place all ingredients in a casserole dish then place in the trivet.
- Cover the Instant Pot with the lid and lock it properly.
- Select "Manual" setting then cook the beef on high and set the time to 30 minutes.
- Once it is done, naturally release the Instant Pot then open the lid.
- Take the casserole dish out from the Instant Pot then serve right away.

Beef Heart

Total Time: 4 hours 10 minutes; Serves: 2; Calories 196; Fat 5.4 g; Carbohydrates 2.1 g; Sugar 0.8 g; Protein 32.6 g; Cholesterol 240 mg

1/2 lb beef heart, cut into cubes	1/8 tsp garlic powder
1/2 small onion, sliced	1/8 tsp ground black pepper
1/4 tsp dried oregano	1/4 tsp salt

- Use the "Slow Cooker" setting on your Instant Pot.
- Add all ingredients to the slow cooker and stir well.
- Cover and cook on low for 4 hours.
- Serve over rice and enjoy.

Gluten Free Pot Roast

Serves: 8 / Preparation time: 10 minutes / Cooking time: 80 minutes, Per Serving: Calories: 130; Total Fat: 3.4g; Saturated Fat: 1.5g; Protein: 12.6g; Carbs: 12.3g; Fiber: 2.7g; Sugar: 4.3g;

3 lbs beef pot roast	Pepper
2 cups homemade beef broth	Salt

- Spray instant pot from inside with cooking spray and set on sauté mode.
- Add roast to the pot and brown the roast on all sides.
- Season with pepper and salt.
- Pour beef broth into the instant pot.
- Seal pot with lid and cook for 70 minutes.
- Allow releasing pressure naturally then open the lid.
- Serve and enjoy.

Lasagna

Serves: 6, Preparation time: 10 minutes, Cooking time: 20 minutes, Per Serving: Calories: 379; Total Fat: 22; Saturated Fat: 13g; Protein: 35g; Carbs: 15g; Fiber: 1g; Sugar: 7g

1 pound lean ground beef	Salt and freshly ground black pepper, to taste
1 onion, diced	
6 cloves garlic, peeled and minced	1 cup ricotta cheese
1 can (28 ounces) crushed tomatoes	6 ounces mozzarella cheese, shredded
2 teaspoons Italian herb blend, plus more for garnish	½ cup finely grated Parmesan cheese
	2 eggs, lightly beaten
3 small zucchini, cut lengthwise into strips	1 teaspoon dried oregano
	6 ounces mozzarella cheese, sliced

- In Instant Pot on sauté setting, cook ground beef, onion and garlic until ground beef is browned, 5-6 minutes. Drain fat if necessary.
- Add crushed tomatoes and herb blend to pot and season to taste with salt and pepper. Remove half of the beef mixture from pot and set aside.
- Arrange half of the zucchini slices over the beef mixture in the pot. Mix ricotta, mozzarella, Parmesan, eggs and oregano and spread over zucchini slices. Arrange remaining zucchini slices over cheese mixture and top with remaining beef mixture.
- Secure pot lid, close pressure valve and cook at high pressure until done, about 10 minutes. When cooking time ends, carefully turn venting knob from sealing to venting position for a quick pressure release.
- Arrange mozzarella slices over lasagna, cover pot and let stand until cheese is melted. Cut lasagna into wedges and sprinkle with Italian herb blend to serve. Enjoy!

Vegetable Beef Roast

Serves: 4 / Preparation time: 15 minutes / Cooking time: 60 minutes, Per Serving: Calories: 549; Total Fat: 14.9g; Saturated Fat: 5.4g; Protein: 72.5g; Carbs: 28.8g; Fiber: 7.1g; Sugar: 18.2g;

2 lbs beef loin roast	1 large onion, sliced
1 tbsp coconut aminos	1 tbsp balsamic vinegar
1 apple, cut into chunks	1 tsp garlic powder
2 medium rutabagas, peeled and cut into chunks	1 tsp onion powder
	1 tbsp dried Italian herb seasoning
1/2 cup homemade broth	1 tsp sea salt

- Place beef roast into the instant pot.
- Rub dried herbs, onion powder, garlic powder, and sea salt on the roast.

- Pour broth, balsamic vinegar, and layer with sliced onion.
- Seal pot with lid and cook on the manual setting for 50 minutes.
- Release pressure using quick release method than open the lid.
- Transfer roast onto the cutting board and cut into the slices.
- Return sliced meat to the instant pot with apple and vegetables.
- Seal pot with lid and cook on the manual setting for another 10 minutes.
- Release pressure using quick release method than open the lid.
- Stir in coconut amino and serve.

Balsamic Beef Roast

1 hour 5 minutes, Serves: 6, Calories 533; Fat 23.2 g; Carbohydrates 0.4 g Sugar 0 g; Protein 75.4 g; Cholesterol 234 mg

3 lbs chuck roast	4 tbsp balsamic vinegar
1 cup beef stock	1/4 Tsp thyme, dried
1 tbsp clarified butter, melted	1/2 Tsp pepper
1 Tsp Rosemary	1 Tsp salt
1 tbsp extra virgin olive oil	

- In a small bowl, mix together thyme, rosemary, pepper, and salt and rub all over roast.
- Add oil in instant pot and select sauté.
- Add roast in pot and brown them on both the sides, about 5 minutes on each side.
- Mix together broth, butter, and vinegar and pour over roast.
- Seal pot with lid and cook on manual high pressure for 40 minutes.
- Allow releasing pressure naturally then open the lid and serve.

Beef Pasta Black Pepper

Serves: 2 / Preparation time: 5 minutes / Cooking time: 15 minutes, Per Serving: Calories: 235; Total Fat: 8.2 g; Saturated Fat: 3.6g; Protein: 11.9g; Carbs: 29g; Fiber: 2.3g; Sugar: 8.8 g

½ cup macaroni	1-¾ cups fresh milk
½ cup ground beef	1-teaspoon black pepper
1 cup chopped onion	2 tablespoons soy sauce

- Heat up the Instant Pot for 30 seconds then select "Sauté" menu.
- Place ground beef, chopped onion, and soy sauce in the Instant Pot then sauté until aromatic. Press the "Cancel" button.
- Pour fresh milk over the beef then add macaroni to the Instant Pot.
- Season with black pepper then cover the Instant Pot with the lid. Lock it properly.
- Select "Manual" setting then select "High" menu and set time for 15 minutes.
- Once it is done, naturally release the Instant Pot then open the lid.
- Stir the pasta and beef then transfer to a serving dish.
- Serve and enjoy immediately.

Taco Bowls

Serves: 6, Preparation time: 10 minutes, Cooking time: 20 minutes, Per Serving: Calories: 325; Total Fat: 21g; Saturated Fat: 6g; Protein: 18g; Carbs: 16g; Fiber: 8g; Sugar: 6g

1 large head cauliflower (about 3 pounds), cut into large chunks	2 teaspoons each of cumin and chili powder
½ teaspoon salt	1 teaspoon each of unsweetened cocoa powder, and dried oregano
1 pound ground beef	¼ teaspoon cayenne pepper
1 small onion, finely diced	Salt and freshly ground black pepper, to taste
2 cloves garlic, minced	
1 can (28 ounces) crushed tomatoes	1 avocado, pitted and sliced

- Pour 1 cup of water into Instant Pot. Place cauliflower in steamer basket and set in pot. Secure pot lid, close pressure valve and cook on manual setting for 1 minute. Carefully turn venting knob from sealing to venting position for a quick pressure release.
- Remove cauliflower from steamer basket to a large bowl, sprinkle with salt and mash to desired consistency with a potato masher. Cover mash to keep warm and set aside.
- Drain water from Instant Pot and set pot to sauté. Crumble ground beef into pot, add onion and cook until lightly browned, 3-4 minutes. Stir garlic into beef mixture and cook for about 1 minute. If necessary, drain fat from beef mixture.
- Add crushed tomatoes, chili powder, cumin, cocoa powder, oregano and cayenne pepper to pot, season to taste with salt and pepper and mix well.
- Secure pot lid, close pressure valve and cook at high pressure for 8 minutes, then carefully turn venting knob from sealing to venting position for a quick pressure release.
- Fluff cauliflower with a fork and scoop into 6 deep bowls. Ladle taco filling over cauliflower and garnish with avocado slices to serve. Enjoy!

Flavorful Jalapeno Beef

Total Time: 6 hours 10 minutes; Serves: 2; Calories 874; Fat 63.4 g; Carbohydrates 9.7 g; Sugar 7.7 g; Protein 60.5 g; Cholesterol 234 mg

1 lb beef chuck roast
6 oz jar roasted bell peppers, drained and chopped
2 jalapenos, sliced
1/2 onion, sliced
1/4 cup Worcestershire sauce
1/4 cup beef broth
1/4 tsp black pepper
1/2 tsp salt

- Use the "Slow Cooker" setting on your Instant Pot.
- Place chuck roast in the slow cooker.
- Pour Worcestershire sauce and beef broth over the roast.
- Season with pepper and salt.
- Top roast with bell peppers, jalapenos, and sliced onions.
- Cover and cook on low for 6 hours.
- Using fork shred the meat.
- Serve and enjoy.

Juicy Roast Beef Sandwiches

Total Time: 5 hours 15 minutes; Serves: 2; Calories 948; Fat 69.2 g; Carbohydrates 17.5 g; Sugar 15.5 g; Protein 60.5 g; Cholesterol 249 mg

1 lb beef chuck roast, boneless
1 1/2 tsp Worcestershire sauce
2 tsp red wine vinegar
3 tbsp lemon juice
1/3 cup ketchup
1 tbsp butter
1 tbsp brown sugar
1/4 cup celery, chopped
1/4 cup onion, chopped
1 cup water
1/8 tsp salt

- Use the "Slow Cooker" setting on your Instant Pot.
- Place beef chuck roast into the slow cooker then pour water over the roast.
- Cover and cook on high for 3 hours or until meat is tender.
- Remove roast from slow cooker and place on chopping board.
- Using fork shred the roast and return shredded roast to the slow cooker.
- Melt butter in the pan. Add onion and celery and sauté until onion is softened.
- Add Worcestershire sauce, salt, vinegar, pepper, lemon juice, brown sugar, and ketchup. Stir well.
- Transfer pan mixture to the slow cooker.

- Cover and cook on low for 2 hours.
- Serve on buns and enjoy.

Round Steak with Peppers

Serves: 4, Preparation time: 15 minutes, Cooking time: 25 minutes, Per Serving: Calories: 310; Total Fat: 15g; Saturated Fat: 4g; Protein: 27g; Carbs: 12g; Fiber: 3g; Sugar: 8g

1 pound round steak, cut into strips	1 cup beef stock
Salt and freshly ground black pepper, to taste	¼ cup soy sauce
	1 teaspoon dried basil
2 tablespoons vegetable oil	1 teaspoon dried oregano
2 bell peppers, cut into strips	½ teaspoon dried thyme
2 cloves garlic, peeled and minced	½ teaspoon ground ginger
1 can (28 ounces) diced tomatoes	

- Season round steak strips with salt and pepper. In Instant Pot on sauté setting, cook strips in oil until lightly browned, about 5 minutes.
- Add bell pepper strips and garlic to pot and cook until slightly softened, 2-3 minutes.
- Add undrained tomatoes, beef stock, soy sauce, basil, oregano, thyme and ginger to pot, season to taste with salt and pepper and mix well.
- Secure pot lid, close pressure valve and cook at stew setting for 15 minutes. When cooking time ends, carefully turn venting knob from sealing to venting position for a quick pressure release.
- On sauté setting, simmer steak and peppers, stirring frequently, to reduce sauce to desired consistency. Serve and enjoy!

Beef Chili

40 minutes, Serves: 4, Calories 217; Fat 5.1 g; Carbohydrates 20 g; Sugar 10.1 g; Protein 27.1 g; Cholesterol 46 mg

1 lb sirloin tips	1 medium onion, chopped
1 Tsp cumin	6 oz tomato paste
2 tbsp chili powder	14 oz can tomatoes, diced and drained
1 jalapeno, diced	1/4 Tsp black pepper
3 garlic cloves, minced	1/4 Tsp salt

- Add all ingredients into the instant pot and stir well.
- Seal pot with lid and cook on manual high pressure for 30 minutes.
- Release pressure using quick release method than open the lid.
- Stir well and serve.

Salty Beef Brisket

Serves: 2 / Preparation time: 5 minutes / Cooking time: 35 minutes, Per Serving: Calories: 150; Total Fat: 10.5 g; Saturated Fat: 4.1g; Protein: 11.7g; Carbs: 1.9g; Fiber: 0.2g; Sugar: 0.6g

¾ lb. beef brisket	1 bay leaf
2 teaspoons minced garlic	1 ½ cup beef broth
1-tablespoon coriander	1 ½ teaspoons salt

- Heat up the Instant Pot for 30 seconds.
- Place beef brisket in the Instant Pot then sprinkle salt, coriander, and minced garlic over the beef brisket.
- Add a bay leaf to the pot then pour beef broth into the pot.
- Cover the Instant Pot then lock it properly.
- Select "Manual" setting then select "High" menu and set time for 35 minutes.
- Once it is done, naturally release the Instant Pot then open the lid.
- Take the cooked beef brisket out from the Instant Pot then place on a flat surface.
- Cut the beef brisket into slices then place on a serving dish.
- Enjoy.

Tasty Mongolian Beef

Serves: 8 / Preparation time: 10 minutes / Cooking time: 30 minutes, Per Serving: Calories: 300; Total Fat: 8.3g; Saturated Fat: 3.1g; Protein: 24g; Carbs: 32g; Fiber: 0.3g; Sugar: 26.4g;

1 1/2 lbs flank steak, sliced
1/2 cup carrot grated
3/4 cup honey
3/4 cup coconut aminos
1/2 tsp ginger, mince, and peel
2 tsp olive oil
1/4 cups arrowroot

- Coat flank steak with arrowroot powder.
- Add olive oil, coconut aminos, ginger, honey, water, green onion and carrots into the instant pot and stir well.
- Place flank steak into the pot.
- Seal pot with lid and cook on manual high for 30 minutes.
- Allow releasing pressure naturally then open the lid.
- Serve and enjoy.

Hot Pepper Shredded Beef

Total Time: 6 hours 5 minutes; Serves: 2; Calories 490; Fat 27.1 g; Carbohydrates 12 g; Sugar 7.5 g; Protein 46.1 g; Cholesterol 151 mg

1 lb beef chuck shoulder roast, boneless and fat trimmed
1 cup beef broth
1/2 medium onion, sliced
2 banana peppers, seed discarded and sliced

- Use the "Slow Cooker" setting on your Instant Pot.
- Add all ingredients to the slow cooker.
- Cover and cook on low for 6 hours.
- Using fork shred the meat and serves.

Spicy Habanero Chili

45 minutes, Serves: 4, Calories 328; Fat 11.4 g Carbohydrates 19.7 g; Sugar 9.7 g; Protein 37.4 g; Cholesterol 101 mg

1 lb ground beef
1 Tsp paprika
1 1/2 Tsp cumin powder
2 Tsp oregano
1 tbsp chili powder
14 oz can tomatoes, diced
3 celery stalks, chopped
3 large carrots, chopped
1 bell pepper, chopped
1 habanero, minced
4 garlic cloves, minced
1 onion, diced
1 tbsp extra virgin olive oil
1 Tsp salt

- Add oil in instant pot and select sauté.
- Add garlic and onion and sauté for 2 minutes.
- Add ground beef and cook until browned.
- Add remaining ingredients and stir well.
- Seal pot with lid and select meat/stew setting and set timer for 35 minutes.
- Allow releasing pressure naturally then open the lid.
- Stir well and serve.

Beef Ragu

Serves: 3 / Preparation time: 10 minutes / Cooking time: 40 minutes, Per Serving: Calories: 515; Total Fat: 7.9g; Saturated Fat: 5.9g; Protein: 72g; Carbs: 13.9g; Fiber: 4g; Sugar: 6.4g;

1 1/2 lbs beef steak, diced	2 bay leaves
1 tsp black pepper	3 garlic cloves, sliced
14 oz tomatoes, chopped	1/2 tsp chili flakes
1 cup beef stock	1 celery stalk, diced
1 tsp coconut aminos	1 large carrot, diced
1/2 tsp ground cinnamon	1 medium onion, diced
1 tsp dried oregano	2 tsp olive oil
1 tsp ground paprika	1 1/2 tsp sea salt

- Add olive oil into the instant pot and select sauté.
- Add onion, celery, carrot, chili flakes and salt sauté for 6 minutes.
- Add remaining ingredients and beef, stir well.
- Seal pot with lid and cook on manual high pressure for 30 minutes.
- Allow releasing pressure naturally then open the lid.
- Turn instant pot on sauté mode and using fork shred the beef into smaller pieces.
- Sauté for 12-15 minutes or until sauce thickened.

Curry Jalapeno Beef Stew

Total Time: 8 hours 25 minutes; Serves: 4; Calories 293, Fat 11.1 g, Carbohydrates 10 g, Sugar 5 g, Protein 37.2 g, Cholesterol 101 mg

1 lb beef stew meat	1 tsp fresh ginger, chopped
1 cup beef broth	2 garlic cloves, minced
1 onion, sliced	1 tbsp vegetable oil
14.5 oz can tomatoes, diced	Pepper
1 tbsp curry powder	Salt
1 fresh jalapeno pepper, diced	

- Use the "Slow Cooker" setting on your Instant Pot.
- Heat oil in the pan over medium heat.
- Add beef to the pan and cook until brown. Transfer to the Instant Pot.
- Season browned beef with pepper and salt.
- In same pan, sauté ginger, garlic, and jalapeno for 2 minutes.
- Add tomatoes and curry powder and stir for a minute. Transfer pan mixture to the Instant Pot.
- Add remaining ingredients and mix well.
- Cover and cook on low for 8 hours.
- Serve and enjoy.

Beef Tender in Sweet Red Sauce

Serves: 2 / Preparation time: 5 minutes / Cooking time: 30 minutes, Per Serving: Calories: 224; Total Fat: 15.2 g; Saturated Fat: 5.4g; Protein: 12.5g; Carbs: 11g; Fiber: 2.9g; Sugar: 7g

¾ lb. beef brisket	½ cup water
1-teaspoon olive oil	¼ teaspoon salt
½ cup chopped onion	½ teaspoon pepper
2 cups chopped tomato	½ teaspoon sugar

- Heat up the Instant Pot for 30 seconds.
- Select "Sauté" menu then pour olive oil into the Instant Pot.
- Put chopped onion into the Instant Pot then sauté until wilted and aromatic.

- Stir in beef brisket then season with salt, pepper, and sugar.
- Sprinkle chopped tomato over the beef brisket and pour water into the Pot.
- Cover the Instant Pot then lock it properly.
- Select "Manual" setting then cook the beef on high for 30 minutes.
- Once it is done, naturally release the Instant Pot then open the lid.
- Transfer to a serving dish then serve.
- Enjoy.

Cinnamon Honey Beef

Serves: 2 / Preparation time: 5 minutes / Cooking time: 30 minutes, Per Serving: Calories: 304; Total Fat: 4.4 g; Saturated Fat: 1.7g; Protein: 13.4g; Carbs: 58.4g; Fiber: 7.6g; Sugar: 46.6g

¾ lb. beef tenderloin	¼ cup cinnamon
¼ cup honey	½ teaspoon nutmeg
2 tablespoons brown sugar	¼ teaspoon salt
¼ cup orange juice	

- Heat up the Instant Pot for 30 seconds.
- Place the beef in the Instant Pot then sprinkle salt, nutmeg, cinnamon, and brown sugar over the beef.
- Drizzle orange juice and honey on top then cover and lock the Instant Pot properly.
- Select "Manual" setting then cook the beef on high and set the time to 30 minutes.
- Once it is done, naturally release the Instant Pot then open the lid.
- Open the lid then transfer the beef to a serving dish.
- Cut the beef into slices then serve.
- Enjoy.

Spicy Beef with Beans

Serves: 2 / Preparation time: 10 minutes / Cooking time: 35 minutes, Per Serving: Calories: 167; Total Fat: 4.7 g; Saturated Fat: 1.4g; Protein: 18.2g; Carbs: 15g; Fiber: 4.6g; Sugar: 6.1g

1-cup beef cubes	1-teaspoon cumin
¾ cup cooked beans	½ teaspoon pepper
¼ cup chopped onion	½ cup salsa
2 teaspoons red chili flakes	1-cup vegetable broth
2 teaspoons chili powder	

- Heat up the Instant Pot for 30 seconds then place all ingredients in the Instant Pot. Stir well.
- Cover the Instant Pot with the lid and make sure that it is locked properly.
- Select "Manual" setting then select "High" menu and set time for 35 minutes.
- Once it is done, naturally release the Instant Pot then open the lid.
- Transfer to a serving dish then serve.
- Enjoy.

Creamy Beef Stroganoff

Serves: 4, Preparation time: 5 minutes, Cooking time: 30 minutes, Per Serving: Calories: 361; Total Fat: 13g; Saturated Fat: 7g; Protein: 28g; Carbs: 8g; Fiber: 4g; Sugar: 2g

1 pound beef stew meat	1 cup beef stock or water
1 onion, julienned	1 teaspoon Worcestershire sauce
4 cloves garlic, peeled and minced	Salt and freshly ground pepper, to taste
1 tablespoon olive oil	½ cup sour cream
2 cups (about 4 ounces) sliced fresh mushrooms	1 teaspoon arrowroot flour
	1 tablespoon water

- In Instant Pot on sauté setting, cook onion, garlic and stew meat in oil until beef is lightly browned.
- Add mushrooms, stock and Worcestershire sauce to pot and season to taste with salt and pepper.

- Secure pot lid, close pressure valve and cook at high pressure until done, about 20 minutes. When cooking time ends, let pressure release naturally.
- Set pot to sauté and stir in sour cream. Combine arrowroot flour and water until smooth and stir into stroganoff to thicken. Serve and enjoy!

Flavorful Slow Cooker Chili

Total Time: 8 hours 10 minutes; Serves: 2; Calories 441; Carbohydrates 53.7 g; Sugar 32.5 g; Protein 38.5 g; Cholesterol 101 mg

1/2 lb ground beef
1 tsp parsley
1/4 tsp cumin
1/8 cup steak sauce
1 tbsp chili powder

15 oz chili sauce
1/2 small onion, diced
8 oz can tomato sauce
1/4 tsp salt

- Use the "Slow Cooker" setting on your Instant Pot.
- Add all ingredients to the slow cooker and stir well to combine.
- Cover and cook on low for 8 hours.
- Serve and enjoy.

Chunky Steak Chili

Serves: 4, Preparation time: 15 minutes, Cooking time: 35 minutes, Per Serving (calculated without optional garnishes): Calories: 255; Total Fat: 9g; Saturated Fat: 4g; Protein: 31g; Carbs: 21g; Fiber: 7g; Sugar: 11g

1 tablespoon chili powder
1 tablespoon ground cumin
1 teaspoon unsweetened cocoa powder
1 teaspoon paprika
1 teaspoon ancho chili powder
1 teaspoon dried oregano
¼ teaspoon cayenne pepper
1 pound round steak, trimmed and cut into 1-inch cubes

1 onion, coarsely diced
4 stalks celery, trimmed and diced
4 cloves garlic, peeled and minced
1 cup beef stock
1 can (6 ounces) tomato paste
1 can (28 ounces) crushed tomatoes
Salt and freshly ground black pepper, to taste

- Mix first 7 ingredients (all the spices) in a bowl and set aside.
- In Instant Pot on sauté setting, cook round steak cubes with half of the spices until meat is browned on all sides. Add onion, celery, garlic, beef stock and tomato paste to pot, season to taste with salt and pepper and mix well.
- Without stirring, add crushed tomatoes to pot. *Do not mix.*
- Secure pot lid, close pressure valve and cook at high pressure for about 12 minutes. When cooking time ends, let pressure release naturally.
- Add remaining spices and mix well. Set pot to sauté, place lid on pot slightly ajar and let chili simmer until reduced to desired consistency, up to about 10 minutes.
- Garnish as desired to serve and enjoy!

Beef Brisket Garlic Stew

Serves: 7 / Preparation time: 10 minutes / Cooking time: 35 minutes, Per Serving: Calories: 417; Total Fat: 14.3g; Saturated Fat: 4.9g; Protein: 61.4g; Carbs: 7.3g; Fiber: 1.3g; Sugar: 2.7g;

3 lbs beef brisket, cut into 2-inches cubes	1/4 cup Italian parsley, chopped
6 garlic cloves	1 bay leaf, dried
2 tsp tomato paste	1 tsp thyme, dried
16 oz stemmed cremini mushrooms, quartered	1 tsp red boat fish sauce
	2 tsp coconut aminos
2 onion, sliced	Black pepper
1 tbsp olive oil	Kosher salt

- Season beef cubes with pepper and salt.
- Add olive oil into the instant pot and set the pot to the sauté mode.
- Add onion, mushrooms and 1/2 tsp kosher salt and sauté for 5 minutes.
- Add tomato paste and garlic and sauté for another 30 seconds.
- Add beef, fish sauce, coconut aminos, bay leaf, and thyme. Stir well.
- Seal pot with lid and select Meat/Stew setting and set the timer for 35 minutes.
- Allow releasing pressure naturally then open the lid.
- Serve and enjoy.

Chili Lime Shredded Beef

Total Time: 6 hours 10 minutes; Serves: 2; Calories 933; Fat 63.4 g; Carbohydrates 28 g; Sugar 22.5 g; Protein 59.8 g; Cholesterol 234 mg

1 lb beef chuck roast	1 tsp chili powder
1 lime juice	2 cups lemon-lime soda
1 garlic clove, crushed	1/2 tsp salt

- Use the "Slow Cooker" setting on your Instant Pot.
- Place beef chuck roast into the slow cooker.
- Season roast with garlic, chili powder, and salt.
- Pour lemon-lime soda over the roast.
- Cover and cook on low for 6 hours.
- Using fork shred the roast.
- Add lime juice over shredded roast and serve.

Bell Pepper Ground Beef Chili

40 minutes, Serves: 10, Calories 253; Fat 9 g Carbohydrates 13.6 g; Sugar 6.3 g; Protein 29.4 g; Cholesterol 81 mg

2 lbs ground beef	5 celery stalks, chopped
1 tbsp cumin	8 carrots, chopped
1 tbsp oregano	10 garlic cloves, minced
2 tbsp chili powder	2 onion, diced
14 oz can tomatoes, diced	2 tbsp extra virgin olive oil
2 jalapenos, minced	1 Tsp black pepper
2 bell peppers, chopped	2 Tsp salt

- Add oil in instant pot and select sauté.
- Add garlic and onion and sauté for 2 minutes.
- Add beef and cook until browned.
- Add remaining ingredients and stir well.
- Seal pot with lid and select bean/chili setting, it takes 30 minutes.
- Allow releasing pressure naturally then open the lid.

- Stir well and serve.

Beef Mushroom Pie

Serves: 2 / Preparation time: 10 minutes / Cooking time: 15 minutes, Per Serving: Calories: 367; Total Fat: 27.5g; Saturated Fat: 13.1g; Protein: 18g; Carbs: 11.4g; Fiber: 0.4g; Sugar: 1g

1-cup ground beef	¼ cup chopped onion
1 cup mashed potatoes	1-½ tablespoons flour
1-tablespoon butter	¼ cup grated cheese
1 organic egg	

- Coat a heatproof casserole dish with cooking spray.
- Place mashed potato in the casserole dish then spread evenly.
- Combine ground beef with chopped onion, egg, and flour then mix well.
- Place the ground beef mixture over the mashed potato then spread evenly too.
- Drop butter over the beef then sprinkle grated cheese on top.
- Turn the Instant Pot on then pour water into it.
- Place a trivet then preheat the Instant Pot.
- Place the casserole dish with pie on the trivet then cover the Instant Pot with the lid. Make sure that it is locked properly.
- Select "Manual" setting then cook the beef on high for 15 minutes.
- Quickly release the Instant Pot then open the lid.
- Remove the casserole dish from the Instant Pot then enjoy warm.

Garlic Beef Short Ribs

Serves: 3 / Preparation time: 10 minutes / Cooking time: 15 minutes, Per Serving: Calories: 318; Total Fat: 12.6g; Saturated Fat: 4g; Protein: 46.4g; Carbs: 2.3g; Fiber: 0.4g; Sugar: 0.4g;

1 lb beef ribs, Diced in 1-inch pieces	2 tsp olive oil
4 crimini mushrooms, chopped	2 scallions, minced
2 garlic cloves, minced	Black pepper
2 tsp coconut aminos	1 tsp sea salt

- Add all ingredients into the instant pot and stir well.
- Seal pot with lid and cook on manual high pressure for 15 minutes.
- Allow releasing pressure naturally then open the lid.
- Serve and enjoy.

Herb Pot Roast

1 hour 5 minutes, Serves: 6, Calories 902; Fat 68.4 g; Carbohydrates 9.1 g; Sugar 4.6 g; Protein 60.2 g; Cholesterol 245 mg

3 lbs beef chuck roast	2 cups vegetable stock
2 tbsp clarified butter	1 onion, diced
1 tbsp Italian seasoning	1 Tsp black pepper
2 garlic cloves, minced	1 Tsp salt
5 large carrots, peeled	

- Place beef chunks in a large dish and sprinkle with spices.
- Add butter in instant pot and select sauté.
- Add onion in a pot and sauté until brown, about 5 minutes.
- Add chunk roast over the onions then pour stock.
- Seal pot with lid and select manual and set timer for 40 minutes.
- Release pressure using quick release method than open the lid.

- Add carrots and stir well.
- Again Seal pot with lid and select manual and set the timer for another 10 minutes.
- Release pressure using quick release method than open the lid.
- Stir well and serve.

Roasted Tomato Beef Curry

Total Time: 6 hours 10 minutes; Serves: 2; Calories 572; Fat 15 g; Carbohydrates 32.1 g; Sugar 6.5 g; Protein 73.4 g; Cholesterol 203 mg

1 lb beef stew meat, cut into cubed
15 oz can roasted tomatoes, diced
1 garlic clove, minced
1/2 tbsp fresh ginger, minced
1/2 tsp cumin
1 tbsp curry powder
1/2 lb small red potatoes, cut into quarters
1/4 tsp black pepper
1/2 tsp salt

- Use the "Slow Cooker" setting on your Instant Pot.
- Add all ingredients to the slow cooker and stir well.
- Cover and cook on low for 6 hours.
- Serve over rice and enjoy.

Spicy Orange Beef

Serves: 5 / Preparation time: 10 minutes / Cooking time: 20 minutes, Per Serving: Calories: 431; Total Fat: 18.2g; Saturated Fat: 6.7g; Protein: 51.5g; Carbs: 12.4g; Fiber: 0.9g; Sugar: 5.6g;

2 lbs flank steak, cut into 1/4 strip
6 garlic cloves, minced
3 tsp cold water
2 tsp arrowroot powder
1 tsp orange zest
1/2 tsp red pepper flakes, crushed
2 tsp olive oil
1/4 cups coconut aminos
3/4 cups orange juice
1 tsp olive oil
2 bell peppers, sliced
1 bunch chopped green onion

- Season flank steak with pepper and salt.
- Add olive oil to the pot and set the pot on sauté mode.
- Add meat into the pot and browned it all sides.
- Remove meat from instant pot and set aside.
- Add garlic to the pot and sauté for 1 minute.
- Add olive oil, orange juice, red pepper flakes and some orange zest to the pot. Stir well.
- Add browned meat. Seal pot with lid and select high pressure and set timer for 13 minutes.
- Release pressure using quick release method than open the lid carefully.
- Add water, arrowroot, bell peppers to pot and stir well.
- Select sauté mode and bring to boil until sauce thickened.
- Garnish with chopped green onion, red pepper flakes, and orange zest.
- Serve and enjoy

Beef Stew

1 hour 10 minutes, Serves: 8, Calories 339; Fat 7.9 g; Carbohydrates 25.5 g; Sugar 5.4 g; Protein 38.7 g; Cholesterol 101 mg

2 lbs beef stew meat, cut into pieces
1/4 cup water
1/4 cup arrowroot powder
1 Tsp oregano
1 tbsp parsley, dried
4 small potatoes, cut into the pieces
2 cups baby carrots
32 oz beef broth
6 oz tomato puree
2 garlic cloves, minced
1 medium onion, chopped
1 Tsp pepper

1 Tsp salt

- Add all ingredients except arrowroot powder and water into the instant pot and stir well.
- Seal pot with lid and select stew setting.
- Allow releasing pressure naturally for 12 minutes then release using quick release method.
- Open lid carefully and stir in arrowroot powder and water mixture and stir well.
- Serve and enjoy.

Juicy Beef Meatballs Marinara

Serves: 2 / Preparation time: 5 minutes / Cooking time: 15 minutes, Per Serving: Calories: 304; Total Fat: 19.1g; Saturated Fat: 8g; Protein: 13.3g; Carbs: 20.4g; Fiber: 4g; Sugar: 12.1g

1-½ lbs. ground beef	½ teaspoon garlic powder
3 teaspoons chopped parsley	1-teaspoon onion powder
½ cup grated cheese	¼ teaspoon oregano
4 tablespoons almond flour	¼ cup water
1 organic egg	1-teaspoon olive oil
¼ teaspoon salt	1-cup marinara sauce
¼ teaspoon pepper	

- Combine ground beef with grated cheese, chopped parsley, almond flour, and egg.
- Season with salt, pepper, garlic powder, onion powder, and oregano then mix until combined.
- Shape the mixture into balls forms then set aside.
- Heat up the Instant Pot for 30 seconds.
- Select "Sauté" menu then pour olive oil into it.
- Arrange the balls in the Instant Pot then cook for a few seconds.
- Flip the balls then cook again for another minute. Press the "Cancel" button.
- Combine marinara sauce with water then pour over the balls.
- Cover the Instant Pot with the lid then lock it properly.
- Select "Manual" setting then cook the oxtail on low for 15 minutes.
- Once it is done, naturally release the Instant Pot then open the lid.
- Transfer the Meatballs to a serving bowl together with the sauce.
- Serve and enjoy warm.

Simple Beef Tacos

2 hours 5 minutes, Serves: 6, Calories 438; Fat 14.2 g; Carbohydrates 3 g; Sugar 0 g; Protein 69.1 g; Cholesterol 203 mg

3 lbs beef roast	4 tbsp taco seasoning
2/3 cup beef stock	

- Place beef roast in instant pot.
- Pour stock over the roast and sprinkle roast with taco seasoning.
- Seal pot with lid and select manual and set timer for 2 hours.
- Allow releasing pressure naturally then open the lid.
- Using fork shred the beef and serves.

Beef Mix Vegetable Soup

10 minutes, Serves: 6, Calories 321; Fat 12.5 g; Carbohydrates 12.2 g; Sugar 4.6 g; Protein 48.2 g; Cholesterol 135 mg

2 lbs ground beef	2 cups mix vegetables
2 cup vegetable stock	1 small onion, diced
3 cans tomatoes, diced	1 tbsp extra virgin olive oil

Pepper	Salt

- Add oil in instant pot and select sauté.
- Add onion and ground beef in a pot and sauté onion until softened.
- Add all remaining ingredients into the pot and stir well.
- Seal pot with lid and cook on manual high pressure for 4 minutes.
- Allow releasing pressure naturally then open the lid.
- Serve and enjoy.

Beef Bolognese Mushroom

Serves: 2 / Preparation time: 5 minutes / Cooking time: 10 minutes, Per Serving: Calories: 341; Total Fat: 7.3g; Saturated Fat: 2.3g; Protein: 27.2g; Carbs: 42g; Fiber: 4.8g; Sugar: 12.7g

¼ lb. ground beef	½ teaspoon pepper
1-cup penne	1-teaspoon olive oil
½ cup chopped mushroom	3 cups low sodium chicken broth
2 teaspoons minced garlic	½ cup tomato paste
1 teaspoon chopped celery	2 tablespoons low sodium soy sauce
¼ teaspoon oregano	3 teaspoons fish sauce
¼ teaspoon basil	1 ½ tablespoons Worcestershire sauce
¼ teaspoon salt	

- Heat up the Instant Pot for 30 seconds then select "Sauté" menu.
- Pour olive oil into the pot then stir in ground beef.
- Season with salt and pepper then sauté until crispy.
- Add minced garlic, chopped mushroom, chopped celery, oregano, and basil then stir for about 30 seconds.
- Pour chicken broth over the beef then add tomato paste, soy sauce, fish sauce, and Worcestershire sauce. Stir to combine then press the "Cancel" button.
- Add penne to the Instant Pot then stir well. Make sure that the penne is completely covered with the liquid.
- Cover the Instant Pot with the lid then lock it properly.
- Select "Manual" setting then cook the beef on high for 6 minutes.
- Once it is done, quickly release the Instant Pot then open the lid.
- Transfer the pasta to a serving dish then enjoy immediately.

Meatloaf

Total Time: 8 hours 10 minutes; Serves: 2; Calories 532; Fat 17.3 g; Carbohydrates 15.6 g; Sugar 1.9 g; Protein 74.3 g; Cholesterol 285 mg

1 egg	3 tbsp dry onion soup mix
1 lb ground beef	1/3 cup quick oats
4 tbsp tomato sauce	

- Use the "Slow Cooker" setting on your Instant Pot.
- In a bowl, combine together oats, onion soup mix, 3 tbsp tomato sauce, ground beef, and egg.
- Shape mixture into the loaf and place into the slow cooker.
- Spread remaining tomato sauce on top of the meatloaf.
- Cover and cook on low for 8 hours.
- Cut loaf into the slices and serve.

Beef Curry

Total Time: 4 hours 15 minutes; Serves: 2; Calories 510; Fat 6.4 g; Carbohydrates 5.8 g; Sugar 2.6 g; Protein 70 g; Cholesterol 203 mg

1 lb stewing beef, cut into cubes	1/2 tbsp garam masala
1/4 cup beef stock	1/2 tsp turmeric
1 tbsp olive oil	1/2 tsp black pepper
1/2 tsp brown sugar	2 tbsp fresh cilantro, chopped
1/4 tsp lemon zest	1/4 cup tomatoes, crushed
1/4 tsp smoked paprika	1 garlic cloves, minced
1/4 tsp cayenne pepper	1/2 onion, chopped
1/4 tsp coriander	1/2 tsp salt
1/4 tsp cumin	

- Use the "Slow Cooker" setting on your Instant Pot.
- Heat oil in the pan over medium-high heat.
- Add garlic, onions, spices, pepper, and salt into the pan and sauté for 3 minutes.
- Stir in brown sugar and crushed tomatoes. Bring to boil.
- Transfer pan mixture to the blender and blend until smooth.
- Brown the beef pieces into the pan.
- Transfer beef into the slow cooker then pours blended paste over the beef.
- Add lemon zest and stock into the slow cooker.
- Cover and cook on low for 4 hours or until meat is cooked.
- Serve over rice and enjoy.

Italian Beef

Serves: 7 / Preparation time: 10 minutes / Cooking time: 65 minutes, Per Serving: Calories: 742; Total Fat: 55.8g; Saturated Fat: 21.8g; Protein: 51.9g; Carbs: 0.7g; Fiber: 0.9g; Sugar: 2.7g;

3 lbs beef chuck roast, boneless and cut into 4 pieces	1 tsp Italian seasoning
1 onion, sliced	1 tsp garlic powder
1 tsp fish sauce	1 tsp onion powder
1 cup beef stock	2 bell pepper, sliced
2 tsp olive oil	Black pepper
	Sea salt

- Season beef pieces with pepper, salt, onion powder, garlic powder and Italian seasoning.
- Add olive oil into the instant pot and select sauté.
- Add season meat into the pot and sear meat on all side until it brown.
- Remove meat from instant pot and set aside.
- Add fish sauce and beef stock into the instant pot and stir well.
- Place trivet into the instant pot. Arrange sliced onion and browned meat on a trivet.
- Seal pot with lid and cook on the manual setting for 60 minutes.
- While meat is cooking toss bell pepper with garlic powder, pepper, and salt.
- Sauté bell pepper slices in a pan with olive oil until getting lightened in color. Set aside.
- Allow releasing pressure naturally then open the lid.
- Using fork shred the meat and serve with bell peppers.

Bacon Cheeseburger Casserole

Serves: 6, Preparation time: 15 minutes, Cooking time: 30 minutes, Per Serving: Calories: 471; Total Fat: 32g; Saturated Fat: 12g; Protein: 31g; Carbs: 3g; Fiber: 2g; Sugar: 4g

1 pound ground beef	2 cloves garlic, peeled and minced
2 tablespoons chopped onion	½ pound bacon, cooked and crumbled

4 eggs, beaten
8 ounces mild cheddar cheese, grated
1 can (6 ounces) tomato paste
½ cup plain whole-milk yogurt
Salt and freshly ground black pepper, to taste

- Mix ground beef, onion and garlic in Instant Pot and season to taste with salt and pepper. Cook on sauté setting, stirring occasionally, until beef is mostly browned. Secure pot lid, close pressure valve and cook at high pressure for 10 minutes. Carefully turn venting knob from sealing to venting position for a quick pressure release.
- Open lid and, if necessary, cook on sauté setting to boil off excess liquid.
- Add bacon to beef mixture and stir to combine.
- Whisk together eggs, tomato paste, yogurt and half of the cheddar cheese and season to taste with salt and pepper. Stir egg mixture into beef mixture and sprinkle with remaining cheese.
- Secure pot lid, close pressure valve and cook at high pressure for about 10 minutes until done. When cooking time ends, let pressure release naturally.
- Serve and enjoy!

Beef and Potatoes

Total Time: 6 hours 15 minutes; Serves: 2; Calories 799; Fat 15.9 g; Carbohydrates 78.7 g; Sugar 9.5 g; Protein 81.7 g; Cholesterol 203 mg

1 lb beef roast
1/2 tsp ground black pepper
1/2 tbsp Worcestershire sauce
1/2 tbsp adobo seasoning
3 garlic cloves, minced
1 packet onion soup mix
16 oz beef broth
2 carrots, cut into pieces
4 medium potatoes, cleaned and cut into pieces
Salt

- Use the "Slow Cooker" setting on your Instant Pot.
- Season beef roast with pepper and salt.
- Brown the beef into the large pan over medium heat and set aside.
- Add remaining ingredients to the slow cooker. Top with beef.
- Cover and cook on low for 6 hours or until beef is cooked.
- Serve and enjoy.

Beef Ribs

25 minutes, Serves: 4, Calories 308; Fat 17.3 g; Carbohydrates 3.1 g; Sugar 0.5 g; Protein 33.6 g; Cholesterol 103 mg

1 lb beef short ribs, boneless and diced
2 scallions, minced
4 mushrooms, chopped
2 garlic cloves, minced
2 tbsp coconut amino
2 tbsp extra virgin olive oil
1 Tsp salt

- Add all ingredients into the instant pot and stir well.
- Seal pot with lid and cook on manual high pressure for 15 minutes.
- Allow releasing pressure naturally then open the lid.
- Serve and enjoy.

Beef Steak Black Pepper

Serves: 2 / Preparation time: 5 minutes / Cooking time: 30 minutes, Per Serving: Calories: 341; Total Fat: 10.6g; Saturated Fat: 3.4g; Protein: 40.8g; Carbs: 19.5g; Fiber: 1.4g; Sugar: 9.2g

¾ lb. beef round steak
2 tablespoons flour
1-teaspoon olive oil
¼ teaspoon salt
1-teaspoon black pepper
2 teaspoon Worcestershire sauce
4 tablespoons ketchup
3 teaspoons minced garlic

½ cup chopped onion	2 tablespoons chopped celery

- Cut the beef steak into medium slices then roll in the flour.
- Heat up the Instant Pot then press "Sauté" button.
- Pour olive oil into the pot place the coated beefsteak in it.
- Stir the beefsteak until brown then press the "Cancel" button.
- Add salt, black pepper, Worcestershire sauce, minced garlic, chopped onion, ketchup, and chopped celery to the pot then cover it with the lid. Lock the Instant Pot properly.
- Choose "Manual" menu and cook the beefsteak on high for 30 minutes.
- Once it is done, naturally release the Instant Pot then open the lid.
- Transfer the beefsteak together with the sauce to a serving dish then serve.
- Enjoy.

Onion Chuck Roast

Total Time: 8 hours 10 minutes; Serves: 2; Calories 630; Fat 32 g; Carbohydrates 50 g; Sugar 7.8 g; Protein 34.9 g; Cholesterol 117 mg

8 oz beef chuck roast	15 baby carrots, sliced
1/2 packet onion soup mix	3 small potatoes, cut into cubed
1/2 medium onion, sliced	

- Use the "Slow Cooker" setting on your Instant Pot.
- Place carrots and potatoes into the bottom of slow cooker.
- Place meat on top of veggies than add remaining ingredients.
- Cover and cook on low for 8 hours.
- Serve and enjoy.

Tomato Beef Brisket

6 hours 20 minutes, Serves: 6, Calories 505; Fat 18.9 g; Carbohydrates 9.8 g; Sugar 5.6 g; Protein 70.9 g; Cholesterol 203 mg

3 lbs beef brisket	2 tbsp extra virgin olive oil
1 cup beef stock	4 garlic cloves, minced
28 oz can tomatoes, diced	Pepper
1 large onion, chopped	Salt

- Season beef brisket with pepper and salt.
- Heat 1 tbsp oil in a pan over medium high heat.
- Once the oil is hot then place brisket and brown them on both the sides.
- In another pan, heat remaining oil over medium heat.
- Once the oil is hot then add onion and sauté until lightly golden brown.
- Place beef brisket into the instant pot.
- Top brisket with sautéed onion, tomatoes, garlic, pepper, salt, and stock.
- Seal pot with lid and select slow cooker setting for 6 hours.
- Cut brisket into the slices and serve.

Braised Beef Ribs

Serves: 8 / Preparation time: 10 minutes / Cooking time: 30 minutes, Per Serving: Calories: 477; Total Fat: 21g; Saturated Fat: 7.9g; Protein: 67.7g; Carbs: 1.7g; Fiber: 0.3g; Sugar: 0.6g;

4 lbs beef short ribs	1 tsp olive oil
3 garlic cloves	Kosher salt
1 onion, quartered	Water

- Season ribs with salt.
- Add olive oil into the instant pot and select sauté.
- Once the oil is hot then add ribs into the pot brown ribs on all sides.
- Remove ribs from instant pot and set aside.
- Add little olive oil, onion, and garlic and sauté for 2 minutes, add browned ribs and 2 inches of water.
- Seal pot with lid and cook on manual high pressure for 30 minutes.
- Allow releasing pressure naturally then open the lid.
- Serve and enjoy.

Hot Beef with Herbs

Serves: 2 / Preparation time: 5 minutes / Cooking time: 30 minutes, Per Serving: Calories: 315; Total Fat: 17.1g; Saturated Fat: 2.1g; Protein: 22.3g; Carbs: 22.9g; Fiber: 5.5g; Sugar: 5.3g

½ lb. beef chunks
¼ cup chopped leek
4 cloves garlic
5 shallots
½ cup red chili
1-teaspoon turmeric

3 candlenuts
3 kaffir lime leaves
2 bay leaves
1-inch galangal
1 lemongrass
1-cup water

- Place garlic, shallots, red chili, turmeric, and candlenuts in a food processor. Pulse until smooth.
- Preheat the Instant Pot for 30 seconds then place the beef chunks in the pot.
- Add spice mixture to the pot together with lime leaves, bay leaves, galangal, and lemongrass.
- Sprinkle chopped leek on top then pour water into the pot.
- Cover the Instant Pot with the lid then lock it properly.
- Select "Manual" setting then cook the beef on high for 30 minutes.
- Once it is done, naturally release the Instant Pot then open the lid.
- Discard the galangal, bay leaves, and kaffir lime leaves.
- Transfer the beef and the remaining spiced gravy to a serving dish.
- Enjoy with a bowl of rice.

Taco Meat

Serves: 5 / Preparation time: 10 minutes / Cooking time: 15 minutes, Per Serving: Calories: 424; Total Fat: 15.7g; Saturated Fat: 4.9g; Protein: 56.8g; Carbs: 12.3g; Fiber: 2.9g; Sugar: 5.7g;

2 lbs ground beef
1 tsp cumin
1tsp paprika
1/2 tsp black pepper
1/2 tsp turmeric
1 tsp dried basil
1 tsp salt
2 tsp oregano

2 tsp chili powder
5 garlic cloves, minced
3 green bell peppers, diced
2 red onion, diced
4 tsp olive oil
1/2 tsp chipotle powder
1/2 tsp cayenne

- Add all ingredients into the instant pot except beef.
- Set pot on sauté mode and sauté pot mixture for 5 minutes.
- Add ground beef and sauté until meat gets brown.
- Seal pot with lid and cook on manual high pressure for 10 minutes.
- Allow releasing pressure naturally then open the lid.
- Stir well and serve.

Oxtail Soup

Serves: 2 / Preparation time: 5 minutes / Cooking time: 25 minutes, Per Serving: Calories: 336; Total Fat: 17.3g; Saturated Fat: 6.5g; Protein: 36.1g; Carbs: 9.2g; Fiber: 3g; Sugar: 3g

2 lbs. oxtail	1-teaspoon nutmeg
½ cup chopped onion	½ cup chopped carrot
1-teaspoon salt	½ cup potato cubes
1-teaspoon pepper	1 tablespoon chopped celery
3 cloves	2 cups water

- Heat up the Instant Pot for 30 seconds.
- Place chopped oxtail in the Instant Pot then sprinkle chopped onion, salt, pepper, cloves, and nutmeg over the oxtail.
- Pour water into the pot then stir well.
- Place a trivet over the oxtail then place chopped carrot and potato cubes in the trivet.
- Cover the Instant Pot with the lid then lock it properly.
- Select "Manual" setting then cook the oxtail on high for 30 minutes.
- Once it is done, naturally release the Instant Pot then open the lid.
- Transfer the Oxtail Soup to a serving bowl then sprinkle chopped celery on top.
- Serve and enjoy.

Beef Tomato Soup

20 minutes, Serves: 4, Calories 327; Fat 24.7 g; Carbohydrates 15.2 g; Sugar 9 g; Protein 14.7 g; Cholesterol 33 mg

1 1/2 cups ground beef, cooked	1 tbsp coconut oil
1/4 cup fresh basil, chopped	1 cup coconut milk
1 cup chicken broth	30 oz tomatoes, diced
3 Tsp garlic, minced	1 Tsp salt
1 cup onion, diced	

- Add coconut milk and tomatoes in a blender and blend until smooth.
- Add oil in instant pot and select sauté.
- Add garlic and onion and sauté for 2 minutes.
- Add remaining ingredients and stir well.
- Seal pot with lid and cook on manual high pressure for 4 minutes.
- Allow releasing pressure naturally then open the lid.
- Stir well and serve.

Chipotle Mexican Beef Stew

Serves: 5 / Preparation time: 10 minutes / Cooking time: 35 minutes, Per Serving: Calories: 530; Total Fat: 26.1g; Saturated Fat: 9.5g; Protein: 61.6g; Carbs: 8.6g; Fiber: 1.9g; Sugar: 4.4g;

2 lbs stew meat, thawed	1 tsp dried oregano
15 oz tomatoes, roasted on the fire	1 tsp smoked paprika
6 oz green chilies, diced	2 tsp cumin
1 cup bone broth	1 medium onion, diced
1/2 tsp chipotle powder	2 tsp olive oil
1/2 tsp white pepper	2 tsp salt

- Coat the meat with all spices in a bowl.
- Add olive oil into the instant pot and select sauté.
- Once the oil is hot then add onion and sauté 2-3 minutes.

- Add the seasoned meat in the pot to sear the meat for 2-3 minutes.
- Pour broth, green chilies, and tomatoes.
- Seal pot with lid and cook on manual high pressure for 30 minutes.
- Allow releasing pressure naturally then open the lid.
- Serve and enjoy.

Sweet Beef Curry

Total Time: 8 hours 15 minutes; Serves: 6; Calories 333, Fat 10.3 g, Carbohydrates 23 g, Sugar 15.7 g, Protein 37.4 g, Cholesterol 0 mg

- 2.2 lbs stew beef
- 1 tbsp raisins
- 1 tbsp relish
- 1 tbsp tomato sauce
- 2 carrots, peeled and chopped
- 1 onion, chopped
- 2 celery stalks, chopped
- 2 apples, chopped
- 1 tbsp Worcestershire sauce
- 1/2 cup water
- 1 tbsp golden syrup
- 2 tbsp brown sugar
- 1 tbsp curry powder
- 2 tsp salt

- Use the "Slow Cooker" setting on your Instant Pot.
- Add all ingredients into the Instant Pot and mix well.
- Cover and cook on low for 8 hours.
- Serve and enjoy.

Spicy Beef Stew

50 minutes, Serves: 4, Calories 481; Fat 14.3 g; Carbohydrates 38.2 g; Sugar 6.4 g; Protein 49.1 g; Cholesterol 101 mg

- 1 lb beef stew meat, cut into cubes
- 2 tbsp hot sauce
- 2 cups bone broth
- 1 Tsp garlic powder
- 2 cups kale, chopped
- 2 celery stalks, chopped
- 4 carrots, chopped
- 3 medium potatoes, chopped
- 1 onion, diced
- 2 tbsp extra virgin olive oil
- 1/2 Tsp black pepper
- 1/2 Tsp salt

- Add oil in instant pot and select sauté.
- Add meat and cook until browned.
- Add remaining ingredients and stir well.
- Seal pot with lid and select meat/stew setting.
- Allow releasing pressure naturally then open the lid.
- Stir well and serve.

Chipotle Barbacoa

1 hour 10 minutes, Serves: 8, Calories 399; Fat 14.4 g; Carbohydrates 7.5 g; Sugar 2.5 g; Protein 57.1 g; Cholesterol 172 mg

- 3 lbs chuck roast, cut into chunks
- 1/2 cup water
- 1 tbsp cumin
- 3 tbsp coconut vinegar
- 3 fresh lime juice
- 3 dried chipotle peppers
- 1 Tsp pepper
- 1 tbsp oregano
- 4 oz green chilies
- 5 garlic cloves
- 1 large onion, sliced
- 1 Tsp salt

- Add all ingredients into the instant pot and stir well.
- Seal pot with lid and select manual and set timer for 60 minutes.

- Allow releasing pressure naturally then open the lid.
- Shred the meat using a fork and stir well.
- Serve and enjoy.

Smoky Beef Brisket

Serves: 8 / Preparation time: 15 minutes / Cooking time: 60 minutes, Per Serving: Calories: 410; Total Fat: 22.5g; Saturated Fat: 9.1g; Protein: 46.8g; Carbs: 1.2g; Fiber: 0.6g; Sugar: 0.1g;

4 lbs grass-fed beef
1 tsp oregano, dried
1 tsp ginger, ground
1 tsp pepper
1 tsp paprika
2 tsp cumin, ground

1 tsp liquid smoke
1 cup beef stock
1/4 tsp chipotle chili powder
2 tsp chili powder
2 tsp salt

- Mix together all spices in a small bowl and sprinkle over the meat and rub well.
- Add 1 tsp olive oil into the instant pot and set the pot on sauté mode.
- When the oil is hot then add a piece of brisket to the pot.
- Sear beef until brown and transfer the brisket piece to the plate.
- Pour beef stock and liquid smoke over the meat.
- Seal pot with lid and select manual and set timer for 60 minutes.
- Allow releasing pressure naturally then open the lid.
- Serve and enjoy.

Meatballs with sauce

45 minutes, Serves: 6, Calories 248; Fat 7.4 g; Carbohydrates 23.3 g; Sugar 14.8 g; Protein 38.1 g Cholesterol 101 mg

For meatballs:
1 1/2 lbs ground beef
2 Tsp adobo spiced
1/4 Tsp black pepper
1/2 Tsp salt
For sauce:
1 cup tomato sauce
1/2 Tsp red pepper flakes

1/4 Tsp pepper
1 Tsp garlic powder
1 Tsp salt
4 garlic cloves, peeled
1 medium onion, chopped
10 mini bell peppers, sliced
4 tomatoes, diced

- Add all meatball ingredients into the bowl and mix well.
- Make small meatballs from mixture and place in instant pot.
- Select sauté mode and cook meatballs until browned.
- Remove meatballs from pot and place on a dish.
- Add all sauce ingredients to the pot and stir well.
- Top with meatballs and seal pot with lid and select stew/meat setting, it takes 35 minutes.
- Stir well and serve.

Mexican Meatloaf

45 minutes, Serves: 8, Calories 326; Fat 7.8 g; Carbohydrates 24.4 g; Sugar 1.9 g; Protein 36 g; Cholesterol 122 mg

1 egg
2 lbs ground beef
1 1/4 cup arrowroot powder
1 onion, diced

1 Tsp black pepper
1 Tsp onion powder
1 Tsp paprika
1 Tsp chili powder

1 Tsp garlic powder
1 Tsp cumin

1 cup salsa
1 Tsp sea salt

- Take one loaf pan which fits into your instant pot and sprays with cooking spray.
- In a bowl, combine together all ingredients and pour into the prepared loaf pan.
- Pour 1 cup water into the instant pot then place a trivet in the pot.
- Place loaf pan on a trivet.
- Seal pot with lid and select meat/stew setting and set timer for 35 minutes.
- Release pressure using quick release method than open the lid carefully.
- Cut meatloaf into slices and serve.

Beanless Beef Chili

Serves: 5 / Preparation time: 10 minutes / Cooking time: 20 minutes, Per Serving: Calories: 355; Total Fat: 10.2g; Saturated Fat: 3.4g; Protein: 45g; Carbs: 21.7g; Fiber: 4.6g; Sugar: 9.2g;

1 1/2 lbs ground beef
2 garlic cloves, chopped
1 tsp cumin, ground
2 tsp chili powder
2 cup zucchini, cut into half moons
1 cup bell peppers, diced
1 1/2 cup carrots, peeled and diced

1/2 cup chopped celery
1 large onion, diced
1 tsp oregano
15 oz tomato puree
15 oz tomatoes with green chilies
1 tsp olive oil
1 tsp salt

- Select sauté mode of the instant pot.
- Add beef and cook until beef is brown. Add garlic and sauté for a minute.
- Drain the excess fat and set aside.
- Add olive oil, carrots, onion, peppers, celery and seasoning to the pot and sauté until veggies softened.
- Add zucchini, tomatoes, tomato puree and beef. Stir well.
- Seal pot with lid and cook on manual high pressure for 20 minutes.
- Release pressure using quick release method than open the lid carefully.
- Add cilantro and chili. Serve and enjoy.

Simple Corned Beef

Serves: 8 / Preparation time: 5 minutes / Cooking time: 90 minutes, Per Serving: Calories: 296; Total Fat: 21.3g; Saturated Fat: 9.1g; Protein: 23g; Carbs: 1.7g; Fiber: 0.3g; Sugar: 0.6g;

3 lbs corned beef brisket
1 onion, quartered
3 garlic cloves, peeled

2 bay leaves
Water

- Add beef into the instant pot with onion, bay leaves, and garlic.
- Add water to cover beef with enough water.
- Seal pot with lid and select manual high for 90 minutes.
- Allow releasing pressure naturally then open the lid.
- Serve and enjoy

Corned Beef with Cabbage

1 hour 50 minutes, Serves: 6, Calories 493; Fat 23.9 g; Carbohydrates 39.3 g; Sugar 10.6 g; Protein 29.5 g; Cholesterol 118 mg

1 head green cabbage, cut into wedges
3 cups baby carrots

2 lbs potatoes, quartered

2 1/2 lbs corned beef brisket, with spice packet
4 cups water
4 garlic cloves

- Place rack in instant pot and pour 4 cups water in a pot.
- Place corned beef brisket into the instant pot on the rack and sprinkle with spice packet.
- Seal pot with lid and cook on manual high pressure for 90 minutes.
- Release pressure using quick release method than open lid carefully.
- Remove brisket from pot and place on a serving dish.
- Add remaining ingredients into the pot.
- Again seal pot and cook on high pressure for 5 minutes.
- Release pressure using quick release method than open the lid carefully.
- Serve and enjoy.

Beef Potato Gratin

Total Time: 4 hours 15 minutes; Serves: 2; Calories 806; Fat 35.8 g; Carbohydrates 58 g; Sugar 5.8 g; Protein 62.3 g; Cholesterol 190 mg

1/2 lb ground beef
1/4 cup beef broth
1 1/2 cups shredded cheese
1/2 tsp parsley
1/4 tsp garlic powder

1/2 tsp paprika
1/2 cup onion, sliced
1 1/2 lbs potatoes, sliced 1/4" thick
1/8 tsp black pepper
1/2 tsp salt

- Use the "Slow Cooker" setting on your Instant Pot.
- Season ground beef with pepper and salt.
- Brown ground beef into the pan over medium heat.
- In a small bowl, combine together parsley, garlic powder, paprika, pepper, and salt.
- Add half sliced potatoes into the slow cooker.
- Sprinkle half sliced onion, half of meat, half of seasoning, and half of the cheese. Repeat the same layers.
- Drizzle with the broth over the layers.
- Cover and cook on low for 4 hours.
- Serve and enjoy.

Chapter 3: Poultry

Tasty Cheeseburger Soup

Total Time: 5 hours 10 minutes; Serves: 2; Calories 775; Fat 44.1 g; Carbohydrates 12.3 g; Sugar 5.3 g; Protein 84 g; Cholesterol 251 mg

- 4 oz cheddar cheese, shredded
- 1 tbsp flour
- 1 cup water
- 1/2 cup milk
- 10 oz can chicken broth
- 1 celery ribs, chopped
- 1/4 cup green bell pepper, chopped
- 1/2 cup onion, chopped
- 1/2 lb ground turkey

- Use the "Slow Cooker" setting on your Instant Pot.
- Brown ground turkey into the pan.
- Transfer turkey to the slow cooker.
- Add remaining ingredients except for cheese into the slow cooker and stir well.
- Cover and cook on low for 4 hours.
- Add cheese and stir well and cook for another 1 hour.
- Serve and enjoy.

Chicken Pot Pie

Total Time: 4 hours 40 minutes; Serves: 2; Calories 338; Fat 11.3 g; Carbohydrates 10.5 g; Sugar 3.1 g; Protein 45.5 g; Cholesterol 126 mg

- 10 oz chicken thighs, boneless and skinless
- 1/3 cup celery, sliced
- 2/3 cup frozen mixed vegetables
- 1 cup chicken broth
- 1/4 tsp dried thyme
- 1/4 cup onion, chopped
- 1/4 tsp poultry seasoning
- 1/8 tsp pepper

- Use the "Slow Cooker" setting on your Instant Pot.
- Add all ingredients except frozen vegetables into the slow cooker and mix well.
- Cover and cook on low for 4 hours.
- Add frozen vegetables and cook on high for another 30 minutes.
- Serve and enjoy.

Spicy Chicken Curry

Total Time: 6 hours 20 minutes; Serves: 4; Calories 387, Fat 14.8 g, Carbohydrates 17.3 g, Sugar 6 g, Protein 44.9 g, Cholesterol 130 mg

- 4 chicken thighs, boneless and cut into chunks
- 3 tbsp flour
- 2 tsp ground coriander
- 2 tsp garam masala
- 2 tsp turmeric
- 2 tsp ground cumin
- 1 tsp ginger, grated
- 1/2 lemon juice
- 4 garlic cloves, crushed
- 2 onion, chopped
- 2 green chilies, chopped
- 14 oz can tomatoes, chopped
- 1 tbsp vegetable oil

- Use the "Slow Cooker" setting on your Instant Pot.
- Add ginger, chilies, garlic, and onion into the blender and blend until smooth.
- Heat oil in the pan over medium heat.
- Add blended puree into the pan and sauté for 3 minutes.
- Add spices and sauté for 2-3 minutes.
- Add flour and tomatoes into the pan and stir well.
- Refill tomato can halfway with water and adds in the pan. Stir well.
- Add chicken into the Instant Pot and season with pepper and salt.
- Pour pan mixture over the chicken with lemon juice.
- Cover and cook on low for 6 hours.

- Serve and enjoy.

Chicken Vindaloo

Serves: 4, Preparation time: 15 minutes, Cooking time: 15 minutes, Per Serving: Calories: 218; Total Fat: 13g; Saturated Fat: 3g; Protein: 15g; Carbs: 4g; Fiber: 2g; Sugar: 0g

1 teaspoon ground ginger	1 onion, finely diced
1 teaspoon ground coriander	4 cloves garlic, peeled and minced
1 teaspoon paprika	1 tablespoon olive oil
1 teaspoon cumin	½ cup water
½ teaspoon turmeric	1 tablespoon red wine vinegar
½ teaspoon cinnamon	Salt and freshly ground black pepper, to taste
½ teaspoon cayenne pepper	
½ teaspoon cardamom	1 pound boneless skinless chicken thighs, cut into large chunks
1/8 teaspoon ground cloves	

- In a small bowl, combine ginger, coriander, paprika, cumin, turmeric, cinnamon, cayenne pepper, cardamom and cloves and set aside.
- In Instant Pot on sauté setting, cook onion and garlic in oil until softened, about 5 minutes. Add spice mixture to pot and cook for about 1 minute, stirring constantly.
- Add water and vinegar to pot and mix well. Thoroughly scrape bottom of pot to loosen any spices or browned bits.
- Add chicken to pot and stir to coat. Secure pot lid, close pressure valve and cook at high pressure until done, about 5 minutes. When cooking time ends, allow pressure to release naturally.
- If desired, remove chicken and boil sauce down on sauté setting to reduce to desired consistency. Serve and enjoy!

Cinnamon Chicken Soup

Serves: 2 / Preparation time: 3 minutes / Cooking time: 15 minutes, Per Serving: Calories: 290; Total Fat: 14.5g; Saturated Fat: 2.3g; Protein: 16.4g; Carbs: 23.4g; Fiber: 2.5g; Sugar: 6.4g

1 lb. chopped chicken	1-teaspoon cinnamon
¼ cup chopped onion	1-teaspoon coriander
1-teaspoon ginger	3 cups low sodium chicken broth
2 teaspoons minced garlic	1-tablespoon fish sauce
½ cup chopped cilantro	¾ teaspoon salt
1-tablespoon sugar	1-tablespoon olive oil

- Open the Instant Pot then select the "Sauté" menu.
- Pour olive oil into the pot then stir in chopped onion and minced garlic. Sauté until wilted and aromatic.
- Next, add chopped chicken to the pot then season with ginger, cilantro, sugar, cinnamon, coriander, fish sauce, and salt.
- Pour chicken broth over the chicken then cover the Instant Pot with the lid and make sure that it is completely locked.
- Press "Cancel" button then choose "Manual" menu and cook on high for 15 minutes.
- Once it is done, naturally release the Instant Pot then open the lid.
- Transfer the chicken soup to a serving dish then serve.
- Enjoy.

Turkey with Sauerkraut

Serves: 8 / Preparation time: 10 minutes / Cooking time: 25 minutes, Per Serving: Calories: 133; Total Fat: 5.1g; Saturated Fat: 0g; Protein: 12.1g; Carbs: 8.3g; Fiber: 2.2g; Sugar: 4.2g;

4 lbs turkey wings	1 tsp arrowroot powder
2 tsp water	1 cup apple cider vinegar

1 tsp dried thyme
1/2 tbsp parsley
1 tsp ground cinnamon
1 1/2 cup frozen cranberries

3 garlic cloves, peeled and minced
1/4 cup raisins
2 cups sauerkraut, drained
1 tsp sea salt

- Add sauerkraut, garlic, and raisins into the instant pot.
- Place turkey over the sauerkraut.
- Sprinkle 1 cup cranberries over the turkey.
- In a bowl, combine together cinnamon, thyme, parsley, apple cider, and sea salt and pour into the pot.
- Seal pot with lid and select poultry setting for 25 minutes.
- Allow releasing pressure naturally then open the lid.
- Preheat the broiler.
- Place turkey in an ovenproof dish and broil for 5 minutes or until lightly brown.
- Add remaining cranberries into the instant pot and set the pot to the sauté mode.
- Mix together water and arrowroot powder and pour into the instant pot and cook until thickened.
- Serve turkey with cranberry and sauerkraut sauce.

Savory Turkey Stew

Serves: 4 / Preparation time: 10 minutes / Cooking time: 30 minutes, Per Serving: Calories: 460; Total Fat: 17.1g; Saturated Fat: 3.9g; Protein: 38.4g; Carbs: 40.2g; Fiber: 5.4g; Sugar: 17.4g;

1 lb ground turkey breast
2 green plantains, peeled and diced
1/4 tsp dried sage
2 tsp dried parsley
2 tsp fresh rosemary, minced
1 tbsp dried thyme
3 cups homemade beef broth

1 bay leaf
2 celery ribs, diced
2 large parsnips, peeled and diced
1 large onion, diced
2 tbsp olive oil
1 tsp sea salt

- Add olive oil into the instant pot and select sauté.
- Add onion, celery, parsnips, and bay leaf into the pot and sauté for 10 minutes.
- Discard bay leaf from pot. Transfer pot content into the blender with broth and blend until smooth. Set aside.
- Add turkey, sage, parsley, rosemary, thyme, and salt into the pot and cook until meat is no longer pink.
- Add plantains and cook for 3 minutes.
- Pour blended mixture into the pot and stir well.
- Bring to boil, uncover for 15 minutes or until stew is creamy.
- Stir well and serve.

Super easy Cashew Chicken

Total Time: 4 hours 10 minutes; Serves: 2; Calories 770; Fat 39 g; Carbohydrates 59.5 g; Sugar 26.4 g; Protein 47.5 g; Cholesterol 87 mg

1/2 lb chicken, boneless and skinless, cut into pieces
1 cup broccoli slaw
1 cup cashews
1 tsp ground ginger
2 garlic cloves, minced
2 tbsp brown sugar

2 tbsp sweet chili sauce
4 tbsp ketchup
2 tbsp rice wine vinegar
1/4 cup soy sauce
1/2 tbsp olive oil
2 tbsp cornstarch
1/2 tsp black pepper

- Use the "Slow Cooker" setting on your Instant Pot.
- Add chicken, cornstarch, and pepper into the ziplock bag and shake well to coat.

- Heat oil in the pan over medium heat.
- Add chicken to the pan and cook until browned.
- Transfer chicken to the slow cooker.
- In a small bowl, combine together soy sauce, ginger, garlic, brown sugar, sweet chili sauce, ketchup, and vinegar.
- Pour bowl mixture over the chicken.
- Cover and cook on low for 4 hours.
- After 3 hours add broccoli slaw and cashews and stir well to combine. Cover again and cook the remainder of the time.
- Serve over rice and enjoy.

Sweet Chicken Wings with Black Pepper

Serves: 2 / Preparation time: 3 minutes / Cooking time: 15 minutes, Per Serving: Calories: 65; Total Fat: 1.6g; Saturated Fat: 0.4g; Protein: 2.6g; Carbs: 10.2g; Fiber: 0.7g; Sugar: 7g

½ lb. chicken wings
¼ teaspoon salt
1-teaspoon black pepper
4 tablespoons low sodium soy sauce
2 tablespoons sugar
2 tablespoons apple cider vinegar
1 bay leaf
½ cup chopped onion

- Place chicken wings in the Instant Pot then sprinkle salt, black pepper, sugar, and chopped onion over the chicken.
- Drizzle soy sauce and apple cider vinegar then add a bay leaf to the pot.
- Cover the Instant Pot with the lid then lock it properly.
- Select "Manual" setting in the Instant Pot then select "High" menu and set the time for 15 minutes.
- Once it is done, naturally release the Instant Pot then open the lid.
- Transfer the cooked chicken to a serving dish then serve.
- Enjoy.

Lemon Chicken

Serves: 4 / Preparation time: 20 minutes / Cooking time: 10 minutes, Per Serving: Calories: 256; Total Fat: 13g; Saturated Fat: 8g; Protein: 25g; Carbs: 8g; Fiber: 0g; Sugar: 0g

2 large boneless skinless chicken breasts, cut into bite-size pieces
2 tablespoons coconut oil
4 cloves garlic, peeled and minced
1 cup chicken stock
2 lemons, zested and juiced
2 tablespoons soy sauce
Salt and freshly ground black pepper, to taste
1 tablespoon arrowroot flour
1 tablespoon water

- In Instant Pot on sauté setting, cook chicken and garlic in coconut oil until lightly browned.
- Add chicken stock, lemon zest, lemon juice and soy sauce to pot and season to taste with salt and pepper.
- Secure pot lid, close pressure valve and cook on poultry setting until done, about 7 minutes. When cooking time ends, allow pressure to release naturally.
- Whisk together the arrowroot flour and water and stir into chicken mixture to thicken. Serve and enjoy!

Classic Chicken Adobo

Total Time: 6 hours 10 minutes; Serves: 2; Calories 506; Fat 18.2 g; Carbohydrates 12.7 g; Sugar 7.4 g; Protein 68.3 g; Cholesterol 202 mg

1 lb chicken thighs
1/4 cup apple cider vinegar
4 tbsp soy sauce
1/4 cup chicken stock
1 bay leaf
1/4 tsp cayenne pepper
1/4 tsp ground black pepper
1 1/2 tbsp brown sugar
3 garlic cloves, minced
1 shallot, minced
1/2 tsp olive oil

- Use the "Slow Cooker" setting on your Instant Pot.
- Add all ingredients to the slow cooker and mix well.
- Cover and cook on low for 6 hours.
- Serve and enjoy.

Lemon Garlic Chicken Breasts

Total Time: 4 hours 10 minutes; Serves: 2; Calories 316; Fat 11.6 g; Carbohydrates 1.1 g; Sugar 0.3 g; Protein 48.4 g; Cholesterol 160 mg

1 lb chicken breast, skinless, boneless, and halves
1/2 tbsp parsley, minced
1/2 tsp chicken bouillon granules
1 garlic clove, minced
1 1/2 tbsp lemon juice
2 tbsp water
1 tbsp butter
1/2 tsp dried oregano
1/8 tsp black pepper
1/4 tsp salt

- Use the "Slow Cooker" setting on your Instant Pot.
- In a small bowl, combine together garlic, oregano, pepper, and salt.
- Rub bowl mixture over the chicken.
- Melt butter in the large pan. Brown the chicken into the pan.
- Transfer chicken to the slow cooker.
- Pour water, bouillon granules, and lemon juice in the same pan. Bring to boil over high heat.
- Pour boiled pan mixture over chicken.
- Cover and cook on low for 4 hours.
- Garnish with parsley and serve.

Tasty Tso's Chicken

Serves: 4 / Preparation time: 10 minutes / Cooking time: 10 minutes, Per Serving: Calories: 363; Total Fat: 14.4g; Saturated Fat: 1.3g; Protein: 37.9g; Carbs: 17.9g; Fiber: 1.3g; Sugar: 5.8g;

1 1/2 lbs chicken breast, cut into 2-inch pieces
2 tsp sesame seeds
1/2 cup water
3 tsp red hot chili, chopped
2 tsp ginger, minced
2 garlic cloves, crushed
1/4 cup green onion, chopped
1/4 cup coconut sugar
1 tbsp almond butter
1 tbsp honey
2 tbsp tomato paste
1/2 cup coconut aminos
2 tbsp olive oil
1 tbsp arrowroot powder

- Coat chicken breast with arrowroot powder.
- Set pot on sauté mode, add olive oil, garlic, and place chicken into the pot.
- Sauté until chicken pieces lightly brown on each side.
- In a bowl, mix together coconut aminos, tomato paste, honey, almond butter, sugar, ginger, chili flakes, and water. Mix well and pour over chicken.
- Seal pot with lid and select manual high for 8 minutes.
- Release pressure using quick release method than open the lid.
- Sprinkle sesame seeds over the chicken.
- Serve and enjoy.

Simple BBQ Chicken

Total Time: 4 hours 10 minutes; Serves: 2; Calories 448; Fat 6 g; Carbohydrates 45.7 g; Sugar 35 g; Protein 48.2 g; Cholesterol 145 mg

1 lb chicken breast
1/2 tsp garlic powder
2 tbsp brown sugar

2 tbsp apple cider vinegar
1/2 bottle BBQ sauce

- Use the "Slow Cooker" setting on your Instant Pot.
- Add all ingredients to the slow cooker and mix well.
- Cover and cook on low for 4 hours.
- Serve and enjoy.

Chicken Garlic Rosemary

Serves: 2 / Preparation time: 5 minutes / Cooking time: 10 minutes, Per Serving: Calories: 175; Total Fat: 8g; Saturated Fat: 1.8g; Protein: 17.9g; Carbs: 7.9g; Fiber: 1.9g; Sugar: 1.4g

¾ lb. chopped boneless chicken
½ cup chopped onion
2 tablespoons minced garlic
1-cup low sodium chicken broth
1 ½ teaspoons olive oil
1 bay leaf

1 tablespoon chopped rosemary
¼ teaspoon thyme
½ teaspoon salt
½ teaspoon pepper
2 tablespoons chopped celery

- Cut the chicken into cubes then set aside.
- Turn on the Instant Pot then select the "Sauté" menu.
- Put olive oil, chopped onion and minced garlic into the pot then sauté until soft and lightly golden.
- Press the "Cancel" button then add chicken cubes to the pot.
- Season with salt, pepper, bay leaf, chopped rosemary, and thyme then cover the Instant Pot with the lid. Make sure to lock it properly.
- Select "Manual" setting then cook on high for 10 minutes.
- Once the chicken is done, turn the Instant Pot then naturally release it.
- Open the lid then transfer the cooked chicken along with the gravy to a serving dish.
- Sprinkle chopped celery over the chicken then serve.
- Enjoy.

Spicy Cauliflower Chicken

Total Time: 6 hours 15 minutes; Serves: 4; Calories 391, Fat 17.3 g, Carbohydrates 26.7 g, Sugar 6.7 g, Protein 31.1 g, Cholesterol 96 mg

1 1/2 lbs chicken thighs, skinless, boneless and cut into halves
1 small cauliflower head, cut into florets
1/4 cup raisins
1 onion, chopped

1 tbsp curry powder
2 tbsp ginger, grated
2 tbsp tomato paste
28 oz can tomatoes, diced
1/2 tsp kosher salt

- Use the "Slow Cooker" setting on your Instant Pot.
- Add all ingredients into the Instant Pot and stir well.
- Cover and cook on low for 6 hours.
- Serve and enjoy.

Ranch Chicken Wings

Serves: 6 / Preparation time: 10 minutes / Cooking time: 15 minutes, Per Serving: Calories: 475; Total Fat: 21.5g; Saturated Fat: 8.6g; Protein: 65.8g; Carbs: 0.7g; Fiber: 0.1g; Sugar: 0.5g;

3 lbs chicken wings
2 tbsp coconut oil, melted
1/2 cup water
1 cup hot sauce
1 packet ranch seasoning

- Add chicken wings into the instant pot.
- In a bowl, combine together hot sauce, coconut oil, and ranch seasoning.
- Pour water and bowl mixture over chicken wings.
- Seal pot with lid and select manual high pressure for 12 minutes.
- Release pressure using quick release method than open the lid.
- Place chicken wings on a baking tray and broil for 2 minutes until lightly brown.
- Serve and enjoy.

Turkey Vaca Frita

Serves: 4 / Preparation time: 10 minutes / Cooking time: 35 minutes, Per Serving: Calories: 576; Total Fat: 10.1g; Saturated Fat: 1.9g; Protein: 84.4g; Carbs: 34.8g; Fiber: 6.1g; Sugar: 21.8g;

4 lbs turkey breasts
4 garlic cloves, minced
3 large onions, peeled and sliced
3 lemons
2 tsp olive oil
1 cup cilantro, minced
1 cup bone broth

- Add turkey breasts and broth into the pot and select poultry setting.
- When finish cooking then releases pressure using quick release method than open the lid.
- Transfer turkey breast from the pot and place it into a bowl.
- Using fork shred the turkey breast.
- Set pot to Sauté mode. Add olive oil into the pot once oil is hot then add onion and garlic sauté until onion softens.
- Add shredded turkey meat and stir for 6-8 minutes.
- Add half of lemon juice and cilantro stir well.
- Toss well and let it sit for 6 minutes and transfer it in to plate.
- Serve and enjoy.

Chicken Curry Tomato with Eggplant

Serves: 2 / Preparation time: 5 minutes / Cooking time: 25 minutes, Per Serving: Calories: 207; Total Fat: 6.8g; Saturated Fat: 1.2g; Protein: 12.3g; Carbs: 28g; Fiber: 14g; Sugar: 10.4g

1 lb. bone in chicken legs
1 ½ teaspoons olive oil
2 teaspoons minced garlic
3 teaspoons sliced shallot
1-teaspoon curry powder
½ teaspoon turmeric
1-teaspoon brown sugar
1-cup coconut milk
1-cup water
2 kaffir lime leaves
¼ cup chopped tomato
1 medium eggplant

- Cut the eggplant into thick slices then set aside. You don't have to peel it.
- Turn the Instant Pot on then select "Sauté" menu.
- Stir in olive oil. Minced garlic, sliced shallot, curry powder, and turmeric then sauté until aromatic. Press the "Cancel" button.
- Add chicken legs to the Instant Pot together with brown sugar and kaffir lime leaves.
- Place a trivet over the chicken then sprinkle chopped tomato and eggplant on the trivet.
- Cover the Instant Pot with the lid then make sure that it is locked properly.

- Select "Manual" setting then cook the chicken on high for 8 minutes.
- Quickly release the Instant Pot then open the lid.
- Press the "Sauté" menu on the Instant Pot then pour coconut milk over the cooked chicken. Stir well.
- Once it is done, turn the Instant Pot off then transfer the Chicken Curry to a serving dish.
- Serve and enjoy.

Mushroom Leek Chicken

25 minutes, Serves: 6, Calories 555; Fat 24.3 g; Carbohydrates 36.8 g; Sugar 11.2 g; Protein 49.7 g; Cholesterol 150 mg

6 chicken breasts, skinless and boneless
1/2 cup almond milk, unsweetened
2 tbsp arrowroot
1 1/4 lbs mushrooms, sliced
1/2 cup chicken broth
3 lbs leeks, sliced
4 tbsp clarified butter
1/4 Tsp pepper
1/2 Tsp pink Himalayan salt

- Season chicken with pepper and salt.
- Add butter in a pot and select sauté.
- Add chicken to the pot and brown them on both the sides.
- Remove chicken from pot and place on a plate.
- Add chicken broth, mushrooms, leeks, and chicken to the pot and stir well.
- Seal pot with lid and cook on manual high pressure for 8 minutes.
- Allow releasing pressure naturally for 4 minutes then release pressure using quick release method than open the lid.
- Transfer chicken from pot and place on a plate.
- Stir almond milk and arrowroot to the pot and select sauté. Stir for 2 minutes.
- Serve chicken on top of mushrooms and leeks.

Turkey Soup

Serves: 4, Preparation time: 20 minutes, Cooking time: 10 minutes, Per Serving: Calories: 259; Total Fat: 11g; Saturated Fat: 8g; Protein: 33g; Carbs: 5g; Fiber: 2g; Sugar: 3g

1 onion, diced
1 medium red bell pepper, diced
4 stalks celery, trimmed and diced
2 cloves garlic, peeled and minced
2 tablespoons butter
1 pound boneless skinless turkey thighs
Salt and freshly ground black pepper, to taste
4 cups chicken stock
½ teaspoon dried oregano
½ teaspoon dried basil
½ teaspoon dried thyme
1 large bay leaf
2 small zucchini, diced
1 cup frozen peas
1 tablespoon fresh cilantro, minced

- In Instant Pot on sauté setting, cook onion, bell pepper, celery and garlic in butter until onion is translucent, about 5 minutes. Move onion mixture to sides of pot.
- Season turkey thighs to taste with salt and pepper, add to pot and cook on both sides until lightly browned, 2-3 minutes per side.
- Add chicken stock, oregano, basil, thyme and bay leaf to pot and season soup to taste with salt and pepper.
- Secure pot lid, close pressure valve and cook on high setting for 15 minutes. When cooking time ends, carefully turn venting knob from sealing to venting position for a quick pressure release.
- Remove turkey thighs from pot and dice or shred as desired. Return turkey to pot and add zucchini and peas. Cover pot and let soup stand until zucchini and peas are warmed, about 5 minutes.
- Remove bay leaf from soup. Ladle soup into bowls and garnish with cilantro. Serve and enjoy!

Chicken Wings Cola

Serves: 2 / Preparation time: 5 minutes / Cooking time: 20 minutes, Per Serving: Calories: 228; Total Fat: 8.8g; Saturated Fat: 1.9 g; Protein: 5.6g; Carbs: 32.8g; Fiber: 0.4g; Sugar: 27g

1 lb. chicken wings	1 cup cola flavor beverage
2 teaspoons minced garlic	1-½ tablespoons low sodium soy sauce
2 tablespoons chopped onion	½ tablespoon rice wine
½ teaspoon ginger	½ tablespoon sesame oil

- Heat up the Instant Pot then select "Sauté" menu.
- Stir in sesame oil, minced garlic, and chopped onion then sauté until wilted and aromatic.
- Add chicken wings to the pot then sauté until brown. Press the "Cancel" button.
- Pour cola flavor beverage together with soy sauce and rice wine then stir well.
- Cover the Instant Pot with the lid then make sure that it is locked properly.
- Select "Manual" setting then cook the chicken on high for 20 minutes.
- Once it is done, naturally release the Instant Pot then open the lid.
- Transfer the cooked chicken wings to a serving dish then pour the gravy over the chicken.
- Serve and enjoy.

Bacon and Mushroom with Honey Mustard Chicken

Serves: 6 / Preparation time: 10 minutes / Cooking time: 10 minutes, Per Serving: Calories: 416; Total Fat: 21g; Saturated Fat: 4.2g; Protein: 47g; Carbs: 7.7g; Fiber: 1g; Sugar: 4g;

2 lbs chicken breasts cut into 4 pieces	1 cup bacon, cooked and diced
1/4 cup water	1 1/2 cup mushrooms, sliced
1/2 cup Newman's honey mustard for dressing	1/2 cup white onion, diced

- Pour 1/4 cup of water in the bottom of the instant pot.
- Place the chicken pieces in the pot, add onion, cooked bacon and mushroom in instant pot over chicken.
- Pour honey mustard dressing over chicken and stir well.
- Seal pot with lid and select manual high pressure for 10 minutes.
- Allow releasing pressure naturally then open the lid.
- Serve and enjoy.

Original Salty Chicken

Serves: 2 / Preparation time: 5 minutes / Cooking time: 25 minutes, Per Serving: Calories: 194; Total Fat: 13.1g; Saturated Fat: 3.5g; Protein: 19.1g; Carbs: 1g; Fiber: 0.3g; Sugar: 0g

4 chicken legs	¾ teaspoon salt
1-teaspoon ginger	½ teaspoon pepper

- Rub the chicken with ginger, salt, and pepper then wrap with aluminum foil.
- Pour water into the Instant Pot then place a trivet in it.
- Heat up the Instant Pot then place the wrapped chicken on the trivet.
- Cover the Instant Pot with the lid then make sure that it is locked properly.
- Select "Manual" setting then cook the chicken on high for 25 minutes.
- Once it is done, naturally release the Instant Pot then open the lid.
- Remove the wrapped chicken from the Instant pot then let it cool for a few minutes.
- Unwrap the chicken then transfer to a serving dish.
- Serve and enjoy.

Turkey Sausage with Cabbage

Serves: 4 / Preparation time: 10 minutes / Cooking time: 15 minutes, Per Serving: Calories: 498; Total Fat: 36g; Saturated Fat: 10.9g; Protein: 25.5g; Carbs: 19.5g; Fiber: 6.4g; Sugar: 11.3g;

1 lb turkey sausage, sliced
2 tsp Dijon mustard
2 tsp honey
3 garlic cloves, minced
1 onion, diced

1 medium cabbage head, sliced
1 tbsp olive oil
Pepper
Salt

- Add olive oil into the instant pot and set the instant pot on sauté mode.
- Add onions and cook sausage until lightly browned.
- Add remaining ingredients and cabbage and sauté until cabbage cooks a bit.
- Season with pepper and salt.
- Serve and enjoy

Mediterranean Chicken Wings

10 minutes, Serves: 10, Calories 161; Fat 12.6 g; Carbohydrates 0.6 g Sugar 0.1 g; Protein 11.3 g; Cholesterol 34 mg

12 chicken wings
1 tbsp basil
1 tbsp oregano
3 tbsp tarragon
1 tbsp chicken seasoning

6 tbsp chicken broth
3 tbsp extra virgin olive oil
1 tbsp garlic puree
Pepper
Salt

- Add all ingredients into the large bowl and mix well.
- Pour 1 cup water into the instant pot and place rack in the pot.
- Place marinated chicken on the rack.
- Seal pot with lid and cook on manual high pressure for 10 minutes.
- Release pressure using quick release method than open the lid carefully.
- Serve and enjoy.

Chicken Wings Barbecue

Serves: 2 / Preparation time: 5 minutes / Cooking time: 15 minutes, Per Serving: Calories: 337; Total Fat: 10.9g; Saturated Fat: 2.9g; Protein: 10.1g; Carbs: 48.4g; Fiber: 1.3g; Sugar: 34.8g

2 lbs. chicken wings
½ cup barbecue sauce
1-cup water
½ cup chopped onion

2-½ tablespoons raw honey
¼ teaspoon salt
½ teaspoon pepper

- Place the chicken wings in an Instant Pot.
- Combine barbecue sauce with water, raw honey, salt, and pepper then mix well.
- Drizzle the barbecue mixture over the chicken wings then cover the Instant Pot with the lid. Make sure that you have locked it properly.
- Select "Manual" setting then cook the chicken on high for 10 minutes.
- Quickly release the Instant Pot then open the lid.
- Preheat a pan over medium heat then transfer the chicken barbecue to the pan. Bring to simmer and stir until the barbecue sauce is thickened.
- Remove the barbecue chicken wings from the pan then transfer to a serving dish.
- Serve and enjoy immediately.

Chicken Taco Soup

Total Time: 4 hours 10 minutes; Serves: 2; Calories 404; Fat 4.9 g; Carbohydrates 51.8 g; Sugar 11.1 g; Protein 36.6 g; Cholesterol 64 mg

1 chicken breast, cooked and shredded
1/2 cup frozen peas
1/2 cup frozen corn

7.5 oz can black beans
8 oz salsa
16 oz chicken broth

1 packet taco seasoning
- Use the "Slow Cooker" setting on your Instant Pot.
- Add all ingredients to the slow cooker and stir well.
- Cover and cook on low for 4 hours.
- Using fork shred the chicken and stirs well.
- Serve and enjoy.

Whole Turkey

Serves: 8, Preparation time: 20 minutes, Cooking time: 48 minutes, Per Serving: Calories: 236; Total Fat: 11g; Saturated Fat: 3g; Protein: 32g; Carbs: 0g; Fiber: 0g; Sugar: 0g

1 whole turkey (about 8 pounds), fresh or defrosted, giblets removed
Salt and freshly ground black pepper, to taste
2 medium onions, cut into wedges
4 stalks celery, trimmed and cut into 2-inch pieces
Fresh or dried herbs of choice, if desired
1 cup chicken stock

- Rinse turkey and pat dry inside and out. Season turkey inside and out to taste with salt and pepper.
- Place onions and celery inside turkey cavity and add fresh or dried herbs of choice, if desired. With kitchen twine, tie drumsticks together and secure wings in tucked position.
- Pour chicken stock into Instant Pot, place trivet in pot and set turkey on trivet.
- Secure pot lid, close pressure valve and cook at high pressure until done, about 48 minutes. When cooking time ends, allow pressure to release naturally.
- Remove turkey from pot to a serving platter and let rest for about 10 minutes. Remove kitchen twine from turkey and remove onion and celery from cavity. Carve turkey as desired and baste with cooking juices, if desired. Serve and enjoy!

Chicken Drumstick Soup

Serves: 4 / Preparation time: 10 minutes / Cooking time: 30 minutes, Per Serving: Calories: 378; Total Fat: 11.3g; Saturated Fat: 3g; Protein: 52.8g; Carbs: 13.1g; Fiber: 3.1g; Sugar: 5.1g;

1 1/2 lbs chicken drumsticks
4 cup chicken broth
1/2 tsp ground black pepper
2 bay leaves

1 small onion, diced
1 parsnip, peeled and diced
2 carrots, peeled and diced
2 celery ribs, sliced

- Add all ingredients into the instant pot.
- Seal pot with lid and select soup setting.
- Allow releasing pressure naturally then open the lid.
- Remove chicken drumsticks from the pot.
- Remove the meat from the drumstick, discard bones. Return the meat to the pot with other ingredients.
- Season with pepper and salt.
- Serve and enjoy.

Slow Cooked Turkey Breast

Serves: 4 / Preparation time: 15 minutes / Cooking time: 4 hours, Per Serving: Calories: 479; Total Fat: 11.6g; Saturated Fat: 2g; Protein: 68.7g; Carbs: 22.4g; Fiber: 2.5g; Sugar: 18.7g;

3 1/2 lbs turkey breast
1 cup turkey broth
1 tsp mustard
1 tsp chicken seasoning
2 tsp paprika

3 tsp honey
4 tsp olive oil
1 tsp garlic, minced
Pepper
Salt

- Rub turkey skin with olive oil and season with pepper and salt.
- Place season turkey into the instant pot and select sauté mode.
- Mix together all ingredients except turkey broth in a bowl.
- Sprinkle the bowl mixture over the turkey.
- Seal pot with lid and select slow cook for 4 hours.
- Allow releasing pressure naturally then open the lid.
- Transfer the turkey to chopping board and cut into the slices.
- Serve and enjoy.

Honey Chicken Apple

Serves: 2 / Preparation time: 10 minutes / Cooking time: 10 minutes, Per Serving: Calories: 291; Total Fat: 4.7g; Saturated Fat: 4.7g; Protein: 20.5g; Carbs: 44.9g; Fiber: 5.4g; Sugar: 33.3g

¾ lb. boneless chicken breast	1 ½ teaspoons olive oil
2 fresh apples	½ teaspoon chopped rosemary
2 teaspoons minced garlic	¼ teaspoon salt
½ cup low sodium chicken broth	½ teaspoon pepper
2 tablespoons raw honey	1-tablespoon cornstarch
1-½ teaspoons low sodium soy sauce	¼ cup water

- Cut the apples into cubes then set aside.
- Preheat the Instant Pot then select the "Sauté" menu.
- Pour olive oil into the Instant Pot then stir in minced garlic into the pot. Sauté until aromatic and lightly golden then press the "Cancel" button.
- Cut the chicken breast into cubes then add to the pot.
- Add apples, honey, soy sauce, rosemary, salt, and pepper then pour chicken broth into the pot.
- Cover the Instant Pot with the lid then lock it properly.
- Select "Manual" setting then set the temperature to high and the time to 10 minutes.
- Meanwhile, mix the cornstarch with water then stir well. Set aside.
- Once the chicken is done, turn off the Instant Pot then quick release the Instant Pot.
- Open the lid then take the chicken out from Instant Pot and place on a serving dish.
- Press "Cancel" button then select the "Sauté" menu again.
- Drizzle cornstarch mixture over the gravy then stir for about a minute.
- Turn off the Instant Pot then drizzle thickened gravy over the chicken.
- Serve and enjoy with a bowl of rice.

Curried Chicken Bowls

Serves: 4, Preparation time: 20 minutes, Cooking time: 25 minutes, Per Serving: Calories: 438; Total Fat: 21g; Saturated Fat: 18g; Protein: 36g; Carbs: 19g; Fiber: 9g; Sugar: 10g

1 large head cauliflower (about 3 pounds), cut into large chunks	2 large boneless skinless chicken breasts, cut into bite-size pieces
½ teaspoon each of salt & ground ginger	8 stalks celery, trimmed and diced
1 medium eggplant, peeled and cut into bite-size cubes	1 large onion, sliced
½ cup plain whole-milk yogurt	3 tablespoons curry powder
Salt and ground black pepper, to taste	1 can (14 ounces) coconut milk
2 tablespoons coconut oil	½ cup chicken stock
	1 lime, cut into wedges

- Pour 1 cup of water into Instant Pot. Place cauliflower in steamer basket and set in pot. Secure pot lid, close pressure valve and cook on manual setting for 1 minute. Carefully turn venting knob from sealing to venting position for a quick pressure release.
- Remove cauliflower from steamer basket to a large bowl, sprinkle with salt and mash with a potato masher. Cover cauliflower to keep warm and set aside.

- Sprinkle ginger, salt, and pepper over eggplant, then stir in yogurt and set aside.
- Drain water from Instant Pot and set to sauté. Melt coconut oil and cook chicken, celery and onion for 4 minutes. Sprinkle curry powder over chicken mixture and season with salt and pepper. Stir to coat chicken mixture with spices and sauté for 1 minute.
- Add coconut milk and chicken stock to pot and mix well. Secure pot lid, close pressure valve and cook on poultry setting until done, about 7 minutes. When cooking time ends, carefully turn venting knob from sealing to venting position for a quick pressure release.
- Set Instant Pot to warm, stir eggplant mixture into pot and season with salt and pepper. Cover pot and let stand for 10 minutes, then fluff cauliflower with a fork and spoon into deep bowls. Ladle curry over cauliflower and garnish with lime wedges to serve.

Easy White Chicken Chili

Total Time: 4 hours 10 minutes; Serves: 2; Calories 784; Fat 13 g; Carbohydrates 108.3 g; Sugar 5 g; Protein 61 g; Cholesterol 71 mg

3/4 cup shredded chicken
3 1/2 oz chicken broth
2 oz pepper jack cheese, cubed

1/4 cup salsa
12 oz great northern beans

- Use the "Slow Cooker" setting on your Instant Pot.
- Add all ingredients to the slow cooker and stir well.
- Cover and cook on low for 4 hours.
- Stir well and serve.

Spiced Chicken Cake

Serves: 2 / Preparation time: 5 minutes / Cooking time: 25 minutes, Per Serving: Calories: 358; Total Fat: 20.9g; Saturated Fat: 9.6g; Protein: 36.2g; Carbs: 6.6g; Fiber: 1.4g; Sugar: 2.6g

2 cups chicken cubes
1-cup low sodium chicken broth
3 tablespoons butter
½ cup chopped onion
2 teaspoons chopped celery
¼ teaspoon salt

½ teaspoon pepper
¾ teaspoon thyme
¾ teaspoon sage
1-teaspoon garlic powder
½ teaspoon olive oil
3 organic eggs

- Heat up the instant pot then select the "Sauté" menu.
- Stir in olive oil and chopped onion then sauté until translucent and aromatic.
- Add butter, chopped celery, salt, pepper, thyme, sage, and garlic powder to the Instant Pot then pour chicken broth into the pot. Stir well then press the "Cancel" button.
- Pour the mixture over the chicken cubes then stir to combine.
- After that, crack the eggs then place in a bowl.
- Using a fork whisk the eggs until incorporated then pour the eggs mixture over the chicken. Mix well.
- Line a baking pan with aluminum foil.
- Next, transfer the chicken and the liquid to the pan. Spread evenly.
- Cover the baking pan with aluminum foil then set aside.
- Pour water into the Instant Pot then place a trivet in it.
- Heat up the Instant Pot then place the baking pan on the trivet.
- Cover the Instant Pot with the lid and make sure that you have locked it properly.
- Select "Manual" setting then cook the chicken on high for 25 minutes.
- Once it is done, naturally release the Instant Pot then open the lid.
- Take the baking pan out from the Instant Pot then let it cool.
- Once it is cool, remove the aluminum foil then take the chicken out from the baking pan.
- Cut into thick slices then place on a serving dish.
- Serve and enjoy.

Chicken Quinoa Curry

Total Time: 4 hours 45 minutes; Serves: 6; Calories 185, Fat 3.1 g, Carbohydrates 14.4 g, Sugar 8.2 g, Protein 24.4 g, Cholesterol 59 mg

1 1/2 lbs chicken breast, diced	1 cup chicken broth
1/3 cup quinoa	1 3/4 cups apples, chopped
1/4 tsp paprika	1 1/4 cups celery, chopped
1 tbsp curry powder	3/4 cup onion, chopped
1/4 cup coconut milk	

- Use the "Slow Cooker" setting on your Instant Pot.
- Add all ingredients except quinoa into the Instant Pot and stir well.
- Cover and cook on low for 4 hours.
- Add quinoa and stir well. Cook for another 35 minutes.
- Stir well and serve.

Cafe Rio Chicken

Serves: 15 / Preparation time: 10 minutes / Cooking time: 20 minutes, Per Serving: Calories: 335; Total Fat: 15.7g; Saturated Fat: 3.8g; Protein: 43.9g; Carbs: 1.9g; Fiber: 0.1g; Sugar: 1.4g;

2 1/2 lbs chicken breasts, boneless and skinless	1 tsp cumin
	1 tsp chili powder
2 1/2 lbs chicken thighs, boneless and skinless	1 cup Italian dressing
	1 tsp kosher salt

1 tsp garlic powder

- Add all ingredients into the instant pot.
- Seal pot with lid and cook on manual high pressure for 18 minutes.
- Allow releasing pressure naturally then open the lid.
- Transfer the chicken to a cutting board and shred chicken.
- Return shredded chicken into the pot juices. Stir well.
- Season chicken with pepper and salt.
- Serve and enjoy.

Chicken Mushroom Stew

Serves: 2 / Preparation time: 5 minutes / Cooking time: 15 minutes, Per Serving: Calories: 174; Total Fat: 3.4g; Saturated Fat: 0.6g; Protein: 13.6g; Carbs: 25.6g; Fiber: 5.3g; Sugar: 10.4g

¾ lb. boneless chicken breast	½ teaspoon salt
½ cup chopped mushroom	1-teaspoon pepper
1 teaspoon avocado oil	1-cup tomato puree
¼ cup chopped onion	1-cup low sodium chicken broth
½ cup chopped carrots	1-tablespoon tomato paste
½ cup chopped potatoes	2 tablespoons chopped parsley

1 tablespoon Italian seasoning

- Cut the chicken into cubes then place in a bowl.
- Preheat an Instant Pot for about 30 seconds then choose the "Sauté" menu.
- Put avocado oil, chopped onion, and chicken cubes the sauté until the chicken is brown. Press the "Cancel" button.
- Add the remaining ingredients to the pot then cover and lock it properly.
- Select "Manual" setting then cook the chicken on high for 15 minutes.
- Once it is done, naturally release the Instant Pot then open the lid.
- Transfer the chicken stew to a serving dish then enjoy immediately.

- If you want to have thickened gravy, take all solid parts out from the Instant Pot and place on a serving dish. Leave the gravy in the Instant Pot.
- Combine a tablespoon of cornstarch with 3 tablespoons water then pour the mixture over the gravy.
- Select "Sauté" menu then stir the gravy.
- Drizzle the gravy over the stew the serve.
- Enjoy.

Yellow Chicken Curry

Total Time: 4 hours 15 minutes; Serves: 6; Calories 296, Fat 8.7 g, Carbohydrates 20.5 g, Sugar 5.1 g, Protein 35.9 g, Cholesterol 101 mg

1 1/2 lbs chicken thighs, boneless, skinless and cut into pieces	1 tsp curry powder
1 lb potatoes, diced	2 tsp garlic, minced
1 medium onion, diced	1 tbsp fresh ginger, minced
13.5 oz can coconut milk	1/2 tsp ground coriander seed
2 tbsp brown sugar	1/2 tsp red pepper
1 tsp ground turmeric	1 tsp kosher salt

- Use the "Slow Cooker" setting on your Instant Pot.
- Add all ingredients into the Instant Pot and stir well.
- Cover and cook on low for 4 hours.
- Serve and enjoy.

Turkey Sandwich Meat

Serves: 4 / Preparation time: 10 minutes / Cooking time: 30 minutes, Per Serving: Calories: 392; Total Fat: 20.9g; Saturated Fat: 3.3g; Protein: 40g; Carbs: 10.3g; Fiber: 1.2g; Sugar: 8.2g;

2 lbs turkey breast	1/3 cup olive oil
1/2 cup seasoning of choice	2 garlic cloves, minced
1 cup chicken broth	

- Season the turkey breast with seasoning.
- Set pot on sauté mode and brown the turkey breast on all sides and transfer to plate.
- Place trivet into the pot. Place turkey breast on the trivet.
- Add minced garlic over turkey breast.
- Seal pot with lid Select manual and set timer for 30 minutes.
- Allow releasing pressure naturally then open the lid.
- Cut turkey breast into the slices and serve.

Spicy Sour Chicken Soup

Serves: 2 / Preparation time: 5 minutes / Cooking time: 15 minutes, Per Serving: Calories: 124; Total Fat: 5.6g; Saturated Fat: 1.5g; Protein: 8.7g; Carbs: 8.9g; Fiber: 1.2g; Sugar: 1.9g

½ lb. chicken wings	½ cup chopped green tomatoes
½ lb. chicken thighs	1-inch galangal
2 teaspoons sliced garlic	2 bay leaves
3 teaspoons sliced shallot	3 cups low sodium chicken broth
3 tablespoons red chili flakes	

- Cut the chicken wings and thighs into small chunks then place in the Instant Pot.
- Sprinkle sliced garlic, sliced shallot, red chili flakes, and green tomatoes over the chicken.
- Cover the Instant Pot with the lid then lock it properly.
- Select "Manual" setting then cook the chicken on high for 15 minutes.

- Once it is done, naturally release the Instant Pot then open the lid.
- Transfer the chicken soup to a serving bowl then serve warm.
- Enjoy.

Creamy Chicken Vegetable Soup

Serves: 8 / Preparation time: 10 minutes / Cooking time: 20 minutes, Per Serving: Calories: 384; Total Fat: 18.1g; Saturated Fat: 11.4g; Protein: 27.6g; Carbs: 27g; Fiber: 3.1g; Sugar: 4.8g;

1 1/2 lbs chicken thighs, boneless and skinless
3 garlic cloves, minced
10 oz cremini mushrooms, sliced
4 carrots, diced
3 stalks celery, chopped
1 chopped onion, medium size
1 tsp olive oil

1 1/2 cup coconut cream
1 tsp fresh rosemary, chopped
1 tsp fresh thyme, chopped
6 cup chicken stock
5 tsp cassava flour
Pepper
Salt

- Add olive oil into the instant pot and set the instant pot on sauté mode.
- Add onion, carrot, mushrooms, and celery and sauté for 5-7 minutes.
- Toss the cubed chicken into cassava flour to coat evenly.
- Add chicken stock and chicken with rosemary into the instant pot and stir well.
- Seal pot with lid and cook on manual high pressure for 15 minutes.
- Allow releasing pressure naturally then open the lid.
- Add 1 cup of hot stock to a bowl and mix cassava flour. Pour cassava flour slurry and coconut cream into the pot and stir well and cook until soup is thickened.
- Serve hot and enjoy.

Creamy Chicken Carrots

Total Time: 4 hours 10 minutes; Serves: 2; Calories 339; Fat 9.4 g; Carbohydrates 15.9 g; Sugar 7.4 g; Protein 46 g; Cholesterol 128 mg

2 chicken breast, skinless, boneless and halves
4 oz mushroom, drained and cut into pieces

10 oz cream of mushroom soup
1/2 lb baby carrots, cut in half

- Use the "Slow Cooker" setting on your Instant Pot.
- Add chicken to the slow cooker.
- Top with mushrooms and carrots.
- Pour mushrooms soup over the chicken.
- Cover and cook on low for 4 hours.
- Serve over rice and enjoy.

Chicken Soup

Total Time: 12 hours 15 minutes; Serves: 6; Calories 225, Fat 5.9 g, Carbohydrates 4.3 g, Sugar 1.9 g, Protein 36.4 g, Cholesterol 102 mg

3 carrots, peeled and sliced
1 tsp ginger, crushed
1/2 tsp garlic, crushed
1/4 tsp turmeric
1/2 onion, diced

12 cups water
5 cloves
2 cinnamon sticks
1/4 tsp black peppercorns
2 chicken breasts

1 lb chicken   1 tbsp sea salt
- Use the "Slow Cooker" setting on your Instant Pot.
- Add all ingredients into the Instant Pot.
- Cover and cook on low for 12 hours.
- Remove chicken from Instant Pot and using fork shred the chicken.
- Return shredded chicken to the Instant Pot and stir well.
- Season with pepper and salt.
- Serve and enjoy.

Honey Mustard Chicken

Total Time: 4 hours 10 minutes; Serves: 2; Calories 626; Fat 17.1 g; Carbohydrates 60.5 g; Sugar 40.4 g; Protein 59.3 g; Cholesterol 145 mg

1 lb chicken breast, skinless, boneless and cut into strips
2 tbsp water
2 tbsp cornstarch
2 tbsp soy sauce
1/4 cup orange juice
1/2 cup ground mustard
1/4 cup honey

- Use the "Slow Cooker" setting on your Instant Pot.
- Add chicken to the slow cooker.
- In a small bowl, combine together soy sauce, orange juice, ground mustard, and honey.
- Pour bowl mixture over the chicken.
- Cover and cook on low for 4 hours.
- Mix together water and cornstarch and pour over chicken mixture and stir well.
- Cook chicken for 2-3 minutes until sauce thickens.
- Serve and enjoy.

Rosemary Chicken

Serves: 4, Preparation time: 10 minutes, Cooking time: 35 minutes, Per Serving: Calories: 276; Total Fat: 7g; Saturated Fat: 0g; Protein: 51g; Carbs: 0g; Fiber: 0g; Sugar: 0g

1 whole roasting chicken (about 4 pounds), giblets removed
2 tablespoons peanut oil
Salt and freshly ground black pepper, to taste
2 tablespoons dried rosemary, divided
1 onion, quartered
2 stalks celery, trimmed and cut into 2-inch pieces
1 cup chicken stock

- Rinse chicken and pat dry. Brush oil over outside of chicken and inside body cavity and season to taste with salt and pepper. Crush half of the dried rosemary and sprinkle inside chicken. Place onion and celery inside chicken and tie drumsticks together with kitchen twine.
- Set Instant Pot to sauté setting. Carefully set chicken in pot breast-side down and cook until skin is browned, 3-4 minutes. Carefully turn chicken breast-side up and cook until skin is browned, about 3-4 more minutes.
- Remove chicken from pot, pour stock into pot and set trivet in pot. Place chicken breast-side up on trivet and tuck in wings. Sprinkle remaining crushed rosemary over chicken and season to taste with salt and pepper.
- Secure pot lid, close pressure valve and cook at high pressure until done, about 25 minutes. When cooking time ends, allow pressure to release naturally.
- Remove chicken from pot to a serving platter and let rest for about 5 minutes. Remove kitchen twine from drumsticks and remove onion and celery from cavity. Carve chicken as desired and baste with cooking juices, if desired. Serve and enjoy!

Sweet Brown Chicken

Serves: 2, Preparation time: 5 minutes, Cooking time: 10 minutes, Per Serving: Calories: 267; Total Fat: 7.2g; Saturated Fat: 1g; Protein: 4.6g; Carbs: 48.3g; Fiber: 1g; Sugar: 36.8g

2 boneless chicken breasts
3 teaspoons cornstarch
3 teaspoons olive oil
½ cup brown sugar
2 teaspoons minced garlic

1 ½ teaspoons ginger
½ cup low sodium soy sauce
½ cup low sodium chicken broth
1-½ teaspoons garlic powder

- Cut the chicken breast into cubes then place in a zipper-lock plastic bag.
- Add cornstarch to the plastic bag then shake until the chicken cubes are completely coated with cornstarch.
- Open the Instant Pot then select the "Sauté" menu.
- Pour olive oil into the pot then stir in chicken cubes. Sauté until crispy.
- Next, sprinkle brown sugar, minced garlic, ginger, and garlic powder over the chicken.
- Drizzle soy sauce and chicken broth then stir well.
- Cover the Instant Pot with the lid and make sure that it is completely locked.
- Press "Cancel" button then choose "Manual" menu and cook on high for 10 minutes.
- Once it is done, naturally release the Instant Pot then open the lid.
- Transfer the Sweet Brown Chicken to a serving dish then serve.
- Enjoy.

Teriyaki Chicken

Total Time: 4 hours 10 minutes; Serves: 2; Calories 522; Fat 17.3 g; Carbohydrates 26.2 g; Sugar 23.1 g; Protein 62.2 g; Cholesterol 178 mg

2 chicken breasts, skinless and boneless
1/2 tsp sesame oil
2 tbsp soy sauce
2 garlic cloves, minced

1/4 cup brown sugar
1/4 cup teriyaki sauce
1/4 cup chicken broth
1/2 tbsp sesame seeds

- Use the "Slow Cooker" setting on your Instant Pot.
- In a bowl, combine together chicken broth, garlic cloves, sesame oil, soy sauce, brown sugar, and teriyaki sauce.
- Add chicken to the bowl and toss well.
- Pour chicken mixture into the slow cooker.
- Cover and cook on low for 4 hours.
- Using fork shred the chicken.
- Sprinkle sesame seeds over the shredded chicken and serve with rice.

Simple Turkey and Gravy

Serves: 4 / Preparation time: 10 minutes / Cooking time: 35 minutes, Per Serving: Calories: 310; Total Fat: 6.2g; Saturated Fat: 1.1g; Protein: 46.8g; Carbs: 14.7g; Fiber: 2.5g; Sugar: 10.2g;

2 lbs turkey breast
2 tsp olive oil
2 tsp dried sage
1 garlic cloves, smashed and peeled
1 celery rib, diced

1 large carrot, diced
1 medium onion, diced
1 1/2 cup bone broth
1 bay leaf
Black pepper

- Set pot on sauté mode brown the turkey breast.
- Transfer turkey breast to plate, leaving fat in instant pot.
- Add onion, celery, and carrot to the pot sauté until for 5 minutes. Add garlic cook for 30 seconds.
- Add broth and bay leaf and stir well, place turkey into the pot.
- Seal pot with lid and cook on high for 35 minutes.
- Release pressure using quick release method than open the lid.
- Transfer turkey breast to the plate.

- Using an immersion blender, puree the pot content until smooth.
- Cook puree until thickened.
- Cut turkey breasts into the slices and pour hot gravy over them.
- Serve and enjoy.

Tasty Chicken Enchilada Soup

30 minutes , Serves: 6, Calories 268; Fat 9.4 g; Carbohydrates 8.9 g; Sugar 4.4 g; Protein 35.9 g; Cholesterol 101 mg

1 1/2 lbs chicken thighs, skinless and boneless	1/2 cup water
1/2 Tsp ground pepper	2 cup chicken broth
1/2 Tsp smoked paprika	3 garlic cloves, minced
1 Tsp oregano	1 onion, sliced
1 tbsp chili powder	1 bell pepper, sliced
1 tbsp cumin	14 oz can tomatoes, crushed
	1/2 Tsp sea salt

- Add all ingredients into the instant pot and stir well.
- Seal pot with lid and cook on manual high pressure for 20 minutes.
- Allow releasing pressure naturally then open the lid.
- Using fork shred the chicken.
- Stir well and serve.

Tasty Coconut Drumsticks

Serves: 2, Preparation time: 5 minutes, Cooking time: 15 minutes, Per Serving: Calories: 343; Total Fat: 29.7g; Saturated Fat: 22.1g; Protein: 13.6g; Carbs: 9.2g; Fiber: 2.6g; Sugar: 4.2g

4 chicken drumsticks	1 lemongrass
½ teaspoon coconut oil	1-teaspoon ginger
¾ cup coconut milk	3 teaspoons fish sauce
2 teaspoons minced garlic	¼ teaspoon pepper
¼ cup chopped onion	1 tablespoon lemon juice

- Chop the lemongrass then place in a blender.
- Add minced garlic, ginger, fish sauce, pepper, and lemon juice then pour coconut milk into the blender. Blend until smooth and incorporated.
- Preheat the Instant Pot then select the "Sauté" menu.
- Pour coconut oil into the pot then stir in chopped onion. Sauté until aromatic.
- Add chicken drumsticks to the pot then pour coconut mixture over the chicken.
- Cover the Instant Pot with the lid then lock it properly.
- Select "Manual" setting then cook on high for 10 minutes.
- Once it is done, naturally release the Instant Pot then open the lid.
- Transfer the cooked chicken drumsticks to a serving dish then serve.
- Enjoy.

Tasty Leftover Turkey Stew

Serves: 6 / Preparation time: 10 minutes / Cooking time: 35 minutes, Per Serving: Calories: 238; Total Fat: 6.6g; Saturated Fat: 2g; Protein: 36g; Carbs: 7.5g; Fiber: 1.8g; Sugar: 4.3g;

1 1/2 lbs turkey, cooked and diced	2 large carrots, peeled and diced
3 garlic cloves, minced	1 small onion, diced
14 oz tomatoes, diced	1 tsp olive oil
5 cup turkey broth	Pepper
3 celery stalks, diced	Salt

- Add olive oil into the instant pot and select sauté mode.
- Add onion, carrot, and celery and sauté for 4 minutes or until onion softens.
- Add diced tomatoes, turkey broth stirs well. Add minced garlic and thymes.
- Seal pot with lid and select soup setting and cook for 30 minutes.
- Release pressure using quick release method than open the lid.
- Discard the thyme.
- Season with pepper and salt.
- Serve and enjoy.

Salsa Verde Chicken

Total Time: 4 hours 10 minutes; Serves: 2; Calories 454; Fat 17.4 g; Carbohydrates 22.2 g; Sugar 1.8 g; Protein 52.1 g; Cholesterol 151 mg

3/4 lb chicken thighs
1/4 cup chicken stock
1 tbsp cornstarch
1/2 lime juice
1/4 cup fresh cilantro, chopped
1/2 tsp dried oregano
1 small onion, sliced

1 poblano chili, seeded and stemmed
1 lb tomatillos, husk removed
1 tsp olive oil
1 garlic cloves, minced
1/4 tsp ground black pepper
1/2 tsp salt

- Use the "Slow Cooker" setting on your Instant Pot.
- Preheat the broiler.
- Combine together onion, poblano chili, tomatillos, olive oil, and garlic and spread over baking sheet.
- Broil onion mixture in a preheated broiler for 10 minutes.
- Add broil ingredients to the blender with chicken stock, cornstarch, lime juice, oregano, pepper, and salt and blend until smooth.
- Place chicken into the slow cooker the pour blended mixture over the chicken.
- Cover and cook on low for 4 hours.
- Serve and enjoy.

Chicken Potato with Lemon Sauce

Serves: 2, Preparation time: 5 minutes, Cooking time: 15 minutes, Per Serving: Calories: 258; Total Fat: 3.5g; Saturated Fat: 0.5g; Protein: 18.4g; Carbs: 37.9g; Fiber: 6g; Sugar: 3.7g

1 lb. chopped chicken
1 lb. potatoes
2 tablespoons lemon juice
1 teaspoon lemon zest
½ cup low sodium chicken broth

1-½ tablespoons Dijon mustard
1 tablespoon Italian seasoning
½ teaspoon salt
½ teaspoon pepper

- Peel the potatoes then cut into wedges. Set aside.
- Preheat the Instant Pot then select the "Sauté" menu.
- Season the chopped chicken with salt and pepper then place in the Instant Pot.
- Pour chicken broth over the chicken then add potato wedges, Dijon mustard, Italian seasoning, lemon juice, and lemon zest to the pot.
- Cover the Instant Pot with the lid then lock it properly.
- Select "Manual" setting then cook on high and set the time to 15 minutes.
- Once it is done, naturally release the Instant Pot then open the lid.
- Transfer the cooked chicken drumsticks to a serving dish then serve.
- Enjoy.

Chicken Chili Verde

Serves: 6 / Preparation time: 10 minutes / Cooking time: 15 minutes, Per Serving: Calories: 307; Total Fat: 11.4g; Saturated Fat: 3.1g; Protein: 44.8g; Carbs: 3.4g; Fiber: 0.3g; Sugar: 1.2g;

16 oz salsa Verde
2 lbs chicken thighs
1/4 tsp garlic powder
1/2 tsp ground cumin
Black pepper
Salt

- Add chicken, garlic powder, cumin, and salsa Verde into the instant pot.
- Seal pot with lid and select poultry setting and set timer for 15 minutes.
- Allow releasing pressure naturally then open the lid.
- Shred the chicken using a fork.
- Season with black pepper and salt.
- Serve and enjoy.

Shredded Chicken Wraps

Serves: 6, Preparation time: 15 minutes, Cooking time: 5 minutes, Per Serving: Calories: 179; Total Fat: 6g; Saturated Fat: 2g; Protein: 25g; Carbs: 3g; Fiber: 2g; Sugar: 1g

3 boneless, skinless chicken breasts
Salt and freshly ground black pepper, to taste
½ cup chicken broth
½ teaspoon chili powder
½ teaspoon ground cumin
12 large leaves romaine lettuce

- Season chicken breasts to taste with salt and pepper and place in Instant Pot.
- Secure pot lid, close pressure valve and cook on high setting until done, about 5 minutes. When cooking time ends, allow pressure to release naturally.
- Remove chicken breasts to a large bowl and shred with forks. Mix chili powder and cumin into chicken, adding leftover broth from the pot if the chicken mixture is too dry.
- Layer pairs of lettuce leaves together, top with chicken and roll up to serve. Enjoy!

Spicy Buffalo Chicken

25 minutes, Serves: 6, Calories 297; Fat 11.3 g; Carbohydrates 1.6 g; Sugar 0.7 g; Protein 44.3 g; Cholesterol 135 mg

2 lbs chicken breasts
1/2 cup chicken broth
1/2 cup buffalo wing sauce
2/3 cup onion, chopped
1/2 cup celery, diced

- Add all ingredients into the instant pot and stir well.
- Seal pot with lid and cook on manual high pressure for 12 minutes.
- Release pressure using quick release method than open the lid carefully.
- Remove chicken from pot and using fork shred the chicken.
- Return chicken to the instant pot and stir well.
- Serve and enjoy.

Tasty Chicken Kheema

Total Time: 4 hours 20 minutes; Serves: 4; Calories 291, Fat 10.8 g, Carbohydrates 11.8 g, Sugar 4.7 g, Protein 35.8 g, Cholesterol 106 mg

1 lb ground chicken
3/4 cup frozen peas
1 bay leaf
3/4 tsp ground cinnamon
3/4 tsp garam masala
3/4 tsp ground turmeric
3/4 tsp chili powder
3/4 tsp ground cumin

3/4 tsp ground coriander
1 jalapeno, seeded and chopped
4 tbsp cilantro, chopped
3/4 cup can tomato sauce
1 tsp ginger, grated

3 garlic cloves, minced
1 medium onion, chopped
2 tsp butter
1 tsp kosher salt

- Use the "Slow Cooker" setting on your Instant Pot.
- Heat butter in a pan over medium heat.
- Add onion to the pan and sauté for 5 minutes.
- Add ginger and garlic and sauté for 2 minutes.
- Add ground chicken and salt and cook for 5 minutes.
- Transfer chicken mixture to the Instant Pot along with remaining ingredients and stir well.
- Cover and cook on high for 4 hours.
- Serve and enjoy.

Japanese Chicken Teriyaki

Serves: 2 / Preparation time: 10 minutes / Cooking time: 15 minutes, Per Serving: Calories: 295; Total Fat: 8.4g; Saturated Fat: 1g; Protein: 27.3g; Carbs: 20.3g; Fiber: 0.3g; Sugar: 10.4g

1 lb. boneless chicken breast
2 teaspoons minced garlic
1-teaspoon ginger
¾ tablespoon cornstarch
¼ cup water
2 tablespoons low sodium soy sauce

2 tablespoons rice wine
2 tablespoons Japanese Sake
1-½ tablespoons sesame oil
1-tablespoon sugar
¼ teaspoon salt

- Preheat the Instant Pot then select the "Sauté" menu.
- Pour sesame oil into the Instant Pot then stir in minced garlic into the pot. Sauté until lightly golden then press the "Cancel" button.
- Cut the chicken breast into slices then add to the pot.
- Season with salt, ginger, and sugar then cover the Instant Pot with the lid then lock it properly.
- Select "Manual" setting then cook on high and set the time to 15 minutes.
- Once it is done, quick release the Instant Pot then open the lid.
- Drizzle low sodium soy sauce, rice wine, and Japanese sake over the chicken then select "Sauté" menu again. Cook and stir for about 2 minutes.
- Combine cornstarch with water then mix well.
- While the cooked chicken is still hot, stir in the cornstarch mixture then stir vigorously. Turn the Instant Pot off.
- Transfer the cooked chicken to a serving dish then serve.
- Enjoy.

Moroccan Chicken

Serves: 8 / Preparation time: 10 minutes / Cooking time: 30 minutes, Per Serving: Calories: 337; Total Fat: 11.7g; Saturated Fat: 3.1g; Protein: 43.7g; Carbs: 13.4g; Fiber: 2.6g; Sugar: 9g;

8 chicken thighs, boneless and skinless
1 lemon, quartered
1/2 cup pitted green olives
8 dates, chopped
1/2 cup chicken stock
24 oz whole tomatoes
2 large carrots, chopped
1 small yellow onions, diced

3 minced garlic cloves
1 tsp olive oil
1/2 tsp coriander, ground
1/2 tsp paprika, smoked
1/2 tsp cumin, ground
1/4 tsp pepper
1/4 tsp sea salt

- Mix salt, spices, and pepper. Drizzle chicken with olive oil and coat mix spices over chicken thighs.
- Set pot on Sauté mode, once the pot is hot then add chicken thighs to the pot and browned it on both the sides.
- Add garlic, onion, and carrots and mix it well.
- Add tomatoes, dates, green olives and chicken stock. Stir well and add a lemon wedge on top.
- Seal pot with lid and cook on the manual setting for 20 minutes.
- Release pressure using quick release method than open the lid. Discard lemon wedges.
- Set pot to sauté and let the sauce reduce up to 8-10 minutes.
- Serve and enjoy.

Asian Chicken Legs

Total Time: 4 hours 10 minutes; Serves: 2; Calories 641; Fat 21.1 g; Carbohydrates 22.7 g; Sugar 19.1 g; Protein 84.6 g; Cholesterol 252 mg

1 1/4 lbs chicken legs
3/4 tsp fresh ginger, minced
1 garlic clove, minced
1 tbsp tomato paste

1 tbsp rice wine vinegar
1/4 cup soy sauce
1/4 cup brown sugar

- Use the "Slow Cooker" setting on your Instant Pot.
- Add sugar, ginger, garlic, tomato paste, vinegar, and soy sauce into the microwave safe bowl and microwave for 1 minute.
- Place chicken in the slow cooker.
- Pour bowl mixture over the chicken.
- Cover and cook on low for 4 hours.
- Transfer chicken to a baking tray and broil for 5 minutes.
- Serve and enjoy.

Shredded Chicken Pineapple

Serves: 2 / Preparation time: 2 minutes / Cooking time: 6 minutes, Per Serving: Calories: 254; Total Fat: 8.5g; Saturated Fat: 2.3g; Protein: 33.3g; Carbs: 9.3g; Fiber: 0.3g; Sugar: 6.3g

½ lb. boneless chicken breast
½ cup unsweetened pineapple juice
2 teaspoons minced garlic

¼ teaspoon salt
½ teaspoon pepper

- Cut the chicken breast into cubes then place in the Instant Pot.
- Add minced garlic, salt, and pepper then pour pineapple juice.
- Cover the Instant Pot with the lid then lock it properly.
- Select "Manual" setting then cook on high and set the time for 6 minutes.
- Once it is done, naturally release the Instant Pot then open the lid.
- Transfer the cooked chicken to a serving dish then serve.
- Enjoy.

Creamy Coconut Chicken Curry

Total Time: 4 hours 15 minutes; Serves: 4; Calories 579, Fat 17.9 g, Carbohydrates 62.4 g, Sugar 9.5 g, Protein 44.2 g, Cholesterol 101 mg

1 lb chicken breasts, skinless and boneless
2 tbsp lemon juice
1 cup green peas
1/2 tsp cayenne
2 tbsp curry powder

15 oz can tomato sauce
1/2 cup chicken stock
1/2 cup coconut milk
2 medium sweet potatoes, diced
15 oz can chickpeas, drained and rinsed
1 medium onion, sliced

1 tsp salt
- Use the "Slow Cooker" setting on your Instant Pot.
- Add all ingredients except peas into the Instant Pot and mix well.
- Cover and cook on high for 4 hours.
- Add peas and stir well.
- Serve and enjoy.

Chicken Vegetable Soup

Total Time: 8 hours 10 minutes; Serves: 2; Calories 128; Fat 2.8 g; Carbohydrates 8.1 g; Sugar 2.6 g; Protein 17 g; Cholesterol 36 mg

1 chicken breast, skinless, boneless, and cut into cubes
1/8 tsp pepper
1/8 tsp thyme
1/4 tsp oregano
3/8 tsp chicken bouillon cubes
1/2 celery stalk, chopped
1/2 carrots, peeled and diced
1 garlic clove, minced
1/4 onion, diced
1/4 cup white corn
14 oz chicken broth
Salt

- Use the "Slow Cooker" setting on your Instant Pot.
- Add all ingredients to the slow cooker and stir well.
- Cover and cook on low for 6 hours.
- Serve and enjoy.

Cranberry Turkey Wings

Serves: 4 / Preparation time: 10 minutes / Cooking time: 25 minutes, Per Serving: Calories: 399; Total Fat: 30.6g; Saturated Fat: 2.1g; Protein: 19.8g; Carbs: 14.8g; Fiber: 4g; Sugar: 7.7g;

2 lbs turkey wings
1 bunch fresh thyme
1 cup fresh orange juice
1 cup walnuts
1 onion, sliced
1 cup dry cranberries
2 tbsp olive oil
Black pepper
Salt

- Add olive oil into the instant pot and select sauté.
- Season turkey wings with pepper and salt.
- Brown the turkey wings from all the sides.
- Remove turkey wings from the pot and set aside.
- Add onion to the pot and sauté for a minute then place turkey wings on the onion.
- Top turkey wings with thyme, walnuts, and cranberries.
- Pour orange juice over the turkey wings.
- Seal pot with lid and cook on high pressure for 20 minutes.
- Allow releasing pressure naturally then open the lid.
- Serve and enjoy.

Sticky Honey Chicken

Serves: 2 / Preparation time: 5 minutes / Cooking time: 10 minutes, Per Serving: Calories: 347; Total Fat: 11.3g; Saturated Fat: 11.3g; Protein: 12.8g; Carbs: 53.1g; Fiber: 2.1g; Sugar: 36g

1 lb. chicken fillet
4 tablespoons raw honey
4 tablespoons chopped onion
¼ teaspoon salt
½ teaspoon pepper
1 ½ teaspoons olive oil
2 teaspoons minced garlic
4 tablespoons low sodium soy sauce

1-tablespoon cornstarch
1-½ tablespoons low sodium chicken broth
1-tablespoon sesame seeds

- Preheat the Instant Pot then select the "Sauté" menu.
- Pour olive oil into the Instant Pot then stir in chopped onion and minced garlic into the pot. Sauté until lightly golden then press the "Cancel" button.
- Cut the chicken into cubes then drizzle soy sauce on top.
- Combine chicken broth and cornstarch then stir well.
- Pour chicken broth mixture over the chicken then season with salt and pepper.
- Cover the Instant Pot with the lid then lock it properly.
- Select "Manual" setting then cook on high and set the time for 8 minutes.
- Once it is done, quick release the Instant Pot then open the lid.
- Drizzle raw honey over the chicken then select "Sauté" menu again. Cook and stir for about 2 minutes. Turn the Instant Pot off.
- Transfer the cooked chicken to a serving dish then sprinkle sesame seeds on top.
- Serve and enjoy.

Tasty Fajita Soup

Total Time: 4 hours 10 minutes; Serves: 2; Calories 448; Fat 16.1 g; Carbohydrates 18.7 g; Sugar 9 g; Protein 56.9 g; Cholesterol 151 mg

0.75 lb chicken thighs, skinless and boneless
1/2 tsp paprika
1/2 tsp cumin
1/2 tbsp chili powder
1/2 tsp olive oil
2 cups chicken broth
1 lime juice

1 garlic clove
1/2 cup salsa
1/4 jalapeno pepper, sliced
1/2 medium onion, chopped
1 1/2 bell pepper, chopped
1/2 tsp black pepper
1/2 tsp sea salt

- Use the "Slow Cooker" setting on your Instant Pot.
- Add all ingredients to the slow cooker and stir well.
- Cover and cook on low for 4 hours.
- Using fork shred the chicken.
- Stir well and serve.

Shredded Chicken Garlic

Serves: 2 / Preparation time: 5 minutes / Cooking time: 25 minutes, Per Serving: Calories: 131; Total Fat: 1.5g; Saturated Fat: 0g; Protein: 26.5g; Carbs: 2.4g; Fiber: 0.4g; Sugar: 0.7g

¾ lb. boneless chicken
1-teaspoon salt

½ teaspoon pepper
2 teaspoons garlic powder

- Season the chicken with ginger, salt, and pepper.
- Pour water into the Instant Pot then place a trivet in it.
- Heat up the Instant Pot then place the seasoned chicken on the trivet.
- Cover the Instant Pot with the lid then lock it properly.
- Select "Manual" setting then cook the chicken on high for 25 minutes.
- Once it is done, naturally release the Instant Pot then open the lid.
- Remove the cooked chicken from the Instant pot then place on a flat surface.
- Using a fork or a sharp knife shred the chicken then place on a platter.
- Serve and enjoy the shredded chicken with rice, as filling for a sandwich, or eat it just the way it is.

Simple Shredded Chicken

25 minutes, Serves: 8, Calories 434; Fat 16.9 g; Carbohydrates 0.1 g; Sugar 0 g; Protein 65.9 g; Cholesterol 202 mg

4 lbs chicken breasts
1/2 cup chicken broth
1/2 Tsp black pepper
1 Tsp salt

- Add all ingredients into the instant pot.
- Seal pot with lid and cook on manual high pressure for 20 minutes.
- Release pressure using quick release method than open the lid.
- Using fork shred the chicken and serves.

Chicken Tomato Pasta

Serves: 2 / Preparation time: 5 minutes / Cooking time: 15 minutes, Per Serving: Calories: 101; Total Fat: 2.3g; Saturated Fat: 0.6g; Protein: 15.8g; Carbs: 3.9g; Fiber: 1g; Sugar: 2g

1 ½ cup diced chicken
¼ teaspoon salt
½ teaspoon pepper
½ teaspoon olive oil
½ cup diced tomatoes
½ cup chopped onion
½ cup diced red bell pepper
½ teaspoon oregano
1 bay leaf
2 tablespoons chopped parsley

- Heat up the Instant Pot then select "Sauté" menu on your Instant Pot.
- Pour olive oil into the pot then stir in chopped onion.
- Sauté until translucent and aromatic then press the "Cancel" button.
- Add diced chicken to the pot together with red bell pepper and diced tomatoes.
- Season with salt, pepper, oregano, and bay leaf then stir well.
- Cover the Instant Pot with the lid then lock it properly.
- Select "Manual" setting then cook the chicken on high for 10 minutes.
- Once it is done, naturally release the Instant Pot then open the lid.
- Stir the chicken then transfer to a serving dish. Sprinkle chopped parsley on top.
- Enjoy the chicken as topping for your favorite pasta.

Tender and Juicy Turkey Breast

Serves: 8 / Preparation time: 10 minutes / Cooking time: 35 minutes, Per Serving: Calories: 404; Total Fat: 6.4g; Saturated Fat: 1.3g; Protein: 64.2g; Carbs: 18.7g; Fiber: 2.4g; Sugar: 14g;

6 1/2 lbs turkey breast, bone-in and skin-on
3 tbsp cold water
1 tbsp arrowroot powder
1 thyme sprig
1 celery rib, chopped
1 large onion, quartered
14 oz homemade chicken broth
Black pepper
Salt

- Season turkey with pepper and salt.
- Place trivet into the instant pot.
- Add broth, thyme, celery, and onion into the pot.
- Place seasoned turkey breast onto the trivet.
- Seal pot with lid and cook on high pressure for 30 minutes.
- Allow releasing pressure naturally then open the lid.
- Transfer turkey to the serving platter.
- Whisk together arrowroot powder and cold water and pour into the pot.
- Select sauté mode of instant pot and cook pot content until it thickened.
- Cut turkey into the slices then pour pot mixture over the slices turkey and serve.

Chicken Salads in Cabbage Blanket

Serves: 2 / Preparation time: 5 minutes / Cooking time: 15 minutes, Per Serving: Calories: 110; Total Fat: 1.3g; Saturated Fat: 0.3g; Protein: 11.6g; Carbs: 13.9g; Fiber: 2.4g; Sugar: 10.5g

1-½ cups diced chicken	3 tablespoons brown sugar
½ cup chopped onion	2 teaspoon red chili flakes
½ teaspoon salt	8 slices large steamed cabbage
½ teaspoon pepper	

- Combine diced chicken with chopped onion, brown sugar, and red chili flakes.
- Season with salt and pepper then mix well.
- Place a sheet of steamed cabbage on a flat surface then put about 2 tablespoons of chicken mixture on it.
- Wrap the chicken with cabbage and roll it tightly. Repeat with the remaining chicken and cabbage.
- Pour water into the Instant Pot then place a trivet in it.
- Turn the Instant Pot on then place the rolled chicken cabbage on the trivet.
- Cover the Instant Pot with the lid then lock it properly.
- Select "Manual" setting then cook the chicken on high for 15 minutes.
- Once it is done, naturally release the Instant Pot then open the lid.
- Take the chicken cabbage out from the Instant Pot then place
- Enjoy the chicken as topping for your favorite pasta.

Black Pepper Chicken Thigh Stew

Total Time: 4 hours 15 minutes; Serves: 8; Calories 322, Fat 11.1 g, Carbohydrates 17.4 g, Sugar 2.4 g, Protein 36.9 g, Cholesterol 101 mg

2 lbs chicken thighs, skinless, boneless and cut into pieces	1 cup chicken broth
1 medium onion, chopped	5 tsp curry powder
3 garlic cloves, minced	2 tsp ground ginger
1/4 tsp ground black pepper	1 bay leaf
15 oz can chickpeas, rinsed and drained	1 tbsp vegetable oil
14 oz can tomatoes, diced	2 tbsp lime juice
	1/2 tsp salt

- Use the "Slow Cooker" setting on your Instant Pot.
- Add all ingredients into the Instant Pot and mix well.
- Cover and cook on high for 4 hours.
- Serve and enjoy.

Easy 3 Ingredients Chicken

Total Time: 4 hours 5 minutes; Serves: 2; Calories 550; Fat 12.9 g; Carbohydrates 17 g; Sugar 5.1 g; Protein 85.6 g; Cholesterol 222 mg

1 1/4 lbs chicken, boneless	8 oz salsa
7 oz condensed cheddar soup	

- Use the "Slow Cooker" setting on your Instant Pot.
- Add all ingredients to the slow cooker.
- Cover and cook on low for 4 hours.
- Using fork shred the chicken and serves.

Moist and Tender Baked Chicken

Serves: 8 / Preparation time: 10 minutes / Cooking time: 20 minutes, Per Serving: Calories: 279; Total Fat: 10.9g; Saturated Fat: 3g; Protein: 42.3g; Carbs: 0.4g; Fiber: 0.1g; Sugar: 0g;

8 chicken legs	1/4 tsp spice mix

2 tsp ground ginger
1 1/4 tsp kosher salt

1/4 tsp ground pepper

- Add all ingredients into the large mixing bowl and mix well.
- Add 1 cup water in instant pot and place steamer rack into the pot.
- Place chicken on parchment paper and wrap around the chicken.
- Place wrapped chicken on shallow dish and place dish on steamer rack.
- Seal pot with lid and select manual high pressure for 20 minutes.
- Allow releasing pressure naturally then open the lid.
- Serve and enjoy.

Chicken Lettuce Wraps

20 minutes, Serves: 4, Calories 269; Fat 8.6 g; Carbohydrates 10.5 g; Sugar 3 g; Protein 33.6 g; Cholesterol 101 mg

1 lb ground chicken
2 tbsp balsamic vinegar
1/4 cup chicken broth
1/4 cup coconut amino
1/2 cup water chestnuts, drain and sliced

1/8 Tsp allspice
1/2 Tsp ground ginger
5 Tsp garlic, minced
3/4 cup onion, diced

- Add all ingredients into the instant pot and stir well.
- Seal pot with lid and select manual and set timer for 10 minutes.
- Release pressure using quick release method than open the lid.
- Add meat into lettuce leaves and serve.

Whole Turkey

Serves: 8 / Preparation time: 10 minutes / Cooking time: 50 minutes, Per Serving: Calories: 781; Total Fat: 22.7g; Saturated Fat: 7.5g; Protein: 133.1g; Carbs: 2.4g; Fiber: 0.5g; Sugar: 1g;

8 lbs fresh turkey
1/2 cup water
1 bay leaf
2 garlic cloves cut in half
1 medium carrot, quartered

1 celery stalk, quartered
1 medium onion, quartered
Black pepper
Salt

- Season turkey with pepper and salt.
- Add half onion and garlic into the turkey cavity.
- Add remaining ingredients into the instant pot then place trivet into the pot.
- Place turkey on a trivet.
- Seal pot with lid and select manual for 48 minutes.
- Allow releasing pressure naturally then open the lid.
- Serve and enjoy.

Sweet Orange Honey Chicken

Total Time: 4 hours 10 minutes; Serves: 2; Calories 636; Fat 17.5 g; Carbohydrates 47.8 g; Sugar 34.3 g; Protein 67.7 g; Cholesterol 202 mg

1 lb chicken breasts, skinless, boneless, and cut into pieces
2 garlic cloves, minced
1/4 tsp sesame oil
2 tbsp soy sauce

2 tbsp honey BBQ sauce
2 tbsp flour
1/4 cup orange marmalade
1/8 tsp red pepper flakes

- Use the "Slow Cooker" setting on your Instant Pot.
- Add all ingredients to the slow cooker and stir well.
- Cover and cook on low for 4 hours.
- Serve with rice and enjoy.

Caesar Chicken

Total Time: 6 hours 10 minutes; Serves: 2; Calories 481; Fat 23.8 g; Carbohydrates 3.2 g; Sugar 2 g; Protein 58 g; Cholesterol 183 mg

2 chicken breasts, skinless and boneless
1/4 tsp dried parsley
2 tbsp fresh basil, chopped
1/4 cup creamy Caesar dressing
1/8 tsp black pepper
1/8 tsp salt

- Use the "Slow Cooker" setting on your Instant Pot.
- Add all ingredients to the slow cooker and stir well.
- Cover and cook on low for 6 hours.
- Using fork shred the chicken.
- Serve and enjoy.

Bacon-Wrapped Stuffed Chicken Breasts

Serves: 6, Preparation time: 20 minutes, Cooking time: 10 minutes, Per Serving: Calories: 365; Total Fat: 25g; Saturated Fat: 12g; Protein: 32g; Carbs: 7g; Fiber: 0g; Sugar: 0g

3 boneless skinless chicken breasts
1 package (8 ounces) cream cheese, softened
1 package (10 ounces) frozen spinach
¼ cup chopped red bell pepper
4 cloves garlic, peeled and minced
6 slices bacon

- Using a sharp knife, slice lengthwise into the thicker end of each chicken breast and fold open.
- Mix cream cheese, spinach, red bell pepper and garlic and season to taste with salt and pepper. Spread about ¼ of the cream cheese mixture on each chicken breast.
- Fold each chicken breast over filling and wrap 2 slices of bacon around each chicken breast.
- Pour 1 cup of water into Instant Pot, place trivet in pot and set chicken breasts on trivet. Secure pot lid, close pressure valve and cook on manual setting until done, about 10 minutes. When cooking time ends, allow pressure to release naturally.
- Let chicken breasts rest for about 5 minutes before cutting into slices to serve. Enjoy!

Easy Chicken Wings

30 minutes, Serves: 6, Calories 207; Fat 7.5 g; Carbohydrates 3 g; Sugar 0 g; Protein 29.2 g; Cholesterol 90 mg

1 1/3 lbs chicken wings
1 1/2 Tsp smoked salt
4 tbsp taco seasoning

- In a dish mix together taco seasoning and smoked salt.
- Coat all chicken wings with seasoning mixture.
- Pour 1 cup water into the pot then place trivet into the pot.
- Place seasoned chicken wings over the trivet.
- Seal pot with lid and cook on manual high pressure for 10 minutes.
- Allow releasing pressure naturally then open the lid.
- Transfer chicken wings to baking sheet and broil chicken wings for 10 minutes.
- Serve hot and enjoy.

Chicken Stew

Total Time: 6 hours 10 minutes; Serves: 2; Calories 284; Fat 4 g; Carbohydrates 30.8 g; Sugar 7.1 g; Protein 31.2 g; Cholesterol 73 mg

1/2 lbs chicken breast, skinless, boneless, and cut into cubes	2 oz mushrooms, sliced
	1 potatoes, peeled and cut into cubes
1/4 cup peas	1/2 celery stalk, diced
1/4 tsp dried thyme	1 carrot, peeled and sliced
3 1/2 oz tomatoes, diced	1/4 onion, diced
7 oz chicken broth	1/8 tsp black pepper
1/4 cup corn	

- Use the "Slow Cooker" setting on your Instant Pot.
- Add all ingredients except peas into the slow cooker and stir well.
- Cover and cook on low for 5 1/2 hours.
- Add peas and stir well and cook for another 30 minutes.
- Serve and enjoy.

Easy Salsa Chicken

Total Time: 6 hours 10 minutes; Serves: 2; Calories 648; Fat 30.8 g; Carbohydrates 29.6 g; Sugar 2 g; Protein 62 g; Cholesterol 195 mg

2 chicken breast, skinless, boneless and halves	7 oz cheddar cheese soup
	1 1/2 tsp taco seasoning
1/4 cup sour cream	1/2 cup salsa

- Use the "Slow Cooker" setting on your Instant Pot.
- Add chicken to the slow cooker and season with taco seasoning.
- Combine together cheese soup and salsa and pour over the chicken.
- Cover and cook on low for 6 hours.
- Remove chicken from slow cooker and using fork shred the chicken.
- Return shredded chicken to the slow cooker and stir well.
- Add sour cream to the slow cooker and stir well.
- Serve over rice and enjoy.

Perfect Chicken Curry

Serves: 5 / Preparation time: 10 minutes / Cooking time: 5 minutes, Per Serving: Calories: 416; Total Fat: 29.8g; Saturated Fat: 18.1g; Protein: 18.2g; Carbs: 24.2g; Fiber: 5g; Sugar: 14.2g;

3/4 lb chicken breast, diced	3 tsp arrowroot powder
1 tbsp honey	3 tbsp olive oil
1 tbsp ginger, grated	3 tbsp curry powder
1 small onion, chopped	1/2 zucchini, chopped
1 cup mushrooms, sliced	10 oz pineapple chunks
1 bell pepper, sliced	1/4 tsp black pepper
14 oz coconut milk	1 tsp salt

- Add olive oil into the instant pot and select sauté mode.
- Add chicken to the pot and sauté for 2-3 minutes.
- Add remaining ingredients and stir well.
- Seal pot with lid and cook on manual high pressure for 5 minutes.
- Allow releasing pressure naturally then open the lid.
- Serve and enjoy.

Chicken Rice Casserole

Total Time: 8 hours 10 minutes; Serves: 2; Calories 862; Fat 23.7 g; Carbohydrates 87.3 g; Sugar 1.5 g; Protein 69 g; Cholesterol 189 mg

2 chicken breasts, halved
1 cup long grain rice
1 tbsp dry onion soup mix
2 oz mushroom, sliced
10 oz cream of chicken soup

- Use the "Slow Cooker" setting on your Instant Pot.
- Spray slow cooker from inside with cooking spray.
- Add mushroom, soup, and rice into the slow cooker and stir well.
- Place chicken in the slow cooker then sprinkles onion soup mix over the chicken.
- Cover and cook on low for 8 hours.
- Serve and enjoy.

Simple Mustard Pulled Turkey

Serves: 4 / Preparation time: 10 minutes / Cooking time: 50 minutes, Per Serving: Calories: 414; Total Fat: 20.6g; Saturated Fat: 6.1g; Protein: 44.1g; Carbs: 11.3g; Fiber: 0.7g; Sugar: 9.7g;

2 lbs turkey thighs, bone-in, and skin removed
1 tbsp tomato paste
1 tbsp mustard
2 tbsp vinegar
2 tbsp honey
12 oz chicken stock
1/2 tsp garlic powder
1 tsp dry mustard
2 tsp ground coriander
1 tsp salt

- Mix together coriander, garlic powder, pepper, mustard, and salt in a small bowl.
- Rub bowl mixture over the turkey thighs.
- Pour stock into the instant pot then place thighs into the pot.
- Seal pot with lid and cook on high pressure for 45 minutes.
- Release pressure using quick release method than open the lid.
- Transfer turkey thighs onto the chopping board then cut into the pieces.
- Select sauté mode of instant pot and cook pot liquid for 4 minutes.
- Stir in honey, vinegar, mustard. and tomato paste and cook for another 1 minutes.
- Return chopped turkey to the pot and stir well.
- Serve and enjoy.

Simple Lime Chicken

20 minutes, Serves: 4, Calories 444; Fat 17.1 g; Carbohydrates 2.6 g; Sugar 0.3 g; Protein 66.1 g; Cholesterol 202 mg

2 lbs chicken breasts, skinless and boneless
1/2 Tsp liquid smoke
5 garlic cloves, minced
1 Tsp onion powder
1 Tsp cumin
1 1/2 Tsp chili powder
2 fresh limes juice
1/4 Tsp black pepper
1 Tsp kosher salt

- Place chicken into the instant pot.
- Add lemon juice and sprinkle all seasoning over the chicken.
- Add garlic and liquid smoke and rub all over the chicken.
- Seal pot with lid and cook on high pressure for 6 minutes.
- Allow releasing pressure naturally then open the lid.

- Using fork shred the chicken.
- Season chicken with pepper and salt.
- Serve and enjoy.

Pulled Chicken Taco Salad

Serves: 4, Preparation time: 15 minutes, Cooking time: 15 minutes, Per Serving: Calories: 597; Total Fat: 34; Saturated Fat: 10g; Protein: 53g; Carbs: 18g; Fiber: 7g; Sugar: 9g

1 tablespoon olive oil	¼ teaspoon cayenne pepper
1 large onion, julienned	Salt and freshly ground black pepper, to taste
1 bell pepper, julienned	
4 cloves garlic, peeled and minced	1 small head green leaf lettuce, torn into bite-size pieces (about 8 cups total)
4 boneless, skinless chicken breasts	
½ cup water	4 ounces cojack cheese, shredded
1 tablespoon chili powder	4 Roma tomatoes, chopped
1 tablespoon cumin	4 tablespoons sour cream
½ tablespoon ancho chili powder	1 avocado, pitted and sliced
½ teaspoon dried oregano	

- Heat oil in Instant Pot on sauté setting and cook onion, bell pepper and garlic until softened, about 5 minutes.
- Mix chili powder, cumin, ancho chili powder, oregano and cayenne pepper. Add chicken and water to pot and sprinkle spice mixture over chicken. Season chicken to taste with salt and pepper and stir lightly to coat chicken with spice mixture.
- Secure pot lid, close pressure valve and cook on high setting until done, about 10 minutes. When cooking time ends, allow pressure to release naturally. Remove chicken from pot and shred with a fork. Mix juices from pot into shredded chicken.
- Divide lettuce among 4 serving plates and top with shredded cheese, tomatoes and about 1 tablespoon sour cream. Garnish salads with avocado slices.
- Serve chicken with a slotted spoon on top of the salads or alongside as desired. Enjoy!

Quick Turkey Breast

Serves: 8 / Preparation time: 10 minutes / Cooking time: 30 minutes, Per Serving: Calories: 391; Total Fat: 6.5g; Saturated Fat: 1.4g; Protein: 60.9g; Carbs: 18.8g; Fiber: 2.6g; Sugar: 13.3g;

6 lbs turkey breast, thawed	2 celery stalks, cut in half
1 tbsp fresh sage	1 carrot cut in half
1 tbsp parsley, chopped	3 garlic cloves, minced
1 tbsp fresh rosemary, chopped	1 onion, diced
4 cups chicken broth	1 tbsp arrowroot powder

- Add all ingredients except arrowroot powder into the instant pot and stir well.
- Seal pot with lid and cook for 30 minutes.
- Allow releasing pressure naturally then open the lid.
- Remove turkey from instant pot and place on a serving platter.
- Add arrowroot powder into the pot and set the pot to the sauté mode and cook until gravy is thickened.
- Pour gravy over the turkey and serve.

Italian Chicken

Serves: 8 / Preparation time: 10 minutes / Cooking time: 20 minutes, Per Serving: Calories: 335; Total Fat: 13.7g; Saturated Fat: 3.4g; Protein: 43.9g; Carbs: 6.7g; Fiber: 1.2g; Sugar: 2.6g;

8 chicken thighs, skinless and boneless	1/2 cup basil leaves, sliced
1/2 cup green olives pitted	1/4 cup fresh Italian parsley, chopped

8 oz cremini mushrooms, quartered
1 tbsp olive oil
1 small onion, chopped
2 medium carrots, chopped
3 garlic cloves, minced

2 cup cherry tomatoes
1 tbsp tomato paste
1/4 tsp fresh ground black pepper
Kosher salt

- Season chicken thighs with pepper salt.
- Set pot on sauté mode. Add olive oil to the pot.
- Add carrot, onion, and mushroom and sauté for 3-4 minutes or until softened.
- Add garlic and tomato paste and stir for 40 seconds.
- Add cherry tomatoes, green olives, and chicken thighs. Mix well.
- Seal pot with lid and select manual and set timer for 15 minutes.
- Allow releasing pressure naturally then open the lid.
- Serve and enjoy

Easy Pot Turkey

Serves: 4 / Preparation time: 10 minutes / Cooking time: 25 minutes, Per Serving: Calories: 582; Total Fat: 37.8g; Saturated Fat: 1.1g; Protein: 42.3g; Carbs: 10.1g; Fiber: 1.2g; Sugar: 2.3g;

2 1/2 lbs turkey quarters
2 bay leaves
2 tbsp olive oil
1 cup homemade chicken stock
1 celery stalk, chopped
1 large carrot, chopped
3 garlic cloves, minced

1 medium onion, diced
1/4 tsp dried sage
1/4 tsp dried thyme
1/4 tsp dried rosemary
1 tbsp arrowroot powder
Black pepper
Kosher salt

- Season turkey with pepper and salt.
- Add olive oil into the instant pot and select sauté.
- Add turkey quarters into the pot and brown them on all the sides.
- Remove turkey from pot and set aside.
- Add onion and garlic into the pot and sauté for a minute.
- Add turkey with remaining ingredients except for arrowroot powder into the pot.
- Seal pot with lid and cook on manual high pressure for 20 minutes.
- Allow releasing pressure naturally then open the lid.
- Remove turkey from pot and place on a serving platter.
- Add arrowroot powder to the pot and stir well and cook until thickened.
- Pour pot contents over turkey and serve.

Chicken Potato Curry

35 minutes, Serves: 8, Calories 658; Fat 34.9 g; Carbohydrates 16.5 g; Sugar 3.1 g; Protein 68.5 g; Cholesterol 202 mg

4 lbs chicken thighs
2 tbsp extra virgin olive oil
2 tbsp curry powder
1 Tsp onion powder
1 Tsp garlic powder

1 Tsp kosher salt
1 tbsp coconut sugar
4 cups potatoes, peeled and diced
1 cup water
2 cups coconut milk

- In a large bowl, combine together chicken, oil, 1 tbsp curry powder, onion powder, garlic powder and salt and set aside for 1 hour.

- Add marinated chicken into the instant pot.
- Set the instant pot on sauté mode and brown the chicken on all sides.
- Add coconut sugar, potatoes, 1 tbsp curry powder and coconut milk into the pot and stir well.
- Seal pot with lid and cook on manual high pressure for 25 minutes.
- Release pressure using quick release method than open the lid.
- Stir well and serve.

Chicken Korma

Serves: 5 / Preparation time: 10 minutes / Cooking time: 30 minutes, Per Serving: Calories: 550; Total Fat: 36.3g; Saturated Fat: 19.2g; Protein: 46.4g; Carbs: 11.2g; Fiber: 2.6g; Sugar: 4.2g;

5 large chicken thighs, boneless and skinless
1 onion, chopped
2 tsp coriander
2 tsp green chilies
1 tsp garlic, minced
2 tsp olive oil
1/2 tsp cumin
1/2 tsp garam masala
1/4 tsp turmeric
1 1/2 cup coconut milk
1/2 tsp ginger
Serving Ingredients:
1/2 cup cashews
Cilantro for garnish

- Add all ingredients except serving ingredients into the instant pot.
- Seal pot with lid and cook on high pressure for 30 minutes.
- Allow releasing pressure naturally then open the lid.
- Using fork shred the chicken, add cashews and cilantro. Mix well.
- Serve and enjoy.

Flavorful Chicken Curry

25 minutes, Serves: 4, Calories 428; Fat 20.3 g; Carbohydrates 10.4 g; Sugar 4.6 g; Protein 50.5 g; Cholesterol 145 mg

2 lbs chicken breast, skinless and boneless
1 Tsp fresh ginger, grated
3 garlic cloves, minced
1/2 cup coconut milk
15 oz tomatoes, diced
1/4 Tsp cayenne pepper
1/2 Tsp turmeric
2 Tsp garam masala
1 Tsp coriander
1 Tsp cumin
2 tbsp extra virgin olive oil
1/2 yellow pepper, chopped
1 small onion, chopped

- Add oil, yellow peppers, and onion into the instant pot and select sauté and cook for 4 minutes.
- Add spices, ginger, garlic, and salt and cook for another 2 minutes.
- Add coconut milk and tomatoes and stir well.
- Add chicken and seal pot with lid and select poultry function.
- Open the lid and using fork shred the chicken.
- Stir well and serve.

Bruschetta Chicken

Serves: 4 / Preparation time: 5 minutes / Cooking time: 10 minutes, Per Serving: Calories: 316; Total Fat: 12.2g; Saturated Fat: 3.2g; Protein: 43.4g; Carbs: 6.3g; Fiber: 1.6g; Sugar: 3.3g;

4 chicken cutlets
1 tsp parsley
1 tsp olive oil
4 garlic cloves, minced
1 tsp dried basil
2 cup Roma tomatoes
1 large carrots, chopped

- Add oil in instant pot and select sauté mode.
- Add garlic, parsley, and basil.
- When onion softens add carrot and tomato cook down a bit.
- Add chicken cutlets and seal pot with lid and select Meat setting for 10 minutes.
- Release pressure using quick release method than open the lid carefully.
- Serve and enjoy.

Instant Pot Whole Chicken

35 minutes, Serves: 8, Calories 556; Fat 21.1 g; Carbohydrates 4.1 g; Sugar 1.6 g; Protein 82.5 g; Cholesterol 252 mg

5 lbs whole chicken
3 cups water
5 garlic cloves, smash
3 celery stalks, chopped
2 large carrots, chopped

1 medium onion, chopped
1 Tsp thyme
1 Tsp oregano
Pepper
Salt

- Add garlic and vegetables into the instant pot.
- Pour water into the instant pot then place a rack over the veggies.
- Season chicken with herbs, pepper, and salt.
- Place chicken into the instant pot rack.
- Seal pot with lid and select meat setting.
- Allow releasing pressure naturally then open the lid.
- Cut chicken into the pieces and serve.

Spicy White Chicken Chili

Total Time: 4 hours 10 minutes; Serves: 2; Calories 757; Fat 5.4 g; Carbohydrates 125.5 g; Sugar 14.2 g; Protein 56.7 g; Cholesterol 40 mg

3/4 cup chicken, boneless and skinless
1/2 tsp chili powder
1/2 tsp cumin
1 1/2 oz chilies, chopped
4 oz salsa Verde

3 1/2 oz chicken broth
12 oz great northern beans, cooked
1/4 medium onion, chopped
1/8 tsp pepper
1/8 tsp salt

- Use the "Slow Cooker" setting on your Instant Pot.
- Add all ingredients to the slow cooker and stir well.
- Cover and cook on low for 4 hours.
- Using fork shred the chicken.
- Stir well and serve.

Easy Curried Chicken

Total Time: 4 hours 15 minutes; Serves: 4; Calories 553, Fat 34.2 g, Carbohydrates 10.2 g, Sugar 2.3 g, Protein 52.4 g, Cholesterol 151 mg

2 tbsp tomato paste
14 oz can coconut milk
3 garlic cloves, minced
2 tbsp fresh ginger, minced
1 tsp cumin
1 tsp turmeric
1 tsp garam masala

1 cinnamon stick
2 bay leaves
1 1/2 lbs chicken thighs
1 medium onion, diced
1/4 cup fresh cilantro, chopped
1 1/2 tsp salt

- Use the "Slow Cooker" setting on your Instant Pot.
- Add all ingredients into the Instant Pot and stir well.
- Cover and cook on low for 4 hours.
- Using fork shred the meat and stir well into the sauce.
- Serve and enjoy.

Thai Red Curry with Chicken

Serves: 5 / Preparation time: 10 minutes / Cooking time: 15 minutes, Per Serving: Calories: 408; Total Fat: 26.6g; Saturated Fat: 18.9g; Protein: 28.8g; Carbs: 15.6g; Fiber: 2.9g; Sugar: 8g;

1 lb chicken thighs, sliced into pieces
2 tsp fish sauce
2 tsp honey
1 tsp lime juice
14 oz coconut milk
3 tsp Thai red curry paste
1 cup green bell pepper, cubed
1 cup carrot, sliced
1/2 cup onion, cubed
4 kaffir lime leaves
12 Thai basil leaves

- Set the instant pot on sauté mode. Add coconut milk and red curry paste mixture stir for 2 minutes.
- Add chicken and stir well.
- Seal pot with lid and cook on manual high pressure for 4 minutes.
- Release pressure using quick release method than open the lid.
- Add fish sauce, honey, bell pepper, lime juice, onion, carrots and kaffir lime leaves.
- Select sauté and cook for about 5-6 minutes until vegetables are crisp and tender.
- Stir with Thai basil leaves and serve.

Perfect Mexican Chicken

25 minutes, Serves: 6, Calories 341; Fat 14.2 g; Carbohydrates 9.7 g; Sugar 3.4 g; Protein 46.1 g; Cholesterol 135 mg

2 lbs chicken breasts
1 fresh lime juice
2/3 cup chicken broth
1/2 Tsp chili powder
2 Tsp cumin
2 Tsp garlic powder
4 oz jalapenos, diced
10 oz tomatoes, diced
1/2 cup green bell pepper
1/2 cup red bell pepper
1/2 cup onion, diced
1 tbsp extra virgin olive oil
1/4 Tsp salt

- Add oil into the instant pot and select sauté.
- Add onion, bell peppers and salt into the pot and sauté for 3 minutes.
- Add remaining ingredients into the pot and stir well.
- Seal pot with lid and cook on manual high pressure for 12 minutes.
- Release pressure using quick release method than open the lid carefully.
- Remove chicken from pot and using fork shred the chicken.
- Return chicken to the instant pot and stir well.
- Serve and enjoy.

Adobo Chicken

Serves: 4 / Preparation time: 10 minutes / Cooking time: 25 minutes, Per Serving: Calories: 467; Total Fat: 17.1g; Saturated Fat: 4.7g; Protein: 66.5g; Carbs: 7.6g; Fiber: 1.3g; Sugar: 4.3g;

2 lbs chicken breasts, boneless and skinless
1 tbsp Goya adobo all-purpose seasoning
1/2 cup water
7 oz green chilies, roasted and diced
1 tsp turmeric
14 oz tomatoes, fire roasted and diced
Black pepper

- Place chicken breast into the instant pot, sprinkle chicken with adobo and turmeric seasoning flip the chicken and sprinkle on another side
- Pour tomatoes and diced chilies over chicken breast add 1/2 cup of water at the bottom of the instant pot.
- Seal pot with lid and cook on the manual setting for 25 minutes.
- Allow releasing pressure naturally then open the lid.
- Transfer chicken breasts to the bowl and using fork shred the chicken.
- Serve and enjoy.

Peanut Butter Chicken

Total Time: 4 hours 30 minutes; Serves: 6; Calories 356, Fat 22.2 g, Carbohydrates 15.4 g, Sugar 8.7 g, Protein 26.2 g, Cholesterol 65 mg

- 3 chicken breasts, skinless and boneless
- 1 tbsp lime juice
- 2 tbsp cornstarch
- 3 garlic cloves, minced
- 1 tbsp ginger, minced
- 1 tbsp rice wine vinegar
- 2 tbsp honey
- 2 tbsp soy sauce
- 1/3 cup creamy peanut butter
- 1 cup coconut milk

- Use the "Slow Cooker" setting on your Instant Pot.
- Add all ingredients except lime juice and cornstarch into the Instant Pot and mix well.
- Cover and cook on low for 4 hours.
- Whisk together cornstarch and 2 tbsp water and pour into the Instant Pot.
- Stir well and cook for another 20 minutes until gravy thickens.
- Serve and enjoy.

Onion Balsamic Chicken

25 minutes, Serves: 6, Calories 303; Fat 11.4 g Carbohydrates 2.3 g; Sugar 0.9 g; Protein 44.5 g; Cholesterol 135 mg

- 2 lbs chicken breasts
- 1/2 Tsp dried thyme
- 1 Tsp garlic, chopped
- 1 medium onion, chopped
- 1/2 cup chicken broth
- 1 tbsp Dijon mustard
- 1/3 cup balsamic vinegar

- Combine together Dijon, chicken broth, and vinegar and pour into the instant pot.
- Add thyme, garlic, onion, and chicken to the pot and stir well.
- Seal pot with lid and cook on manual high pressure for 12 minutes.
- Release pressure using quick release method than open the lid.
- Remove chicken from pot and using fork shred the chicken.
- Return shredded chicken to the instant pot and stir well.
- Serve and enjoy.

Chicken Cacciatore

Serves: 8 / Preparation time: 5 minutes / Cooking time: 10 minutes, Per Serving: Calories: 167; Total Fat: 5.9g; Saturated Fat: 1.5g; Protein: 22.2g; Carbs: 5.9g; Fiber: 1.1g; Sugar: 3.7g;

- 4 chicken breasts, skinless, boneless, and cubed
- 1/2 onion, sliced
- 3 bell peppers, sliced
- 24 oz hot sauce
- 1/2 tsp chili powder
- 1 tsp garlic salt

- Add cubed chicken into the instant pot and pour hot sauce over the chicken.

- Add onion and bell pepper into the instant pot, sprinkle garlic salt and chili powder over the chicken. Stir well.
- Seal pot with lid and cook on manual high pressure for 3 minutes.
- Release pressure using quick release method than open the lid.
- Serve and enjoy.

Turkey Thighs

Serves: 6, Preparation time: 10 minutes, Cooking time: 40 minutes, Per Serving: Calories: 321; Total Fat: 21g; Saturated Fat: 5g; Protein: 310g; Carbs: 3g; Fiber: 2g; Sugar: 0g

1 teaspoon rubbed sage
1 teaspoon dried rosemary, crushed
1 teaspoon thyme
Salt and freshly ground pepper, to taste
3 turkey thighs, skin removed
2 tablespoons olive oil
1 onion, peeled and diced
4 cloves garlic, peeled and minced
2 cups chicken stock

- Combine sage, rosemary and thyme, rub over turkey thighs and season to taste with salt and pepper.
- In Instant Pot on sauté setting, brown thighs in 1 tablespoon olive oil on all sides.
- Remove thighs from pot and set aside. Add remaining olive oil to pot and sauté onion and garlic until translucent, about 5 minutes. Return thighs to pot, add stock and season to taste with salt and pepper.
- Secure pot lid, close pressure valve and cook on high setting until done, about 30 minutes. When cooking time ends, let pressure release naturally. Cut meat from bones into slices to serve. Enjoy!

Rutabaga Chicken Soup

30 minutes, Serves: 4, Calories 411; Fat 11.4 g; Carbohydrates 20.7 g; Sugar 10.4 g; Protein 53.9 g; Cholesterol 150 mg

1 1/2 lbs chicken drumsticks
4 cups chicken broth
2 bay leaves
1 small onion, diced
1 rutabaga, peeled and diced
1 parsnip, peeled and diced
2 medium carrots, peeled and diced
2 celery ribs, sliced
1/2 Tsp black pepper

- Add all ingredients into the instant pot and stir well.
- Seal pot with lid and select soup function.
- Allow releasing pressure naturally then open the lid.
- Remove meat from chicken drumsticks and discard bones.
- Return meat to the pot and stir well.
- Season with pepper and salt.
- Serve and enjoy.

Chicken Leg Quarters with Lemon and Rosemary

Serves: 6 / Preparation time: 10 minutes / Cooking time: 15 minutes, Per Serving: Calories: 390; Total Fat: 16.6g; Saturated Fat: 4.3g; Protein: 55.2g; Carbs: 1.7g; Fiber: 0.2g; Sugar: 1.2g;

2 1/2 lbs chicken legs, skin removed
1/2 cup chicken broth
1 tsp honey
1 tsp lemon zest
1 tsp garlic, minced
1 lemon juice
1 1/2 tsp dried rosemary
3 tsp olive oil
1/4 tsp pepper
1/4 tsp thyme, dried
3/4 tsp salt

- Add all ingredients into the instant pot.

- Seal pot with lid and cook on manual high pressure for 14 minutes.
- Allow releasing pressure naturally then open the lid.
- Serve and enjoy

Flavorful Chicken Cacciatore

Total Time: 5 hours 10 minutes; Serves: 2; Calories 683; Fat 19 g; Carbohydrates 52.1 g; Sugar 30.5 g; Protein 80 g; Cholesterol 202 mg

1 3/4 lb chicken thighs	6 oz cremini mushrooms
1 tbsp capers	1 medium red pepper
1 fresh rosemary sprig	14 oz tomato paste
1 garlic clove	1 cup chicken broth
1 cherry pepper	Pepper
1 small onion, chopped	Salt

- Use the "Slow Cooker" setting on your Instant Pot.
- Whisk together tomato paste and broth in a bowl.
- Season chicken with pepper and salt.
- Place season chicken into the slow cooker.
- Add remaining ingredients to the slow cooker then pour tomato paste mixture over chicken.
- Cover and cook on low for 5 hours.
- Serve and enjoy.

Red Pepper Chicken Tacos

25 minutes, Serves: 8, Calories 287; Fat 10.9 g; Carbohydrates 12.3 g; Sugar 7.1 g; Protein 35.6 g; Cholesterol 101 mg

2 lbs chicken breasts	1/2 cup chicken stock
1 Tsp hot sauce	1 tbsp extra virgin olive oil
1/2 Tsp red pepper, crushed	1 onion, chopped
1/2 Tsp cilantro	14 oz tomato paste
1 tbsp coriander	Pepper
2 tbsp cumin	Salt

- Add oil in instant pot and select sauté.
- Add onion to the pot and sauté for 3 minutes.
- Add chicken and brown the both sides.
- Add remaining ingredients and mix well.
- Seal pot with lid and select poultry function.
- Release pressure using quick release method than open the lid carefully.
- Remove chicken from pot and shred.
- Return shredded chicken to the pot and stir well.
- Serve and enjoy.

Salsa Verde Shredded Chicken

Serves: 4 / Preparation time: 10 minutes / Cooking time: 15 minutes, Per Serving: Calories: 475; Total Fat: 17.4g; Saturated Fat: 4.7g; Protein: 67.6g; Carbs: 8.7g; Fiber: 1.1g; Sugar: 2.8g;

2 lbs chicken breasts	1 Jalapeno, diced and seeded
2 tsp cumin	16 oz salsa Verde
2 tbsp fresh lime juice	Pepper
1/2 onion, chopped	Salt

- Add onion, lime juice, Jalapeno, cumin, and salsa Verde in instant pot add chicken over it.
- Seal pot with lid and select poultry and set timer for 15 minutes.
- Allow releasing pressure naturally then open the lid.
- Using fork shred the chicken. Season with pepper and salt.
- Serve and enjoy

Onion Garlic Chicken

20 minutes, Serves: 6, Calories 300; Fat 11.5 g; Carbohydrates 1.7 g; Sugar 0.6 g; Protein 44.8 g; Cholesterol 135 mg

2 lbs chicken breasts, skinless and boneless
1 cup chicken broth
1 tbsp garlic, chopped
1 small onion, chopped
1/2 Tsp salt

- Add all ingredients into the instant pot and stir well.
- Seal pot with lid and cook on manual high pressure for 12 minutes.
- Allow releasing pressure naturally then open the lid.
- Remove chicken from pot and using fork shred the chicken.
- Return chicken to the instant pot and stir well.
- Serve and enjoy.

Salsa Chicken

Serves: 4 / Preparation time: 5 minutes / Cooking time: 10 minutes, Per Serving: Calories: 341; Total Fat: 12.7g; Saturated Fat: 3.5g; Protein: 50.2g; Carbs: 4.1g; Fiber: 1g; Sugar: 2g;

1 1/2 lbs chicken breasts, boneless and skinless
1 tbsp Mexican seasoning
1 cup salsa

- Season the chicken breast using Mexican seasoning on both sides.
- Place seasoned chicken into the instant pot and spread the salsa over chicken breast.
- Seal pot with lid and cook on manual high pressure for 10 minutes.
- Allow releasing pressure naturally then open the lid.
- Transfer chicken to the bowl and using fork shred the chicken.
- Serve and enjoy.

Spicy Shredded Chicken

30 minutes, Serves: 8, Calories 237; Fat 10.2 g; Carbohydrates 1.5 g; Sugar 0.9 g; Protein 33 g; Cholesterol 101 mg

2 lbs chicken breasts
1/2 cup hot sauce
1/2 red bell pepper, chopped
1/2 onion, chopped
1 tbsp extra virgin olive oil

- Add oil in instant pot and select sauté.
- Add onion and bell peppers to the pot and sauté for 4 minutes.
- Add chicken and hot sauce and stir well.
- Seal pot with lid and cook on high pressure for 12 minutes.
- Release pressure using quick release method than open the lid carefully.
- Remove chicken from pot and using fork shred the chicken.
- Return chicken to the instant pot and stir well.
- Serve and enjoy.

Chicken Tikka Masala

Serves: 4, Preparation time: 10 minutes, Cooking time: 20 minutes, Per Serving: Calories: 388; Total Fat: 15.6g; Saturated Fat: 6.7g; Protein: 50.5g; Carbs: 10.4g; Fiber: 2.8g; Sugar: 4.6g;

2 lbs chicken breast, boneless and skinless
1 tsp ginger, grated
3 garlic cloves, minced
1/2 cup coconut milk
15 oz tomatoes, diced
1/4 tsp cayenne pepper
2 tsp garam masala

1 tsp coriander
1/2 tsp turmeric
1 tsp cumin
2 tsp olive oil
1/2 yellow pepper, chopped
1 small onion, chopped
1 1/2 tsp sea salt

- Set instant pot to sauté mode.
- Add olive oil, yellow pepper and onion cook for 4 minutes or until onion softens.
- Add ginger, garlic, salt, and spices and cook for another 2 minutes.
- Add tomatoes and coconut milk and stir well.
- Place chicken into the instant pot.
- Seal pot with lid and select poultry setting.
- Allow releasing pressure naturally then open the lid.
- Transfer chicken on chopping board and using fork shred the chicken.
- Use a hand blender, puree the sauce. Return shredded chicken to the pot and stir well.
- Serve and enjoy.

Olive Lemon Chicken

20 minutes, Serves: 4, Calories 499; Fat 34.3 g; Carbohydrates 1.9 g; Sugar 0.9 g; Protein 44 g; Cholesterol 191 mg

4 chicken breasts, skinless and boneless
1/2 cup onion, sliced
1 can green olives, pitted
1 cup chicken broth
1/2 lemon juice

1/2 cup clarified butter
1/2 Tsp cumin
1/4 Tsp black pepper
1 Tsp sea salt

- Season chicken with pepper and salt.
- Set the instant pot on sauté mode then place season chicken into the pot and brown them on both the sides.
- Add all remaining ingredients and seal pot with lid.
- Cook on manual high pressure for 10 minutes.
- Release pressure using quick release method than open the lid.
- Serve and enjoy.

Butter Chicken

Total Time: 4 hours 30 minutes; Serves: 6; Calories 480, Fat 33.3 g, Carbohydrates 17.2 g, Sugar 7.1 g, Protein 30.6 g, Cholesterol 103 mg

4 large chicken thighs, skinless, boneless and cut into pieces
14 oz can coconut milk
1 cup plain yogurt
15 green cardamom pods
6 oz can tomato paste
1 tsp garam masala
2 tsp tandoori masala

1 tsp curry paste
2 tsp curry powder
3 garlic cloves, minced
1 onion, diced
3 tbsp vegetable oil
2 tbsp butter
Salt

- Use the "Slow Cooker" setting on your Instant Pot.
- Heat butter and oil in a pan over medium heat.
- Add chicken, garlic, and onion to the pan and cook until onion softens.
- Stir in tomato paste, garam masala, tandoori masala, curry paste, and curry powder.
- Transfer chicken mixture into the Instant Pot.
- Stir in yogurt, coconut milk, and cardamom pods.
- Season with salt.
- Cover and cook on high for 4 hours.
- Serve and enjoy.

Easy Shredded Chicken

Serves: 5, Preparation time: 5 minutes, Cooking time: 25 minutes, Calories: 418; Total Fat: 9.2g; Saturated Fat: 0g; Protein: 77.4g; Carbs: 0.2g; Fiber: 0.1g; Sugar: 0.1g;

4 lbs chicken breast, boneless
1/2 tsp black pepper
1/2 cup chicken broth or water
1 tsp salt

- Add all ingredients into the instant pot.
- Seal pot with lid and cook on high pressure for 20 minutes.
- Release pressure using quick release method than open the lid.
- Place the chicken on chopping board and using forks to shred the chicken.
- Serve and enjoy.

Chicken Vegetable Curry

Total Time: 3 hours 25 minutes; Serves: 4; Calories 635, Fat 37.9 g, Carbohydrates 32 g, Sugar 2.3 g, Protein 45.2 g, Cholesterol 111 mg

2 cups mushrooms, sliced
1 cup green peas
3 chicken breasts, skinless, boneless and cut into pieces
2 tsp ground cayenne
1/2 tsp black pepper
3 tbsp curry powder
1 packet dry onion soup mix
14 oz can coconut milk
10.75 oz can chicken soup
10.75 oz can mushroom soup
1 onion, chopped
1 tbsp butter

- Use the "Slow Cooker" setting on your Instant Pot.
- Melt butter in the pan over medium heat.
- Add onion and cook for 5 minutes. Transfer to the Instant Pot.
- Add remaining ingredients and stir well.
- Cover and cook on high for 1 1/2 hours then reduce heat to low and cook for another 1 1/2 hours.
- Serve and enjoy.

Tasty Chicken Fajitas

20 minutes, Serves: 6, Calories 177; Fat 1 g; Carbohydrates 11.2 g; Sugar 5.5 g; Protein 31.9 g; Cholesterol 64 mg

2 lbs chicken tenderloins
1 fresh lime juice
1 onion, sliced
3 bell peppers, sliced
3 garlic cloves, minced
10 oz can tomatoes, diced
1 packet taco seasoning

- Place chicken into the instant pot then sprinkles taco seasoning over chicken.
- Add lime juice, onion, peppers, garlic, and tomatoes over the chicken.

- Seal instant pot with lid and cook on manual high pressure for 8 minutes.
- Release pressure using quick release method than open the lid carefully.
- Serve and enjoy.

Chicken Tandoori

Total Time: 8 hours 20 minutes; Serves: 4; Calories 514, Fat 34.8 g, Carbohydrates 7.1 g, Sugar 3.8 g, Protein 44.9 g, Cholesterol 130 mg

14 oz coconut milk	2 tsp tomato paste
4 chicken thighs	2 tsp garam masala
1 tsp fresh ginger, grated	1 tsp ground coriander
1 tsp paprika	1 tsp ground cumin
1 tsp cayenne pepper	

- Use the "Slow Cooker" setting on your Instant Pot.
- Add all ingredients into the Instant Pot and mix well.
- Cover and cook on low for 8 hours.
- Serve and enjoy.

Herbed Turkey Breast

Serves: 4 / Preparation time: 10 minutes / Cooking time: 10 minutes, Per Serving: Calories: 483; Total Fat: 20g; Saturated Fat: 3.2g; Protein: 59.3g; Carbs: 14.6g; Fiber: 1.7g; Sugar: 12.1g;

3 lbs turkey breast, boneless	1 cup homemade chicken stock
2 tbsp herb seasoning blend	Black pepper
4 tbsp olive oil	Salt

- Pour chicken stock into the instant pot then place trivet into the pot.
- Season turkey breast with pepper and salt and place on a trivet.
- Drizzle turkey breast with olive oil and sprinkle with herb seasoning blend.
- Seal pot with lid and cook on manual high pressure for 10 minutes.
- Release pressure using quick release method than open the lid.
- Serve and enjoy.

Delicious Whole Chicken

Serves: 8 / Preparation time: 10 minutes / Cooking time: 25 minutes, Per Serving: Calories: 452; Total Fat: 18g; Saturated Fat: 4.8g; Protein: 66.4g; Carbs: 1.7g; Fiber: 0.4g; Sugar: 0.7g;

4 lbs whole chicken	1 cup chicken broth
1 tsp paprika	1 onion, sliced
1 3/4 tsp olive oil	1 lemon halved, sliced
1/2 tsp pepper	1 1/2 tsp salt
1 tsp garlic, granulated	

- Place the lemon and onion into the cavity of the chicken.
- In a bowl, combine together all spices with olive oil and stir mixture well and rub the spice mixture on breast side of chicken.
- Set the instant pot on sauté mode.
- Place chicken breast side down into the instant pot. carefully rub the oil and spices on another side of the chicken.
- Cook for 3-4 minutes and allow breast side to crisp up chicken skin then cook other side for 2 minutes.
- Add the chicken broth. Seal pot with lid and cook on manual high pressure for 25 minutes.
- Allow releasing pressure naturally then open the lid.

- Serve and enjoy.

Lemon Garlic Quarter Chicken

Total Time: 4 hours 10 minutes; Serves: 2; Calories 244;Fat 16.7 g; Carbohydrates 6.9 g; Sugar 0.8 g' Protein 18.7 g; Cholesterol 105 mg

2 chicken leg quarters	1 lemon, cut in half
2 fresh rosemary sprigs	Pepper
2 garlic heads, cut in half	Salt

- Use the "Slow Cooker" setting on your Instant Pot.
- Place garlic, lemon, and rosemary in the bottom of slow cooker.
- Place chicken on top of garlic and lemon.
- Season chicken with pepper and salt.
- Cover and cook on low for 4 hours.
- Serve and enjoy.

Green Chicken Curry

30 minutes, Serves: 4, Calories 583; Fat 36.9 g; Carbohydrates 19.9 g; Sugar 5.6 g; Protein 45.3 g; Cholesterol 126 mg

1 1/4 lbs chicken thighs, skinless, boneless and cut into pieces	2 tbsp green curry paste
1/4 cup fresh cilantro, chopped	1 medium onion, sliced
1 large sweet potato, peeled and diced	3 small zucchini, diced
14 oz can coconut milk	1 tbsp extra virgin olive oil
1 tbsp coconut palm sugar	1 Tsp sea salt

- Add 1 tbsp oil in instant pot and set the pot on sauté mode.
- Add zucchini in a pot and sauté for 6 minutes then remove from pot and set aside.
- Add remaining oil to the pot.
- Add onion and sauté for 5 minutes.
- Stir in coconut sugar, curry paste, and salt and cook for few minutes.
- Add coconut milk and stir well.
- Add sweet potatoes and chicken and stir well.
- Seal pot with lid and cook on high pressure for 10 minutes.
- Release pressure using quick release method than open the lid.
- Stir in cilantro and zucchini.
- Serve and enjoy.

Quick and Easy Turkey Breast

Serves: 18 / Preparation time: 10 minutes / Cooking time: 35 minutes, Per Serving: Calories: 163; Total Fat: 2.6g; Saturated Fat: 0.5g; Protein: 26.3g; Carbs: 7.1g; Fiber: 1g; Sugar: 5.7g;

6 lbs turkey breast	1 1/2 cups chicken broth
1 tsp thyme	Black pepper
1 onion, quartered	Salt
1 celery rib, cut into pieces	

- Place trivet into the instant pot.
- Pour chicken broth into the instant pot with thyme, onion, and celery.
- Season turkey breast with pepper and salt.
- Place seasoned breast onto the trivet.

- Seal pot with lid and select manual and set timer for 30 minutes.
- Allow releasing pressure naturally then open the lid.
- Cut turkey breast into the pieces and serve.

Chicken Drumsticks

Serves: 4 / Preparation time: 10 minutes / Cooking time: 10 minutes, Per Serving: Calories: 282; Total Fat: 6.6g; Saturated Fat: 1.7g; Protein: 31.8g; Carbs: 21.2g; Fiber: 0.1g; Sugar: 17.5g;

10 chicken drumsticks
2 garlic cloves, minced
1/4 cup coconut aminos

1/4 cup honey
1/2 cup balsamic vinegar

- In a bowl, combine together garlic, honey, coconut aminos, and vinegar. Pour into the instant pot.
- Add chicken drumsticks in instant pot and stir well.
- Seal pot with lid and cook on high pressure for 10 minutes.
- Release pressure using quick release method than open the lid carefully.
- Remove chicken drumsticks from instant pot and place on baking tray.
- Select sauté mode of the instant pot to thicken the sauce.
- Broil chicken drumsticks for 2 minutes.
- Once sauce thickens then turns off the instant pot.
- Pour sauce over chicken drumsticks and serve.

Tasty Chicken Tikka Masala

Total Time: 6 hours 25 minutes; Serves: 6;Calories 557, Fat 27.8 g, Carbohydrates 24.5 g, Sugar 12.7 g, Protein 51.1 g, Cholesterol 178 mg

2 lbs chicken thighs, skinless and boneless, cut into 2-inch pieces
10 oz frozen peas, thawed
1 1/2 cups heavy cream
1 tbsp cornstarch
1 tbsp sugar
28 oz can tomatoes
1 tsp ginger, grated
3 tbsp garam masala

1/2 tsp red pepper flakes
6 garlic cloves, minced
1 large onion, diced
2 tbsp vegetable oil
1 cup plain yogurt
1 tbsp ground cumin
1 tbsp ground coriander
1 tsp kosher salt

- Use the "Slow Cooker" setting on your Instant Pot.
- In a large bowl, combine together chicken, yogurt, cumin, ground coriander, and salt. Marinade for 10 minutes.
- Heat 1 tbsp oil in the pan over medium-high heat.
- Place marinated chicken into the pan and cook until lightly brown on both the sides.
- Transfer chicken into the Instant Pot.
- In the same pan, heat remaining oil. Add onions, red pepper flakes, and garlic and saute for 5 minutes.
- Add ginger, garam masala, and salt and cook for 1 minute.
- Add sugar and tomatoes, turn heat to high and bring to boil. Transfer into the Instant Pot.
- Cover and cook on low for 6 hours.
- Whisk together 1/4 cup heavy cream and cornstarch and add to the Instant Pot along with remaining peas and heavy cream.
- Stir to mix and cover and cook for another 10 minutes.
- Serve and enjoy.

Easy Dinner Turkey Roast

Serves: 4 / Preparation time: 10 minutes / Cooking time: 35 minutes, Per Serving: Calories: 353; Total Fat: 17.5g; Saturated Fat: 4.4g; Protein: 38.7g; Carbs: 8.1g; Fiber: 0.1g; Sugar: 0.5g;

1 1/2 lbs turkey roast, boneless
2 tbsp olive oil
1 tbsp arrowroot powder
1/8 cup onion, minced
2 cups chicken broth
1/8 tsp black pepper
Salt

- Add olive oil into the instant pot and select sauté.
- Add onion to the pot and sauté until brown.
- Deglaze pot with broth.
- Add remaining ingredients except for arrowroot powder.
- Seal pot with lid and select meat setting.
- Release pressure using quick release method than open the lid.
- Remove turkey from pot and place on a serving platter.
- Add arrowroot powder into the pot and set the instant pot on sauté mode until gravy thickened.
- Pour gravy over the turkey and serve.

Garlic Lemon Dump Chicken

20 minutes, Serves: 4, Calories 390; Fat 23.5 g; Carbohydrates 0.7 g; Sugar 0.2 g; Protein 42.4 g; Cholesterol 130 mg

4 chicken breasts, skinless and boneless
2 tbsp fresh lemon juice
1 tbsp fresh parsley, chopped
1/4 cup extra virgin olive oil
2 Tsp garlic, minced

- Add all ingredients into the large zip lock bag and mix well.
- Place bag in the refrigerator for 2 hours.
- Remove marinated chicken from refrigerator and pour into the instant pot.
- Add little water to the pot until you have one cup liquid in the pot.
- Seal pot with lid and cook on manual high pressure for 10 minutes.
- Release pressure using quick release method than open the lid carefully.
- Serve and enjoy.

Orange Chicken Chunks

Total Time: 6 hours 15 minutes; Serves: 2; Calories 430; Fat 12.4 g; Carbohydrates 25.8 g; Sugar 12.7 g; Protein 51.4 g; Cholesterol 131 mg

0.75 lb chicken, boneless and cut into chunks
1 1/2 tbsp ketchup
1/2 tsp balsamic vinegar
1 1/2 tbsp brown sugar
3 oz orange juice
1/4 cup flour
1 tbsp olive oil
1/2 tsp salt

- Use the "Slow Cooker" setting on your Instant Pot.
- Coat chicken pieces with flour.
- Heat olive oil in the pan over medium heat.
- Brown the chicken pieces into the pan then transfer chicken into the slow cooker.
- Combine together all remaining ingredients and pour over chicken.
- Cover and cook on low for 6 hours.
- Serve and enjoy.

Chicken Noodle Soup

Total Time: 4 hours 10 minutes; Serves: 2; Calories 211; Fat 4.1 g; Carbohydrates 22.6 g; Sugar 3.7 g; Protein 19.9 g; Cholesterol 53 mg

1 chicken breast, skinless, boneless and cut into cubes
3/4 cup dry noodles
1 bay leaf
1/2 onion, chopped
1 celery stalk, chopped
1 carrot, peeled and sliced
16 oz chicken broth
1/4 tsp pepper
1/4 tsp salt

- Use the "Slow Cooker" setting on your Instant Pot.
- Add all ingredients to the slow cooker except noodles.
- Cover and cook on low for 4 hours.
- After first 3 hours add noodles, stir well and cook.
- Stir well and serve.

Shredded Turkey

Serves: 4 / Preparation time: 15 minutes / Cooking time: 60 minutes, Per Serving: Calories: 349; Total Fat: 11.3g; Saturated Fat: 1.8g; Protein: 39.8g; Carbs: 20g; Fiber: 1.4g; Sugar: 17.3g;

2 lbs turkey breast
1 tsp liquid smoke
2 tsp hot sauce
1/2 tsp celery seed
1 tsp mustard powder
1 tsp onion powder
1 tsp garlic powder

2 tbsp honey
1/2 cup vinegar
1/2 cup broth
2 tbsp olive oil
Black pepper
Salt

- In a bowl, combine together liquid smoke, hot sauce, celery seed, mustard powder, onion powder, garlic powder, honey, vinegar, black pepper, and salt.
- Rub bowl mixture over the turkey breast.
- Add olive oil into the instant pot and select sauté.
- Add turkey into the pot and brown on all the sides.
- Pour broth into the pot.
- Seal pot with lid and cook on high pressure for 40 minutes.
- Release pressure using quick release method than open the lid.
- Remove turkey from pot and place on a platter.
- Select sauté mode of pot and cook until pot content is thickened.
- Using fork shred the turkey and returns shredded turkey into the pot and stir well.
- Serve and enjoy.

Tasty Ranch Chicken

Total Time: 4 hours 10 minutes; Serves: 2; Calories 635; Fat 24.4 g; Carbohydrates 3.7 g; Sugar 0 g; Protein 89.1 g; Cholesterol 273 mg

3 chicken breasts, skinless and boneless
1/4 cup water
2 garlic cloves, minced
1 1/2 tbsp dry ranch seasoning
1 1/2 tbsp taco seasoning

- Use the "Slow Cooker" setting on your Instant Pot.
- Add chicken to the slow cooker.

- In a small bowl, whisk together remaining ingredients and pour over chicken.
- Cover and cook on low for 4 hours.
- Using fork shred the chicken and serves.

Basil Chicken Breasts

Serves: 3, Preparation time: 10 minutes, Cooking time: 15 minutes, Calories: 281; Total Fat: 11g; Saturated Fat: 3g; Protein: 42.3g; Carbs: 0.4g; Fiber: 0.1g; Sugar: 0.1g;

3 chicken breasts, boneless and skinless
1 cup water
1/8 tsp dried basil
1/4 tsp garlic powder
1/8 tsp dried oregano
1 tsp avocado oil
1/8 tsp black pepper
1/4 tsp salt

- Add oil into the instant pot and select sauté mode.
- Season the chicken breasts with black pepper, oregano, garlic powder, basil, and salt.
- Place seasoned chicken breasts into the pot.
- Brown chicken breast for 4 minutes on each side then remove from pot and set aside.
- Place trivet into the pot. Pour 1 cup water into the pot.
- Place chicken breasts on a trivet.
- Seal pot with lid and cook on manual high pressure for 5 minutes.
- Allow releasing pressure naturally then open the lid.
- Serve and enjoy

Juicy and Tender Chicken Breasts

20 minutes, Serves: 3, Calories 319; Fat 15.5 g; Carbohydrates 0.3 g; Sugar 0.1 g; Protein 42.3 g; Cholesterol 130 mg

3 chicken breasts, skinless and boneless
1 cup water
1/8 Tsp basil, dried
1/8 Tsp oregano, dried
1 tbsp extra virgin olive oil
1/4 Tsp black pepper
1/4 Tsp garlic salt

- Add oil into the instant pot and select sauté function.
- Season chicken breasts from one side and place into the instant pot.
- Sauté chickens for 3 minutes then turn to another side.
- Season chicken with the second side and sauté for another 3 minutes.
- Transfer chicken to a dish and pour 1 cup water into the pot.
- Place trivet into the pot.
- Place season chicken breasts over the trivet.
- Seal pot with lid and cook on manual high pressure for 5 minutes.
- Allow releasing pressure naturally then open the lid.
- Serve and enjoy.

Chicken Dinner

Total Time: 8 hours 10 minutes; Serves: 2; Calories 596; Fat 11.5 g; Carbohydrates 68.3 g; Sugar 8.2 g; Protein 53.1 g; Cholesterol 136 mg

2 chicken breast, skinless, boneless, and cut into halves
1/8 tsp garlic powder
14 oz cream chicken soup
1/2 cup frozen peas
1 medium celery stalk, chopped
3 medium potatoes, cut into chunks
10 baby carrots, halves

- Use the "Slow Cooker" setting on your Instant Pot.

- Add peas, carrots, potatoes, and celery into the slow cooker.
- Add chicken breasts on top of vegetable.
- Combine together chicken soup and garlic powder and pour over the chicken.
- Cover and cook on low for 8 hours.
- Serve and enjoy.

Easy Turkey Drumsticks

Serves: 6 / Preparation time: 10 minutes / Cooking time: 20 minutes, Per Serving: Calories: 124; Total Fat: 4.1g; Saturated Fat: 0g; Protein: 19.5g; Carbs: 2.4g; Fiber: 0.1g; Sugar: 2g;

6 turkey drumsticks
1/2 cup chicken broth
1/2 cup water
1/2 tsp garlic powder

1 tsp ground black pepper
2 tsp honey
1 tbsp kosher salt

- Season drumsticks with garlic powder, pepper, salt, and honey.
- Pour water and broth into the instant pot and then place drumsticks into the pot.
- Seal pot with lid and cook on manual high pressure for 20 minutes.
- Allow releasing pressure naturally then open the lid.
- Serve and enjoy.

Garlicky Sweet Chicken

Total Time: 4 hours 10 minutes; Serves: 2; Calories 352; Fat 10.8 g; Carbohydrates 18.6 g; Sugar 17.7 g; Protein 42.5 g; Cholesterol 130 mg

2 chicken thighs, skinless and boneless
1 tsp soy sauce
1 tbsp apple cider vinegar

1/4 cup brown sugar
1 garlic clove, minced

- Use the "Slow Cooker" setting on your Instant Pot.
- Add chicken to the slow cooker.
- In a small bowl, combine together all remaining ingredients and pour over chicken.
- Cover and cook on low for 4 hours.
- Using fork shred the chicken and serves.

Chicken Coconut Curry

40 minutes, Serves: 6, Calories 437; Fat 25.7 g; Carbohydrates 7.6 g; Sugar 3.1 g; Protein 44.3 g; Cholesterol 130 mg

6 chicken thighs, skinless and boneless
15 fresh basil leaves
1 lime juice
1 tbsp curry powder
1 tbsp fresh ginger, grated

1 tbsp garlic, chopped
1 jalapeno, chopped
1 onion, sliced
13 oz can coconut milk
1 Tsp salt

- Add all ingredients except basil and lime juice into the instant pot and stir well.
- Seal pot with lid and select soup button, it takes 30 minutes.
- Allow to releasing pressure naturally then open the lid.
- Stir well and using fork lightly shred the chicken.
- Add basil and lime juice and stir well.
- Serve hot and enjoy.

Lemon Garlic Chicken Thighs with Green Beans

25 minutes, Serves: 6, Calories 504; Fat 27 g; Carbohydrates 18.4 g; Sugar 2.2 g; Protein 46.7 g; Cholesterol 156 mg

2 lbs chicken thighs, boneless
1/2 cup chicken stock
1 lb green beans
1 lb potatoes
1 Tsp herb de Provence
1 lemon juice

5 garlic cloves, crushed
3 tbsp extra virgin olive oil
4 tbsp ghee
1/4 Tsp black pepper
1/2 Tsp salt

- Add ghee and oil in instant pot and select sauté.
- Add garlic, lemon juice, pepper, and salt into the pot and stir well.
- Add chicken and sauté for minutes.
- Add remaining all ingredients and stir well.
- Seal pot with lid and cook on manual high pressure for 15 minutes.
- Stir well and serve.

Chicken Dumplings

Total Time: 4 hours 40 minutes; Serves: 2; Calories 734; Fat 43.4 g; Carbohydrates 84.6 g; Sugar 6.7 g; Protein 56.2 g; Cholesterol 160 mg

2 chicken breast, skinless and boneless
5 biscuits, break into pieces
2 tbsp flour

14 oz cream of chicken soup
1/2 onion, diced
1 tbsp butter

- Use the "Slow Cooker" setting on your Instant Pot.
- Add chicken, onion, soup, and butter into the slow cooker, and fill with enough water to cover.
- Cover and cook on low for 4 hours.
- About half hour before serving, roll each biscuit pieces in the flour then drop into the slow cooker.
- Cover again and cook for another 30 minutes.
- Serve and enjoy.

Turkey and Bone Broth Gravy

Serves: 4 / Preparation time: 10 minutes / Cooking time: 20 minutes, Per Serving: Calories: 349; Total Fat: 4g; Saturated Fat: 0.8g; Protein: 48.2g; Carbs: 28.4g; Fiber: 4.7g; Sugar: 14.5g;

2 lbs turkey breast, skinless and boneless
1 bay leaf
1/2 cup bone broth
1/2 tsp dried sage
1 tsp dried parsley
2 tsp dried thyme
1 tsp sea salt

For gravy:
1/2 rosemary sprig
1 bay leaf
1 cup bone broth
1 1/4 cup sweet potato, peeled and diced
2 cups onion, diced
1/2 tsp sea salt

- Add all gravy ingredients into the instant pot and stir well.
- Seal pot with lid and cook on manual high pressure for 5 minutes.
- Release pressure using quick release method than open the lid.
- Transfer pot content into the blender and blend until smooth and set aside.
- Season turkey with parsley, thyme, sage, and salt.
- Pour broth into the instant pot then place trivet into the pot.
- Place turkey on trivet and seal pot with lid and select poultry setting.
- Release pressure using the quick release method than open the lid.
- Cut turkey into the slices and serve with gravy.

Creamy Chicken Mushroom

Total Time: 4 hours 10 minutes; Serves: 2; Calories 418; Fat 14.4 g; Carbohydrates 14.6 g; Sugar 2.1 g; Protein 54.7 g; Cholesterol 156 mg

1 lb chicken breast, skinless and boneless
1/2 cup chicken broth
1 packet dry onion mix
10 oz can cream of chicken soup
4 oz mushrooms, sliced

- Use the "Slow Cooker" setting on your Instant Pot
- Add all ingredients to the slow cooker and mix well.
- Cover and cook on low for 4 hours.
- Serve and enjoy.

Chapter 4: Pork

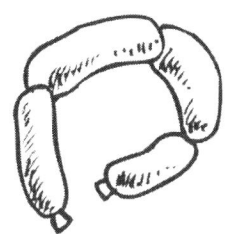

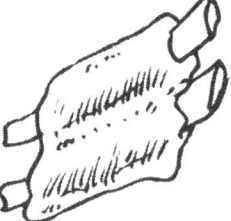
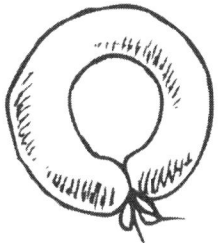

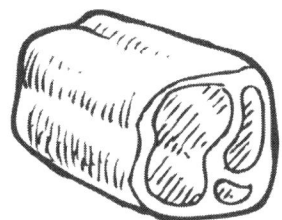

Pork Tender in Tropical Sauce

Serves: 2 / Preparation time: 5 minutes / Cooking time: 25 minutes, Per Serving: Calories: 291; Total Fat: 5g; Saturated Fat: 1.7g; Protein: 31.7g; Carbs: 30.7g; Fiber: 3.6g; Sugar: 20.4g

½ lbs. pork tenderloin	½ teaspoon rosemary
½ cup tomato puree	½ teaspoon nutmeg
1 cup unsweetened pineapple juice	½ teaspoon cinnamon
½ cup pineapple chunks	2 cloves
¼ cup chopped onion	

- Heat up the Instant Pot then select "Sauté" menu.
- Cut the pork into slices then place in the Instant Pot.
- Add tomato puree and pineapple juice to the pot then sprinkle chopped onion, rosemary, nutmeg, cloves, and cinnamon on top.
- Cover the Instant Pot with the lid then make sure that it is locked properly.
- Select "Manual" setting then cook the pork on high for 25 minutes.
- Quickly release the Instant Pot then open the lid.
- Add pineapple chunks to the pot then stir well. Do not need to reheat it again.
- Transfer to a serving dish then enjoy warm.

Tasty Sausage Soup

Total Time: 4 hours 10 minutes; Serves: 2; Calories 682; Fat 39.8 g; Carbohydrates 45.3 g; Sugar 5 g; Protein 34.9 g; Cholesterol 116 mg

1/2 lb Italian sausage, browned	1/4 cup heavy cream
2 cups kale, chopped	2 3/4 cups chicken broth
2 potatoes, cubed	1/4 tsp red pepper flakes
1 carrot, grated	1/4 tsp salt

- Use the "Slow Cooker" setting on your Instant Pot.
- Add all ingredients to the slow cooker and stir well.
- Cover and cook on low for 4 hours.
- Stir well and serve.

Pineapple Pork

Serves: 8 / Preparation time: 10 minutes / Cooking time: 90 minutes, Per Serving: Calories: 342; Total Fat: 24.9g; Saturated Fat: 9g; Protein: 26.5g; Carbs: 1.4g; Fiber: 0.1g; Sugar: 1.1g;

2 lbs pork shoulder, cut into 2 pieces	1/2 cup water
1 tsp fish sauce	1/2 cup pineapple, diced
1 tsp olive oil	1 tsp salt
1 tsp liquid smoke	

- Add olive oil into the instant pot and select sauté mode of the instant pot.
- Sear pork each half for 3 minutes on each side until lightly brown.
- Season pork with salt.
- Add pork, fish sauce, pineapple, liquid smoke and water to the pot.
- Seal pot with lid and cook on the manual setting for 90 minutes.
- Allow releasing pressure naturally then open the lid.
- Remove pork from instant pot and using forks shred the meat.
- Serve and enjoy.

Smoked Sausage & Cabbage

Serves: 4, Preparation time: 15 minutes, Cooking time: 8 minutes, Per Serving: Calories: 310; Total Fat: 28g; Saturated Fat: 11g; Protein: 12g; Carbs: 6g; Fiber: 2g; Sugar: 3g

2 tablespoons butter
1 pound smoked Polish pork sausage links, cut into 1-inch pieces
1 small onion, cut into strips
1 large head cabbage, cored and cut into strips
2 cups chicken stock
Salt and freshly ground black pepper, to taste

- Melt butter in Instant Pot on sauté setting and cook sausage and onion until lightly browned on all sides, about 5 minutes.
- Add cabbage and stock to pot, mix well and season to taste with salt and pepper.
- Secure pot lid and close pressure valve and cook pork high pressure for about 3 minutes. When cooking time ends, carefully turn venting knob from sealing to venting position for a quick pressure release.
- Serve smoked sausage & cabbage with a slotted spoon. Enjoy!

Pork Stew

55 minutes, Serves: 6, Calories 510; Fat 15.9 g; Carbohydrates 5.8 g Sugar 2.1 g; Protein 82.1 g; Cholesterol 221 mg

4 lbs pork cheeks, cut into pieces
1 lemon juice
6 garlic cloves, peeled
1 small onion, diced
1 large leek, cut into chunks
8 oz mushrooms, sliced
1 1/2 cups chicken broth
2 tbsp extra virgin olive oil
1 Tsp sea salt

- Add oil in instant pot and select sauté.
- Add meat into the pot and cook until browned.
- Add remaining ingredients and stir well.
- Seal pot with lid and select meat/stew, it takes 45 minutes.
- Release pressure using quick release method than open the lid carefully.
- Remove meat from pot and place on a plate.
- Using fork shred the meat.
- Add pot vegetable and juices into the blender and blend until smooth.
- Add shredded meat in blended liquid and stir well.
- Serve and enjoy.

Pork Clear Soup with Collard Green

Serves: 2 / Preparation time: 10 minutes / Cooking time: 25 minutes, Per Serving: Calories: 271; Total Fat: 6.4g; Saturated Fat: 2.1g; Protein: 46.2g; Carbs: 6g; Fiber: 2g; Sugar: 0.1g

¾ lb. pork tenderloin
2 cups chopped collard green
2 tablespoons minced garlic
1-teaspoon pepper
1-teaspoon salt
3 cups water

- Cut the pork tenderloin into cubes then place in the Instant Pot.
- Sprinkle minced garlic, salt, and pepper then pour water into the Instant Pot.
- Place a trivet over the pork feet then place chopped collard green in it.
- Cover the Instant Pot with the lid then make sure that it is locked properly.
- Select "Manual" setting then cook the pork on high for 25 minutes.
- Naturally release the Instant Pot then open the lid.
- Combine collard green with the soup then stir well.
- Transfer to a serving dish then enjoy warm.

Citrusy Pork Carnitas

1 hour 40 minutes, Serves: 6, Calories 477; Fat 34.5 g; Carbohydrates 3.8 g; Sugar 2.4 g; Protein 35.6 g; Cholesterol 142 mg

- 2 lbs pork shoulder, boneless and cut into chunks
- 1 tbsp ghee
- 1 lime juice
- 2 oranges juice
- 1 tbsp Mexican seasoning
- 1/4 Tsp black pepper
- 3/4 Tsp sea salt

- Season pork with Mexican seasoning, black pepper, and salt.
- Place seasoned pork in instant pot.
- Pour lime juice and orange juice over the pork.
- Seal pot with lid and select manual and set timer for 50 minutes.
- Allow releasing pressure naturally then open the lid.
- Using fork shred the pork and stir well in pot juices.
- Select sauté mode and sauté until all liquid is absorb about 20 minutes.
- Once all liquid is absorbed then add ghee and stir for 5 minutes.
- Serve hot and enjoy.

Appetizing Pork with Cabbage

Serves: 2 / Preparation time: 10 minutes / Cooking time: 25 minutes, Per Serving: Calories: 229; Total Fat: 17.9g; Saturated Fat: 13.4g; Protein: 10.9g; Carbs: 8.9g; Fiber: 2.6g; Sugar: 3.3g

- ¾ lb. pork tenderloin
- 1-teaspoon olive oil
- 2 teaspoons minced garlic
- 2 teaspoon sliced shallot
- ½ teaspoon turmeric
- ½ teaspoon ginger
- ½ teaspoon pepper
- ½ teaspoon salt
- 1 lemongrass
- 1-½ cups water
- ½ cup coconut milk
- 2 teaspoons soy sauce
- 1-cup cabbage

- Cut the pork tenderloin into cubes then set aside.
- Preheat the Instant Pot then select the "Sauté" menu.
- Pour olive oil into the Instant Pot then stir in minced garlic, sliced shallot, turmeric, ginger, and lemongrass. Sauté until aromatic then press the "Cancel" button.
- Add pork cubes to the Instant Pot then pour water into the pot.
- Season with salt and pepper then cover the Instant Pot with the lid. Lock it properly.
- Select "Manual" setting then cook the pork on high for 25 minutes.
- Quickly release the Instant Pot then open the lid.
- Press the "Sauté" menu again then add cabbage to the pot and drizzle soy sauce on top. Stir well.
- Transfer to a serving dish then enjoy.

Ginger-Honey Pork Tenderloin

Serves: 3 / Preparation time: 10 minutes / Cooking time: 30 minutes, Per Serving: Calories: 385; Total Fat: 8.1g; Saturated Fat: 2.8g; Protein: 59.6g; Carbs: 13.1g; Fiber: 0.2g; Sugar: 4g;

- 1 1/2 lbs Pork Tenderloin, cut into quarter
- 2 tsp garlic cloves, minced
- 1/2 cup cilantro, chopped
- 2 tsp lemon juice
- 2 tsp honey
- 1 tsp ginger, peel and diced
- 1/2 cup coconut aminos

- Add coconut aminos, honey, ginger, lemon juice, cilantro and garlic into the bowl.
- Add pork and marinate at least 1 hour.

- Place pork tenderloin into the instant pot.
- Seal pot with lid and select Meat/Stew setting and set the timer for 30 minutes.
- Allow releasing pressure naturally then open the lid.
- Serve and enjoy.

Sweet Pork Belly

Serves: 2 / Preparation time: 5 minutes / Cooking time: 25 minutes, Per Serving: Calories: 194; Total Fat: 14.4g; Saturated Fat: 3.7g; Protein: 4.8g; Carbs: 12.6g; Fiber: 2.1g; Sugar: 5.7g

¾ lb. pork belly
1-teaspoon olive oil
½ teaspoon salt
½ teaspoon pepper
½ cup chopped onion
3 tablespoons soy sauce
2 tablespoons barbecue sauce
2 tablespoons sesame seeds

- Cut the pork belly into thick slices then set aside.
- Heat up the Instant Pot then select the "Sauté" setting.
- Place the sliced pork belly in the Instant Pot then sauté until the pork generates oil.
- Take the beef out from the Instant Pot then place in a casserole dish. Press the "Cancel" button then clean the Instant Pot.
- Pour water into an Instant Pot then place a trivet in it.
- Place the casserole dish with pork belly in the trivet then drizzle soy sauce and barbecue sauce over the pork.
- Sprinkle chopped onion on top then cover the Instant Pot with the lid. Lock it properly.
- Select "Manual" setting then cook the pork on high and set the time to 25 minutes.
- Once it is done, naturally release the Instant Pot then open the lid.
- Take the casserole dish out from the Instant Pot then garnish with sesame seeds.
- Serve and enjoy immediately.

Savory Pork Loin

Serves: 4, Preparation time: 10 minutes, Cooking time: 30 minutes, Per Serving: Calories: 162; Total Fat: 6g; Saturated Fat: 2; Protein: 23g; Carbs: 0g; Fiber: 0g; Sugar: 0g

1 boneless pork loin roast (1 pound)
2 cloves garlic, peeled and minced
1 tablespoon dried rosemary, crushed
Salt and freshly ground pepper, to taste
1 cup chicken stock

- Pierce pork loin all over with a fork or tip of a sharp knife. Mix garlic and rosemary and rub over pork loin, pressing mixture into piercings. Season pork loin to taste with salt and pepper.
- Place pork loin in Instant Pot and add chicken stock. Secure pot lid, close pressure valve and cook on stew setting for 30 minutes. When cooking time ends, let pressure release naturally.
- Cut pork loin into slices to serve. Enjoy!

Thai Pork Stew

50 minutes, Serves: 5, Calories 570; Fat 23.5 g; Carbohydrates 20.2 g; Sugar 1.4 g; Protein 64.2 g; Cholesterol 363 mg

2 lbs pork butt
8 cups water
5 garlic cloves, sliced
1 medium onion, quartered
1 cup cilantro, chopped
1 1/2 Tsp ginger, sliced
2 tbsp cacao powder
1 1/2 cups coconut amino
2 tbsp five spice powder
1 tbsp black peppercorns
1 tbsp coriander seeds
6 eggs, boiled
2 tbsp extra virgin olive oil
1/4 Tsp salt

- Add coriander seeds, ginger, garlic, and black peppercorns into the blender and blend until smooth.
- Add 1 tbsp oil in instant pot and select sauté.

- Add meat into the pot and browned the meat on all sides.
- Remove meat from pot and place on a plate.
- Add remaining oil in instant pot.
- Add blended ingredients to the pot and sauté for 1 minute.
- Return meat to the pot with remaining ingredients and stir well.
- Seal pot with lid and select meat/stew setting and set timer for 35 minutes.
- Allow releasing pressure naturally then open the lid.
- Stir well and serve.

Hot Pork Ginger

Serves: 2 / Preparation time: 5 minutes / Cooking time: 30 minutes, Per Serving: Calories: 164; Total Fat: 6.7g; Saturated Fat: 1.9g; Protein: 24.4g; Carbs: 8.7g; Fiber: 1.5g; Sugar: 2g

1-½ pork tenderloin	4 shallots
1-teaspoon olive oil	¼ cup red chili
3 cloves garlic	1-teaspoon ginger

- Place garlic, shallots, red chili, and ginger in a food processor then pulse until smooth.
- Add olive oil to the spice mixture then mix well.
- Brush the pork tenderloin with the spice mixture then wrap it with aluminum foil.
- Pour water into the Instant Pot then place a trivet in it.
- Place the wrapped pork in the trivet then cover the Instant Pot with the lid and lock it properly.
- Select "Manual" setting then cook the pork on high and set the time to 30 minutes.
- Once it is done, naturally release the Instant Pot then open the lid.
- Take the pork out from the Instant Pot then unwrap the pork.
- Cut the pork into slices or shred it.
- Eat with rice, sandwich, or just the way it is.
- Enjoy.

Tangy and Sticky Chicken

Total Time: 4 hours 15 minutes; Serves: 2; Calories 527; Fat 8.8 g; Carbohydrates 33.8 g; Sugar 28.6 g; Protein 74.3 g; Cholesterol 218 mg

1 1/2 lbs chicken breast	2 garlic cloves, minced
2 tbsp tomato paste	1 tbsp ginger, minced
2 tbsp water	2 tbsp soy sauce
1/4 tsp cayenne pepper	6 tbsp brown sugar

- Use the "Slow Cooker" setting on your Instant Pot.
- Add 3 tbsp sugar, 1 tbsp soy sauce, garlic, cayenne pepper, ginger, and chicken into the ziplock bag and shake well to coat.
- Pour chicken mixture into the slow cooker and cook on low for 4 hours.
- Place chicken in baking dish.
- In a small bowl, combine together remaining sugar, tomato paste, water, and soy sauce.
- Brush bowl mixture over the chicken.
- Broil chicken for 5 minutes and serve.

Simple Pork Ribs

Serves: 8 / Preparation time: 5 minutes / Cooking time: 35 minutes, Per Serving: Calories: 571; Total Fat: 43.3g; Saturated Fat: 15.9g; Protein: 42.3g; Carbs: 0.2g; Fiber: 0g; Sugar: 0.2g;

| 2 1/2 lbs spareribs, boneless | 15 oz homemade chicken broth |
| 1 tbsp liquid smoke | 1 tbsp sea salt |

- Season spareribs with salt.

- Add liquid smoke and broth into the instant pot. Place trivet into the instant pot.
- Place seasoned spareribs on a trivet.
- Seal pot with lid and select meat setting for 35 minutes.
- Allow releasing pressure naturally then open the lid.
- Serve and enjoy.

Apple Ginger Pork Stew

Serves: 2 / Preparation time: 5 minutes / Cooking time: 30 minutes, Per Serving: Calories: 184; Total Fat: 7.5g; Saturated Fat: 2.4g; Protein: 6.6g; Carbs: 24.7g; Fiber: 4.5g; Sugar: 13g

¾ lb. pork	2 tablespoons soy sauce
¼ teaspoon salt	2 teaspoons minced garlic
½ teaspoon pepper	1 fresh apple
1-teaspoon olive oil	1-teaspoon ginger
¼ cup beef broth	1 tablespoon lemon juice

- Heat up the Instant Pot for 30 seconds then select "Sauté" menu.
- Stir in olive oil and minced garlic then sauté until wilted.
- Add beef to the Instant Pot then season with salt, pepper, and ginger.
- Drizzle soy sauce and lemon over juice over the beef then pour beef broth into the pot.
- Cut the apples into cubes then sprinkle on top.
- Cover the Instant Pot then lock it properly.
- Select "Manual" setting then cook the pork on high for 30 minutes.
- Once it is done, naturally release the Instant Pot then open the lid.
- Transfer the beef along with the apple and liquid to a serving dish.
- Serve and enjoy.

Apple Cider Shredded Pork

8 hours 10 minutes, Serves: 8, Calories 471; Fat 15.3 g; Carbohydrates 8 g; Sugar 6.1 g; Protein 71 g; Cholesterol 209 mg

4 lbs pork butt, boneless	1/2 Tsp chili powder
1 1/2 cups apple cider, unsweetened	1 1/2 Tsp garlic powder
1 large onion, sliced	1 1/2 Tsp smoked paprika
For rub:	1/2 Tsp black pepper
1/2 Tsp ground ginger	1 tbsp sea salt

- In a small bowl, mix together all spice ingredients.
- Rub spice mixture all over the pork.
- Add onion sliced into the instant pot then place season pork over onions.
- Pour apple cider over the pork.
- Seal pot with lid and select slow cooker setting and set the timer for 8 hours.
- Remove pork from pot and using fork shred the pork.
- Serve and enjoy.

Smothered Pork Chops

Serves: 4, Preparation time: 15 minutes, Cooking time: 25 minutes, Per Serving: Calories: 308; Total Fat: 190g; Saturated Fat: 11g; Protein: 25g; Carbs: 4g; Fiber: 2g; Sugar: 0g

4 boneless top loin pork chops (about 4 ounces each)	Salt and freshly ground black pepper, to taste
1 teaspoon poultry seasoning	2 tablespoons coconut oil
	1 large onion, sliced

4 cloves garlic, peeled and minced	1 teaspoon paprika
8 ounces fresh sliced mushrooms	1 teaspoon arrowroot flour
1 cup chicken stock	½ cup heavy cream

- Rub poultry seasoning into pork chops and season to taste with salt and pepper. Melt 1 tablespoon coconut oil in Instant Pot on sauté setting and cook pork chops until brown on both sides, about 6 minutes. Remove pork chops from pot and set aside.
- Melt remaining coconut oil in pot and sauté onion, garlic and mushrooms until softened and onions are translucent, about 5 minutes.
- Return pork chops to pot and add chicken stock and paprika. Secure pot lid, close pressure valve and cook on meat/stew setting for about 12 minutes. When cooking time ends, let pressure release naturally.
- Move the chops to the edge of the pot. Add cream and arrowroot flour to juices in pot, season to taste with salt and pepper and whisk to thicken the gravy.
- Serve the chops smothered with the gravy. Enjoy!

Special Pork in Tomato Sticky Sauce

Serves: 2 / Preparation time: 5 minutes / Cooking time: 30 minutes, Per Serving: Calories: 210; Total Fat: 7.1g; Saturated Fat: 1.5g; Protein: 12.7g; Carbs: 26.4g; Fiber: 3.1g; Sugar: 13.5g

¾ lb. pork tenderloin	1-teaspoon sugar
2 teaspoons olive oil	¼ teaspoon salt
1-tablespoon fish sauce	3 tablespoons tomato sauce
2 tablespoons barbecue sauce	1-cup tomato puree
3 teaspoons minced garlic	1-tablespoon cornstarch
½ teaspoon pepper	¼ cup water

- Cut the pork into slices then set aside.
- Heat up the Instant Pot for 30 seconds then select "Sauté" menu.
- Pour olive oil then stir in sliced pork and minced garlic. Sauté until brown.
- Season with fish sauce, barbecue sauce, pepper, salt, sugar, tomato sauce, and tomatoes puree then stir well.
- Cover the Instant Pot then lock it properly.
- Select "Manual" setting then cook on high for 30 minutes.
- Once it is done, quickly release the Instant Pot then open the lid.
- Select the "Sauté" menu again then pour cornstarch and water mixture over the pork stir well.
- Transfer to a serving dish along with the sauce then serve.
- Enjoy.

Pork Ribs

Serves: 8 / Preparation time: 5 minutes / Cooking time: 45 minutes, Per Serving: Calories: 796; Total Fat: 50.8g; Saturated Fat: 17.9g; Protein: 75.8g; Carbs: 4.4g; Fiber: 1g; Sugar: 2.6g;

5 lbs pork ribs, cut into thirds	2 tsp mustard powder
1 tsp pepper	1 tbsp honey
1 tsp onion powder	2 tbsp sweet paprika
1 tsp garlic powder	1/2 tsp celery salt
1 tsp cumin	2 tsp salt
1 tsp chili powder	

- In a bowl, mix together sweet paprika, celery salt, onion powder, garlic powder, cumin, chili powder, mustard powder, honey, and salt.
- Rub seasoning all over the ribs.
- Pour water into the instant pot then place trivet into the pot.
- Place seasoned ribs on a trivet.
- Seal pot with lid and select manual and set timer for 45 minutes.

- Release pressure using quick release method than open the lid.
- Serve and enjoy.

Savory Pork Belly in Fresh Basil

Serves: 2 / Preparation time: 5 minutes / Cooking time: 30 minutes, Per Serving: Calories: 200; Total Fat: 14.9g; Saturated Fat: 12.8g; Protein: 4.4g; Carbs: 16.3g; Fiber: 2.7g; Sugar: 4.6g

¾ lb. pork belly	1-inch galangal
2 cups fresh basil	2 teaspoon red chili flakes
5 cloves garlic	¼ teaspoon salt
6 shallots	½ cup coconut milk
1-teaspoon coriander	½ cup water
¼ teaspoon turmeric	

- Cut the pork into small cubes then place in the Instant Pot.
- Place garlic, shallots, turmeric, red chili flakes, and salt in a food processor then pulse until smooth.
- Transfer the spice mixture to the pot then mix with the pork.
- Add galangal and basil then pour water and coconut milk over the pork. Stir well.
- Cover the Instant Pot then lock it properly.
- Select "Manual" setting then cook the pork on high for 30 minutes.
- Once it is done, naturally release the Instant Pot then open the lid.
- Transfer to a serving dish along with the basil and the liquid then serve.
- Enjoy.

Pork Chops with Mushroom

30 minutes, Serves: 4, Calories 360; Fat 25.6 g; Carbohydrates 6.7 g; Sugar 2.3 g; Protein 25.7 g; Cholesterol 69 mg

4 pork chops	8 oz mushrooms, sliced
10 oz cream of mushroom soup, low sodium	3 garlic cloves, minced
	1/2 onion, chopped
1 fresh thyme sprig	1 tbsp extra virgin olive oil
1 cup bone broth	Pepper
1 Tsp garlic powder	Salt

- Add oil in instant pot and select sauté.
- Add garlic and onion and sauté for 2 minutes.
- Season pork chops with pepper and salt.
- Add thyme, broth, and pork chops in a pot.
- Seal pot with lid and cook on manual high pressure for 20 minutes.
- Allow releasing pressure naturally then open the lid.
- Remove pork chops from pot and place on a serving plate.
- Add mushroom soup in a pot and stir well.
- Pour gravy over pork chops and serve.

Simple Pork Garlic

Serves: 2 / Preparation time: 5 minutes / Cooking time: 30 minutes, Per Serving: Calories: 267; Total Fat: 8.1g; Saturated Fat: 3g; Protein: 39.2g; Carbs: 8.1g; Fiber: 0.4g; Sugar: 0.2g

1 lb. pork tenderloin	1-cup water
¼ cup minced garlic	½ teaspoon salt
2 tablespoons coriander	¼ teaspoon ginger
3 lemongrasses	

- Place all ingredients in an Instant Pot then stir well.
- Cover the Instant Pot then lock it properly.

- Select "Manual" setting then cook the pork on high for 30 minutes.
- Once it is done, naturally release the Instant Pot then open the lid.
- Take the cooked pork out from the Instant Pot then place on a flat surface.
- Cut the pork into slices then fry until crispy or eat it just the way it is.
- Serve and enjoy with a bowl of rice.

Peppercini Pot Roast

1 hour 30 minutes, Serves: 6, Calories 653; Fat 38 g; Carbohydrates 6.2 g; Sugar 0.6 g; Protein 67.8 g; Cholesterol 239 mg

3 lbs pork roast
1/2 cup water
1/2 jar pepperoncini
1/2 cup clarified butter
1 packet ranch seasoning

- Place pork roast into the instant pot.
- Sprinkle ranch seasoning over the pork.
- Place butter on top of roast.
- Pour water around the pork roast.
- Seal pot with lid and select manual and set timer for 90 minutes.
- Using fork shred the meat and serve.

Easy Pork Sausage

Serves: 2 / Preparation time: 5 minutes / Cooking time: 25 minutes, Per Serving: Calories: 159; Total Fat: 10.4g; Saturated Fat: 3.8g; Protein: 13.1g; Carbs: 2.7g; Fiber: 0.3g; Sugar: 0.9g

1 lb. ground pork
3 teaspoons minced garlic
½ teaspoon nutmeg
½ teaspoon pepper
¼ teaspoon salt
¼ teaspoon sugar
1 egg

- Combine all ingredients then mix well.
- Divide the mixture into 4 then shape into long logs and wrap with aluminum foil.
- Pour water into an Instant Pork then place a trivet in it.
- Place the pork logs in the trivet then cover the Instant Pot properly.
- Select "Manual" setting then cook the beef on high for 25 minutes.
- Once it is done, naturally release the Instant Pot then open the lid.
- Take the sausage out from the Instant Pot then cook for another dish or eat just the way it is.
- Enjoy right away.

Garlic Balsamic Pork Chops

Serves: 4 / Preparation time: 5 minutes / Cooking time: 20 minutes,Per Serving: Calories: 502; Total Fat: 32.5g; Saturated Fat: 9.3g; Protein: 18.3g; Carbs: 35.9g; Fiber: 0.1g; Sugar: 34.9g;

4 pork chops, boneless
1 tsp dried parsley
1 tbsp garlic, minced
1/2 cup balsamic vinegar
1/2 cup honey
1/4 cup olive oil
Pepper
Salt

- Season pork chops with pepper and salt.
- Add oil into the instant pot and select sauté.
- Add pork chops into the instant pot and sear on each side for 1 minute.
- Add remaining ingredients into the pot and stir well.
- Seal pot with lid and cook on manual high pressure for 15 minutes.
- Release pressure using quick release method than open the lid.

- Serve and enjoy.

Salty and Spicy Pork

Serves: 2 / Preparation time: 5 minutes / Cooking time: 20 minutes, Per Serving: Calories: 125; Total Fat: 6.8g; Saturated Fat: 1.4g; Protein: 10.6g; Carbs: 6.1g; Fiber: 0.4g; Sugar: 0.2g

1 lb. pork tenderloin	1-teaspoon salt
2 teaspoons olive oil	¼ cup red chilies
¼ cup minced garlic	

- Cut the pork into slices then set aside.
- Preheat an Instant Pot for 30 seconds then choose the "Sauté" menu.
- Pour olive oil into the Instant Pot then stir in minced garlic and sliced pork. Sauté until brown and crispy then Press the "Cancel" button.
- Place the pork in a baking dish then season with salt.
- Cut the red chilies into slices then sprinkle over the pork.
- Pour water into the Instant Pot then place a trivet in it.
- Place the baking dish in the trivet then cover the Instant Pot properly.
- Select "Manual" setting then cook the pork on high for 25 minutes.
- Once it is done, naturally release the Instant Pot then open the lid.
- Take the baking dish out from Instant Pot then serve.
- Enjoy right away.

BBQ Boneless Ribs

Serves: 4, Preparation time: 5 minutes, Cooking time: 40 minutes, Per Serving: Calories: 227; Total Fat: 9g; Saturated Fat: 3g; Protein: 26g; Carbs: 13g; Fiber: 4g; Sugar: 5

1 medium onion, sliced	¼ teaspoon ground chipotle chili pepper
2 cloves garlic, peeled and minced	Salt and freshly ground black pepper, to taste
1 tablespoon butter	
1 pound boneless pork ribs	1 can (28 ounces) crushed tomatoes
1 teaspoon chili powder	2 tablespoons lemon juice
½ teaspoon paprika	1 tablespoon cider vinegar
¼ teaspoon ground cumin	1 tablespoon soy sauce

- In Instant Pot on sauté setting, cook onion in butter until onion is translucent, about 4 minutes. Add garlic to pot and cook about 1 minute more. Season ribs to taste with salt and pepper, add to pot and sauté until ribs are lightly browned, 2-3 minutes.
- Mix chili powder, paprika, cumin and chipotle Chile pepper and sprinkle over ribs, turning ribs to coat with spices. Sauté ribs for about 1 more minute.
- Add crushed tomatoes, lemon juice, vinegar and soy sauce to pot and stir gently.
- Secure pot lid, close pressure valve and cook on high pressure until done, about 30 minutes. When cooking time ends, let pressure release naturally.
- Serve and enjoy!

Pulled Pork with Apple Cider Vinegar

1 hour 50 minutes, Serves: 8, Calories 688; Fat 50.8 g; Carbohydrates 1.4 g; Sugar 0.4 g; Protein 53.4 g; Cholesterol 204 mg

4 lbs pork shoulder, cut into pieces	1 Tsp garlic powder
2 tbsp apple cider vinegar	1 Tsp paprika
1 1/2 cups chicken stock	1 tbsp chili powder
1 tbsp coconut oil	2 Tsp sea salt
2 Tsp mustard powder	

- Add oil in instant pot and select sauté.
- In a bowl, mix together mustard powder, garlic powder, paprika, chili powder, and salt.
- Rub spice mixture all over the pork.
- Add seasoned pork pieces into the pot and cook until browned.
- Add vinegar and chicken stock in a pot.
- Seal pot with lid and set the timer for 1 hour 40 minutes.
- Release pressure using quick release method than open the lid carefully.
- Stir well and serve.

Delicious Pork Shoulder

Serves: 8 / Preparation time: 15 minutes / Cooking time: 60 minutes, Per Serving: Calories: 504; Total Fat: 36.4g; Saturated Fat: 13.4g; Protein: 39.8g; Carbs: 1.6g; Fiber: 0.1g; Sugar: 0.7g;

3 lbs pork shoulder, boneless and cut into 2-inch cubes	1/4 cup lime juice
	1/4 cup orange juice
1/2 tsp ground cumin	Fresh cilantro, chopped
5 garlic cloves, minced	1 tsp salt

- Add lime juice, orange juice, garlic, cumin powder and salt into the instant pot.
- Add pork and stir well.
- Seal pot with lid and cook on manual high for 45 minutes.
- Allow releasing pressure naturally then open the lid.
- Remove pork from instant pot. Set the instant pot on sauté mode and reduce the liquid until thickened, about 15 minutes.

- Pour liquid into the bowl.
- Broil the pork about 5 minutes or until it browned.
- Serve with reduced sauce and enjoy

Pork Meatballs in Sticky Sauce

Serves: 2 / Preparation time: 5 minutes / Cooking time: 25 minutes, Per Serving: Calories: 274; Total Fat: 21.5g; Saturated Fat: 11.6g; Protein: 13.6g; Carbs: 6.7g; Fiber: 1.1g; Sugar: 3.1g

¾ lbs. ground pork
¼ cup chopped onion
1 organic egg
1 tablespoons breadcrumb
¼ cup coconut milk
¾ teaspoon brown sugar

- Combine ground pork with egg and breadcrumbs then mix well.
- Shape the mixture into balls forms then arrange in the Instant Pot.
- Pour coconut milk over the meatballs then sprinkle brown sugar and chopped onion on top.
- Cover the Instant Pot with the lid then make sure that it is locked properly.
- Turn on the Instant Pot then choose "Manual" setting.
- Cook the pork meatballs on low and set the time to 25 minutes.
- Once it is done, naturally release the Instant Pot then open the lid.
- Transfer the pork meatballs along with the sauce to a serving dish then serve.
- Enjoy.

Tasty Pork Carnitas

45 minutes, Serves: 6, Calories 901; Fat 65 g; Carbohydrates 4 g; Sugar 2 g; Protein 71 g; Cholesterol 272 mg

4 lbs pork shoulder, cut into chunks
1 bay leaf
1/4 Tsp ground cinnamon
1 Tsp chili powder
2 Tsp ground cumin
1 Tsp dried oregano
4 garlic cloves, minced
1/2 onion, sliced
1 grapefruit juice
3 Tsp kosher salt

- Add all ingredients into the instant pot and stir well.
- Seal pot with lid and select manual and set timer for 35 minutes.
- Allow releasing pressure naturally then open the lid.
- Using slotted spoon remove meat from pot and place on a baking dish.
- Using fork shred the meat and broil shredded meat in hot broiler until crisp.
- Serve and enjoy.

Simple Pulled Pork

Serves: 2 / Preparation time: 10 minutes / Cooking time: 45 minutes, Per Serving: Calories: 106; Total Fat: 2.3g; Saturated Fat: 0.9g; Protein: 9.9g; Carbs: 11.7g; Fiber: 0.5g; Sugar: 8.9g

1 lb. pork tenderloin
3 teaspoons minced garlic
1-teaspoon black pepper
½ teaspoon nutmeg
¾ cup water
2 tablespoons brown sugar
½ teaspoon salt

- Heat up the Instant Pot then select "Sauté" menu.
- Cut the pork into slices then place in the Instant Pot.
- Add tomato puree and pineapple juice to the pot then sprinkle chopped onion, rosemary, nutmeg, cloves, and cinnamon on top.
- Cover the Instant Pot with the lid then make sure that it is locked properly.
- Select "Manual" setting then cook the pork on high for 25 minutes.
- Quickly release the Instant Pot then open the lid.
- Add pineapple chunks to the pot then stir well. Do not need to reheat it again.

- Transfer to a serving dish then enjoy warm.

Flavorful Shredded Pork

Serves: 8 / Preparation time: 5 minutes / Cooking time: 30 minutes, Per Serving: Calories: 546; Total Fat: 21.5g; Saturated Fat: 7.8g; Protein: 65.2g; Carbs: 15.4g; Fiber: 0.1g; Sugar: 5.7g;

4 lbs pork roast, boneless and cut into chunks	1/2 cup homemade chicken stock
1/4 cup lime juice	1 cup orange juice
	1/3 cup taco seasoning

- Season pork chunks with taco seasoning.
- Add seasoned pork, lime juice, chicken stock, and orange juice into the instant pot. Stir well.
- Seal pot with lid and select meat setting and set timer for 30 minutes.
- Allow releasing pressure naturally then open the lid.
- Using fork shred the meat and serve.

Pork Belly Black Pepper

Serves: 2 / Preparation time: 10 minutes / Cooking time: 35 minutes, Per Serving: Calories: 189; Total Fat: 15.5g; Saturated Fat: 5.6g; Protein: 4.4g; Carbs: 7.9g; Fiber: 1.3g; Sugar: 1.4g

1 lb. pork belly	½ cup chopped onion
1 ½ teaspoons black pepper	1-teaspoon thyme
¼ teaspoon salt	1-tablespoon cornstarch
½ cup beef broth	3 tablespoons water

- Cut the pork belly into medium cubes then place in the Instant Pot.
- Sprinkle chopped onion, salt, and black pepper then pour beef broth over the pork.
- Add thyme to the pork then stir well.
- Cover the Instant Pot with the lid then make sure that it is locked properly.
- Select "Manual" setting then cook the beef on high for 35 minutes.
- Quickly release the Instant Pot then open the lid.
- Take the pork belly out from the Instant Pot then place on a serving dish but leave the liquid in the Instant Pot.
- Combine cornstarch with water then stir into the Instant Pot. Mix well.
- Drizzle the liquid over the pork then serve.
- Enjoy.

Pork Chops with Gravy

25 minutes, Serves: 4, Calories 551; Fat 46.1 g; Carbohydrates 13.4 g; Sugar 3.8 g; Protein 23 g; Cholesterol 80 mg

4 pork chops	1 tbsp seasoned salt
2 tbsp arrowroot powder	For gravy:
1 1/4 cups chicken broth	1 1/2 tbsp clarified butter
2 tbsp extra virgin olive oil	1 tbsp arrowroot powder
2 garlic cloves, minced	1 cup coconut milk
1/2 cup onion, sliced	1/4 Tsp black pepper
8 oz mushrooms, sliced	1/2 Tsp sea salt

- In a bowl, whisk together all gravy ingredients and set aside.
- Season pork chops with seasoned salt.
- Add oil in instant pot and select sauté.
- Add pork chops in a pot and cook until brown.
- Remove pork chops from pot and place on a plate.
- Add garlic and onion and sauté for minutes.

- Add broth, gravy mixture, pork chops, and mushroom in instant pot.
- Seal pot with lid and cook on manual high pressure for 8 minutes.
- Allow releasing pressure naturally then open the lid.
- Remove pork chops from pot and place on a plate.
- Select sauté mode of the instant pot.
- Add arrowroot powder in a pot and stir until gravy thickens.
- Pour gravy over pork chops and serve.

Pork Feet Stew with Vegetables

Serves: 2 / Preparation time: 10 minutes / Cooking time: 30 minutes, Per Serving: Calories: 292; Total Fat: 19.4g; Saturated Fat: 5.4g; Protein: 22.2g; Carbs: 6.4g; Fiber: 1.3g; Sugar: 2.3g

¾ lb. pork feet
1-teaspoon olive oil
½ cup chopped carrot
2 tablespoons chopped onion
¼ cup soy sauce
¼ teaspoon salt
½ teaspoon pepper
2 cups water

- Heat up an Instant Pot for 30 seconds then press the "Sauté" menu.
- Pour olive oil into the Instant Pot then stir in chopped onion. Sauté until softened and aromatic.
- Add pork feet to the Instant Pot then drizzle soy sauce over the pork feet.
- Season with salt and pepper then pour water into the Instant Pot.
- Place a trivet over the pork feet then place the chopped carrot in it.
- Cover the Instant Pot with the lid then make sure that it is locked properly.
- Select "Manual" setting then cook the pork on high for 30 minutes.
- Naturally release the Instant Pot then open the lid.
- Combine carrots with the pork feet and the liquid then stir well.
- Transfer to a serving dish then enjoy warm.

Creamy Chicken

Total Time: 4 hours 10 minutes; Serves: 2; Calories 852; Fat 61.8 g; Carbohydrates 17.3 g; Sugar 1.3 g; Protein 55.5 g; Cholesterol 271 mg

2 chicken breasts, boneless and skinless
14 oz can cream of chicken soup
8 oz cream cheese, softened
1 packet dry Italian seasoning
Black pepper

- Use the "Slow Cooker" setting on your Instant Pot.
- Place chicken in the slow cooker.
- Sprinkle Italian seasoning over the chicken.
- In a saucepan, cook cream cheese and chicken soup over low heat until cheese is completely smooth.
- Pour soup mixture over the chicken.
- Cover and cook on low for 4 hours.
- Using fork shred the chicken.
- Serve over rice and enjoy.

Cinnamon Honey Pork Chops

Serves: 4 / Preparation time: 10 minutes / Cooking time: 15 minutes, Per Serving: Calories: 798; Total Fat: 56.7g; Saturated Fat: 21.2g; Protein: 51.4g; Carbs: 18.4g; Fiber: 0.6g; Sugar: 17.5g;

2 lbs pork chops, boneless
1/4 tsp ground cloves
1/2 tsp cinnamon
1/2 tsp ginger, minced
2 tbsp Dijon mustard
1/4 cups honey
1/4 tsp ground black pepper
1/2 tsp sea salt

- Season pork chops with pepper and salt and place in instant pot.
- Select sauté mode of instant pot and brown the pork chops on both the sides.
- In a bowl, combine together honey, cloves, cinnamon, ginger, and Dijon mustard.
- Pour honey mixture over the pork chops.
- Seal pot with lid and select manual and set timer for 15 minutes.
- Allow releasing pressure naturally then open the lid.
- Serve and enjoy.

Baby Back Ribs

Serves: 6, Preparation time: 10 minutes, Cooking time: 60 minutes, Per Serving: Calories: 427; Total Fat: 27g; Saturated Fat: 10g; Protein: 40g; Carbs: 6g; Fiber: 0g; Sugar: 1g

- 1 teaspoon salt
- 1 teaspoon paprika
- 1 teaspoon chili powder
- ½ teaspoon freshly ground black pepper
- ½ teaspoon cumin
- ¼ teaspoon cayenne pepper
- 2 tablespoons olive oil
- 3 pounds baby back pork ribs
- 6 ounces bacon, chopped
- 1 onion, coarsely chopped
- 4 cloves garlic, peeled and minced
- 1-1/2 cups beef or vegetable stock
- 3 tablespoons tomato paste
- 1 tablespoon arrowroot flour
- 1/4 cup water

- Combine salt, paprika, chili powder, black pepper, cumin and cayenne pepper and rub over ribs. Heat 1 tablespoon oil in instant pot on sauté setting and cook half of the ribs until meat is browned on all sides, 4-5 minutes. Repeat with remaining oil and ribs. Remove ribs from pot and set aside.
- Sauté bacon in pot until lightly browned. Stir onion and garlic into pot with bacon and sauté until translucent, 2-3 minutes.
- Add stock and tomato paste to pot, stir to loosen browned bits and return ribs to pot. Secure pot lid, close pressure valve and cook at high pressure until meat is very tender, about 40 minutes. Cook longer if necessary. When cooking time ends, let pressure release naturally.
- Remove ribs to a plate, cover and set aside. Skim fat from juices in pot if necessary. Thoroughly mix arrowroot flour into water and stir into pot juices to thicken. Return ribs to pot and stir gently to coat ribs with sauce. Cover pot and let stand for about 10 minutes, stirring occasionally. Serve and enjoy!

Chinese Steamed Pork Bags

Serves: 2 / Preparation time: 5 minutes / Cooking time: 15 minutes, Per Serving: Calories: 227; Total Fat: 8.8g; Saturated Fat: 3g; Protein: 12.8g; Carbs: 24.4g; Fiber: 1.3g; Sugar: 0.6g

- ¾ lb. ground pork
- 2 teaspoons minced garlic
- 1-tablespoon fish sauce
- ½ teaspoon pepper
- ½ teaspoon salt
- 2 tablespoons chopped leek
- 8 sheets dumpling wrapper

- Combine ground pork with minced garlic, fish sauce, pepper, salt, and chopped leek then mix well.
- Divide the mixture into 8 then wrap each part with dumpling wrapper.
- Pour water into the Instant Pot then place a trivet in in.
- Arrange the pork bags in the trivet then cover the Instant Pot properly.
- Select "Manual" setting then cook the pork on high for 15 minutes.
- Once it is done, naturally release the Instant Pot then open the lid.
- Remove the pork bags from the Instant Pot then arrange on a serving dish.
- Enjoy right away.

Green Chile Pork Stew

35 minutes, Serves: 6, Calories 305; Fat 8.5 g; Carbohydrates 36.5 g; Sugar 7.8 g; Protein 19.8 g; Cholesterol 50 mg

- 1 lb lean pork stew meat, cut into 1/2 inch pieces
- 4 cups potatoes, diced
- 3 cups chicken stock

3 1/2 cups salsa Verde
3/4 cup green Chile, roasted chopped
3 large onion, chopped
1 tbsp extra virgin olive oil

1/2 Tsp garlic powder
1/2 Tsp black pepper
1/4 cup arrowroot powder
1/2 Tsp kosher salt

- Add pork, arrowroot powder, pepper, and garlic powder in a large zip lock bag.
- Seal bag and shake well and set aside.
- Add oil in instant pot and select sauté.
- Add pork pieces in a pot and cook until browned, about 5 minutes.
- Add remaining all ingredients into the pot and stir well.
- Seal pot with lid and cook on manual high pressure for 20 minutes.
- Allow releasing pressure naturally then open the lid.
- Stir well and serve.

Crispy Pork in Sweet Sour Sauce

Serves: 2 / Preparation time: 5 minutes / Cooking time: 20 minutes, Per Serving: Calories: 192; Total Fat: 4.7g; Saturated Fat: 1.1g; Protein: 13.3g; Carbs: 26.8g; Fiber: 4.8g; Sugar: 15.8g

¾ lb. pork tenderloin
1-teaspoon olive oil
1 medium carrot
¼ cup green peas
½ cup chopped onion
1 teaspoon minced garlic

½ teaspoon pepper
¼ teaspoon salt
1-cup tomato puree
¼ cup water
1-tablespoon sugar

- Cut the pork into slices then set aside.
- Peel and cut the carrot into sticks then set aside.
- Heat up the Instant Pot then choose "Sauté" menu.
- Pour olive oil into the Instant Pot then stir in minced garlic and chopped onion. Sauté until aromatic and soft. Press the "Cancel" button.
- Add the remaining ingredients to the Instant Pot then cover it properly.
- Select "Manual" setting then cook the pork on high for 20 minutes.
- Once it is done, naturally release the Instant Pot then open the lid.
- Transfer to a serving dish then serve.
- Enjoy right away.

Easy Balsamic Pork Tenderloin

Serves: 4 / Preparation time: 10 minutes / Cooking time: 10 minutes, Per Serving: Calories: 515; Total Fat: 17.5g; Saturated Fat: 4.5g; Protein: 75.7g; Carbs: 9.8g; Fiber: 0.3g; Sugar: 8.9g;

2 1/2 lbs pork tenderloin
1/4 cup water
1 tsp ground sage
1 tbsp Dijon mustard
2 garlic cloves, minced

1/4 cup balsamic vinegar
2 tbsp honey
1 cup homemade chicken stock
2 tbsp olive oil
1 tsp kosher salt

- Add oil into the instant pot and select sauté.
- Add remaining ingredients and mix well.
- Seal pot with lid and select manual for 7 minutes.
- Release pressure using quick release method than open the lid.
- Serve and enjoy.

Simple Cheesy Pork Meatloaf

Serves: 2 / Preparation time: 5 minutes / Cooking time: 20 minutes, Per Serving: Calories: 299; Total Fat: 20.4g; Saturated Fat: 9.7g; Protein: 20g; Carbs: 8.9g; Fiber: 1.1g; Sugar: 2g

¾ lb. ground pork
1 egg
2 tablespoons breadcrumbs
½ cup chopped onion
½ teaspoon salt
½ teaspoon pepper
2 cheese slices

- Line a loaf pan with aluminum foil then set aside.
- Combine ground pork with breadcrumbs, chopped onion, salt, and pepper then mix well.
- Place half of the mixture in the prepared loaf pan then spread evenly.
- Lay cheese slices on it then cover with the remaining mixture.
- Pour water into the Instant Pot then place a trivet in it.
- Place the loaf pan in the trivet then cover the Instant Pot properly.
- Select "Manual" setting then cook the pork loaf on high for 20 minutes.
- Once it is done, naturally release the Instant Pot then open the lid.
- Remove the loaf pan from the Instant Pot then let it cool for a few minutes.
- Take the meatloaf out from the pan then place on a serving dish.
- Cut into thick slices then serve.
- Enjoy.

Perfect Pork Ragu

55 minutes, Serves: 10, Calories 119; Fat 2.4 g; Carbohydrates 7.2 g Sugar 2.1 g; Protein 14.9 g; Cholesterol 37 mg

18 oz pork tenderloin
1 tbsp fresh parsley, chopped
2 bay leaves
2 fresh thyme sprigs
7 oz jar roasted red peppers, drained
28 oz tomatoes, crushed
5 garlic cloves, smashed
1 Tsp extra virgin olive oil
1/4 Tsp black pepper
1 Tsp kosher salt

- Season pork with pepper and salt.
- Add oil in instant pot and select sauté.
- Add pork in instant pot and cook until brown.
- Add remaining ingredients and stir well.
- Seal pot with lid and cook on manual high pressure for 45 minutes.
- Allow releasing pressure naturally then open the lid.
- Using fork shred the pork and serve.

Hot Chili Pork Ribs

Serves: 2 / Preparation time: 5 minutes / Cooking time: 25 minutes, Per Serving: Calories: 198; Total Fat: 12.3g; Saturated Fat: 3.9g; Protein: 18g; Carbs: 4.5g; Fiber: 1.5g; Sugar: 1.9g

1-½ lbs. pork ribs
½ teaspoon salt
1-teaspoon coriander
1 bay leaf
1-cup water
¼ cup red chilies
2 cloves garlic
1-teaspoon vegetable oil

- Place pork ribs in the Instant Pot then season with salt, coriander, and a bay leaf.
- Pour water into the Instant Pot then cover and lock properly.
- Select "Manual" setting then cook the pork ribs on high for 25 minutes.
- Meanwhile, place red chilies and garlic in a food processor then pulse until smooth.
- Transfer the chili mixture to a bowl then add vegetable oil to it. Mix well.
- Once the pork is done, naturally release the Instant Pot then open the lid.
- Transfer to a serving dish then top with the chilies and garlic mixture.
- Serve and enjoy warm.

Honey Lime Shredded Pork with Chicken Stock

Serves: 4 / Preparation time: 10 minutes / Cooking time: 30 minutes, Per Serving: Calories: 461; Total Fat: 32.4g; Saturated Fat: 11.2g; Protein: 33.3g; Carbs: 8.1g; Fiber: 0.8g; Sugar: 4.8g;

1 1/2 lbs pork shoulder, diced
1 cup chicken stock
1 tbsp honey
1/2 lime juice
1 tsp allspice
1 tsp dried oregano
1 tsp onion powder
1 1/2 tsp red chili flakes
1 tsp ground coriander
1 tsp cumin powder
1 bay leaf
5 garlic cloves, diced
1 onion, diced
1 tbsp olive oil
1 tsp sea salt

- Add olive oil into the instant pot and select sauté.
- Add onion to the pot and sauté for 2 minutes.
- Add pork and cook for 2 minutes.
- Add spices and garlic. Stir well.
- Add remaining ingredients and stir well.
- Seal pot with lid and cook on manual high pressure for 20 minutes.
- Release pressure using quick release method than open the lid.
- Using fork shred the meat.
- Return shredded meat to the instant pot and select sauté for 5-8 minutes.
- Serve and enjoy.

Pulled Pork Carnitas

Serves: 8, Preparation time: 30 minutes, Cooking time: 40 minutes, Per Serving: Calories: 381; Total Fat: 22g; Saturated Fat: 8g; Protein: 37g; Carbs: 7g; Fiber: 3g; Sugar: 0g

3 pounds pork tenderloin, cut into 2-inch cubes
1 teaspoon salt
½ teaspoon freshly ground pepper
¼ teaspoon cayenne pepper
1 cup chicken stock
4 cloves garlic, peeled and minced
1 orange, juiced and zested
1 lime, juiced and zested
Salt and freshly ground black pepper, to taste
8 ounces sour cream
2 avocados, cut into slices

- Toss pork cubes with salt and pepper to coat. Cook pork in instant pot on sauté setting until browned on all sides.
- Mix chicken stock, garlic, orange juice, orange zest, lime juice and lime zest and pour into pot with pork. Secure pot lid, close pressure valve and cook at high pressure until done, about 30 minutes. When cooking time ends, let pressure release naturally.
- Shred cooked pork with two forks, season with salt and pepper to taste and stir.
- Serve onto plates with a slotted spoon. Dollop servings with sour cream and garnish with avocado slices. Enjoy!

Pork Roast Black Pepper

Serves: 2 / Preparation time: 10 minutes / Cooking time: 45 minutes, Per Serving: Calories: 399; Total Fat: 13.5g; Saturated Fat: 4.6g; Protein: 41.5g; Carbs: 26.6g; Fiber: 2.1g; Sugar: 5.7g

½ lb. pork
1-teaspoon olive oil
½ cup Mozzarella cheese
½ cup Parmesan cheese
1 egg
1-teaspoon oregano
¼ teaspoon salt
½ teaspoon pepper
Uncooked lasagna noodles
1-cup pasta sauce

- Preheat the Instant Pot for about 30 seconds then select the "Sauté" menu.
- Pour olive oil into the pot then brown the ground pork.
- Remove from the Instant Pot then press the "Cancel" button.
- Combine Parmesan cheese and Mozzarella cheese with egg, salt, pepper, and oregano then mix well.
- Prepare a small baking pan then line with lasagna noodles.
- Spread pasta sauce over the lasagna noodles then layer with ground pork and cheese. Repeat with the remaining ingredients.
- Pour water into the Instant Pot then place a trivet in it.
- Place the lasagna in the trivet then cover the Instant Pot properly.
- Select "Manual" setting then cook the pork loaf on high for 45 minutes.
- Once it is done, naturally release the Instant Pot then open the lid.
- Take the lasagna out from the Instant Pot then enjoy.

Pork Chops with Brussels sprouts

35 minutes, Serves: 4, Calories 439; Fat 31.9 g; Carbohydrates 12.1 g; Sugar 3.7 g; Protein 27.8 g; Cholesterol 98 mg

1 lb pork chops, boneless
1 tbsp arrowroot powder
1 cup chicken stock
1 cup carrot, chopped
2 cups Brussels sprouts, halve

1/2 Tsp thyme, dried
2 Tsp garlic, minced
1 cup onion, sliced
1 tbsp coconut oil
1 Tsp salt

- Season pork chops with salt.
- Add oil in instant pot and select sauté.
- Add pork chops to the pot and cook until brown.
- Remove pork chops from pot and place on a plate.
- Add thyme, garlic, and onion and sauté for 2 minutes.
- Add broth and pork chops.
- Seal pot with lid and select manual and set timer for 15 minutes.
- Release pressure using quick release method than open the lid.
- Add carrots and Brussels sprouts and stir well.
- Seal pot again and select a manual and set timer for 3 minutes.
- Release pressure using quick release method than open the lid.
- Remove vegetables and pork chops from pot and place on a serving plate.
- Add arrowroot powder and stir until thickened.
- Pour gravy over vegetables and pork chops.
- Serve and enjoy.

Garlic Cumin Grapefruit Shredded Pork

Serves: 10 / Preparation time: 10 minutes / Cooking time: 8 hours, Per Serving: Calories: 408; Total Fat: 29.2g; Saturated Fat: 10.7g; Protein: 32g; Carbs: 2.5g; Fiber: 0.4g; Sugar: 1.2g;

3 lbs pork shoulder, boneless
1 bay leaf
1/2 tbsp cumin
1/2 tbsp fresh oregano

1 lime juice
2/3 cup grapefruit juice
6 garlic cloves
1 tbsp kosher salt

- Cut pork into the pieces and place into the bowl.
- Add cumin, oregano, lime juice, grapefruit juice, garlic, and salt into the blender and blend until smooth.
- Pour marinade mixture over pork and mix well. Marinate in refrigerator for 1 hour.
- Transfer marinated pork into the instant pot with bay leaf.
- Seal pot with lid and select slow cooker setting and cook on low for 8 hours.
- Release pressure using quick release method than open the lid.

- Using fork shred the pork and serves.

Apple Pork Ribs

35 minutes, Serves: 4, Calories 504; Fat 27.5 g; Carbohydrates 25 g; Sugar 21.1 g; Protein 38.7 g; Cholesterol 0 mg

2 lbs rack of pork back ribs, cut in half and remove membrane

1/2 cup apple cider vinegar
3 1/2 cups apple juice

- Pour apple cider vinegar and apple juice in instant pot.
- Place trivet into the instant pot.
- Place pork ribs on a trivet.
- Seal pot with lid and select manual and set timer for 30 minutes.
- Allow releasing pressure naturally then open the lid.
- Serve and enjoy.

Simple Kalua Pork

1 hour 40 minutes, Serves: 8, Calories 576; Fat 19.1 g; Carbohydrates 6.7 g; Sugar 3.7 g; Protein 89.7 g Cholesterol 261 mg

5 lbs pork butt, remove bone and cut into chunks
1 green cabbage, sliced

1 cup water
1 Tsp smoked paprika
1 tbsp sea salt

- Season pork with paprika and salt.
- Pour water into the instant pot.
- Place season pork in the pot.
- Seal pot with lid and select manual and set timer for 90 minutes.
- Allow releasing pressure naturally then open the lid.
- Remove pork from pot and place in a bowl.
- Add sliced cabbage to the pot and stir well.
- Seal pot and cook on manual high pressure for 3 minutes.
- Release pressure using quick release method than open the lid carefully.
- Add cook cabbage to the pork and stir well.
- Serve and enjoy.

Crispy Pulled Pork

1 hour 10 minutes, Serves: 10, Calories 755; Fat 52.6 g; Carbohydrates 14 g; Sugar 8.2 g; Protein 54.4 g; Cholesterol 204 mg

5 lbs pork shoulder, cut into pieces
2 tbsp extra virgin olive oil
2 bay leaves
2 cinnamon sticks
1 large jalapeno pepper, seeded and chopped
10 garlic cloves, minced

1 large onion, chopped
4 large oranges
For rub:
2 Tsp oregano
1 tbsp ground cumin
2 tbsp kosher salt
1/4 Tsp black pepper

- Add pork pieces into the mixing bowl.
- Sprinkle all rub ingredients over pork pieces and rub well.
- Add 1 tbsp oil in instant pot and select sauté.
- Add pork pieces to the pot and sauté for 3 minutes.
- Add 1 orange juice in a pot and deglaze the pot.
- Add bay leaves, cinnamon, jalapeno, garlic, and onions and stir well.
- Add remaining three oranges juice and stir well.

- Seal pot with lid and cook on high pressure for 40 minutes.
- Allow releasing pressure naturally then open the lid.
- Remove meat from pot and place into a strainer and drain all liquid.
- Place drain meat in the large pot and using fork shred the meat.
- Heat remaining oil in a pan over medium high heat.
- Add shredded meat in a pan and sauté for minutes.
- Serve and enjoy.

Kale Garlic Pork

Serves: 6 / Preparation time: 10 minutes / Cooking time: 60 minutes, Per Serving: Calories: 660; Total Fat: 45.4g; Saturated Fat: 15.6g; Protein: 47.7g; Carbs: 13.8g; Fiber: 2g; Sugar: 1.3g;

2 1/2 lbs pork shoulder, boneless and cut into 1 1/2" chunks
1 lb kale, stems removed and cut into strips
2/3 cup homemade chicken broth
1 tbsp vinegar
1 tsp rosemary, minced
20 garlic cloves
1 large onion, chopped
2 tbsp olive oil
2 fresh thyme springs
Black pepper
Salt

- Season pork chops with pepper and salt.
- Add olive oil into the instant pot and select sauté.
- Add seasoned pork chops into the instant pot and browned them from both the sides.
- Transfer pork chops onto the plate.
- Add thyme and onion into the instant pot and sauté for 5 minutes.
- Add rosemary and garlic and cook for 1 minute. Add vinegar and stir well.
- Add pork and broth and stir well to combine.
- Seal pot with lid and cook on manual high pressure for 40 minutes.
- Release pressure using quick release method than open the lid.
- Now add kale and again seal pot with lid and cook on manual high pressure for 10 minutes.
- Release pressure using quick release method than open the lid.
- Using fork shred the pork and serves.

Sirloin Tip Roast

35 minutes, Serves: 6, Calories 234; Fat 5.4 g; Carbohydrates 2.8 g; Sugar 2.1 g; Protein 44.7 g; Cholesterol 61 mg

3 lbs pork sirloin tip roast
1/2 cup apple juice
1 cup water
1 tbsp extra virgin olive oil
1/4 Tsp chili powder
1/2 Tsp garlic powder
1/2 Tsp onion powder
1/2 Tsp black pepper
1/2 Tsp salt

- In a small bowl, mix together all spices.
- Rub spice mixture over the pork from both the sides.
- Add oil in instant pot and brown the pork in the pot.
- Pour apple juice and water into the instant pot.
- Seal pot with lid and cook on high pressure for 25 minutes.
- Release pressure using quick release method than open the lid.
- Serve and enjoy.

Tender and Juicy shredded Pork

1 hour 10 minutes, Serves: 8, Calories 721; Fat 53.9 g; Carbohydrates 3.1 g; Sugar 0.7 g; Protein 53.2 g; Cholesterol 204 mg

4 lbs pork shoulder, trimmed	1 chili, mild
3 tbsp extra virgin olive oil	1 medium onion, quarters
2 tbsp lime juice	4 garlic cloves, peeled
2 tbsp dried oregano	2 Tsp black pepper
1 small dried hot chili	1 tbsp salt

- Add 2 tbsp oil, pepper, lime juice, oregano, chilies, onion, garlic and salt into the blender and blend until smooth.
- Rub marinade over pork and cover and place in refrigerator for 30 minutes.
- Add remaining oil in instant pot and place marinated pork in the pot.
- Seal pot with lid and cook on manual high pressure for 60 minutes.
- Allow releasing pressure naturally then open the lid.
- Using fork shred the pork and serves.

Ham & Asparagus Soup

Serves: 6, Preparation time: 20 minutes, Cooking time: 60 minutes, Per Serving (calculations based on 3 oz. ham per serving): Calories: 296; Total Fat: 17g; Saturated Fat: 7g; Protein: 22g; Carbs: 10g; Fiber: 3g; Sugar: 3g

1 tablespoon butter	4 cups chicken stock
1 onion, diced	2 pounds asparagus stalks
4 stalks celery, trimmed and diced	1 bay leaf
2 cloves garlic, peeled and minced	½ teaspoon dried thyme
1 meaty ham bone	Salt and ground black pepper, to taste

- Melt butter in instant pot on sauté setting and cook onion, celery and garlic until softened, about 5 minutes.
- Add ham bone and stock to pot and simmer for 3 minutes.
- Peel and trim asparagus stalks as necessary, cut in half and add to pot with thyme. Season soup to taste with salt and pepper.
- Secure pot lid, close pressure valve and cook on soup setting for about 45 minutes. When cooking time ends, let pressure release naturally. Remove ham bone and shred ham with a fork. If desired, blend soup with an immersion blender to desired consistency. Stir ham into soup, serve and enjoy!

Tasty Pork Stew

Serves: 16 / Preparation time: 10 minutes / Cooking time: 50 minutes, Per Serving: Calories: 254; Total Fat: 11.2g; Saturated Fat: 4g; Protein: 33.1g; Carbs: 3.6g; Fiber: 1.1g; Sugar: 1.7g;

4 lb pork loin roast, cut into pieces	15 oz tomatoes, chopped
3/4 cup water	1 onion, diced
1 tbsp paprika	3 poblano pepper, diced
2 tbsp adobo seasoning	3 oz green chilies, diced
2 tbsp chili powder	Salt

- Add all ingredients into the instant pot and stir well.
- Seal pot with lid and select manual and set timer for 50 minutes.
- Allow releasing pressure naturally then open the lid.
- Using fork shred meat lightly and stir well.
- Serve and enjoy.

Tomato Pulled Pork

1 hour 30 minutes, Serves: 8, Calories 345; Fat 24.7 g; Carbohydrates 2.3 g; Sugar 1 g; Protein 27 g; Cholesterol 102 mg

1/2 cup water	1/2 cup can tomatoes, diced

1 tbsp mustard powder
1 Tsp garlic powder
1 tbsp onion powder

1/2 Tsp black pepper
2 Tsp salt

- Mix together all dry ingredients and rub over pork.
- Place pork in instant pot and pour remaining ingredients over pork.
- Seal pot with lid and cook on high for 1 hour.
- Allow releasing pressure naturally then open the lid.
- Using fork shred the pork and stir well in pot juices.
- Serve and enjoy.

Perfect Cuban Pork

8 hours 10 minutes, Serves: 6, Calories 652; Fat 51.1 g; Carbohydrates 7.4 g; Sugar 2.8 g; Protein 38.8 g; Cholesterol 161 mg

3 lbs pork shoulder roast, using knife make slits all over pork
1 bay leaf
1 small onion, sliced
6 garlic cloves, smashed
1/4 Tsp red pepper flakes
1 Tsp dried oregano

1 Tsp cumin
1/2 cup lime juice
1/2 cup orange juice
2 tbsp extra virgin olive oil
1/8 Tsp black pepper
1 1/2 Tsp salt

- In a bowl, whisk together garlic, pepper, red pepper flakes, oregano, cumin, salt, lime juice, orange juice and oil.
- Rub bowl mixture over pork and place pork in instant pot.
- Add remaining bowl juice over pork with onion and bay leaf.
- Seal pot with lid and select slow cooker setting and set the timer for 8 hours.
- Using fork shred the pork and serves.

Jerk Pork Roast

55 minutes, Serves: 12, Calories 455; Fat 33.5 g; Carbohydrates 0 g; Sugar 0 g; Protein 36 g; Cholesterol 136 mg

4 lbs pork shoulder
1/2 cup bone broth

1 tbsp extra virgin olive oil
1/4 cup Jamaican jerk spice blend

- Rub oil and jerk spice blend over pork and place pork in instant pot.
- Select sauté and brown the meat on all sides.
- Add broth into the pot.
- Seal pot with lid and cook manual high pressure for 45 minutes,
- Allow releasing pressure naturally then open the lid.
- Using fork shred the meat and serve.

Crustless Ham & Swiss Quiche

Serves: 8, Preparation time: 15 minutes, Cooking time: 30 minutes, Per Serving: Calories: 262; Total Fat: 16g; Saturated Fat: 8g; Protein: 26g; Carbs: 2g; Fiber: 0g; Sugar: 2g

8 eggs, beaten
1 cup plain whole-milk yogurt
Salt and freshly ground black pepper, to taste

2 cups fully cooked diced ham
1 cup shredded Swiss cheese

- Pour 1 cup water into Instant Pot and set trivet in bottom of pot.
- Whisk together eggs and yogurt and season to taste with salt and pepper.
- Grease a soufflé dish that will fit inside the Instant Pot. Arrange the ham and half of the Swiss cheese in the soufflé dish. Pour egg mixture into soufflé dish and cover dish loosely with aluminum foil. Carefully set soufflé dish on trivet in Instant Pot.
- Secure pot lid, close pressure valve and cook at high pressure for about 30 minutes. When cooking time ends, let pressure release naturally.
- Carefully remove soufflé dish from pot and remove foil from soufflé. Sprinkle remaining Swiss cheese over soufflé. Cover soufflé with foil and let stand 1-2 minutes to allow cheese to melt.
- Cut soufflé into wedges to serve. Enjoy!

Ranch Pork Chops

10 minutes, Serves: 6, Calories 426; Fat 37.6 g; Carbohydrates 0 g; Sugar 0 g; Protein 21.5 g; Cholesterol 110 mg

6 pork chops, boneless
8 tbsp clarified butter
1 tbsp extra virgin olive oil
1 cup bone broth
1 packet ranch seasoning
Pepper
Salt

- Season pork chops with pepper and salt.
- Heat oil in a pan over medium heat place pork chops on hot pan and brown them on both the sides, about 5 minutes.
- Remove pan from heat and set aside.
- Place pork chops in instant pot.
- Sprinkle ranch seasoning over the pork chops.
- Add butter and broth into the pot.
- Seal pot with lid and cook on manual high pressure for 5 minutes.
- Allow releasing pressure naturally then open the lid.
- Serve and enjoy.

Herb Pork Tenderloin

50 minutes, Serves: 4, Calories 329; Fat 8.1 g; Carbohydrates 0.9 g; Sugar 0.1 g; Protein 59.5 g; Cholesterol 166 mg

2 lbs pork tenderloin
1 Tsp dried rosemary
1 Tsp dried basil
1 Tsp dried oregano
1 Tsp garlic, minced
1 tbsp onion, minced
1 cup hot water
Pepper
Salt

- Season pork with pepper and salt.
- Place pork into the instant pot with hot water.
- In a small bowl, mix together rosemary, basil, oregano, garlic, and onion.
- Add herb mixture to the pork.
- Seal pot with lid and cook on manual high pressure for 40 minutes.
- Release pressure using quick release method than open the lid.
- Remove pork from pot and cut into the slices.
- Serve and enjoy.

Herb Pork Loin

Serves: 6 / Preparation time: 10 minutes / Cooking time: 40 minutes, Per Serving: Calories: 401; Total Fat: 21.4g; Saturated Fat: 8g; Protein: 42.9g; Carbs: 6.7g; Fiber: 1.8g; Sugar: 3g;

2 lbs pork loin
1 tsp dried thyme

2 tsp paprika
2 tsp garlic powder
3 large carrots cut into chunks
1 medium onion, sliced
1 tsp parsley, chopped

1 cup homemade chicken stock
1 tsp rosemary, dried
Olive oil
Pepper
Salt

- Season pork with garlic powder, pepper, salt, and paprika.
- Add 1 tsp oil into the instant pot and select sauté mode.
- Once the oil is hot then add seasoned pork and sear for 2-3 minutes on each side until it browned.
- Pour chicken stock into the pot, add thyme and rosemary over pork and top with carrots and onions.
- Seal pot with lid and cook on high pressure for 40 minutes.
- Release pressure using quick release method than open the lid carefully.
- Serve and enjoy.

Smoked Pulled Pork

1 hour 20 minutes, Serves: 12, Calories 390; Fat 28.4 g; Carbohydrates 0.8 g; Sugar 0.1 g; Protein 31.2 g; Cholesterol 119 mg

3 1/2 lbs pork shoulder
2 garlic cloves, minced
2 tbsp liquid smoke

2 tbsp coconut amino
1 cup chicken broth

- Place pork into the instant pot.
- Pour remaining ingredients over the pork.
- Seal pot with lid and select manual button and set timer for 70 minutes.
- Allow releasing pressure naturally then open the lid.
- Remove pork from pot and place on cutting board.
- Using fork shred the meat and serves.

Pork Carnitas

1 hour 5 minutes, Serves: 10, Calories 270; Fat 16.3 g; Carbohydrates 1.2 g; Sugar 0.5 g; Protein 28 g; Cholesterol 96 mg

2 1/2 lbs pork shoulder blade roast, boneless and trimmed
2 chipotle peppers
3/4 cup beef stock
1/2 Tsp dry oregano

1 Tsp cumin
1 Tsp garlic powder
2 bay leaves
1/4 Tsp black pepper
2 Tsp kosher salt

- Season pork with pepper and salt.
- In a large pan, brown the pork over high heat, about 5 minutes.
- Remove pork from pan and place on a plate.
- Season pork with garlic powder, oregano, and cumin.
- Add broth, bay leaves and chipotle and stir well.
- Return pork in a pot.
- Seal pot with lid and cook on high pressure for 50 minutes.
- Allow releasing pressure naturally then open the lid.
- Discard bay leaves and using fork shred the pork.
- Stir and serve.

Garlic Thyme Pork Shoulder

Serves: 4, Preparation time: 10 minutes, Cooking time: 45 minutes, Per Serving: Calories: 325; Total Fat: 19; Saturated Fat: 8g; Protein: 33g; Carbs: 0g; Fiber: 0g; Sugar: 0g

- 1 boneless pork shoulder (about 2 pounds)
- 4 cloves garlic, minced
- 2 tablespoons peanut oil
- Salt and freshly ground black pepper, to taste
- 1 cup chicken stock
- 1 teaspoon dried thyme

- Score pork shoulder all over with a sharp knife in a diamond pattern and rub with garlic. Brush peanut oil over pork and season to taste with salt and pepper.
- In Instant Pot on sauté setting, cook pork shoulder, turning frequently until browned on all sides, about 10 minutes total. Sprinkle thyme over pork shoulder and season to taste with salt and pepper, turning pork shoulder to season on all sides.
- Pour 1 cup water into pot, secure pot lid and close pressure valve. Cook pork shoulder at high pressure until done, about 35 minutes. When cooking time ends, allow pressure to release naturally.
- Remove pork shoulder from pot to a serving platter and let rest for about 10 minutes. Cut pork shoulder into thick slices, serve and enjoy!

Pork Chops with Apples

Serves: 4 / Preparation time: 5 minutes / Cooking time: 10 minutes, Per Serving: Calories: 331; Total Fat: 23.6g; Saturated Fat: 8g; Protein: 18.8g; Carbs: 11.1g; Fiber: 2.3g; Sugar: 7g;

- 4 pork chops
- 1/4 cup homemade chicken broth
- 1 tsp cinnamon
- 1 apple, cored and sliced
- 1 tsp garlic, minced
- 1 onion, sliced
- 1 tbsp olive oil
- Pepper
- Salt

- Season pork chops with pepper and salt. Set aside.
- Add olive oil into the instant pot and select sauté.
- Add onions and sauté for 5 minutes.
- Add garlic and sauté for a minute.
- Add cinnamon and apple slices and sauté for 2 minutes.
- Pour broth and stir well.
- Add pork chops and seal pot with lid and cook on high for 3 minutes.
- Allow releasing pressure naturally then open the lid.
- Serve and enjoy.

Loaded Cauliflower Bowls

Serves: 6, Preparation time: 15 minutes, Cooking time: 10-12 minutes, Per Serving: Calories: 362; Total Fat: 27g; Saturated Fat: 15g; Protein: 20g; Carbs: 6g; Fiber: 3g; Sugar: 1g

- 1 large head cauliflower (about 3 pounds), cut into large chunks
- Salt and freshly ground black pepper, to taste
- 1 package (3 ounces) cream cheese, cut into 1/2" pieces
- 2 tablespoons butter, divided
- ½ small onion, finely diced
- 12 ounces fully cooked ham, cut into 1/2" cubes
- 4 ounces mild cheddar cheese, shredded
- ¼ cup green onions, cut into rings
- 4 tablespoons sour cream

- Pour 1 cup water into Instant Pot. Place cauliflower in steamer basket and set in pot. Season cauliflower to taste with salt and pepper.

- Secure pot lid, close pressure valve and cook on steam setting for 6 minutes. When cooking time ends, carefully turn venting knob from sealing to venting position for a quick pressure release.
- Remove cauliflower from steamer basket to a large bowl, add cream cheese and 1 tablespoon butter and puree with an immersion blender until smooth. Cover cauliflower mash to keep it warm and set aside.
- Set Instant Pot to sauté, melt butter and cook onion until transparent, 2-3 minutes. Add ham to pot and stir until ham is lightly browned, 2-3 minutes.
- Scoop cauliflower mixture into 6 deep bowls and sprinkle ham mixture and cheese over cauliflower. Garnish bowls with green onions and sour cream to serve. Enjoy!

Shredded Pork

1 hour 5 minutes, Serves: 6, Calories 680; Fat 48.8 g; Carbohydrates 4.1 g; Sugar 1.4 g; Protein 53.4 g; Cholesterol 204 mg

- 3 lbs pork shoulder
- 1/2 tbsp garlic powder
- 1/2 tbsp cumin
- 1/2 tbsp paprika
- 1/2 cup chicken stock
- 2 lime juice
- 2 chipotle peppers in adobo
- 1 onion, sliced

- Place pork shoulder in instant pot.
- Add remaining ingredients over the pork.
- Seal pot with lid and select meat setting and set timer for 55 minutes.
- Allow releasing pressure naturally then open the lid.
- Using fork shred the pork and place on baking sheet.
- Broil pork for 5 minutes and serve.

Chapter 5: Seafood

Red Hot Fish

Serves: 2 / Preparation time: 5 minutes / Cooking time: 10 minutes, Per Serving: Calories: 257; Total Fat: 18.7g; Saturated Fat: 2.1 g; Protein: 4.7g; Carbs: 20.6g; Fiber: 2.3g; Sugar: 2.1g

1 lb. fresh fish	¾ teaspoon turmeric
2 tablespoons olive oil	¼ cup red chilies
5 cloves garlic	1 lemongrass
5 shallots	¾ cup basil
1 ginger	

- Preheat an Instant Pot for 30 seconds then select "Sauté" menu.
- Pour olive oil into the Instant Pot then wait until hot.
- Add fish to Instant Pot then sauté until both sides are lightly golden.
- Take the fish out from the Instant Pot then place in a baking dish.
- Discard the oil then clean the Instant Pot.
- Pour water into the Instant Pot then place a trivet in it.
- Place garlic, shallots, ginger, turmeric, and red chilies in a food processor then pulse until smooth.
- Spread the spice mixture over the fish then add lemongrass and basil on top.
- Place the baking dish in the trivet then cover the Instant Pot with the lid and lock it properly.
- Select "Manual" setting then cook the pork on high and set the time to 5 minutes.
- Once it is done, naturally release the Instant Pot then open the lid.
- Remove the baking dish from the Instant Pot then serve right away.
- Enjoy.

Creamy Coconut Fish Curry

Serves: 4 / Preparation time: 10 minutes / Cooking time: 15 minutes, Per Serving: Calories: 726; Total Fat: 50.8g; Saturated Fat: 30.4g; Protein: 29.7g; Carbs: 46.8g; Fiber: 7.1g; Sugar: 7g;

1 1/2 lbs fish fillets, rinsed and cut into pieces	6 bay leaves
2 cups coconut milk	1 tbsp fresh ginger, grated
3 tbsp curry powder	2 garlic cloves
1/2 tsp ground fenugreek	2 medium onions, sliced
1 tsp chili powder	2 green chilies, sliced
1/2 tsp ground turmeric	1 tomato, chopped
2 tsp ground cumin	Salt
1 tbsp ground coriander	

- Spray instant pot from inside with cooking spray. Set the instant pot on sauté mode.
- Add ginger, garlic, and onion to the pot and sauté for 1 minute.
- Add all ground spices and sauté for 2 minutes.
- Add coconut milk and stir well.
- Add fish, tomatoes, and green chilies. Stir well.
- Seal pot with lid and cook on manual high pressure for 5 minutes.
- Release pressure using quick release method than open the lid.
- Season with salt.
- Stir well and serve.

Sweet Soy Fish

Serves: 2 / Preparation time: 5 minutes / Cooking time: 10 minutes, Per Serving: Calories: 258; Total Fat: 22g; Saturated Fat: 4.3g; Protein: 10.7g; Carbs: 5g; Fiber: 0.6g; Sugar: 0.9g

1 lb. fresh trout	2 teaspoons minced garlic
3 tablespoons vegetable oil	3 teaspoons sliced shallot

1-inch galangal
1 bay leaf
2 teaspoons chopped red chili
3 tablespoons soy sauce

- Preheat an Instant Pot for 30 seconds then select the "Sauté" menu.
- Pour vegetable oil into the Instant Pot then brown the trout.
- Take the browned trout out from the Instant Pot then set aside.
- Discard the oil then return the browned trout into the Instant Pot.
- Sprinkle minced garlic, sliced shallot, and red chili over the trout then add galangal and bay leaf.
- Drizzle soy sauce over the trout then cover the Instant Pot properly.
- Select "Manual" setting then cook the spaghetti on high for 5 minutes.
- Once it is done, quickly release the Instant Pot then open the lid.
- Transfer to a serving dish then enjoy immediately.

Salmon with Broccoli

Serves: 1 / Preparation time: 5 minutes / Cooking time: 5 minutes, Per Serving: Calories: 267; Total Fat: 11.3g; Saturated Fat: 1.6g; Protein: 37.1g; Carbs: 6.1g; Fiber: 2.4g; Sugar: 1.6g;

1 salmon fillet
1 cup broccoli florets
Black pepper
Salt

- Pour 1 cup water into the instant pot then place steamer rack into the pot.
- Season salmon and broccoli with pepper and salt.
- Place season salmon and broccoli into the steamer rack.
- Seal pot with lid and cook for 2 minutes.
- Allow releasing pressure naturally then open the lid carefully.
- Serve and enjoy.

Stuffed Squids in Tomato

Serves: 2 / Preparation time: 5 minutes / Cooking time: 7 minutes, Per Serving: Calories: 153; Total Fat: 4.5g; Saturated Fat: 1.6g; Protein: 8.3g; Carbs: 22.7g; Fiber: 3.3g; Sugar: 7.1g

4 medium squids
¼ cup breadcrumbs
1 tablespoon chopped parsley
1 tablespoon grated cheese
2 teaspoons minced garlic
1 organic egg
¼ teaspoon pepper
¼ teaspoon salt
1-cup tomato puree
¼ teaspoon oregano
¼ teaspoon rosemary

- Clean the squids then set aside.
- Combine breadcrumbs with chopped parsley, cheese, minced garlic, egg, salt, and pepper. Mix well.
- Fill the squids with breadcrumbs mixture then place in an Instant Pot.
- Add tomato puree then season with oregano and rosemary.
- Cover the Instant Pot with the lid then lock it properly.
- Select "Manual" setting then cook the pork loaf on high for 7 minutes.
- Once it is done, naturally release the Instant Pot then open the lid.
- Serve and enjoy the crabs.

Sea Bass Coconut Curry

Serves: 3 / Preparation time: 5 minutes / Cooking time: 10 minutes, Per Serving: Calories: 344; Total Fat: 34.3g; Saturated Fat: 29.5g; Protein: 3.5g; Carbs: 10.4g; Fiber: 3.4g; Sugar: 4.7g;

14.5 oz coconut milk
1/4 cup fresh cilantro, chopped
1 lb sea bass, cut into 1-inch cubes
1/2 tsp white pepper

1 tsp ground ginger
1 tsp ground turmeric
2 garlic cloves, minced

1 tbsp red curry paste
1 lime juice
1/2 tsp sea salt

- In a large mixing bowl, whisk together coconut milk, red curry paste, ginger, turmeric, garlic, and lime juice.
- Place sea bass into the instant pot.
- Pour coconut milk mixture over the sea bass.
- Seal pot with lid and cook on manual high pressure for 3 minutes.
- Release pressure using quick release method than open the lid.
- Garnish with cilantro and serve.

Vegetable Shrimps Tom Yum Soup

Serves: 2 / Preparation time: 5 minutes / Cooking time: 5 minutes, Per Serving: Calories: 142; Total Fat: 2.7g; Saturated Fat: 0.6g; Protein: 18.1 g; Carbs: 11.4g; Fiber: 1.2g; Sugar: 5.2g

½ cup fresh shrimps
¼ cup chopped carrot
3 cups vegetable broth
1 lemongrass
2 kaffir lime leaves
1-inch galangal

5 red chilies
1 tablespoons fish sauce
½ teaspoon sugar
¼ cup chopped mushroom
1-tablespoon fish sauce
¼ cup chopped onion

- Place all ingredients in the Instant Pot then cover it properly.
- Select "Manual" setting then cook on high for 5 minutes.
- Once it is done, quickly release the Instant Pot then open the lid.
- Transfer to a serving bowl then enjoy hot.

Mahi Fillets

Serves: 2 / Preparation time: 10 minutes / Cooking time: 5 minutes, Per Serving: Calories: 79; Total Fat: 0.9g; Saturated Fat: 0.2g; Protein: 11.6g; Carbs: 7g; Fiber: 1.8g; Sugar: 1.4g;

2 mahi-mahi fillets
1 tbsp orange juice
2 tbsp hot chili sauce
1 tbsp chili powder
1/2 lime juice

1 tbsp ginger, grated
2 garlic cloves, minced
Black pepper
Salt

- Season fish fillets with pepper and salt and set aside.
- In a small bowl, mix together all remaining ingredients.
- Pour 1 cup water into the instant pot.
- Place steamer rack into the instant pot.
- Place fish fillets into the steamer rack then pour bowl mixture over the fish fillets.
- Seal pot with lid and cook on manual high pressure for 5 minutes.
- Release pressure using quick release method than open the lid.
- Serve and enjoy.

Steamed Lemon Crabs

Serves: 2 / Preparation time: 5 minutes / Cooking time: 3 minutes, Per Serving: Calories: 248; Total Fat: 4.2g; Saturated Fat: 0.5g; Protein: 46.5g; Carbs: 5.4g; Fiber: 1.6g; Sugar: 1.5g

1-½ lbs. fresh crabs

2 fresh lemons

½ teaspoon salt
- Pour water into the Instant Pot then place a trivet in it.
- Season the fresh crabs with salt then place in the trivet.
- Cut the lemon into slices then arrange over the crabs.
- Cover the Instant Pot with the lid then lock it properly.
- Select "Manual" setting then cook the pork loaf on high for 3 minutes.
- Once it is done, naturally release the Instant Pot then open the lid.
- Serve and enjoy the crabs.

Shrimp Scampi

Serves: 4, Preparation time: 20 minutes, Cooking time: 10 minutes, Per Serving: Calories: 403; Total Fat: 28g; Saturated Fat: 10g; Protein: 36g; Carbs: 8g; Fiber: 8g; Sugar: 3g

1 tablespoon butter	½ teaspoon paprika
1 tablespoon olive oil	Salt and freshly ground black pepper, to taste
4 cloves garlic, peeled and minced	
½ teaspoon red pepper flakes	½ cup plain yogurt
1 pound frozen large shrimp, peeled and deveined	½ cup finely grated Parmesan cheese
	½ lemon, zested in strips and juiced
1 cup white wine	Parsley sprigs, for garnish

- In Instant Pot on sauté setting, mix butter and olive oil until butter is melted. Add garlic and red pepper flakes and sauté until garlic is lightly browned, 1-2 minutes.
- Add shrimp, chicken stock and paprika to pot and season to taste with salt and pepper. Secure pot lid, close pressure valve and cook for 2 minutes on high pressure.
- When cooking time ends, carefully turn valve from sealing to venting position for a quick pressure release.
- Set Instant Pot to sauté, add yogurt and Parmesan cheese to shrimp mixture and stir until cheese is melted.
- Drizzle lemon juice over shrimp scampi and garnish with lemon zest strips and parsley sprigs to serve. Enjoy!

Simple Steamed Salmon Fillet

Serves: 1 / Preparation time: 5 minutes / Cooking time: 10 minutes, Per Serving: Calories: 205; Total Fat: 8.9g; Saturated Fat: 1.3g; Protein: 28.2g; Carbs: 5.5g; Fiber: 1.7g; Sugar: 1.5g;

5 oz salmon fillet	Pepper
1 lemon cut in half	Salt

- Season salmon with pepper and salt.
- Squeeze lemon juice over the salmon.
- Pour 1 1/2 cup water into the instant pot then place trivet into the pot.
- Place salmon onto the trivet.
- Seal pot with lid and cook on manual high pressure for 3 minutes.
- Release pressure using quick release method than open the lid carefully.
- Serve and enjoy.

Quick Buttery Salmon

Serves: 2 / Preparation time: 5 minutes / Cooking time: 5 minutes, Per Serving: Calories: 253; Total Fat: 17.1g; Saturated Fat: 5.8g; Protein: 20.9 g; Carbs: 6.1g; Fiber: 1.8g; Sugar: 1.8g

¾ lb. salmon steak	2 fresh lemons
1-tablespoon butter	½ cup water
2 tablespoons lemon juice	¼ teaspoon salt

½ teaspoon black pepper

- Cut the lemons into slices then place in the bottom of the Instant Pot.
- Pour water into the pot then place a trivet in it.
- Brush the salmon steak with butter then sprinkle salt and pepper over the salmon.
- Place the salmon in the trivet then cover the Instant Pot properly.
- Select "Manual" setting then cook on high for 5 minutes.
- Once it is done, quickly release the Instant Pot then open the lid.
- Splash lemon juice over the salmon.
- Serve and enjoy.

Tasty Seafood Chowder

Serves: 2 / Preparation time: 5 minutes / Cooking time: 5 minutes, Per Serving: Calories: 272; Total Fat: 16.7g; Saturated Fat: 7.6g; Protein: 18.8g; Carbs: 10.6g; Fiber: 1.6g; Sugar: 2.7g

¼ cup chopped shrimps
¼ cup chopped squids
¼ cup tuna chunks
¼ cup chopped onion
1 tablespoon chopped celery
¼ cup diced carrot
2 teaspoons minced garlic
1 ½ cups potato cubes
¼ cup corn kernels
1-tablespoon butter
2 cups vegetable broth
¼ teaspoon salt
½ teaspoon pepper
2 tablespoons heavy cream

- Preheat an Instant Pot for 30 seconds then select the "Sauté" menu.
- Add butter to the Instant Pot then stir in chopped onion and minced garlic. Press the "Cancel" button.
- Add shrimps, squids, tuna, celery, carrot, potato cubes, and corn kernels to the Instant Pot then pour vegetable broth.
- Season with salt and pepper then cover the Instant Pot properly.
- Select "Manual" setting then cook on high for 5 minutes.
- Once it is done, quickly release the Instant Pot then open the lid.
- Stir in heavy cream into the pot then mix until thickened.
- Transfer to a serving dish then enjoy immediately.

Spicy Salmon Fillets

Serves: 4 / Preparation time: 5 minutes / Cooking time: 10 minutes, Per Serving: Calories: 245; Total Fat: 11.2g; Saturated Fat: 1.7g; Protein: 34.9g; Carbs: 2.3g; Fiber: 0.8g; Sugar: 1 g;

4 salmon fillets
1 cup water
2 tbsp chili pepper
2 tbsp lemon juice
1 lemon, cut into slices
Pepper
Salt

- Season salmon with lemon juice, chili pepper, pepper, and salt.
- Pour water into the instant pot then place steamer rack into the instant pot.
- Place salmon fillets on the steamer rack.
- Arrange lemon slices onto the salmon fillets.
- Seal pot with lid and select manual and set timer for 5 minutes.
- Release pressure using quick release method than open the lid.
- Serve and enjoy.

Easy Tuna Tender

Serves: 2 / Preparation time: 35 minutes / Cooking time: 3 minutes, Per Serving: Calories: 209; Total Fat: 18.7g; Saturated Fat: 18.7g; Protein: 8.9g; Carbs: 1.9g; Fiber: 0.3g; Sugar: 0.3g

¾ lb. tuna fillet
2 tablespoons low sodium soy sauce

1-tablespoon canola oil
½ teaspoon black pepper
¼ teaspoon salt

- Place soy sauce, canola oil, black pepper, and salt in a zipper-lock plastic bag then mix to combine.
- Add tuna fillet to the plastic bag then shake until the tuna is completely coated with the spice. Marinate for 30 minutes.
- Pour water into the Instant Pot then place a trivet in it.
- Arrange the tuna in the trivet then cover the Instant Pot with the lid and lock it properly.
- Select "Manual" setting then cook the tuna on high for 3 minutes.
- Once it is done, naturally release the Instant Pot then serve immediately.

Fish Chowder

Serves: 4, Preparation time: 10 minutes, Cooking time: 20 minutes, Per Serving: Calories: 347; Total Fat: 15g; Saturated Fat: 6g; Protein: 33g; Carbs: 19g; Fiber: 4g; Sugar: 9g

- 1 medium head cauliflower (about 2 pounds), cored and cut into chunks
- 8 ounces bacon, diced
- 1 medium onion, diced
- 1 medium red bell pepper, diced
- 2 stalks celery, trimmed and diced
- 2 cloves garlic, peeled and minced
- 4 cups chicken stock
- 1 pound tilapia fillets
- 2 cups plain whole-milk yogurt
- 1 tablespoon arrowroot flour
- Salt and freshly ground black pepper, to taste

- Pour 1 cup water into Instant Pot. Place cauliflower in steamer basket and set in pot. Secure pot lid, close pressure valve and cook cauliflower on high pressure for 5 minutes. When cooking time ends, allow pressure to release naturally. Drain water from pot if necessary. Remove cauliflower from basket and puree with an immersion blender to desired consistency.
- Cook bacon in Instant Pot on sauté setting until crisp. Add onion, bell pepper, celery and garlic and sauté until vegetables are softened, about 3 minutes.
- Add cauliflower, chicken stock and tilapia to pot and season to taste with salt and pepper. Secure pot lid, close pressure valve and cook chowder on high pressure for 5 minutes. When cooking time ends, let pressure release naturally. Set Instant Pot to warm.
- Stir arrowroot flour into yogurt and mix thoroughly. Add yogurt mixture to chowder and stir 2 to 3 minutes until thickened. Break up fish fillets if necessary.
- Serve and enjoy!

Flavourful Salmon Fillets

Serves: 2 / Preparation time: 10 minutes / Cooking time: 5 minutes, Per Serving: Calories: 261; Total Fat: 11.9g; Saturated Fat: 1.6g; Protein: 35.2g; Carbs: 4.7g; Fiber: 0.8g; Sugar: 2.1g;

- 2 salmon fillets
- 2 tsp chipotle paste
- 1 lemon
- Black pepper
- Salt

- Pour 1 cup water into the instant pot then place trivet into the pot.
- Place salmon fillets on the trivet.
- Squeeze lemon juice over the salmon fillets.
- Season with chipotle paste, black pepper, and salt.
- Seal pot with lid and cook on manual high pressure for 3 minutes.
- Release pressure using quick release method than open the lid.
- Serve and enjoy.

Creole Jambalaya

Serves: 4, Preparation time: 15 minutes, Cooking time: 30 minutes, Per Serving: Calories: 341; Total Fat: 17g; Saturated Fat: 6g; Protein: 35g; Carbs: 6g; Fiber: 0g; Sugar: 2g

3 teaspoons paprika	1 pound fresh or frozen medium shrimp, peeled and deveined
2 teaspoon dried thyme	1 onion, diced
2 teaspoon dried oregano	1 green bell pepper, diced
1 teaspoon cayenne pepper, or to taste	4 stalks celery, trimmed and diced
1 teaspoon freshly ground black pepper	4 cloves garlic, peeled and minced
½ teaspoon red pepper flakes	1 can (14.5 ounces) diced tomatoes, undrained
½ teaspoon salt, or to taste	1 cup chicken stock
8 ounces Andouille or kielbasa sausage, cut into ½" slices	1 teaspoon Worcestershire sauce
1 tablespoon olive oil	2 bay leaves
8 ounces boneless skinless chicken thighs, cut into 1" chunks	1 lemon, juiced
	Fresh parsley sprigs for garnish, if desired

- Mix paprika, thyme, oregano, cayenne pepper, black pepper, red pepper flakes and salt and set aside.
- In Instant Pot on sauté setting, cook sausage in oil until browned, about 5 minutes. Remove sausage from pot with a slotted spoon and set aside.
- Add more oil to pot if necessary and cook chicken until browned, about 5 minutes. Remove chicken from pot with a slotted spoon and set aside.
- Sauté shrimp in pot very briefly, for just a few seconds. Remove shrimp from pot with a slotted spoon and set aside.
- Cook onion, bell pepper, celery and garlic in pot until onion is translucent, about 3-4 minutes. Add spice mixture to pot and stir to coat. Add tomatoes, chicken stock, bay leaves, Worcestershire sauce and reserved sausage and chicken to pot and mix thoroughly. Secure pot lid, close pressure valve and cook on high pressure for 7 minutes.
- When cooking time ends, carefully turn venting knob from sealing to venting position for a quick pressure release and gently stir shrimp and lemon juice into pot. Replace lid on pot and let stand until shrimp is heated through, about 10 minutes.
- Ladle servings of jambalaya into shallow bowls and garnish with parsley sprigs. Serve and enjoy!

Clam Potato Chowder

Serves: 2 / Preparation time: 10 minutes / Cooking time: 10 minutes, Per Serving: Calories: 168; Total Fat: 1.3g; Saturated Fat: 0.1g; Protein: 16.6g; Carbs: 21.5g; Fiber: 2g; Sugar: 2.7g

¼ cup clam juice	½ cup chopped potatoes
8 clams	1 teaspoon minced garlic
½ cup chopped onion	¼ teaspoon pepper
1 tablespoon chopped celery	¼ teaspoon salt
½ cup water	2 tablespoons flour

- Place all ingredients except water and flour in the Instant Pot. Stir well.
- Cover the Instant Pot with the lid then lock it properly.
- Select "Manual" setting then cook on high for 5 minutes.
- Once it is done, quickly release the Instant Pot then open the lid.
- Combine the flour with water then mix well.
- Select "Sauté" then pour the flour mixture into the pot. Stir well.
- Let the gravy bubble then stirring occasionally. Turn the Instant Pot off.
- Transfer to a serving bowl then enjoy hot.

Salty Spicy Salmon Balls

Serves: 2 / Preparation time: 5 minutes / Cooking time: 15 minutes, Per Serving: Calories: 183; Total Fat: 7.6g; Saturated Fat: 1.7g; Protein: 20.6g; Carbs: 7.9g; Fiber: 0.9g; Sugar: 2.2g

1 lb. salmon fillet	1-teaspoon cayenne powder
2 tablespoons sesame flour	¼ cup tomato sauce
1 egg	¼ cup water
1-teaspoon olive oil	2 tablespoons soy sauce
2 teaspoons minced garlic	1-tablespoon fish sauce
2 teaspoons sliced shallot	½ teaspoon salt

- Place salmon fillet, egg and sesame flour in a food processor then pulse until smooth.
- Shape the mixture into balls forms then set aside.
- Heat up an Instant Pot then select "Sauté".
- Pour olive oil into the Instant Pot then stir in minced garlic and sliced shallots. Sauté until wilted then press the "Cancel" button.
- Add the salmon balls then add the remaining ingredients.
- Cover the Instant Pot with the lid then make sure that it is locked properly.
- Turn on the Instant Pot then choose "Manual" setting.
- Cook the fish balls on high and set the time to 15 minutes.
- Once it is done, naturally release the Instant Pot then open the lid.
- Transfer the salmon balls together with the lid to a serving dish then serve.
- Enjoy.

Pepper Lemon Salmon

Serves: 4 / Preparation time: 10 minutes / Cooking time: 10 minutes, Per Serving: Calories: 196; Total Fat: 9.5g; Saturated Fat: 1.4g; Protein: 23.1g; Carbs: 6.2g; Fiber: 1.6g; Sugar: 3.3g;

1 lb salmon fillet, skin on	2 tsp olive oil
1 carrot, cut into julienned	3/4 cup water
1 bell pepper, cut into julienned	1/2 tsp black pepper
1 zucchini, cut into julienned	1/4 tsp salt
1/2 lemon, sliced	

- Pour water into the instant pot then place steamer rack into the instant pot.
- Place salmon on the steamer rack.
- Drizzle salmon with olive oil and season with pepper and salt.
- Seal pot with lid and cook on manual high pressure for 3 minutes.
- Release pressure using quick release method than open the lid carefully.
- Carefully remove steamer rack and set aside.
- Add vegetables into the instant pot and select sauté and sauté vegetables for 1-2 minutes.
- Serve salmon with sautéed vegetables and enjoy.

Coconut Lime Catfish Curry

Serves: 4, Preparation time: 5 minutes, Cooking time: 15 minutes, Per Serving: Calories: 254; Total Fat: 24g; Saturated Fat: 19g; Protein: 18g; Carbs: 8g; Fiber: 2g; Sugar: 4g

1 tablespoon coconut oil	1 can (15 ounces) unsweetened coconut milk
1 red bell pepper, seeds and ribs removed, coarsely chopped	1 small lime, zested and juiced
1 large onion, coarsely chopped	1 pound catfish fillets, rinsed and cut into bite-size pieces
2 cloves garlic, peeled and minced	
3 tablespoons curry powder	

Salt and freshly ground black pepper, to taste

1 cup cherry tomatoes, chopped and drained

- Melt coconut oil in Instant Pot on sauté setting. Add bell pepper, onion and garlic to pot and sauté, stirring frequently, until softened.
- Add curry powder to pot and sauté for about 1 minute, stirring constantly. Stir coconut milk and lime zest into pot, scraping the bottom of the pot to loosen any browned bits.
- Add catfish pieces to pot, mixing thoroughly to coat pieces with sauce. Season sauce to taste with salt and pepper.
- Secure pot lid, close pressure valve and cook for 5 minutes at low pressure. When cooking time ends, allow pressure to release naturally.
- Drizzle lime juice over curry to serve. Garnish with chopped tomatoes as desired. Enjoy!

Chewy Fish in Tomato Light Soup

Serves: 2 / Preparation time: 5 minutes / Cooking time: 10 minutes, Per Serving: Calories: 261; Total Fat: 10g; Saturated Fat: 3g; Protein: 21.6g; Carbs: 23.2g; Fiber: 2.5g; Sugar: 5.2g

¾ lbs. fish fillet
1 organic egg
1-tablespoon tapioca flour
¼ lb. fresh shrimps
2 teaspoons minced garlic
½ teaspoon pepper
½ teaspoon salt
¾ cups tomato puree
3 cups water

- Place fish fillet, egg and tapioca flour in a food processor then pulse until smooth.
- Shape the mixture into balls forms then arrange in a casserole dish. Set aside.
- Pour water into the Instant Pot then season with minced garlic, pepper, and salt.
- Add shrimps and tomato puree in the Instant Pot then place a trivet in the Instant Pot.
- Place the casserole dish with fish balls in the trivet.
- Cover the Instant Pot with the lid then make sure that it is locked properly.
- Turn on the Instant Pot then choose "Manual" setting.
- Cook the fish balls on high and set the time to 10 minutes.
- Once it is done, naturally release the Instant Pot then open the lid.
- Take the casserole dish out from the Instant Pot then transfer the fish balls to a serving bowl.
- Pour the gravy over the fish balls then serve hot.
- Enjoy.

Spicy Fish in Savory Tomato Gravy

Serves: 2 / Preparation time: 5 minutes / Cooking time: 5 minutes, Per Serving: Calories: 191; Total Fat: 9.3g; Saturated Fat: 3.8g; Protein: 25g; Carbs: 18.5g; Fiber: 2.1g; Sugar: 2.8g

1 lb. fish fillet
1-teaspoon vegetable oil
½ cup chopped tomato
2 teaspoons chopped green chili
¼ cup chopped onion
1 teaspoon minced garlic
½ teaspoon ginger
1 bay leaf
½ teaspoon coriander
¼ teaspoon cumin
¼ teaspoon turmeric
1-teaspoon chili powder
1-cup coconut milk
¼ teaspoon salt
1 tablespoon lemon juice

- Preheat the Instant Pot for about 30 seconds then select the "Sauté" menu.
- Pour vegetable oil into the Instant Pot then stir in minced garlic and chopped onion.
- Sauté until wilted and aromatic. Press the "Cancel" button.
- Pour coconut milk into the pot then season with ginger, bay leaf, coriander, cumin, turmeric, chili powder, salt, and lemon juice. Stir to deglaze.
- Add fish fillet, green chili, and chopped tomato to the Instant Pot then cover it properly.

- Select "Manual" setting then cook the pork loaf on high for 5 minutes.
- Once it is done, naturally release the Instant Pot then open the lid.
- Transfer to a serving dish then enjoy.

Crispy Salmon with Honey Glaze

Serves: 2 / Preparation time: 5 minutes / Cooking time: 15 minutes, Per Serving: Calories: 228; Total Fat: 7.6g; Saturated Fat: 1.4g; Protein: 17.7g; Carbs: 23.8g; Fiber: 0.8g; Sugar: 1.2g

¾ lb. salmon fillet
1-teaspoon olive oil
½ teaspoon salt
½ teaspoon pepper
1-cup sesame flour
½ cup chopped onion
¼ cup raw honey
2 tablespoons sesame seeds

- Cut the salmon into slices then place in a plastic bag.
- Combine sesame flour with salt and pepper then add to the plastic bag. Shake until the salmon is completely coated with flour.
- Heat up the Instant Pot then select the "Sauté" setting.
- Pour olive oil into the Instant Pot then stir in the coated salmon. Sauté until the salmon is crispy.
- Take the crispy salmon out from the Instant Pot then place in a casserole dish.
- Pour water into an Instant Pot then place a trivet in it.
- Place the casserole dish in the trivet then drizzle honey over the salmon.
- Sprinkle chopped onion on top then cover the Instant Pot with the lid. Lock it properly.
- Select "Manual" setting then cook the beef on high and set the time to 10 minutes.
- Once it is done, naturally release the Instant Pot then open the lid.
- Take the casserole dish out from the Instant Pot then sprinkle sesame seeds on top,
- Serve right away.

Steamed Lobster Tails

Serves: 4, Preparation time: 10 minutes, Cooking time: 4 minutes, Per Serving: Calories: 90; Total Fat: 3g; Saturated Fat: 0g; Protein: 14; Carbs: 0g; Fiber: 0g; Sugar: 0g

1-1/2 cups chicken broth
1 lemon, zested and juiced
2 pounds fresh raw lobster tails in the shells (about 4 tails)
Large bowl of ice water
Salt and freshly ground black pepper, to taste

- Pour 1-1/2 cups chicken broth into Instant Pot and stir in lemon zest. Place trivet in pot and set lobster tails on trivet with shell sides down. Secure pot lid, close pressure valve and cook on high pressure for 4 minutes.
- When cooking time ends, carefully turn venting knob from sealing to venting position for a quick pressure release. Immediately remove lobster tails from pot and place in ice water so they stop cooking.
- Cut down the center of the underside of the tails with a kitchen shears. Remove meat from shells and arrange on serving plates. Drizzle lemon juice on lobster meat and season to taste with salt and pepper. Serve and enjoy!

Simple Salmon Fillets

Serves: 4, Preparation time: 10 minutes, Cooking time: 5 minutes, Per Serving: Calories: 120; Total Fat: 4g; Saturated Fat: 0g; Protein: 21g; Carbs: 0g; Fiber: 0g; Sugar: 0g

1 package (16 ounces) frozen salmon fillets
12 sprigs fresh dill (or 2 teaspoons dried dill weed)
1 lemon, zested and juiced
Salt and ground black pepper, to taste

- Pour 1 cup of water into Instant Pot and set steamer basket in pot.
- Arrange salmon fillets in steamer basket. Place 2 sprigs of dill on each fillet, sprinkle with lemon juice and lemon zest and season to taste with salt and pepper.

- Secure pot lid, close pressure valve and cook on manual setting for 5 minutes. Carefully turn venting knob from sealing to venting position for a quick pressure release.
- Dot salmon fillets with butter and serve immediately. Enjoy!

Quick Salmon with Dill

Serves: 4 / Preparation time: 10 minutes / Cooking time: 5 minutes, Per Serving: Calories: 269; Total Fat: 14.6g; Saturated Fat: 2.2g; Protein: 34.7g; Carbs: 0.4g; Fiber: 0.1g; Sugar: 0.3g;

4 salmon fillets
1 tbsp olive oil
1 bunch dill weed
3/4 cup water

1/4 cup lemon juice
1/4 tsp ground black pepper
1/4 tsp salt

- Add water and lemon juice into the instant pot.
- Place steamer rack into the instant pot.
- Place salmon fillets on the steamer rack.
- Sprinkle fresh dill on salmon fillets.
- Season salmon with pepper and salt.
- Seal pot with lid and select manual and set timer for 5 minutes.
- Release pressure using quick release method than open the lid.
- Serve with olive oil.

Salsa Poached Cod

Serves: 4, Preparation time: 5 minutes, Cooking time: 5 minutes, Per Serving: Calories: 188; Total Fat: 4g; Saturated Fat: 1g; Protein: 26g; Carbs: 10g; Fiber: 2g; Sugar: 6g

1 jar (16 ounces) salsa
1 package (16 ounces) frozen cod fillets, thawed

1 teaspoon chili powder
Salt and freshly ground black pepper, to taste

- Pour salsa into Instant Pot. Rub chili powder into cod fillets and season to taste with salt and pepper. Place cod fillets into pot and stir lightly to coat with salsa.
- Secure pot lid, close pressure valve and cook on manual setting for 5 minutes.
- When cooking time ends, carefully turn venting knob from sealing to venting position for a quick pressure release.
- Spoon salsa from pot over cod fillets to serve. Enjoy!

Warm Steamed Fish Ginger

Serves: 2 / Preparation time: 5 minutes / Cooking time: 5 minutes, Per Serving: Calories: 208; Total Fat: 11.2g; Saturated Fat: 2g; Protein: 22.2g; Carbs: 5.2g; Fiber: 0.7g; Sugar: 1.7g

1 lb. salmon fillet
2 teaspoons minced garlic
3 tablespoons soy sauce

¾ teaspoon ginger
1 teaspoon red chili flakes
¼ teaspoon salt

- Pour water into the Instant Pot then place a trivet in it.
- Line a baking pan with aluminum foil then place the salmon fillet in it.
- Sprinkle minced garlic, ginger, salt, and red chili flakes over the salmon fillet then drizzle soy sauce on top.
- Place the pan on the trivet then cover the Instant Pot with the lid. Lock it properly.
- Select "Manual" menu then cook the salmon on high for 5 minutes.
- Once it is done, naturally release the Instant Pot then open the lid.
- Transfer the steamed salmon together with the liquid to a serving dish.
- Serve and enjoy.

Steamed Crabs Garlic

Serves: 2 / Preparation time: 5 minutes / Cooking time: 3 minutes, Per Serving: Calories: 268; Total Fat: 18.9g; Saturated Fat: 7.1g; Protein: 17.1g; Carbs: 6.4g; Fiber: 0.4g; Sugar: 1g

1-½ lbs. fresh crabs	¼ teaspoon salt
¼ cup minced garlic	½ cup water
2 tablespoons fish sauce	1 tablespoon lemon juice
¼ cup butter, melted	

- Place crabs in an Instant Pot then season with salt and minced garlic.
- Add fish sauce and drop butter over the crabs then pour water into the Instant Pot.
- Cover the Instant Pot with the lid then lock it properly.
- Select "Manual" setting then cook the spaghetti on high for 3 minutes.
- Once it is done, quickly release the Instant Pot then open the lid.
- Splash lemon juice over the crabs then toss them.
- Transfer to a serving dish then enjoy immediately.

Salmon with Chili Lime Sauce

Serves: 2 / Preparation time: 10 minutes / Cooking time: 5 minutes, Per Serving: Calories: 312; Total Fat: 18.3g; Saturated Fat: 2.6g; Protein: 35.1g; Carbs: 3.9g; Fiber: 0.7g; Sugar: 0.7g;

2 salmon fillets	1 tbsp parsley, chopped
1 cup water	1 tbsp hot water
Black pepper	1 tbsp olive oil
Sea salt	2 garlic cloves, minced
For sauce:	1 lime juice
1/2 tsp cumin	1 jalapeno, seed removed and diced
1/2 tsp paprika	

- Add all sauce ingredients into the bowl. Mix well and set aside.
- Season salmon fillets with pepper and salt.
- Add water into the instant pot then place season salmon into the pot.
- Seal pot with lid and cook on high for 5 minutes.
- Release pressure using quick release method than open the lid.
- Transfer salmon on serving dish and drizzle with chili lime sauce.
- Serve and enjoy.

Brown Caramel Salmon

Serves: 2 / Preparation time: 5 minutes / Cooking time: 5 minutes, Per Serving: Calories: 295; Total Fat: 12.9g; Saturated Fat: 2g; Protein: 34.6g; Carbs: 11.1g; Fiber: 0.3g; Sugar: 9.5g

¾ lb. salmon fillets	½ teaspoon ginger
1-teaspoon vegetable oil	¼ teaspoon lemon zest
2 tablespoons brown sugar	1 tablespoon lemon juice
1-tablespoon fish sauce	¼ teaspoon pepper
2 tablespoons soy sauce	

- Season the salmon with salt and pepper. Set aside.
- Combine vegetable oil with brown sugar, fish sauce, soy sauce, ginger, lemon zest, and lemon juice. Mix well.
- Preheat the Instant Pot for about 30 seconds then select the "Sauté" menu.
- Pour vegetable oil mixture into the Instant Pot then sauté until caramelized. Press the "Cancel" button.
- Add the salmon to the Instant Pot then stir well.
- Cover the Instant Pot with the lid then lock it properly.

- Select "Manual" setting then cook the pork loaf on high for 5 minutes.
- Once it is done, naturally release the Instant Pot then open the lid.
- Transfer the salmon to a serving dish along with the caramel liquid.
- Serve and enjoy.

Teriyaki Salmon

Serves: 4, Preparation time: 10 minutes, plus ½-2 hours for marinating, Cooking time: 15 minutes, Per Serving: Calories: 268; Total Fat: 9g; Saturated Fat: 2g; Protein: 25g; Carbs: 12g; Fiber: 0g; Sugar: 5g

- ¼ cup soy sauce
- ¼ cup water
- ¼ cup mirin, sake or sherry
- 1 tablespoon sesame oil
- 4 cloves garlic, peeled and minced
- 1 lime, zested and juiced
- 2 tablespoons xylitol (or sweetener of choice)
- 1 tablespoon freshly grated ginger
- 4 green onions, minced
- 2 teaspoons fish sauce
- 1 tablespoon sesame seeds
- 1 teaspoon blackstrap molasses
- Salt, freshly ground black pepper and cayenne pepper, to taste
- 1 pound thick salmon fillets
- 1 tablespoon arrowroot flour
- 2 tablespoons water

- For the marinade, mix soy sauce, water, mirin, sesame oil, garlic, lime juice, lime zest, xylitol, ginger, half of the green onions (set remaining onions aside for garnish), fish sauce, sesame seeds and molasses and season to taste with salt, black pepper and cayenne pepper.
- Place salmon fillets in 2 pans that will fit inside Instant Pot. Pour about ¼ of the marinade over salmon in each pan. Set remaining marinade aside.
- Cover salmon and refrigerate for 30 minutes to 2 hours.
- To cook salmon, pour 1 cup water into Instant Pot and set trivet in pot. Set one pan of salmon on trivet and set other pan across the top of first pan in an X pattern. Secure pot lid, close pressure valve and cook for 8 minutes on high pressure.
- When cooking time ends, carefully turn venting knob from sealing to venting position for a quick pressure release. Remove salmon from pot and cover it with foil to keep it warm.
- Drain water from pot and set pot to sauté. Mix arrowroot flour into water and whisk in pot with remaining marinade. Simmer for 1-2 minutes until sauce reaches desired consistency.
- Drizzle sauce over salmon fillets and garnish with green onions to serve. Enjoy!

Green Chili Tuna Pasta

Serves: 2 / Preparation time: 5 minutes / Cooking time: 10 minutes, Per Serving: Calories: 341; Total Fat: 7.3g; Saturated Fat: 2.3g; Protein: 27.2g; Carbs: 42g; Fiber: 4.8g; Sugar: 12.7g

- ¼ lb. tuna chunks
- ¼ lb. uncooked spaghetti
- 2 teaspoons minced garlic
- 1 teaspoon chopped celery
- ¼ teaspoon oregano
- ¼ teaspoon basil
- ¼ teaspoon salt
- ½ teaspoon pepper
- 1-teaspoon olive oil
- 1-½ cups water
- ½ cup chopped green chili
- 3 teaspoons fish sauce
- 1 ½ tablespoons Worcestershire sauce

- Heat up the Instant Pot for 30 seconds then select "Sauté" menu.
- Pour olive oil to the pot then stir in tuna chunks, chopped onion, minced garlic, and chopped green chili.
- Season with salt and pepper then sauté until crispy.
- Pour water into the pot then add uncooked spaghetti and the remaining ingredients.
- Cover the Instant Pot with the lid then lock it properly.
- Select "Manual" setting then cook the spaghetti on high for 6 minutes.
- Once it is done, quickly release the Instant Pot then open the lid.
- Transfer the pasta to a serving dish then enjoy immediately.

Original Savory Shrimps

Serves: 2 / Preparation time: 5 minutes / Cooking time: 2 minutes, Per Serving: Calories: 283; Total Fat: 5g; Saturated Fat: 1.4g; Protein: 51.8g; Carbs: 4.2g; Fiber: 0.2g; Sugar: 0g

1 lb. fresh shrimps
1 teaspoon minced garlic
½ teaspoon pepper
¼ teaspoon salt
½ teaspoon olive oil

- Peel the shrimps then discard the head.
- Pour water into the Instant Pot then place a trivet in it.
- Coat a small heatproof pan with cooking spray then place the peeled shrimps in it.
- Rub the shrimps with minced garlic, pepper, and salt then place the pan on the trivet.
- Turn the Instant Pot on then select "Manual" setting.
- Cook the shrimps on high and set the time to 2 minutes.
- Once it is done, naturally release the Instant Pot then serve immediately.

Mediterranean Cod

Serves: 6, Preparation time: 15 minutes, Cooking time: 15-18 minutes, Per Serving: Calories: 288; Total Fat: 15g; Saturated Fat: 5g; Protein: 24g; Carbs: 11g; Fiber: 2g; Sugar: 7g

2 tablespoons olive oil
1 red onion, julienned
1 can (28 ounces) diced tomatoes
1 lemon, zested and juiced
1 teaspoon dried oregano
½ teaspoon dried basil
½ teaspoon dried thyme
Salt and freshly ground black pepper, to taste
1-½ pounds fresh or frozen cod fillets
6 ounces feta cheese, crumbled
12 Kalamata olives, pitted and sliced

- Heat olive oil in Instant Pot on sauté setting. Add onion and cook until softened, 1-2 minutes, stirring constantly.
- Add undrained tomatoes, lemon zest, lemon juice, oregano, basil and thyme to pot and season to taste with salt and pepper. Mix sauce thoroughly and cook for about 10 minutes, stirring occasionally.
- Place cod fillets in pot and stir lightly to cover with sauce. Secure pot lid, close pressure valve and cook on high pressure for 5 minutes if using frozen cod, 3 minutes if using fresh cod.
- When cooking time ends, carefully turn venting knob from sealing to venting position for a quick pressure release.
- Ladle cod fillets and sauce onto plates. Garnish with feta cheese and Kalamata olives to serve. Enjoy!

Squids Tomato Veggie

Serves: 2 / Preparation time: 5 minutes / Cooking time: 5 minutes, Per Serving: Calories: 100; Total Fat: 2.4g; Saturated Fat: 0.5g; Protein: 13.9g; Carbs: 5g; Fiber: 0.4g; Sugar: 0.9g

½ lb. fresh squids
½ teaspoon olive oil
1 teaspoon minced garlic
½ teaspoon ginger
1-teaspoon pepper
¼ cup unsweetened tomato juice

- Wash and clean the squids. Discard the ink.
- Heat up the Instant Pot for 30 seconds then press the "Sauté" button.
- Pour olive oil into the Instant Pot then stir in minced garlic. Sauté until wilted and aromatic. Press the "Cancel" button.
- Add squids to the pot then season with ginger and pepper.
- Pour tomato juice into the Instant Pot then cover the Instant Pot with the lid.
- Lock the Instant Pot properly then select "Manual" setting.

- Cook the shrimps on high and set the time to 5 minutes.
- Once it is done, naturally release the Instant Pot.
- Open the lid and transfer the squids and the gravy to a serving dish.
- Serve and enjoy immediately.

Ginger Scallion Tilapia

Serves: 4, Preparation time: 15 minutes, plus 20-30 minutes for marinating, Cooking time: 5 minutes, Per Serving: Calories: 187; Total Fat: 9g; Saturated Fat: 2g; Protein: 22g; Carbs: 3 g; Fiber: 0g; Sugar: 0g

- 4 tablespoons soy sauce
- 2 tablespoons dry white wine
- 4 cloves garlic, peeled and minced
- 4 teaspoons natural creamy peanut butter
- 1 teaspoon white wine vinegar
- 1 teaspoon minced ginger
- 1 pound tilapia fillets
- 6 scallions, julienned
- 1 knob ginger (about 1-1/2" long), julienned
- 1 tablespoon peanut oil
- 1 tablespoon sesame seeds

- For the marinade, whisk soy sauce, white wine, garlic, peanut butter, vinegar and ginger. Place tilapia fillets in a shallow dish, pour marinade over fillets and turn fillets over to coat. Cover dish and refrigerate for 20-30 minutes.
- Pour 2 cups water into Instant Pot and set steamer basket in pot. Remove tilapia fillets from marinade, reserving the marinade. Secure pot lid, close pressure valve and cook on low pressure for 2 minutes. When cooking time ends, carefully turn venting knob from sealing to venting position for a quick pressure release.
- Remove steamer basket from pot and drain water from pot. Set pot to sauté and cook scallions and ginger in peanut oil until softened, about 2 minutes. Stir reserved marinade into pot and heat to a boil, stirring frequently.
- Arrange tilapia fillets on plates. Ladle sauce over tilapia and sprinkle with sesame seeds to serve. Enjoy!

Chapter 6: Lamb

Ginger Goat (or Lamb) Curry

Total Time: 5 hours 15 minutes; Serves: 6; Calories 230, Fat 5.9 g, Carbohydrates 10.6 g, Sugar 5.8 g, Protein 33.6 g, Cholesterol 92 mg

- 2 lbs goat (or lamb) meat
- 2 Serrano pepper, minced
- 1 tsp paprika
- 1 tsp chili powder
- 1 tsp turmeric powder
- 1 tsp cumin powder
- 1 tbsp coriander powder
- 2 cardamom pods
- 2 garlic cloves, minced
- 1 tbsp ghee
- 1 bay leaf
- 3 whole cloves
- 1 tsp fresh ginger, minced
- 1 large onion, chopped
- 1 cup water
- 1 tsp garam masala
- 28 oz can tomatoes, diced
- 2 tsp salt

- Use the "Slow Cooker" setting on your Instant Pot.
- Add cardamom and cloves into the grinder and grind well.
- Add all ingredients into the Instant Pot except water, garam masala, and tomatoes.
- Cover and cook on high for 4 hours.
- Add water, garam masala, and tomatoes and stir well.
- Cook for another 1 hour until meat is tender.
- Serve and enjoy.

Easy Instant Pot Leg of Lamb

Serves: 4 / Preparation time: 10 minutes / Cooking time: 45 minutes, Per Serving: Calories: 518; Total Fat: 24.1; Saturated Fat: 7.1g; Protein: 65.6g; Carbs: 6.4g; Fiber: 0.8g; Sugar: 3.2g;

2 lbs leg of lamb
1 cup homemade broth
1 orange juice
4 thyme sprigs
1 medium onion, quartered

2 tbsp olive oil
1 tsp ground black pepper
4 garlic cloves, sliced
1/2 tsp sea salt

- Using knife make slits into the leg of lamb and inserts garlic slices in them.
- Season leg of lamb with pepper and salt.
- Add 1 tbsp of oil into the instant pot and select sauté.
- Add onion into the instant pot and sauté for 4 minutes.
- Remove onion from the pot and set aside.
- Add remaining oil into the instant pot and sear leg of lamb for 2-3 minutes on each side.
- Return onions into the pot with orange juice, broth, and thyme.
- Seal pot with lid and select meat/stew setting and set the timer for 40 minutes.
- Allow releasing pressure naturally then open the lid.
- Stir well and serve.

Easy Lamb Stew

Total Time: 4 hours 15 minutes; Serves: 4; Calories 577, Fat 28.8 g, Carbohydrates 22.2 g, Sugar 13.6 g, Protein 66.5 g, Cholesterol 204 mg

- 2 lbs lamb, boneless
- 2 medium onions, chopped
- 3 garlic cloves, chopped
- 1 tsp fresh ginger, grated
- 1 tsp dried mint
- 2 tbsp vegetable oil
- 2 tsp ground cumin
- 2 tsp ground coriander
- 1 tsp ground turmeric
- 28 oz can tomatoes, crushed
- 1.5 tbsp maple syrup
- 1 tsp garam masala
- 1 tsp red chili flakes
- 2 tsp salt

- Use the "Slow Cooker" setting on your Instant Pot.
- Heat oil in the pan over medium heat.
- Add ginger, garlic, and onion to the pan and sauté for 5 minutes.
- Add lamb and cook until browned. Transfer pan mixture into the Instant Pot.
- Add remaining ingredients and stir well.
- Cover and cook on high for 4 hours.
- Serve warm and enjoy.

Tomato Lamb Rogan Josh

Serves: 4 / Preparation time: 10 minutes / Cooking time: 15 minutes, Per Serving: Calories: 266; Total Fat: 12.3g; Saturated Fat: 3.5g; Protein: 32.9g; Carbs: 5.1g; Fiber: 1.7g; Sugar: 2.1g;

1 lb leg of lamb, deboned and cut into cubes	2 garlic cloves, minced
1/2 tsp garam masala	1 1/2 tsp fennel seeds
For sauce:	1 1/2 tsp cumin seeds
1/2 cup water	2 whole cloves
2 tbsp tomato puree	1-inch cinnamon stick
2 tomatoes, diced	3 green cardamom pods, cracked open
1 tsp ground ginger	2 bay leaves
1 tsp ground cumin	1 tbsp olive oil
1 tsp ground coriander	Salt
1/2 tsp ground chili	
1/2 tsp garam masala	

- Add meat and garam masala into the large mixing bowl and mix well. Marinate in refrigerator for overnight.
- Add oil into the instant pot and select sauté.
- Once the oil is hot then add all whole spices and cook until aroma is released.
- Add garlic and stir for a minute.
- Add remaining ground spices and cook for few minutes.
- Stir in water, tomato puree, and tomatoes.
- Add marinated lamb and stir well.
- Seal pot with lid and select manual and cook for 10 minutes.
- Release pressure using quick release method than open the lid.
- Season with salt and serve.

Perfect Taco Mince

Serves: 6 / Preparation time: 10 minutes / Cooking time: 10 minutes, Per Serving: Calories: 299; Total Fat: 22.1g; Saturated Fat: 10.1g; Protein: 20.6g; Carbs: 7.4g; Fiber: 1.8g; Sugar: 3.6g;

1 1/2 lbs lamb minced	1/2 tbsp olive oil
1/4 tsp smoked paprika	2 large tomatoes
1/2 tsp garlic powder	3 garlic cloves, chopped
1/2 tsp onion powder	1 bell pepper, chopped
1/2 tsp ground cumin	1 onion, chopped
1/2 tsp dried basil	1/4 tsp black pepper
1 tsp paprika	1 tsp salt
1 tsp oregano	

- Add olive oil into the instant pot and select sauté mode.
- Add bell pepper, garlic, onion, and lamb and sauté for 2-3 minutes.
- Add tomato and all seasoning. Stir well.

- Seal pot with lid and select manual and set timer for 15 minutes.
- Release pressure using quick release method than open the lid carefully.
- Stir well and serve.

Cilantro Almond Lamb Curry

Total Time: 8 hours 15 minutes; Serves: 6; Calories 489, Fat 35.4 g, Carbohydrates 16.1 g, Sugar 7.1 g, Protein 28.1 g, Cholesterol 88 mg

2 lbs lamb meat, cut into 1 1/2" cubes	1/4 cup dried coconut, unsweetened
1/4 cup cilantro, chopped	5 garlic cloves, crushed
20 almonds	1 tsp fresh ginger, grated
1/4 tsp saffron threads	1 tsp garam masala
1 cup plain yogurt	1 tsp cumin seeds
1/2 tsp turmeric	3 green Chile pepper
2 large onion, sliced	4 dried red Chile pepper
6 tbsp vegetable oil	Salt
3 tomatoes, chopped	

- Use the "Slow Cooker" setting on your Instant Pot.
- Add tomatoes, grated coconut, garlic, ginger, garam masala, cumin seeds, green chilies, and red chilies into the blender and blend until smooth.
- Heat oil in a pan over medium heat.
- Add onion to the pan and sauté for 5 minutes or until softened.
- Add spice paste to the pan and cook for 3 minutes.
- Stir in meat and salt. Cook over medium heat for 8 minutes.
- Mix in almonds, saffron, and yogurt until well combined.
- Transfer pan mixture into the Instant Pot and stir well.
- Cover and cook on low for 8 hours.
- Serve and enjoy.

Coconut Milk Lamb Curry

Serves: 4 / Preparation time: 10 minutes / Cooking time: 30 minutes, Per Serving: Calories: 496; Total Fat: 27.4g; Saturated Fat: 17.2g; Protein: 50.8g; Carbs: 12g; Fiber: 3.5g; Sugar: 5.6g;

1 1/2 lbs lamb chunks, boneless	1 small zucchini, chopped
1 cup coconut milk	1 small carrot, chopped
1 cup tomatoes	1 tbsp fresh ginger, grated
1 tsp garam masala	2 garlic cloves, crushed
1 red chili, deseeded and chopped	1 onion, chopped
1 tbsp coriander	Black pepper
1 tbsp cumin	Salt

- Spray instant pot from inside with cooking spray.
- Set instant pot sauté mode.
- Add ginger, garlic, and onion and sauté until softened.
- Add zucchini, lamb, carrot, and spices and mix until good coat.
- Add coconut milk, tomatoes, and chili. Stir well.
- Seal pot with lid and select manual high for 20 minutes.
- Allow releasing pressure naturally then open the lid.
- Season with pepper and salt.
- Serve and enjoy.

Shredded Lamb

Total Time: 6 hours 15 minutes; Serves: 6; Calories 671, Fat 27.1 g, Carbohydrates 6.7 g, Sugar 2.3 g, Protein 94.4 g, Cholesterol 299 mg

4.4 lbs lamb shoulder	1 tsp ground coriander
3 tsp vegetable oil	6 peppercorns
1 cup chicken stock	1 tsp fennel seeds
1 tbsp ginger, sliced	1 bay leaf
4 garlic cloves, crushed	1 tsp cumin seeds
2 large onions, sliced	1 cinnamon stick
Spice Rub:	6 cloves
1 tsp red chili powder	1-star anise

- Use the "Slow Cooker" setting on your Instant Pot.
- Add allspice rub ingredients into the grinder and grind to coarse powder.
- Rub spice powder onto the lamb from both the sides.
- Heat oil in the pan over medium-high heat.
- Place lamb onto the pan and brown them on both the sides and set aside.
- Add remaining ingredients into the Instant Pot.
- Place lamb into the Instant Pot.
- Cover and cook on high for 6 hours or until meat is tender.
- Remove lamb from Instant Pot and using fork shred the meat.
- Return shredded meat to the Instant Pot and stir well.
- Serve with rice and enjoy.

Spicy Lamb Curry

Serves: 10 / Preparation time: 15 minutes / Cooking time: 10 hours, Per Serving: Calories: 372; Total Fat: 15.1g; Saturated Fat: 5g; Protein: 51.8g; Carbs: 4.5g; Fiber: 1.4g; Sugar: 1.8g;

4 lbs leg of lamb, trimmed	3 tsp ground fennel
1 tsp ground cardamom	16 oz tomatoes
1/2 tsp cayenne	3 Serrano peppers, minced
1 tsp ground turmeric	1 tbsp ginger, minced
1/2 tsp ground nutmeg	3 garlic cloves, minced
1/4 tsp ground coriander	1 onion, diced
1/8 tsp ground cloves	1 tbsp olive oil
1/4 tsp cinnamon	1 tsp salt
2 tsp ground cumin	

- Add olive oil into the instant pot and select sauté.
- Add lamb into the pot and brown all sides.
- Remove brown lamb from pot and set aside.
- Add Serrano peppers, ginger, garlic and onions and sauté until translucent.
- Add tomatoes and bring to simmer.
- Add spices and stir well.
- Return lamb to the instant pot.
- Seal pot with lid and select slow cooker setting and cook on low for 10 hours.
- Serve and enjoy.

Shredded Lime Mint Lamb

Serves: 4 / Preparation time: 10 minutes / Cooking time: 70 minutes, Per Serving: Calories: 328; Total Fat: 12.6g; Saturated Fat: 4.5g; Protein: 48.4g; Carbs: 2.7g; Fiber: 1.1g; Sugar: 0.2g;

1 1/2 lbs lamb, boneless
2 tsp garlic, crushed
20 fresh mint leaves, sliced
1 cup lime juice
1/4 tsp ground black pepper
1/4 tsp sea salt

- Season lamb with pepper and salt.
- Set the instant pot on sauté mode.
- Spray instant pot from inside with cooking spray.
- Add season lamb into the instant pot and sear for 3-4 minutes.
- Deglaze instant pot with 1 cup warm water.
- Add garlic, mint leaves, and lime juice. Stir well.
- Seal pot with lid and select meat setting and set timer for 45 minutes.
- Release pressure using quick release method than open the lid.
- Using fork shred the meat and serves.

Lamb Shanks with Ginger

Serves: 4 / Preparation time: 10 minutes / Cooking time: 65 minutes, Per Serving: Calories: 373; Total Fat: 13.9g; Saturated Fat: 3.4g; Protein: 26.4g; Carbs: 37.9g; Fiber: 5.8g; Sugar: 24.6g;

3/4 lb lamb shanks
2 tbsp ginger, minced
2 tbsp apple cider vinegar
2 tbsp coconut aminos
2 tsp fish sauce
2 garlic cloves, minced
1 large onion, sliced
2 tbsp olive oil
1 1/2 cup water
10 dried figs cut into lengthwise

- Add 1 tbsp olive oil into the instant pot and select sauté.
- Add shanks into the instant pot and brown all sides. Transfer shanks onto the plate.
- Add onion and ginger and sauté for 3 minutes.
- Mix together vinegar, coconut aminos, fish sauce, and ginger, stir in water and figs.
- Return lamb shank into the instant pot.
- Seal pot with lid and cook on manual high pressure for 1 hour.
- Allow releasing pressure naturally then open the lid.
- Serve and enjoy.

Classic Lamb Curry

Total Time: 6 hours 15 minutes; Serves: 6; Calories 568, Fat 25.7 g, Carbohydrates 8.7 g, Sugar 1.3 g, Protein 71.5 g, Cholesterol 225 mg

3.3 lbs lamb, diced
2 bay leaves
2 cardamom pods
1 cinnamon stick
1 cup chicken stock
1 tsp red chili powder
1 tsp paprika
1 tsp garam masala
4 tsp ground cumin
4 tsp ground coriander
1 tsp turmeric
6 garlic cloves, crushed
1 tsp ginger, grated
1 large onion, sliced
3 tbsp vegetable oil
1/4 cup all-purpose flour
Salt

- Use the "Slow Cooker" setting on your Instant Pot.
- Add flour and lamb into the large zip-lock bag and shake well and set aside.
- Meanwhile, heat 2 tbsp oil in the large frying pan over high heat.
- Add lamb to the pan and cook until browned on both the sides, about 7 minutes.
- Transfer lamb into the Instant Pot.

- Heat remaining oil in the pan over medium-high heat.
- Add garlic, ginger, and onion to the pan and sauté for 2 minutes.
- Add turmeric, red chili powder, paprika, garam masala, cumin, and coriander and sauté for 2 minutes.
- Add chicken stock and stir well.
- Transfer pan mixture to the Instant Pot.
- Add bay leaves, cardamom, and cinnamon stick.
- Cover and cook on low for 6 hours.
- Serve and enjoy.

Coconut Milk Lamb Curry

Serves: 6 / Preparation time: 10 minutes / Cooking time: 25 minutes, Per Serving: Calories: 315; Total Fat: 15.8g; Saturated Fat: 7.6g; Protein: 33.6g; Carbs: 9.7g; Fiber: 2.7g; Sugar: 3.7g;

1 1/2 lbs lamb stew meat, cut into cubed
1 medium zucchini, diced
3 medium carrots, sliced
1 medium onion, diced
3/4 tsp ground turmeric
1 1/2 tbsp curry powder
1 tbsp olive oil

1/2 fresh lime juice
1/2 cup coconut milk
1 tbsp fresh ginger, grated
4 garlic cloves, minced
1/4 tsp ground black pepper
1/4 tsp sea salt

- Add meat, lime juice, coconut milk, ginger, garlic, black pepper, and salt into the large mixing bowl and mix well. Marinate in refrigerator for 1 hour.
- Add marinated meat into the instant pot with carrots, onions, curry powder, and olive oil.
- Seal pot with lid and cook on manual high pressure for 20 minutes.
- Allow releasing pressure naturally then open the lid.
- Set instant pot on sauté mode and stir in zucchini and simmer for 5 minutes.
- Serve and enjoy.

Lamb Chops

Serves: 4 / Preparation time: 10 minutes / Cooking time: 10 minutes, Per Serving: Calories: 730; Total Fat: 35.7g; Saturated Fat: 10.5g; Protein: 95.9g; Carbs: 1.3g; Fiber: 0.4g; Sugar: 0.7g;

3 lbs lamb chops
1 shallot, peeled and halved
1 cup homemade stock
1 tbsp tomato paste

3 tbsp olive oil
2 rosemary sprig
3 tsp kosher salt

- Season lamb chops with salt.
- Add olive oil into the instant pot and select sauté.
- Add lamb chops and rosemary into the instant pot and sauté lamb chops until brown on all the sides.
- Once lamb chops are browned then add shallot and tomato paste and cook for 1-2 minutes.
- Deglaze with homemade beef stock.
- Add lamb chops into the instant pot and mix well.
- Seal pot with lid and cook on high for 2 minutes.
- Release pressure using quick release method than open the lid.
- Serve and enjoy.

Classic Lamb Rogan Josh

Serves: 4 / Preparation time: 10 minutes / Cooking time: 30 minutes, Per Serving: Calories: 240; Total Fat: 8.7g; Saturated Fat: 3.1g; Protein: 32.9g; Carbs: 6.3g; Fiber: 1.6g; Sugar: 2g;

1 lb leg of lamb, cut into cubes	1 tbsp tomato paste
1/4 cup water	1/4 cup water
1 tsp cayenne pepper	2 tbsp lemon juice
1/2 tsp ground cinnamon	2 tsp ginger, minced
1 tsp turmeric	1 onion, diced
1 tsp smoked paprika	4 garlic cloves, minced
2 tsp garam masala	1 tsp salt
1/4 cup cilantro, chopped	

- Add all ingredients into the large mixing bowl and marinate for 1 hour.
- Add marinated lamb mixture into the instant pot and mix well.
- Seal pot with lid and cook on manual high pressure for 20 minutes.
- Allow to release pressure naturally then open the lid.
- Stir well and serve.

Spinach Lamb Curry

Total Time: 4 hours 20 minutes; Serves: 8; Calories 479, Fat 23 g, Carbohydrates 10.6 g, Sugar 6.4 g, Protein 53.8 g, Cholesterol 157 mg

2 cups plain yogurt	2 tsp ground cumin
6 cups baby spinach	1 tsp fresh ginger, grated
3 lbs lamb meat, boneless and cut into pieces	4 garlic cloves, minced
	3 onions, chopped
2 cups beef broth	1/3 cup vegetable oil
1 1/2 tsp ground turmeric	Salt
1 1/2 tsp cayenne pepper	

- Use the "Slow Cooker" setting on your Instant Pot.
- Heat oil in the pan over medium-high heat.
- Add garlic and onions to the pan and sauté for 5 minutes.
- Add turmeric, cayenne, cumin, and ginger and sauté for 1 minute.
- Add broth to the pan and stir well.
- Add meat into the Instant Pot with salt.
- Pour pan mixture over the meat.
- Cover and cook on high for 4 hours.
- Just before serving add spinach and cook until wilted, about 5 minutes.
- Add yogurt and stir well.
- Serve and enjoy.

The "Dirty Dozen" and "Clean 15"

Every year, the Environmental Working Group releases a list of the produce with the most pesticide residue (Dirty Dozen) and a list of the ones with the least chance of having residue (Clean 15). It's based on analysis from the U.S. Department of Agriculture Pesticide Data Program report.

The Environmental Working Group found that 70% of the 48 types of produce tested had residues of at least one type of pesticide. In total there were 178 different pesticides and pesticide breakdown products. This residue can stay on veggies and fruit even after they are washed and peeled. All pesticides are toxic to humans and consuming them can cause damage to the nervous system, reproductive system, cancer, a weakened immune system, and more. Women who are pregnant can expose their unborn children to toxins through their diet, and continued exposure to pesticides can affect their development.

This info can help you choose the best fruits and veggies, as well as which ones you should always try to buy organic.

The Dirty Dozen

Strawberries	Grapes
Spinach	Pears
Nectarines	Cherries
Apples	Tomatoes
Peaches	Sweet bell peppers
Celery	Potatoes

The Clean 15

Sweet corn	Mangoes
Avocados	Eggplant
Pineapples	Honeydew
Cabbage	Kiwi
Onions	Cantaloupe
Frozen sweet peas	Cauliflower
Papayas	Grapefruit
Asparagus	

Measurement Conversion Tables

Volume Equivalents (Liquid)

US Standard	US Standard (ounces)	Metric (Approx.)
2 tablespoons	1 fl oz	30 ml
¼ cup	2 fl oz	60 ml
½ cup	4 fl oz	120 ml
1 cup	8 fl oz	240 ml
1 ½ cups	12 fl oz	355 ml
2 cups or 1 pint	16 fl oz	475 ml
4 cups or 1 quart	32 fl oz	1 L
1 gallon	128 fl oz	4 L

Oven Temperatures

Fahrenheit (F)	Celsius (C) (Approx)
250°F	120°C
300°F	150°C
325°F	165°C
350°F	180°C
375°F	190°C
400°F	200°C
425°F	220°C
450°F	230°C

Volume Equivalents (Dry)

US Standard	Metric (Approx.)
¼ teaspoon	1 ml
½ teaspoon	2 ml
1 teaspoon	5 ml
1 tablespoon	15 ml
¼ cup	59 ml
½ cup	118 ml
1 cup	235 ml

Weight Equivalents

US Standard	Metric (Approx.)
½ ounce	15 g
1 ounce	30 g
2 ounces	60 g
4 ounces	115 g
8 ounces	225 g
12 ounces	340 g
16 ounces or 1 pound	455 g

Recipe Index

Adobo Chicken   173
Almond Rice Pudding   30
Appetizing Pork with Cabbage   192
Apple Breadcrumb Meatloaf   107
Apple Cabbage and Beet Stew   30
Apple Cider Shredded Pork   195
Apple Ginger Pork Stew   195
Apple Pork Ribs   209
Applesauce   89
Asian Chicken Legs   160
Asparagus Cream Soup   62
Asparagus Lemon Tender   41
Baby Back Ribs   204
Bacon and Mushroom with Honey Mustard Chicken   146
Bacon Cheeseburger Casserole   128
Bacon-Wrapped Stuffed Chicken Breasts   166
Baked Beans   63
Balsamic Beef Roast   116
Balsamic Tomato & Red Pepper Soup   88
Banana Bread   44
Barley Walnut Salad   36
Barley with Mushrooms   43
Basil Chicken Breasts   185
Bean Soup   53
Beanless Beef Chili   135
Beef and Broccoli 98
Beef and Potatoes   129
Beef Balls Light Soup   106
Beef Bolognese Mushroom   127
Beef Chili   118
Beef Coconut Fritter   104
Beef Couscous Stuffed Bell Peppers 112
Beef Curry   128
Beef Heart   114
Beef in Gravy   99
Beef Mix Vegetable Soup   126
Beef Mushroom Pie   124
Beef Pasta Black Pepper   116
Beef Potato Gratin   136
Beef Ragu   120
Beef Ribs   129
Beef Short Ribs   103

Beef Steak Black Pepper   129
Beef Stew   111
Beef Stew   125
Beef Stroganoff   99
Beef Tender in Sweet Red Sauce   120
Beef Tomato Soup   132
Beet Borscht   86
Bell Pepper Ground Beef Chili   123
Bitter Melon and Mushroom in Wrap   73
Black Pepper Chicken Thigh Stew   164
Blueberry Cobbler   92
Boneless BBQ Beef Ribs   101
Braised Beef Ribs 130
Broccoli Beef Curry Stew   109
Broccoli Cauliflower Soup   18
Broccoli Cheese Soup   75
Broccoli in Tomato Sauce   61
Broccoli Kale Soup   83
Broccoli with Garlic Sauce   59
Brown Caramel Salmon   229
Bruschetta Chicken   171
Brussels sprouts with Parmesan Cheese   74
Brussels sprouts with Pine nuts   71
Bulgur with Vegetables   64
Butter Chicken   178
Butter Garlic Green Beans   64
Butter Garlic Potatoes   49
Buttered Peas Rice   44
Butternut Squash Creamy Soup   87
Butternut Squash Risotto   63
Butternut Squash Soup   39
Buttery Beef Ribs with Potatoes   104
Cabbage Carrots Celery Soup   27
Caesar Chicken   166
Cafe Rio Chicken   151
Calico Beans   30
Cauliflower "Mac" and Cheese   46
Cauliflower Casserole   76
Cauliflower Curried Soup   43
Cauliflower Lentil Curry   43
Cauliflower Potato Curry Soup   25
Cazuela 80
Cherry Almond Rice   49

Chewy Fish in Tomato Light Soup 226
Chicken Cacciatore 174
Chicken Chili Verde 158
Chicken Coconut Curry 186
Chicken Curry Tomato with Eggplant 144
Chicken Dinner 185
Chicken Drumstick Soup 148
Chicken Drumsticks 182
Chicken Dumplings 187
Chicken Garlic Rosemary 143
Chicken Korma 171
Chicken Leg Quarters with Lemon and Rosemary 175
Chicken Lettuce Wraps 165
Chicken Mushroom Stew 151
Chicken Noodle Soup 184
Chicken Pot Pie 138
Chicken Potato Curry 170
Chicken Potato with Lemon Sauce 157
Chicken Quinoa Curry 151
Chicken Rice Casserole 168
Chicken Salads in Cabbage Blanket 164
Chicken Soup 153
Chicken Stew 167
Chicken Taco Soup 147
Chicken Tandoori 180
Chicken Tikka Masala 178
Chicken Tomato Pasta 163
Chicken Vegetable Curry 179
Chicken Vegetable Soup 161
Chicken Vindaloo 139
Chicken Wings Barbecue 147
Chicken Wings Cola 146
Chickpea Coconut Quinoa Curry 61
Chickpea Curry 93
Chickpea Kale Sweet Potato Stew 41
Chickpea Lentil Chili 57
Chickpea Pumpkin Lentil Curry 54
Chickpea Spinach Cauliflower Curry 87
Chickpea Spinach Soup 45
Chickpea Stew 33
Chickpeas and Tofu 44
Chili Lime Shredded Beef 123
Chili with Cornmeal Dumplings 64
Chilled Quinoa Salad 91
Chinese Steamed Pork Bags 204

Chipotle Barbacoa 133
Chipotle Mexican Beef Stew 132
Chunky Steak Chili 122
Cilantro Almond Lamb Curry 236
Cinnamon Carrots and Apples 17
Cinnamon Chicken Soup 139
Cinnamon Honey Beef 121
Cinnamon Honey Pork Chops 203
Citrusy Pork Carnitas 192
Clam Potato Chowder 224
Classic Chicken Adobo 141
Classic Lamb Curry 238
Classic Lamb Rogan Josh 240
Classic Shepherd's Pie 100
Coconut Crumble Nectarines 48
Coconut Eggplant Curry 82
Coconut Lime Cabbage 31
Coconut Lime Catfish Curry 225
Coconut Milk Lamb Curry 236
Coconut Milk Lamb Curry 239
Coconut Tapioca Pudding 70
Collard Green with Egg 92
Corn on the Cob with Avocado Dressing 50
Corned Beef with Cabbage 135
Cranberry Apple Crisp 24
Cranberry Turkey Wings 161
Creamy Beef Stroganoff 121
Creamy Bow Tie Pasta 34
Creamy Carrot Squash Soup 29
Creamy Cauliflower Broccoli Soup 90
Creamy Cauliflower Soup 67
Creamy Chicken 203
Creamy Chicken Carrots 153
Creamy Chicken Mushroom 188
Creamy Chicken Vegetable Soup 153
Creamy Coconut Chicken Curry 160
Creamy Coconut Fish Curry 218
Creamy Coconut Pumpkin Curry 72
Creamy Curry Cauliflower Soup 92
Creamy Kale Soup 33
Creamy Mashed Potato 20
Creamy Onion Soup 24
Creamy Rice and Beans 31
Creamy Split Pea Curry 20
Creamy Tomato Soup 34
Creole Jambalaya 224

Creole Red Beans 93
Crisp and Tender Potatoes 83
Crispy Pork in Sweet Sour Sauce   205
Crispy Pulled Pork   209
Crispy Salmon with Honey Glaze   227
Crustless Ham & Swiss Quiche   212
Curried Chicken Bowls   149
Curried Potatoes   48
Curried Zucchini Eggplant   49
Curry Jalapeno Beef Stew   120
Delicious Black Lentil Curry   16
Delicious Carrot Potato Medley   56
Delicious Lemon Lentils   75
Delicious Pork Shoulder   200
Delicious Spiced Potatoes and Cauliflower   81
Delicious Sweet Potato Curry   36
Delicious Three Bean Chili   22
Delicious Tofu Coconut Curry   63
Delicious Whole Chicken   180
Easy 3 Ingredients Chicken 164
Easy and Hearty Beef Stew   98
Easy Balsamic Pork Tenderloin   205
Easy Black Bean Soup   72
Easy Cauliflower Rice   79
Easy Chicken Wings   166
Easy Curried Chicken   172
Easy Dinner Turkey Roast   183
Easy Instant Pot Leg of Lamb   234
Easy Lamb Stew   234
Easy Lentils Rice   84
Easy Pork Sausage   198
Easy Pot Turkey   170
Easy Salsa Chicken   167
Easy Shredded Chicken   179
Easy Southwestern Soup   69
Easy Taco Soup   18
Easy Tuna Tender 222
Easy Turkey Drumsticks   186
Easy White Chicken Chili   150
Easy Whole Cauliflower Curry   69
Easy Winter Veggie Soup   21
Eggplant Caponata   87
Eggplant Chickpea Curry   80
Fish Chowder   223
Flavorful Chicken Cacciatore   176
Flavorful Chicken Curry   171

Flavorful Jalapeno Beef   117
Flavorful Red Lentils Curry 27
Flavorful Shredded Pork   202
Flavorful Slow Cooker Chili   122
Flavorful Vegetable Curry   47
Flavourful Salmon Fillets   223
Flavourful Vegetable Korma   48
Frijoles Borrachos (Mexican "Drunken Beans")   16
Frittata with Cheese and Broccoli   39
Fruity Butternut Squash   94
Garam Masala Potatoes   25
Garlic Balsamic Pork Chops   198
Garlic Beef Short Ribs   124
Garlic Cumin Grapefruit Shredded Pork   208
Garlic Lemon Dump Chicken   183
Garlic Smashed Potatoes   62
Garlic Thyme Pork Shoulder   215
Garlicky Sweet Chicken   186
Ginger Goat (or Lamb) Curry   234
Ginger Scallion Tilapia   232
Ginger-Honey Pork Tenderloin   192
Gluten Free Chickpea Curry   58
Gluten Free Masala Lentils 84
Gluten Free Pot Roast   115
Green Beans Barley Soup   82
Green Chicken Curry   181
Green Chile Pork Stew   204
Green Chili Tuna Pasta   230
Green Lentil Curry   79
Green Pea and Cauliflower Korma   55
Ground Beef with Green Beans   109
Ham & Asparagus Soup   211
Harvest Couscous 75
Hearty Potato Curry   83
Hearty Spaghetti Sauce   110
Hearty Vegetarian Chili   71
Herb Garlic Pot Roast   108
Herb Pork Loin   213
Herb Pork Tenderloin   213
Herb Pot Roast   124
Herbed Turkey Breast   180
Honey Chicken Apple   149
Honey Lime Shredded Pork with Chicken Stock   207
Honey Mustard Chicken   154

Honey Roasted Peanut Broccoli Salad 35
Hot Beef Ribs 107
Hot Beef with Herbs 131
Hot Chili Pork Ribs 206
Hot Pepper Shredded Beef 119
Hot Pork Ginger 194
Instant Pot Roast 106
Instant Pot Sambar 49
Instant Pot Whole Chicken 172
Italian Beef 128
Italian Chicken 169
Italian Vegetable Soup 37
Japanese Chicken Teriyaki 159
Jerk Pork Roast 212
Juicy and Tender Chicken Breasts 185
Juicy Beef Meatballs Marinara 126
Juicy Roast Beef Sandwiches 117
Kale Garlic Pork 210
Kale Potato Soup 27
Lamb Chops 239
Lamb Shanks with Ginger 238
Lasagna 115
Lemon Chicken 141
Lemon Garlic Chicken Breasts 142
Lemon Garlic Chicken Thighs with Green Beans 186
Lemon Garlic Quarter Chicken 181
Lentil Butternut Squash Curry 65
Lentil Cauliflower Curry 51
Lentil Chicken Vegetable Curry 67
Lentil Chili 85
Lentil Curry 22
Lentil Potato Coconut Curry 60
Lentil Soup with Spinach 86
Lentil Sweet Potato Beans Stew 17
Lentil Sweet Potato Soup 66
Lentil Vegetable Soup 75
Loaded Cauliflower Bowls 215
Low Carb Beef 113
Mahi Fillets 220
Mashed Cauliflower 29
Measurement Conversion Tables 242
Meatballs with sauce 134
Meatloaf 127
Mediterranean Chicken Wings 147
Mediterranean Cod 231
Mexican Beef Stew 114
Mexican Meatloaf 134
Mexican Rice 51
Mexican Rice and Beans 38
Mix Vegetable Curry 38
Mixed Beans in Hot Sauce 35
Moist and Tender Baked Chicken 164
Mongolian Beef 101
Moroccan Chicken 159
Mushroom Eggplant Potato Curry 102
Mushroom Leek Chicken 145
Mushroom Potato Stew 22
Mushroom Soup 28
Mushroom Stroganoff 19
Mushroom Veggie Soup with Tofu 82
Navratan Korma 16
North Indian red Beans 60
Nutritious Veggie Soup 80
Nutty Mocha Oatmeal 52
Olive Lemon Chicken 178
Onion Balsamic Chicken 174
Onion Chuck Roast 130
Onion Garlic Chicken 177
Orange Chicken Chunks 183
Orange Sweet Potatoes 78
Original Brussel Sprouts Salads 70
Original Salty Chicken 146
Original Savory Shrimps 231
Oxtail Soup 132
Paprika Taco Meat 103
Parmesan Marinara Spaghetti Squash 57
Pea Chickpea Vegetable Curry 85
Peanut Butter Chicken 174
Pepper Lemon Salmon 225
Peppercini Pot Roast 198
Perfect Beef Stew 105
Perfect Carrot Soup 18
Perfect Chicken Curry 167
Perfect Cuban Pork 212
Perfect Curried Baked Beans 40
Perfect Mashed Potatoes 77
Perfect Mexican Chicken 173
Perfect Pork Ragu 206
Perfect Taco Mince 235
Piña Colada Upside Down Cake 73
Pineapple Pork 190

Plum Slump 73
Polenta Porridge 67
Pork Belly Black Pepper 202
Pork Carnitas 214
Pork Chops with Apples 215
Pork Chops with Brussels sprouts 208
Pork Chops with Gravy 202
Pork Chops with Mushroom 197
Pork Clear Soup with Collard Green 191
Pork Feet Stew with Vegetables 203
Pork Meatballs in Sticky Sauce 201
Pork Ribs 196
Pork Roast Black Pepper 207
Pork Stew 191
Pork Tender in Tropical Sauce 190
Pot Roast 108
Potato Cheese Soup 93
Potato Chile Stew 52
Potato Okra Curry 47
Potato Red Lentil Curry 23
Potato Soup with Lentils 41
Potato Vegetable Soup 32
Pulled Chicken Taco Salad 169
Pulled Pork Carnitas 207
Pumpkin Apple Curry Soup 26
Pumpkin Pudding 57
Pumpkin Vegetable Stew 42
Punjabi Red Bean Curry 78
Quick and Easy Turkey Breast 181
Quick Buttery Salmon 221
Quick Salmon with Dill 228
Quick Steamed Broccoli 89
Quick Turkey Breast 169
Quinoa Pilaf 42
Ranch Chicken Wings 144
Ranch Pork Chops 213
Recipe Index 243
Red Bean Rice 71
Red Beans and Lentils 68
Red Beans Bowl 46
Red Beans Cabbage Soup 46
Red Beans with Bell Pepper 55
Red Hot Fish 218
Red Pepper Chicken Tacos 176
Red Wine Poached Pears 37
Refreshing Beef Mango 102

Refried Black Beans 90
Rhubarb Strawberry Apple Crisp 81
Riced Cauliflower 84
Roasted Potato Wedges 74
Roasted Tomato Beef Curry 125
Roasted Vegetables 24
Root Vegetables 80
Rosemary Chicken 154
Round Steak with Peppers 118
Rutabaga Chicken Soup 175
Salmon with Broccoli 219
Salmon with Chili Lime Sauce 229
Salsa Chicken 177
Salsa Poached Cod 228
Salsa Verde Chicken 157
Salsa Verde Shredded Chicken 176
Salty and Spicy Pork 199
Salty Beef Brisket 118
Salty Spicy Salmon Balls 225
Sauteed Green Beans and Eggplant 42
Savory Kale Garlic 36
Savory Pork Belly in Fresh Basil 197
Savory Pork Loin 193
Savory Turkey Stew 140
Scrumptious Spinach Paneer 26
Sea Bass Coconut Curry 219
Shredded Chicken Garlic 162
Shredded Chicken Pineapple 160
Shredded Chicken Wraps 158
Shredded Lamb 237
Shredded Lime Mint Lamb 237
Shredded Pork 216
Shredded Turkey 184
Shrimp Scampi 221
Simple BBQ Chicken 143
Simple Beef Bean Chili 108
Simple Beef Bourguignon 103
Simple Beef Curry 101
Simple Beef Fajitas 100
Simple Beef Tacos 126
Simple Black Eyed Peas 37
Simple Cheesy Pork Meatloaf 206
Simple Chickpea Curry 51
Simple Corned Beef 135
Simple Instant Pot Lentil 66
Simple Kalua Pork 209

Simple Lime Chicken	168	Spicy Lamb Curry	237
Simple Mustard Pulled Turkey	168	Spicy Lentil Stew	89
Simple Pork Garlic	197	Spicy Orange Beef	125
Simple Pork Ribs	194	Spicy Salmon Fillets	222
Simple Pulled Pork	201	Spicy Shredded Chicken	177
Simple Quinoa Risotto	77	Spicy Sour Chicken Soup	152
Simple Salmon Fillets	227	Spicy Vegetable Curry	59
Simple Shredded Chicken	163	Spicy White Chicken Chili	172
Simple Slow Cooker Lentils	61	Spicy Winter Chickpeas	53
Simple Steamed Salmon Fillet	221	Spinach Coconut Lentil Soup	63
Simple Strawberry Sauce	32	Spinach Curry with Lentils	75
Simple Turkey and Gravy	155	Spinach Lamb Curry	240
Simple Yellow Lentil	50	Spinach Lentils	85
Sirloin Tip Roast	210	Split Pea Soup	94
Sloppy Joe Filling	58	Spring Veggie Soup	90
Slow cooked Fancy Beef	111	Squash Curry Soup	20
Slow Cooked Garlic Cinnamon Beef	99	Squids Tomato Veggie	231
Slow Cooked Turkey Breast	148	Steamed Artichokes	68
Smoked Pulled Pork	214	Steamed Beef in Coconut	114
Smoked Sausage & Cabbage	191	Steamed Crabs Garlic	229
Smokey Lentil Soup	88	Steamed Kale with Bacon	26
Smoky Beef Brisket	134	Steamed Lemon Crabs	220
Smothered Pork Chops	195	Steamed Lobster Tails	227
Soft Broccoli Quiche	45	Steamed Winter Veggies	56
Spaghetti	89	Sticky Honey Chicken	161
Spaghetti Squash Marinara	19	Sticky Mango Rice	74
Special Pork in Tomato Sticky Sauce	196	Stuffed Bell Peppers	98
Spiced Chicken Cake	150	Stuffed Squids in Tomato	219
Spiced Coconut Lentils	91	Summer Vegetable Soup	77
Spiced Cranberry Oatmeal	30	Super easy Cashew Chicken	140
Spiced Green Peas Rice	38	Super Tender Italian Pot Roast	110
Spicy and Tender Italian Beef	108	Sweet Beef Curry	133
Spicy Beef Chuck Roast	105	Sweet Brown Chicken	154
Spicy Beef Roast	107	Sweet Chicken Wings with Black Pepper	141
Spicy Beef Stew	133	Sweet Crispy Beef	113
Spicy Beef with Beans	121	Sweet Glazed Carrots	39
Spicy Black Eyed Peas	56	Sweet Orange Honey Chicken	165
Spicy Buffalo Chicken	158	Sweet Pork Belly	193
Spicy Cauliflower Chicken	143	Sweet Potato Chili	94
Spicy Chicken Curry	138	Sweet Potato Peanut Stew	23
Spicy Curried Chickpeas	58	Sweet Soy Fish	218
Spicy Eggplant Potatoes	62	Taco Beans & Rice Bowls	95
Spicy Fish in Savory Tomato Gravy	226	Taco Bowls	116
Spicy Green Beans in Red Gravy	77	Taco Meat	131
Spicy Habanero Chili	119	Tangy and Sticky Chicken	194
Spicy Keema Lentils	96	Tangy Raspberry Lemon Curd	79

Tasty Beef Ragu   110
Tasty Black Eyed Pea Curry   88
Tasty Carrot Lentils Soup   81
Tasty Cheeseburger Soup   138
Tasty Chicken Enchilada Soup   156
Tasty Chicken Fajitas   179
Tasty Chicken Kheema   158
Tasty Chicken Tikka Masala   182
Tasty Coconut Drumsticks   156
Tasty Fajita Soup   162
Tasty Leftover Turkey Stew   156
Tasty Mongolian Beef   119
Tasty Pork Carnitas   201
Tasty Pork Stew   211
Tasty Ranch Chicken   184
Tasty Sausage Soup   190
Tasty Seafood Chowder   222
Tasty Spinach Potato   40
Tasty Sweet Potato Soup   95
Tasty Tofu Curry   24
Tasty Tso's Chicken   142
Tempeh with Figs   47
Tempered Lentils   95
Tender and Juicy shredded Pork   210
Tender and Juicy Turkey Breast   163
Tender Greek Pot Roast   112
Tender Korean Beef   113
Teriyaki Chicken   155
Teriyaki Salmon   230
Thai Pork Stew   193
Thai Red Curry with Chicken   173
The "Dirty Dozen" and "Clean 15"   241
Tomato Basil Soup   96
Tomato Beef Brisket   130
Tomato Casserole with Onion   65
Tomato Lamb Rogan Josh   235
Tomato Lentil Soup   54
Tomato Pulled Pork   211
Tomato Rice with Zucchini   76
Tomato Sauce   27
Turkey and Bone Broth Gravy   187
Turkey Sandwich Meat   152
Turkey Sausage with Cabbage   146
Turkey Soup   145
Turkey Thighs   175
Turkey Vaca Frita   144

Turkey with Sauerkraut   139
Turkish Split Pea Stew   53
Turmeric Lentil Bean Chili   40
Tuscan Pinto Beans   28
Vegetable Beef Roast   115
Vegetable Coconut Curry   21
Vegetable Curried Rice   70
Vegetable Fajitas   72
Vegetable Scraps Stock   38
Vegetable Shrimps Tom Yum Soup   220
Vegetable Stew with Chickpeas   50
Vegetarian Chili   86
Vegetarian Chili Bowl   52
Vegetarian Curry   55
Veggie Corn Soup   54
Veggie Quinoa Pilaf   33
Veggie Soup   32
Veggie Steak Soup   104
Warm Broccoli Salad   66
Warm Steamed Fish Ginger   228
White Bean Wraps   68
Whole Turkey   148
Whole Turkey   165
Wild Rice Soup   69
Wild Rice with Mushrooms   65
Winter Veggie Soup   17
Yellow Chicken Curry   152
Yummy Cheese Soup   29
Yummy Slow Cooked Potatoes   21
Zucchini Curried Soup   35
Zucchini Noodles   59

Made in the USA
Lexington, KY
15 January 2018